Continued on next page

How Do I... (continued)

MASTERING
PALM ORGANIZERS

MASTERING™
PALM
ORGANIZERS

Gayle Ehrenman

Michael Zulich

SYBEX®

San Francisco • Paris • Düsseldorf • Soest • London

Associate Publisher: Roger Stewart
Contracts and Licensing Manager: Kristine O'Callaghan
Acquisitions & Developmental Editor: Brenda Frink
Editor: Malka Geffen
Technical Editor: Sheryl McKeown
Book Designer: Kris Warrenburg
Graphic Illustrator: Tony Jonick
Electronic Publishing Specialist: Cyndy Johnsen, Adrian Woolhouse
Project Team Leader: Jennifer Durning
Proofreader: Jennifer Campbell
Indexer: Ted Laux
CD Technician: Ginger Warner
CD Coordinator: Kara Schwartz
Cover Designer: Design Site
Cover Illustrator: Sergie Loobkoof, Design Site

Library of Congress Card Number: 99-67592
ISBN: 0-7821-2569-7

Manufactured in the United States of America

10 9 8 7 6 5 4 3 2 1

This book is dedicated to the memory of Teresa Ehrenman, who always believed in us and made us believe that we could do anything. We hope we've made you proud.

ACKNOWLEDGMENTS

A book this big is really a team effort, so let's hear it for all those who helped make the whole thing possible.

First, we'd like to thank the team at Sybex. Our deepest gratitude goes to Developmental Editor Brenda Frink for convincing us that there's nothing wrong with having a book that's bigger than the device it's based on, and for helping us figure out just what goes into making a book.

Thanks also to editor extraordinaire Malka Geffen for helping us stick to our focus, our voice, and sometimes even our schedule. And for knowing when to be patient and when to push.

Since this book is all about the Palm organizer, we couldn't have done it without the help of the folks at Palm Computing, their public relations team at A&R Partners, and all the developers working on the platform. In particular, we'd like to express our gratitude to Minnie Lee and Lisa Rathjens at Palm; Kristen Garrigus and Jason Caskey at A&R Partners; Amy Navarro at Puma Technology; and Luis Quiroga, Jeff Tieszen, and Kathleen Hill at Metrowerks.

Now, for the members of our personal teams:

I would like to extend a special thanks to Bob Benton for helping me learn how to put thoughts into words, way back when. Bob—guess it must be snowing in hell!

—*Michael Zulich*

I would like to extend my thanks to Bill Dyszel for getting me hooked on the Palm. To my father, Howie, and brother, Alan, thanks for your patience. I really will come fix your PCs soon. Special appreciation goes out to Nails for cuddling and holding down papers. And thanks, Lilikoi, for not eating the whole manuscript.

—*Gayle Ehrenman*

Finally, we'd would like to acknowledge that despite popular belief, it is possible to write a really long book and stay friends. We wouldn't have it any other way.

CONTENTS AT A GLANCE

TABLE OF CONTENTS

INTRODUCTION

Welcome to *Mastering Palm Organizers*, the book for beginning, intermediate, and advanced Palm users, as well as those interested in developing applications for the Palm platform.

Some people describe Palm organizers as an addiction—and they're not far off. Once you've embraced this tiny dynamo and discovered how much it can do to improve your productivity, you'll never go back to one of those 10-pound, 10-inch filo-whatever's again. We should know; we have a drawer full of paper organizers to prove it.

The Palm crams in all of the date book, address book, memo pad, and to do list abilities of those analog behemoths, as well as a whole lot more. And it fits it all into a pocket-sized device. Straight from the box, the Palm organizer has everything you need to finally get your act together. You don't ever need to buy an accessory or install another application onto the device, if you don't want to. But, if you have a desktop PC, be it a Windows machine or a Macintosh, you've already increased your Palm's capability exponentially. And if you really embrace the whole Palm culture and install just a few simple applications (which don't even cost much), you can turn this device from a powerful organizer into a financial wizard, a musical instrument, an e-mail appliance, a database viewer...we'll stop here, lest we start sounding like one of those late-night infomercials. Rest assured, the Palm organizer can do just about anything but shine your shoes and cut through tin cans. Let's see your big old paper planner top that!

Whether you have a Palm IIIx, a Palm V, a Palm VII, or some variation thereof, you'll find something in this book to make your life a little easier.

We'll cover everything from getting started with Graffiti, the Palm's own written language, to writing your very first Palm application—with lots of stops in between. We'll teach you how to use the applications that come with your organizer, as well as how to expand your Palm's capabilities through third-party applications and accessories. There are tips and tricks here for every level of user, from those who need help figuring out what the buttons on the front of the Palm do, to those who have been members of the Palm cult from the early days.

Consider this your invitation to embark on a Palm adventure.

Your Boarding Pass

All you need to start your journey is a Palm organizer. Any one will do; we cover the applications and functions of all the organizers from the Palm III on up, and devote a whole chapter to the special wireless communication capabilities of the Palm VII. To get the most out of this book, as well as your Palm organizer, you'll also need a desktop computer—any variety of Windows PC or Macintosh will do. And don't forget the cradle that comes with your Palm device; it's crucial for installing new applications on your device and for backing up your data to your desktop computer.

We provide lots of basic information here for Palm users of all levels. For beginning, intermediate, and advanced users, there are step-by-step instructions for using all the applications that come installed on your organizer, tips and shortcuts to make you more productive, descriptions of applications and accessories for expanding the capabilities of your organizer, and instructions for caring for your Palm. Basically, if there's something you want to know about the Palm organizer, chances are you'll find it here.

Your Itinerary

This is a big book, and we certainly don't expect you to read it all in one sitting. So, to make it easier to find just the information you need, we've put a great deal of thought into organizing the wealth of interesting stuff we provide for you. The book breaks down as follows:

Part I: Palm Out of the Box: The Basics   This part provides an introduction to the Palm platform and the various Palm organizers. We cover basic skills and concepts and offer a guided tour to get you started.

Part II: The Applications   This part focuses on all the applications that come installed on the Palm organizer. We teach you how to use them, as well as how to back up data to your desktop computer and how to use the Palm Desktop software on the desktop computer of your choice.

Part III: Your Palm and the Outside World   This third part covers everything you need to know to use your Palm organizer for communicating beyond the desktop. We teach you how to use your organizer for e-mail, Web surfing, faxing, and printing. We devote one whole chapter to using the wireless communication capabilities of the Palm VII.

Part IV: Alternate Uses for Your Palm   This part covers some of the things your device can do beyond serving as an organizer. We provide information on some of our favorite business, graphics, and personal enrichment applications; suggest a dozen or so games; and recommend a handful of accessories we think enhance the Palm experience.

Part V: Advanced Techniques   This part provides hardcore information on enhancing your Palm's performance and writing your own applications. We walk you through the process of creating a Palm application using three of the leading Palm development tools.

Not every part of this book will appeal to every level of user. Those who have never used a Palm organizer before or who are just getting to know the device should start with Part I and work their way through to Part IV. Those who have some familiarity with the Palm organizer can start with Part II to get a refresher course in the applications. Even those who feel comfortable with the applications should give this part a gander; there are lots of tips and tricks that you may not know. If you're ready to move beyond the applications that come installed on your Palm, turn to Part III for the lowdown on using your organizer for communications, and keep reading through Part IV for information on more fun things you can add to your Palm device.

All of these parts were designed to be very user friendly and avoid technical jargon as much as possible. Where we just couldn't avoid a highly technical topic, we tried to set it off so you can read it or skip it as your comfort level and needs dictate.

You'll notice we haven't mentioned Part V in a while. That's because Part V, which covers programming and system enhancement, gets quite technical. We assume that you have some technical background and are comfortable with geek-speak in this part. If you have no interest in getting under the covers of the Palm operating system, you can just pretend this part of the book doesn't exist. The deeper you get into this part, the more technical it gets. If you have a passing interest in juicing up your Palm's performance, read through Chapter 21. If you need to HotSync your Palm to an application other than the Palm Desktop software, read Chapter 22. Those of you who have done a little programming and think you'd like to try your hand at creating a simple Palm application should jump in to Chapter 23 and Chapter 24; if you're feeling adventurous, continue on to Chapter 25. If you're an experienced C programmer, turn those pages to Chapter 26, where we'll walk you through creating an application in Code Warrior, the premier development tool for the Palm platform. But remember we warned you: This chapter is not for the newbie.

Your Roadmap

Now that you know where you should start your Palm adventure, let us offer some tips on navigating through the terrain.

Throughout this book, you'll find step-by-step instructions for carrying out a particular task. Those instructions look like this:

1. First finish step one.

2. Then move on to step two.

When we ask you to make a selection from a software menu, you'll see the following: Pick ➤ From Menu. The arrow lets you know you're making a series of menu selections.

You'll also find Notes, Tips, and Warnings that will help you along your journey.

 NOTE Notes contain important information and comments that help you understand something about the application we're discussing.

 TIP Tips provide a shortcut, an alternate approach, or a bit of insight into using an application more effectively. We've also used Tips to explain how to complete a task on a Macintosh computer when the process differs significantly from using a Windows PC.

 WARNING Warnings are like red lights. They alert you to a potential problem that you should be aware of—and avoid like the plague.

We also have provided a few digressions along the way—information that we consider important to fully appreciating the Palm organizer and how it functions, but not necessarily vital to mastering the device. We've included this type of information as a sidebar:

What Is a Sidebar?

Consider a sidebar to be a scenic overlook. In these tinted boxes, you'll find information related to a topic, but not vital to understanding it. If you have time for a little extra information and want to make your journey more interesting, take a minute to stop and read the sidebars. If all you want to do is get to your destination as quickly as possible, skip over them and come back when you've finished your appointed task.

You'll find that whenever we include a Web address, it will look a little different from the rest of the text. So, if you're trying to quickly find out where you can download something, look for *www.web-address.com.*

We've followed the same convention in the chapters on programming. Any code will be broken out as:

```
important lines of code
```

This should make it easy for you to figure out what you need to program and what you need to read to understand what you're programming. Or something like that.

That should get you on the road and heading in the right direction.

Fasten Your Seatbelt

Before you turn the page and begin your Palm adventure, make sure your tray table and seat back are in the upright and locked position. And that you have put the batteries into your organizer (or charged them, for you Palm V users).

Now get ready for a journey into the wonderful world of the Palm organizer. Once you've experienced the advantages of the Palm, you'll never go back to paper.

Don't be alarmed if you get hooked on the Palm and constantly seek new tricks, tips, and toys for your Palm pal. We warned you it was addictive.

PART I

Palm Out of the Box: The Basics

LEARN TO:

- *Navigate Your Palm Organizer*

- *Set Screen Parameters*

- *Set the Country, Date, and Time*

CHAPTER 1

Meet Your Palm Pal

We think that every relationship should start with a proper introduction (call us old-fashioned, if you must). So, we'll start with a guided tour of your Palm device. We're starting with the hardware because, quite frankly, no matter what anyone says, it's what's on the outside that gets your attention first when you meet someone new (or something new, in this case). After showing you the hardware, we'll walk you through the software installed on your Palm device—all that stuff underneath its pretty face. After all, every lasting relationship is based on the whole package—and we know you want your Palm relationship to last.

Meet the Models

Palm devices come in a variety of different models. Let's start by naming them and exploring the differences between them. We'll let you decide which device is the right one for you.

The earliest versions of the device were the PalmPilot 1000, 5000, Personal, and the PalmPilot Professional. These devices were all extremely limited in memory and functionality. Consider them the great-grandparents of your Palm device, the abacuses of the Palm age. You may find these devices in the wild, but you probably won't find them for sale anywhere.

The Palm III marked the beginning of the modern era of Palm devices. It was the first in the family to offer 2MB of memory, a backlight, and infrared beaming for sending files or applications through the air to other Palm III users. Rumor has it, that by the time this book hits print, the Palm III may be history. Chances are you'll still be able to buy one, but Palm won't make them anymore.

The Palm IIIx is an updated version of the Palm III, with some technology improvements and enhancements. This one has 4MB of memory (trust us, you'll care about memory by the time you've finished reading this book), a higher contrast, brighter screen, an internal expansion slot, and comes with a conduit for Microsoft Outlook. Otherwise, it looks exactly like the Palm III.

The Palm IIIe is the newest member of the Palm family, and is the lowest priced (at least at retail). Targeted at the entry-level user, it has all the standard Palm applications and the improved screen of the Palm IIIx, but only 2MB of memory, no expansion slot or upgrade capability, and no Outlook conduit. There is also a Palm IIIe Special Edition, which is just a Palm IIIe with a fun, clear plastic case that lets you see the innards of the device.

Continued

CONTINUED

The Palm V is the sleekest, most high-fashion member of the Palm family. In addition to being about half as thick as any of the other Palm devices, it's also the only one that runs on rechargeable batteries. There is a trade-off, though: The Palm V only has 2MB of memory inside its svelte titanium case, and it doesn't have an expansion slot. There is also a Palm Vx, which is a Palm V with 8MB of memory.

The Palm VII is the largest of the Palm devices, measuring about a half-inch longer than the Palm III and just as thick. Like that device, it offers 2MB of memory. So why would anyone want this thing? Three words: Wireless Internet connection. The Palm VII has a built-in two-way wireless radio and an antenna for accessing e-mail and the Web.

Looking Around

Now that we've gotten that little introduction out of the way, let's get on with our guided tour of the hardware. Here's what we'll be talking about in this section:

- The hard buttons
- The screen
- The contrast wheel
- The infrared beaming port
- The stylus
- The antenna
- The batteries
- The serial port

Every Palm device from the Palm III through the Palm VII has all of these elements—with the exception of the antenna, which is a Palm VII-only innovation. The rest of the hardware elements do the same things from device to device.

On the surface, Palm devices are incredibly simple. They're little enough to fit in your hand, streamlined enough to be easy to use, and convenient enough to carry with you everywhere. The best part is that they don't have a whole lot of buttons, keystrokes, or commands you need to master. Ah, but the things they can do...

The front of your Palm organizer, no matter which model, is going to have the same two elements: a screen and some hard plastic buttons (see Figure 1.1). Of course, there's much more to it; but be patient, and we'll explain everything.

NOTE The illustration we use in this chapter depicts a Palm VII. Palm III, IIIx, and V devices offer the same functions, though they may look a bit different. We'll point out any differences as we go along, so you can follow along at home on whichever Palm device is closest to your heart.

FIGURE 1.1

The front of the Palm VII

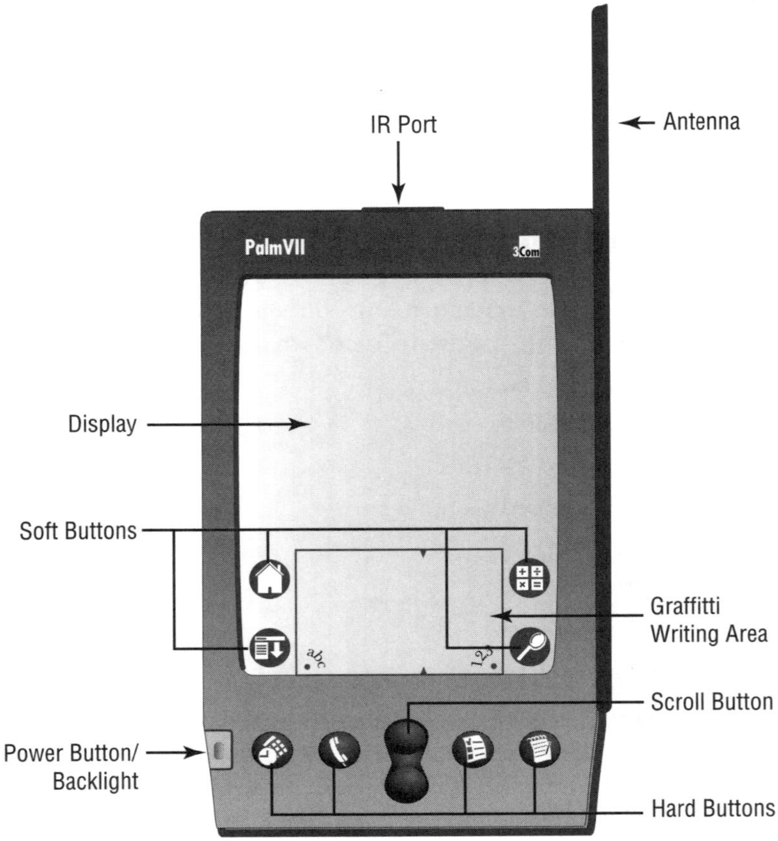

IR Port   ← Antenna

Display

Soft Buttons

Graffitti Writing Area

Scroll Button

Power Button/ Backlight

Hard Buttons

The back of your Palm device is equally simple. There you'll find the stylus, an infrared beaming port (IR Port, for short), the contrast wheel, the HotSync connector, a battery hatch, and a mysterious little hole with the word RESET written in tiny letters next to it (see Figure 1.2).

NOTE If you have a Palm V device, you won't see a battery hatch. That's because the Palm V uses a non-replaceable rechargeable battery, rather than the standard AAA batteries used by the rest of the Palm family. You will see something other Palm users don't: an accessory slot, which is used to help hold things, like an optional modem, in place.

FIGURE 1.2

The back of the Palm VII

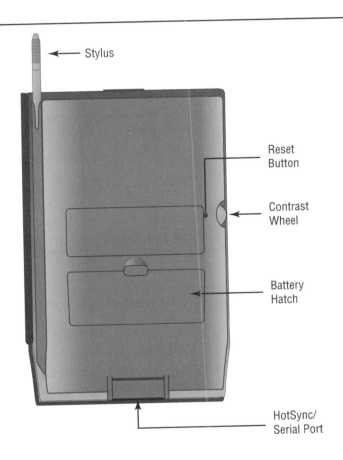

Stylus

Reset Button

Contrast Wheel

Battery Hatch

HotSync/ Serial Port

 NOTE Attention Palm V owners: Your device doesn't have a contrast wheel. It has a button at the top right, which you push to launch the contrast control application.

The Hard Buttons

Let's start our tour at the very bottom of your Palm device and work our way up. Here you'll find the hard buttons, perhaps the most important things on the case of your Palm device.

There are six buttons to choose from:

- One Power button
- Four Application buttons
- One Scrolling button

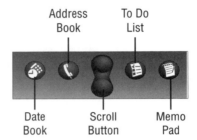

Address
Book

To Do
List

Date
Book

Scroll
Button

Memo
Pad

As you might imagine, the Power button (it's the lovely turquoise-colored one on the left edge of the device) is used to turn the device on and off. You may notice that it has a little sunburst on it—there's a reason for that. The power button is also used to turn on the backlight (which doesn't exist on Palm devices before the III). To turn the device on or off, just give the button a quick press. To turn on the backlight, hold down the power button for two seconds. You'll notice that the screen will take on a lovely bluish tint.

 TIP The backlight is designed to make text easier to read in dim lighting. Using it can drain your batteries in a hurry, so don't keep it running all the time. If you're having trouble seeing the screen under normal lighting conditions, adjust the contrast.

Moving in from the Power button, we come to the Application buttons. Though they're interrupted in the layout by the Scroll button, we'll talk about all the Application buttons together, since they work the same way.

All the Application buttons are used to (you guessed it) launch Palm applications. You don't even need to have your Palm device turned on to make these buttons work.

Pressing one of the Application buttons will turn on the Palm device and start up the application you've selected.

Push each of the Application buttons once, quickly, to launch an application. Pushing a button multiple times offers a quick way to change views. For example, pushing the Date Book button three times will quickly take you from Daily View to Monthly View. You can read more about changing views in Chapters 5 and 6, which cover the four major applications.

From left to right, the four Application buttons are: the Date Book, the Address Book, the To Do List, and the Memo Pad.

The Date Book button is the one with the little clock and calendar grid on it (it's the leftmost of the Application buttons). The Date Book does just what you'd expect it to do—it keeps track of your appointments. For more on using the Date Book, see Chapter 5.

The Address Book button (the one with the telephone handset on it) is the second button from the left. The Address Book stores telephone numbers, addresses, and assorted contact information. For more on using the Address Book, see Chapter 5.

Moving past the Scroll button (we'll get to that after we're done with the Application buttons), we come to the To Do List button (second from the right). It's the one with the little check box list on it. The To Do List keeps track of all the little jobs and tasks you mean to do, but never quite get around to completing. For more on using the To Do List, see Chapter 6.

The Application button on the far right of the device is the Memo Pad button. The Memo Pad is where you can jot down important ideas, notes to yourself, the beginnings of "The Great American Novel," or whatever text you'd like. For more on using the Memo Pad, see Chapter 6.

 TIP We've just described the applications that the hard buttons are set to launch by default. You can program the Application buttons to launch other programs. If you want to find out how it's done, turn to Chapter 7.

Wedged between the buttons for the Address Book and the To Do List lies a little rocker switch called the Scroll button. It's the one with the up and down arrows, in the center of the bottom of the Palm case.

The Scroll button works pretty much as you'd expect: Push on the up arrow of the rocker to scroll up through a list; push on the down arrow to move down through the list. Sometimes the scrolling goes slowly, line by line; sometimes a push on the scroll button will take you to a new screen. It depends on which application you're in, and where in a list you're scrolling from. Once you've built up a lengthy list of addresses, you'll really appreciate this button.

The Screen

The Screen on all the Palm devices is divided into three main areas (see Figure 1.3):

The Display Area   Where you view the contents of an application, for example the entries in the Address Book.

The Soft Buttons   Used to access Palm operating system functions and applications.

The Graffiti Writing Area   Where you enter text into a Palm application.

FIGURE 1.3

The Palm screen is divided into three areas.

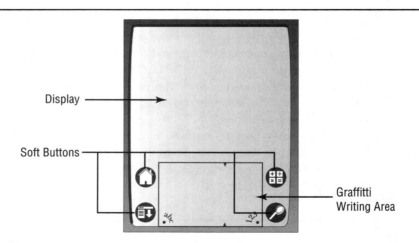

These areas are used to show you information and receive information from you. To use most of the areas of the screen, you'll need to keep your stylus handy.

The Display

The display takes up the bulk of the Palm organizer's screen (shown above in Figure 1.3). Think of the display as your window into your Palm organizer. Launch an application, and you'll see it in the display. Want to cut and paste text from a memo? You'll do that here with the help of your stylus.

As you can guess, the display works as both a viewing area and an area where you can interact with the information stored on your Palm.

What you see in the display area will differ depending on which application you're running, but we can make a few generalizations. You can generally see the name of the application that's running in the upper-left corner of the display; the upper-right corner will show category information for that particular application. The bottom of the display will show buttons for interacting with the data stored in that application. For example, when you're in the Address Book, you'll see a LookUp option, which is used to locate a name in the Address Book.

Of course, these are just generalizations. We provide more details on what you see on the screen in the chapters on the individual applications.

The Soft Buttons

Below the main display area, but above those hard little plastic buttons on the Palm device's case, we come to the soft buttons. They're not really soft in the way a kitten is soft and squishy; really, they're not any softer than the hard buttons. But, they're called soft because they aren't physical buttons (and we needed to distinguish them from the hard buttons somehow). They actually look more like little pictures than real buttons.

The soft buttons are the four icons on the bottom of the screen. There are two on the left of a box (that's the Graffiti writing area, we'll describe it in more detail later in this chapter), and two on the right.

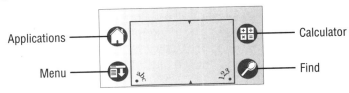

The soft buttons differ from the hard buttons in a couple of significant ways. First, with one exception (which we'll explain in just a bit), the soft buttons aren't used to launch individual applications—they're used to access Palm operating system functions. Second, the soft buttons only work when the Palm device is already turned on (using the Power button or a hard button, of course; a Palm device is immune to the whispering of sweet nothings into its screen).

The top button on the left of the Graffiti writing area is the Applications soft button (it's the one that looks like a house on a Palm VII; on a Palm III, it's represented by a curved arrow and the word Applications). Tap on this button with your stylus, and your display area will instantly be filled with icons representing all the applications installed on your Palm organizer (see Figure 1.4).

FIGURE 1.4

To see all the applications installed on your Palm device, tap the Applications soft button.

Since there are so many applications installed on a Palm VII, you'll need to scroll down through the display (hint, hint: The scroll button would come in handy about now). On a Palm III, IIIx, IIIe, or V, you'll see different and fewer applications right out of the box. Of course, you can quickly change that by installing new applications. When you do, you'll see icons for them on this screen. We'll explain how to install new applications in Chapter 9.

Below the Applications soft button lies the Menu soft button. On a Palm VII, it's the one that looks like a standard Windows-style drop-down menu with a downward pointing arrow. On a Palm III, it looks more like a warped drop-down menu, with the word menu printed below the graphic. The Menu soft button does the same thing, but looks a bit slicker now.

Most applications offer menus for doing things like creating a new item or editing an existing one (Cut, Copy, Paste, and Undo are common menu commands). To access these menus, tap the Menu soft button to see what menus are available. Tap on the menu you want (Record, Edit, and Options are typical) to drop down that menu (see Figure 1.5). Funny how that works. From there, you can carry out whatever action you choose.

FIGURE 1.5

Tap the Menu soft button to see what menus are available for an application.

Sometimes, though, you may tap the Menu soft button and get nothing. This doesn't mean the button is busted; it just means that no menus are available for that particular part of the application. We'll go into more detail on menus in the chapters on the individual applications.

Moving right along to the right side of the Graffiti box, we find the most idiosyncratic of the soft buttons—the Calculator button. This button (top right) is the one with the four mathematical symbols on it. On the Palm III, you'll find the word Calculator below the graphic.

This button is unusual because it launches a single application rather than providing access to an operating system function. Bet you can't guess which application the Calculator button launches? Why yes, you're right: it launches the Calculator. And guess what else? The Palm Calculator works and looks just like a regular calculator (see Figure 1.6).

FIGURE 1.6

The Palm Calculator does all the stuff you'd expect a calculator to do.

The last soft button is the one in the bottom-right corner—the Find button. It's the one with the magnifying glass. Pretty clever graphic, huh? On a Palm III, you also get the word Find below the graphic, in case you couldn't figure it out for yourself.

Find works from any screen and any application on the Palm organizer. Tap it, and you get a blank line to enter what you're looking for (see Figure 1.7). Find can locate names, numbers, dates… any text you have stored anywhere in your Palm organizer.

FIGURE 1.7

Use Find to track down any text in any application.

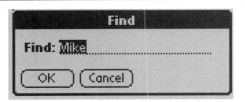

You don't even have to enter an entire word for Find to do its thing. Enter the first few letters of a word, and Find will bring back a list of all possible matches. Then, you can pick the one that most closely matches your input (see Figure 1.8).

FIGURE 1.8

Find will return a list of all possible matches.

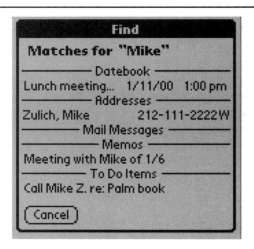

The Graffiti Writing Area

That little box in between the soft buttons (the one with the abc in one lower corner and 123 in the other) is the Graffiti Writing Area. It's the area of the screen you'll interact with (that means use your stylus on and swear at) the most. This is the place where you enter any text you want to include, for example a name or phone number in an Address Book entry.

Notice that about two thirds of the way across the Graffiti box there's a triangle at the top and bottom (see Figure 1.9). These triangles divide the Graffiti screen into areas for writing letters on the left side (hence the abc) and numbers on the right (notice the 123).

FIGURE 1.9

The Graffiti writing area

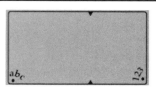

You can write punctuation and special characters on either side. We explain more about Graffiti in Chapter 2. For now, just know that the Graffiti alphabet is a lot like English; only a few of the characters are written differently. It may seem as familiar and easy to master as hieroglyphics at first, but with a little practice (much less than you ever did on the piano), you'll become fluent in the ways of Graffiti. And if you're the one-in-a-million who can't get the hang of it, there's always a tiny built-in keyboard you can use to tap your way through data entry.

The Contrast Wheel

Like your television set, your Palm organizer's display can sometimes be a bit tough to look at. Getting it straight is a lot easier than adjusting your TV. You don't get controls for color, brightness, sharpness, or horizontal or vertical hold on your Palm. All you get is one little dial: the contrast wheel (located on the left edge of the case). Your Palm doesn't need all those color controls for a very simple reason—it doesn't display color (yet). All it shows is gray—many different levels of gray—but still, just gray. The contrast wheel can handle that.

 TIP Remember that the Palm V doesn't offer a contrast wheel. It has a button you push to bring up a Contrast dialog box on screen. From there, you adjust the sliders till the screen looks clear and well defined.

The contrast wheel's job is pretty simple: it fine-tunes the grays so there's a clear differentiation between the light tones and the dark tones. Without that differentiation, all you'd see is a blank or dark screen. And what would be the point of that?

The contrast wheel couldn't be easier to use: Just turn the little wheel up or down until the Palm's display is sharp and clear, and easy to read. There are no calibration tools or predefined contrast settings—it's all left to your personal preference.

 WARNING If your Palm screen comes up black when you turn the power on, it probably just means the contrast wheel got jostled when you were pulling the device out of your briefcase. Try adjusting the contrast before you panic. And consider buying a case for your Palm, so this isn't a constant problem.

The Infrared Beaming Port

The Palm organizer provides another means of communicating with the outside world: wireless communications. On a Palm III, IIIe, IIIx, or V, you can send data and applications to other Palm users via the infrared (IR) port. On a Palm VII, you also get true wireless communication via a built-in transmitter and external antenna (which we describe in the next section).

The infrared beaming port is the red plastic window located on the top edge of your Palm device. It communicates with other Palm devices via infrared light (hence the name), and requires a direct line of site with the other device. This process, which in Palm-speak is called beaming, is explained in greater detail in Chapter 8.

You're probably familiar with IR from your television set and cable box. It's the same technology your remote control uses to "talk" to those devices. Your Palm (on its own), can't change the channels on your television. It can only talk to another Palm device unless you soup it up with some software and peripherals, which we discuss in Chapter 19.

Antenna

At this point, you're probably turning your Palm device around and around wondering how you could have missed the antenna. Relax, you're not crazy. If you have a Palm VII, your device has an antenna. Any other Palm version doesn't have one because it doesn't need one—you only need the antenna for wireless connectivity, which devices other than the Palm VII can't do straight out of the box. The antenna is only a part of the Palm VII hardware.

Located on the right edge of the Palm VII, the antenna is used for wireless reception. Raise the antenna, and the Palm VII turns on and goes to the Palm.Net Application Launcher screen. We'll explain all this wireless stuff in more detail in Chapters 12 and 13.

For now, all we'll say is that the antenna is very important if you want to use your Palm VII for wirelessly checking e-mail or accessing the Internet. If you don't want to do those things, why'd you buy a Palm VII anyway?

Oh, and when you're not using the wireless features, please lower the antenna; your Palm doesn't need it to run the standard applications. Besides, you wouldn't want the antenna to snap off, now would you?

The Stylus

Since your Palm organizer uses handwriting and touch as its source of input, you need something to write and tap with. How convenient that the Palm comes with its very own slim, stylish stylus.

The stylus is that pen-shaped silver and gray instrument tucked into the slot on the back-right side of your Palm device. Just pull it out of that slot, and you're ready to go.

Stop and take a look at the business end of the stylus. Did you notice that there's no ink? At this point, you're probably shaking your head and saying, "Of course there's no ink. The Palm's an electronic device that responds to touch. It isn't paper." Of course, you're right. But you'd be amazed at the number of otherwise intelligent people we know who have misplaced their styluses and used ballpoint pens as a replacement. Very bad idea. You wind up with ink and scratches all over your screen. And when the Palm's screen is ruined, the device is useless; you can't replace the screen.

You can, however, replace your stylus if you lose it, or if you find it's too skinny for your hand. There are lots of sources for replacement styluses. See Chapter 20 for information on some of our favorites.

For now, though, keep in mind that your stylus is an important part of your Palm, and remember to put it back into its cozy little slot when you're finished using it. Didn't your mom always tell you to put your toys away when you were done playing with them? Now you know the importance of that lesson.

Batteries

By now, you're probably wondering what makes the Palm organizer run? In the case of every Palm except the Palm V, it's two AAA batteries, safely tucked away behind the rectangular hatch on the back of the device.

Palm V devices, on the other hand, use a single rechargeable lithium ion battery to keep their motors running. You can't replace this battery, but the folks at Palm swear it's good for at least 500 full charges. That's a lot of juice. To charge the Palm V, you park it in its cradle for around 5 hours. Take it out again and you're ready for anything.

Batteries Are a Terrible Thing to Waste

A Palm organizer can run a long time on a single pair of AAA batteries—unless you spend a lot of time downloading e-mail via modem or wirelessly on a Palm VII. Playing games also drains your battery. The backlight, too, can suck the life out of your batteries in a hurry.

And unless you have a Palm V (which uses the cradle to charge its battery), keep your Palm organizer out of the cradle when you're not HotSyncing it. (HotSyncing is the process of exchanging data or applications between your Palm and your desktop PC. We explain the HotSync process in detail in Chapter 9.) The cradle may seem like a safe, secure place to store your organizer, but it's really a big battery drainer. It has something to do with the fact that the serial port connection stays open when the device is in the cradle, but that's a level of technical detail we don't need to explore here.

Some folks will tell you there's a way to remedy that situation. Unfortunately, it involves opening up your cradle and snipping a wire. If you're the type who likes to take stuff apart just to see how it works, go right ahead. You can find very clear instructions and photos to follow at www.conklinsystems.com/pilot/drainfix.shtml.

Of course, once you open that cradle, the warranty is void. So we say, buy a case for your organizer to rest in, and leave all the wires alone.

If you remember nothing else about your Palm and its batteries, remember this: Back up all your data to your desktop PC often. The process is called HotSyncing, and we explain how in Chapter 9. The battery indicator on your Palm (which you can see at the top of the Application Launcher screen) isn't the most accurate thing in the world. And when your batteries die, so does all your precious data.

When you change batteries, you have roughly 1-2 minutes from the time you take out the old batteries till you install a fresh set into the Palm before its memory is wiped clean and your data is gone forever. So get the new batteries out of the package and close at hand before you open that battery hatch.

And even then, don't remove both batteries at the same time. Take out one old battery and replace it with a fresh one, before taking out the other spent AAA. This is a fairly safe way to keep your data safe. But before you do anything, HotSync!!! We can't say this strongly enough.

The Reset Button

Its official name is the Reset Button, but if you take a good look, you'll notice it's really more of a hole. Whatever you call it, it's a useful piece of hardware for when your Palm organizer just isn't behaving itself.

If you install enough third-party software on your organizer, it may just lock up and refuse to do anything. When that happens, you'll need to stick something small into the reset hole to essentially reboot your Palm organizer, just as you would reboot a misbehaving desktop PC.

There are several different kinds of resets and different conditions for using each. We explain them all in Appendix B.

The Serial Port

On its own, the Palm is a powerful tool for organizing your life. But hook it up to the outside world and you've got a first-rate communication tool.

The Palm was never meant to exist in a vacuum; it was designed to share information with your desktop PC. So whether you're on the go or trapped at a desk, you can always have access to your Palm tools and data.

The Palm uses two bits of hardware to communicate with your desktop PC: its serial port (also known as the HotSync Connector) and its cradle. We'll talk about the cradle next; for now, let's focus on the serial port.

Don't expect the serial port on your Palm to look at all like the connector you hook a modem up to on a standard computer. See that little spring-loaded hatch at the bottom of the Palm? Push in on it gently (GENTLY!), and you'll see some flat gold wires inlaid on a green circuit board. That's the serial port.

The serial port is the Palm's primary tool for connecting with external devices, such as the HotSync cradle or a HotSync cable for exchanging data with your desktop PC, an external modem for surfing the Web, a GPS for knowing where you are at all times... the list goes on and on. We'll tell you about some of the cool peripherals you can hook up to the serial port in Chapter 20.

For now, just think of the Palm's serial port as the piece of equipment necessary to exchange information with a desktop PC.

The HotSync Cradle

To complete that information exchange between your Palm and your desktop PC, you'll need a HotSync cradle. The cradle is that chunk of plastic packaged with your Palm organizer. You can get a good look at it in Figure 1.10.

FIGURE 1.10

The HotSync cradle

You'll notice that the cradle has some pins sticking up from its center and a long cord with a standard (PC-style) serial port connector on its end. The pins plug in to the serial port on the Palm, and the connector hooks up to the serial port on the back of your Windows computer.

TIP If you have a Macintosh, you'll need to get a special adapter to hook up the cradle to your desktop computer. It's included in the MacPac, which we discuss in Chapter 9.

In essence, the HotSync cradle is a middleman, enabling one serial port (the Hot-Sync connector on your Palm) to send data to another serial port (in this case, located on the back of your desktop PC).

Starting Your Palm

Now that you're familiar with all the external parts of your Palm organizer, it's time to move on to the good stuff—the operating system and the applications. So, press that Power button and hang on. The fun is just beginning.

Setting Up House

The first thing you'll want to do is teach your Palm organizer who's boss. Fortunately, you don't need to talk sternly to the device or make threatening gestures toward it. All you need to do is pull out the stylus, press the Power button, and enter a bit of information.

This section provides some instruction and details on setting system options.

Screen Parameters

The first time you power up your Palm, you'll see a series of setup screens filled with instructions for configuring your device. The first thing they'll have you do is define the screen parameters. To set screen parameters, just tap the stylus firmly in the center of the targets displayed on the Palm's screen (see Figure 1.11).

FIGURE 1.13

Just tap to set the screen parameters.

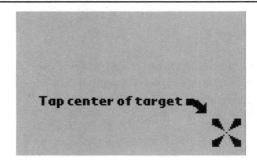

Setting the screen parameters is important for accurate text input. Since your Palm organizer is pressure sensitive, it needs to know where the boundaries of the screen are so it can register pen input accurately. Setting the screen parameters will help your Palm more accurately convert your Graffiti input into text (assuming you write the letters correctly, of course).

Country, Date, and Time

The next step is setting the country, date, and time (see Figure 1.12). You don't need to know Graffiti to do any of this. If you can tap, you're all set.

FIGURE 1.12

Set the country, date, and time.

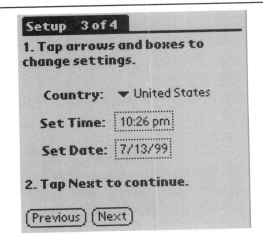

To set the country:

1. Tap on the down arrow next to the words United States (the default country setting). This brings up a pick list of countries.

2. Scroll through the country list by tapping on the arrow in the upper-right corner of the list.

3. Tap on the name of the country where you reside to return to the Setup screen.

To set the time:

1. Tap in the text box currently displaying the wrong time (it's next to the words Set Time). This will bring up a Set Time dialog box, as illustrated in Figure 1.1.3

FIGURE 1.13

The Set Time dialog box

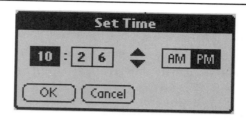

2. The first box, where you enter the hour, will be highlighted. To change the hour, tap the up or down arrows as appropriate, until the hour is correct.

3. Follow the same procedure to set the minutes.

4. Tap on AM or PM to set the time of day.

5. Tap on OK to accept the new time and return to the Setup screen.

Next, you'll need to set the date. To change the date:

1. Tap in the date box that appears next to the words Set Date. This will bring up a full year calendar (see Figure 1.14).

FIGURE 1.14

Pick the current date from the calendar.

2. Tap on the name of the month you want. The yearly calendar will be replaced with a calendar for the month you selected.

3. Tap on the current date on the calendar.

This will take you back to the Setup screen, where you should see the current date and time displayed. Tap Next to finish the setup process.

 TIP You'll see a button that says Today at the bottom of the calendar. Ignore it for now. Your Palm organizer doesn't know what day it is until after you set it for the first time.

You can set other preferences, but these are the only ones that are absolutely necessary to configure. We explain more about personalizing your Palm device in Chapter 4.

Exploring the Applications

Now that your Palm knows what day it is, it's time to start exploring the applications. This section will provide a quick overview of each of the applications that come installed on your Palm. Subsequent chapters will explain how to use each of the applications in greater detail.

To see all the applications installed on your organizer, just tap the Applications soft button (remember, it's the one that looks like a little house). Doing so will take you to the main Application Launcher screen (see Figure 1.15).

FIGURE 1.15

The Application Launcher screen displays icons for all the applications installed on your organizer.

The applications installed on a Palm III, IIIx, and V are:

- Address Book
- Calculator
- Date Book
- Expense
- Graffiti
- HotSync
- Mail
- Memo Pad
- Preferences
- Security
- To Do List
- Welcome

 NOTE On some Palm III devices, there's an application called Giraffe, which takes the place of the Graffiti Trainer. Both are tools that help you master Graffiti.

Palm VII devices have all these applications, plus a few more. We'll explain all those extra offerings later in this chapter.

You can launch any of these applications from the Application Launcher. To access the Launcher, tap on the Application soft button (the one that looks like a little house), then tap on the icon for the application you want to launch.

You can launch the Address Book, Date Book, To Do List, and Memo Pad by pressing the appropriate hard buttons. And, to launch the Calculator, you can just tap on the Calculator soft button, without even opening the Application Launcher.

Address Book

If you're familiar with paper-based address books or contact managers (such as Outlook and ACT!) that run on the PC, you understand what Palm's Address Book is all about. It's more full-featured than a paper address book (just try dealing with peripatetic relatives in one of those! We ran out of space under "M" because of one relative who wouldn't stay put); but, it's not as robust as a PC-based contact manager.

Still, if you need to keep names, addresses, and phone numbers readily available, the Palm Address Book is up to the task.

Press the Address Book hard button to open up your spanking new application. Amazingly enough, there will already be listings on the page. It's not telepathy, it's just the work of the folks from Palm Computing. They didn't want you to feel unloved.

The Address Book has a few cool features, too. For example, it lets you attach a note to an entry, so you can keep all the information on a person in one place. Say you need directions to that new client's office; you can store that info in a note attached to their Address Book listing.

 NOTE   For more on the Address Book, turn to Chapter 5.

Calculator

If you're mathematically challenged like one of the authors of this book (who shall remain nameless), you'll be thrilled with the Palm's built-in calculator. It can handle basic math—addition, subtraction, multiplication, and division. It doesn't have any higher-order mathematical capabilities, so if you really need to compute square roots or the depreciation of an asset, you'll need to install a more specialized calculator. We'll tell you about a few in Chapter 16.

For now, go ahead and tap on the Calculator icon to open the application. Looks just like a non-Palm calculator, but with really big buttons, doesn't it?

 NOTE To learn about some of the nifty tricks the built-in Calculator can do, turn to Chapter 7.

Date Book

Have a busy schedule and a memory like a sieve? Then the Date Book is for you. As you probably guessed, this application lets you schedule appointments and activities—and it even remembers them for you.

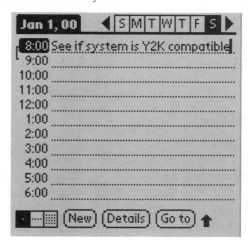

The Date Book is easy to use and lets you view a day, a week, or a month's worth of appointments at a time. It can even remind you about upcoming meetings, birthdays, and special events. So now you have no excuse for missing your anniversary.

Press the Date Book hard button once to open to an empty page representing today. Isn't it nice to see a day that isn't totally booked up?

 NOTE For more information on using the Date Book, see Chapter 5.

Expense

Don't wait until you get home from a business trip to figure out how much you spent. Instead, use the Expense application, to log the date, amount, and type of your expenses. With this application, you'll never have to look at a receipt and wonder: Was this dinner in Dallas or entertainment in New York?

The most useful feature of Expense is that it lets you transfer any data you input in the application to a Microsoft Excel spreadsheet on your desktop computer.

 NOTE To find out more about using Expense, turn to Chapter 7.

Graffiti

Graffiti is the written language of the Palm. Most people have a love/hate relationship with the language; they hate it when they're first trying to learn it, but then grow to love it as they become proficient.

The Graffiti training application can help flatten out the learning curve, turning you into a Graffiti master in no time. You won't be rewarded with a laser saber when you finish all the training lessons, but you will be able to quickly enter information into any Palm application.

Why not start up the application and practice your Graffiti now? You'll need it down the road. Just tap on the Graffiti icon to launch the application, then follow the on-screen instructions to start your tutorial.

 NOTE For a complete guide to Graffiti, as well as text entry tricks, see Chapter 2.

HotSync

In many ways, HotSync is the most important application installed on your Palm organizer. It's the tool that lets you synchronize the data on your organizer with the Palm Desktop software, or another personal information manager (PIM), installed on your PC.

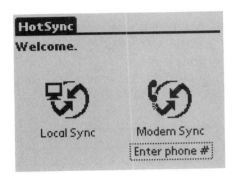

You can HotSync using the cradle that comes with your Palm organizer or by using a modem or network connection. HotSync works equally well, whichever technique you choose.

Just remember to HotSync early and often. It's the only way to keep your precious data safe should something awful happen—like you drop your Palm or just let its batteries die (shame on you!).

 NOTE For full details on using HotSync, see Chapter 9.

Mail

The mail application does just one thing—it manages e-mail that you send via your preferred e-mail application on your desktop PC. It can't send e-mail over the Internet because it doesn't dial out to any Internet services. So, Mail isn't a true e-mail application; think of it instead as an e-mail organizer.

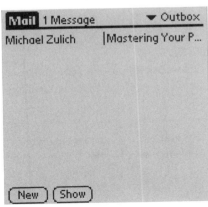

If you want to read e-mail, delete a message, or compose a reply, Mail can handle it. Of course, you'll need to HotSync with your PC to actually send or receive e-mail. In spite of these limitations, Mail offers a way to stay in touch with your e-mail when you're away from your desk.

Go ahead and take a look at the Mail application now. Surprise! Your inbox already has a message.

 NOTE For more on using Mail, see Chapter 12.

Memo Pad

The Memo Pad is the Palm organizer's answer to a word processor. Memo Pad isn't meant for use when writing a book (not even this one!), since each memo is limited to 4K in size. But, for jotting down meeting notes, ideas to include in a report, or any other text that doesn't fit into the Address Book or Date Book, Memo Pad is just the thing.

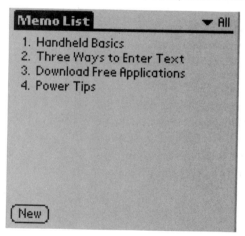

Since you can cut and paste text from the Memo Pad into the Address Book or Date Book, it also works great for temporary storage, like one of those little yellow stickies.

 NOTE We explain the Memo Pad in more detail in Chapter 6.

Preferences

The Preferences application is the key to making your Palm organizer truly yours. Anything on the Palm that can be configured gets configured here. You can do everything from setting the date and time (which you did when you first powered up your Palm), to configuring which application launches when you push the hard buttons or the Calculator soft button.

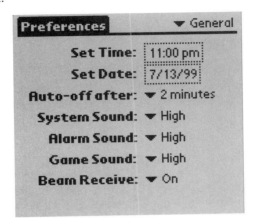

 NOTE There are many more options you can configure. We'll explain them in Chapter 4.

Security

If you're concerned about security on your desktop PC, you're also concerned about your Palm organizer. Luckily, the Security application can password protect your Palm and hide private information from prying eyes. So, you won't need to worry that sensitive data (like your Grandma's recipe for chocolate chip cookies) will fall into the wrong hands should you leave your Palm unattended.

NOTE For more on safeguarding your Palm organizer with the Security application, see Chapter 7.

To Do List

We all have too much to do, but have too little time to get it all done. The To Do List can't help with the time thing, but it can help you keep track of all the tasks you need to complete and help you prioritize them. It even lets you categorize your To Dos, so on Saturday you don't have to see the list of 20 things you need to get done at the office Monday morning.

Start up the To Do List and take a quick look around. The first time you launch the application, you'll see a lovely little reminder to register your Palm organizer. Go ahead and do it, then tap in the little box at the front of the item to mark it complete.

 NOTE For more on using the To Do List, see Chapter 6.

Welcome

When you powered up your Palm organizer for the first time, the Welcome application was automatically running. If you need a new introduction to your Palm organizer, or just want some handholding to change the date and time, the Welcome application can help you out.

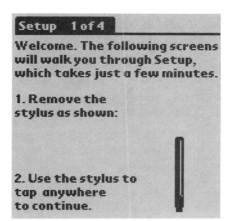

The Welcome application is a good tool to get things started, but once you've configured the date and time, and calibrated the screen, you can go ahead and delete it. We explain how to do just that in Chapter 9.

What's All That Other Stuff on My Palm VII?

In addition to all the applications we've outlined in this chapter, your Palm VII includes the following wireless-specific applications located in the Application Launcher. You'll need to extend the antenna to use any of the following:

- Activate—For setting up your Palm.Net Internet service account. You'll need to have a credit card handy, and you'll have to wait about an hour after first putting the batteries in your Palm VII so the wireless transmitter can charge enough to make a connection.

- Diagnostics—Where you can get the details on the strength of your wireless connection and its transmission rate. This application is useful when you're having trouble connecting to Palm.Net.

- Palm.Net—Where to go to check on your usage and charges, and to get answers to some support questions related to the Palm.Net wireless Internet service.

- iMessenger—The wireless Internet e-mail application for use with the Palm.Net service. Unlike the Mail application, iMessenger logs on directly to the Internet to send and receive mail—no desktop PC required. To find out more about using iMessenger, turn to Chapter 13.

Continued

CONTINUED

- Query Applications—The Palm VII doesn't actually surf the Web; instead, it uses Query Applications to access Internet sites and information. Basically, you make a request for information, and these applications go out to the Web, get the information you want, and deliver it to your Palm VII. For more information on using Query Applications, see Chapter 13.

CHAPTER **2**

Mastering Graffiti

To make your Palm organizer a truly useful device, you need to fill it with data. It has an Address Book for you to add listings for your nearest and dearest. It has a Date Book for you to log all those very important appointments. But how do you get the information in there since the Palm doesn't have a keyboard... or does it?

There are three ways to input data in your Palm organizer:

- You can enter it into the Palm Desktop software on your PC and bring it over to your organizer via HotSync.
- You can tap away on the Palm's little on-screen keyboard.
- You can use the Graffiti writing system.

We'll cover entering information with the on-screen keyboard and Graffiti in this chapter. To find out how to HotSync data from the Palm Desktop, see Chapter 9. We'll discuss Graffiti first.

Let's clear up a couple of common misconceptions before we go any further. First, Graffiti is a writing system with its own alphabet and conventions. It isn't handwriting recognition software, which means that you have to learn how it wants letters written; it isn't ever going to learn anything from you. To make things easier, think of Graffiti as a cat; as long as you do exactly what it wants, you'll get along fine.

The second misconception is that Graffiti is hard to learn. Wrong. Most of the letters in the Graffiti alphabet are just simplified versions of the standard Latin alphabet (that's the one we use to write in English). There are a few unusual characters, but even these are easy to master. We'll offer some tips on improving your Graffiti accuracy later in this chapter.

The third, and final, misconception is that you can write Graffiti anywhere on the Palm screen. Wrong again. You can use you stylus to tap on any part of the screen, for example to make a selection in a pick list (we explain pick lists in Chapter 3). But you can only write Graffiti in the Graffiti writing area at the bottom of the Palm screen (see Figure 2.1).

FIGURE 2.1

The Graffiti writing area

Writing Letters and Numbers

Take a good look at Figure 2.1 and notice that the Graffiti writing area is divided two-thirds of the way across by little arrows at the top and bottom. Notice, too, that in the lower-left corner of the writing area there are the letters abc. This is a reminder that you use the left side of the screen to write letters. The numbers 123 in the lower-right corner of the screen tell you that the area to the right of those dividing arrows is used for writing numbers. Of course, you also use Graffiti to write punctuation marks and symbols. You can write those on either side of the screen. (We'll explain how in the next two sections. For now, let's concentrate on letters and numbers).

 NOTE Your Palm organizer comes with Graffiti stickers and a reference card. Carry the card with you; put the stickers on the back of your Palm VII or on the inside cover of your Palm IIIx. Don't be embarrassed; you're learning a new language and cheat sheets are totally permissible.

You'll notice a few interesting things on those Graffiti stickers (and the charts within the user manual) of Graffiti letters and numbers. Each character has a heavy dot somewhere in it. This indicates the starting point for the character. You don't actually draw the dot; just put your stylus in that spot and start writing from there. You write most Graffiti letters with one continuous stroke, so don't pick up your stylus until you've drawn the whole letter. When you lift your stylus off the screen and then set it down again, Graffiti thinks you're starting a new letter.

Writing Letters

Take a look at Figure 2.2 to see the full Graffiti alphabet. Now look at the Graffiti A. It looks almost exactly like a regular A. The only difference is that the Graffiti A is missing the crossbar—you can't draw that part of the letter without lifting the stylus (and that's a no-no).

FIGURE 2.2

The Graffiti alphabet

Notice also the dot at the lower left of the character. That indicates the place where you start writing the character; you move up the leg to a peak, and then down the other side. That's all there is to it.

You probably noticed that when you write a Graffiti A, you write a capital letter. But, the text letter that appears on screen is lowercase. So how do you get capital letters when there's no shift key?

You use a special Graffiti stroke called Cap Shift, and then write the same Graffiti character you would for a lowercase letter.

The Cap Shift stroke looks like this:

Kind of looks a bit like an exclamation point that had its dot meld with its line, doesn't it?

To write a Cap Shift, start your stylus at the bottom of the Graffiti writing area and draw straight up. When the Cap Shift is turned on, an up arrow appears in the lower-right corner of the display (as in Figure 2.3).

FIGURE 2.3

The Capital Shift in action.

To write a capital A:

1. Enter the Cap Shift character using Graffiti.

2. Write the Graffiti character for A.

You must enter a Cap Shift before you enter the letter you want capitalized. Graffiti will enter one uppercase letter, then revert to lowercase text. So, if you want multiple capital letters (for entering initials, for example), you must enter the Cap Shift and write the first letter; then enter Cap Shift again and write the second letter, and so on. Or, you can use the Cap Lock stroke.

The Graffiti Cap Lock stroke is just the Cap Shift character entered twice in succession. In Graffiti terms, it looks like this:

When Cap Lock is active, you'll see an underlined up arrow in the lower-right corner of the screen (as in Figure 2.4).

FIGURE 2.4

All Caps, all the time

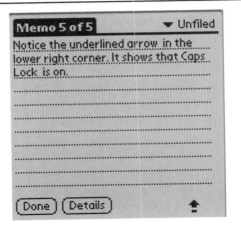

To turn off Cap Lock, you just enter the Cap Shift stroke once.

 TIP Sometimes, Palm applications just assume you want a capital letter (for example, when you enter a name in the Address Book), so they turn on the Cap Shift for you. If you'd prefer a lowercase letter, enter the Cap Shift stroke twice to return to lowercase letters. If you enter it once, you'll just succeed in turning on Cap Lock.

Writing Numbers

You write numbers the same way you write letters with Graffiti—put the stylus down and don't pick it up until you've written an entire character. The only difference is that you use the right side of the Graffiti area to write numbers. You can see all the Graffiti numbers in Figure 2.5.

FIGURE 2.5

Pick a number, any number

Graffiti Tips

Here are ten tips on improving your Graffiti ability.

1. Write large—larger characters are recognized more easily.
2. Hold the stylus at a 90-degree angle to the screen; don't write at a slant.
3. Don't lift the stylus mid-character. When you lift the stylus off the screen, Graffiti thinks you are done writing that character and starts another.
4. If you accidentally turn on Cap Lock or Punctuation Shift, just write a Backspace (position your stylus at the right side of the Graffiti writing area, and drag it to the left—in essence, write a backwards dash) to turn it off.
5. Stay in the box—keep letters on the abc side and numbers on the 123 side of the writing area.
6. Write your Vs backward for better recognition.
7. Write a 3 on the letters side to get a B.
8. Write an 8 on the letters side to get a Y.
9. Make the tail at the top of a Q long, and don't worry about closing the circle.
10. Write a 6 on the letters side to get a G.

Punctuating Your Thoughts

Writing punctuation in Graffiti is a bit more complicated than writing letters or numbers. With a little practice, you can write any punctuation mark you can type on a computer keyboard.

There are two things you need to know about punctuation and Graffiti:

- Punctuation marks can be written in either the letter or number side of the Graffiti writing area.

- Before you can write a punctuation character, you need to turn on the Punctuation Shift.

To turn on Punctuation Shift, just tap once anywhere in the Graffiti writing area. It's just like writing a period. When Punctuation Shift is active, you'll see a dot in the lower-right corner of the display, as in Figure 2.6. Any Graffiti strokes you write with Punctuation Shift active will be translated to punctuation marks. Punctuation Shift automatically turns off after your next stroke. There is no Punctuation Shift lock.

FIGURE 2.6

Look for the Punctuation Shift.

The two punctuation characters you'll use most often are the period and the dash. To write a period:

1. Tap once anywhere in the Graffiti writing area to turn on Punctuation Shift.

2. Tap again to write a period.

To write a dash:

1. Tap once anywhere in the Graffiti writing area to turn on Punctuation Shift.

2. Draw a dash anywhere in the Graffiti writing area, starting at the left and moving to the right.

There are also some frequently used symbols that you write as if they were punctuation. The $, the &, and the @ sign that's part of every e-mail address in the free world are all considered punctuation in the wonderful world of the Palm organizer.

To add an @ sign to an e-mail address, for example, to write me@mydomain.com:

1. Write the word me using Graffiti.

2. Tap once anywhere in the Graffiti writing area to turn on Punctuation Shift.

3. Write the letter O.

4. Write mydomain, punctuate the period, and write com.

To see the full range of characters that Graffiti considers punctuation, see Figure 2.7.

FIGURE 2.7
Punctuate this!

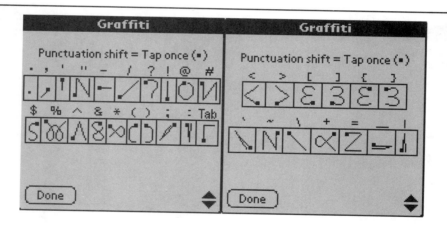

Navigating with Graffiti

This will come as a surprise to even some experienced Palm users: You can use Graffiti for navigating through text and applications. For example, you can use Graffiti to add a space between words, start a new sentence on a new line, and even move from one field of an Address Book record to the next.

TIP Using Graffiti to navigate between fields of an open Address Book record is not documented within the stroke navigation characters. With a contact open in Edit mode, you can use the Next Field (straight down and up) or Previous Field (straight up and down) Graffiti strokes to move from one line to the next, for instance, from Last Name to First Name.

As with punctuation, Graffiti requires special characters to move the cursor through an application. These are called Navigation Strokes. You can see the full range of Navigation Strokes in Figure 2.8.

FIGURE 2.8

Navigation by the strokes

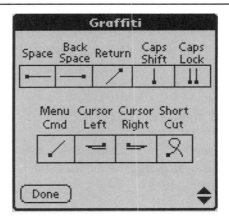

Navigation Strokes can be written anywhere in the Graffiti writing area. The ones you'll probably use most often are the space, backspace, and return. We'll walk you through the Graffiti steps for those now.

To add a space between words:

1. Tap on the display to position your cursor at the point you want to add the space.

2. In the Graffiti writing area, draw a short dash, moving from left to right.

3. Start writing your next word immediately following the newly added space.

To backspace to erase an errant letter:

1. Tap on the display to position your cursor to the right of the letter or word you want to get rid of.

2. In the Graffiti writing area, draw a short dash, moving from right to left (yes, it's the exact opposite of a space).

3. If you want to delete more than one letter, draw the backspace character again and repeat until you've deleted all the letters you no longer want.

A return in Graffiti serves the same purpose as hitting the Enter key on your desktop system's keyboard: It carries your cursor to the next line.

To add a return at the end of a sentence:

1. Tap on the display to position your cursor at the point you want to add the return.

2. In the Graffiti writing area, draw a slash by moving your stylus from the top-right corner diagonally down toward the left.

3. Start entering text on the next line where the cursor is now positioned.

You'll have no problem learning the rest of the Graffiti Navigation Strokes on your own.

Using Special Characters

There are some characters that can't be classified as letters, numbers, or punctuation. Such characters include mathematical symbols (+, %), copyright marks, and more. These characters are written using the Extended Shift character, which is also known as the Symbol Shift.

The Extended Shift is written as a downward slash, starting at the top left and finishing at the bottom right. It looks like this:

After you've entered an Extended Shift, you'll see a slash in the lower-right corner of the screen. This lets you know that you're writing symbols and special characters. You can see the Graffiti strokes for these characters in Figure 2.9.

FIGURE 2.9

*The extended cast of
characters*

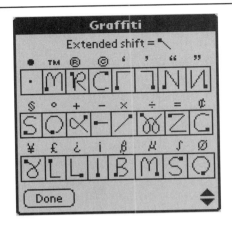

TIP   Some characters, like quotation marks, can be written either as standard punctuation or as extended characters. Both approaches work just fine. And we have absolutely no idea why the Palm folks thought you needed two ways to ask a question.

Working in Applications

There's one Graffiti stroke you'll find invaluable when working in applications. It's called the Command Shift stroke, and it's written as a slash, starting from the bottom left and moving diagonally up to the right. Don't get it confused with the Extended Shift, which looks similar but is written diagonally from top to bottom. The Command Shift stroke looks like this:

The Command Shift tells the Palm that whatever you enter next is an application command (for example, cut, copy, paste, or delete). In essence, the Command Shift lets you perform actions you'd normally access through the menus.

To cut a word in the Address Book, for example, you'd select the word using your stylus (just drag across the word you want to select with your stylus, the same way you would use a mouse to select a word on your desktop PC), then enter the Command Shift followed by X. This will accomplish the same result as choosing Edit ➤ Cut from the Menu Bar.

Many of the Graffiti strokes for commands are the same from application to application. Cut, copy, and paste are always Command Shift ➤ X, C, P, respectively.

To find out what actions can be carried out using the Command Shift in an application, open the Menu Bar for that application and look at the list of commands on the right side of each drop-down menu. These tell you what Graffiti strokes to enter to use that command. You can see an example in Figure 2.10.

FIGURE 2.10

The Graffiti version of a command

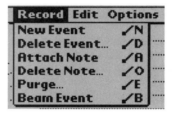

Using ShortCuts

There's one last special Graffiti character we'll introduce you to here. It's called the Graffiti ShortCut and is used to quickly add standard words and phrases, like the date and time, to your records. It works a lot like the AutoText feature in Microsoft Word. You can use ShortCuts in the Address Book, Date Book, Memo Pad, and To Do List.

Graffiti comes with a handful of preconfigured ShortCuts for adding the date, time, or words like Meeting, Breakfast, Lunch, or Dinner to your record. These Short-Cuts are:

ShortCut Name	ShortCut Text
br	Breakfast
di	Dinner
ds	Date Stamp
dts	Date and Time Stamp
lu	Lunch
me	Meeting
ts	Time Stamp

The Breakfast, Dinner, Lunch, and Meeting ShortCuts add those words to your record at the point where your cursor is positioned. Date Stamp adds the current date to your record; Time Stamp adds the time; and Date and Time Stamp adds both.

TIP You can access the list of ShortCuts through the Preferences application. From the Application Launcher, tap on Preferences, then choose ShortCuts from the category drop-down list.

To use these ShortCuts, you first enter the ShortCut character, which looks like a cursive lowercase L or a Graffiti K standing upright, followed by the abbreviation for the ShortCut. So, if you wanted to add the time to your memo, you'd write:

You can also create your own ShortCuts, perhaps to add your name to an e-mail. We'll explain how in Chapter 4.

Working with the On-Screen Keyboard

When all else fails, and you just can't get the hang of Graffiti—in its entirety or just for entering particular characters—it's time to launch the tiny on-screen keyboard. Look back at Figure 2.1 at the start of this chapter. Notice the little dots underneath the abc and 123? Tap on one of those dots, and you launch the on-screen keyboard. You can see it in Figure 2.11.

FIGURE 2.11

The on-screen keyboard

The on-screen keyboard works just like any other typing device, except you use the stylus rather than all 10 of your fingers. There are even keys for adding capital letters, spaces, returns, and backspaces to your text. Any text you can enter using Graffiti, you can also tap out with the on-screen keyboard. You can't, however, use the keyboard for navigating through applications or for adding ShortCut text to your records.

If you tap on the dot under the abc in the Graffiti writing area, the keyboard will open in alphabet mode; tap on the dot under the 123, and you'll see a numeric keyboard. You can switch between the two with the keyboard already open by tapping on either the abc or 123 command buttons at the bottom center of the on-screen keyboard. You'll also see a button marked Int'l next to those two buttons. This one is used for accessing accent marks and special characters that don't exist in English.

The on-screen keyboard will only appear when you're in an application that lets you enter text. For example, it will appear when you have a To Do record open, but not when you're looking at the To Do List.

When you're finished tapping out text, just tap Done to close the on-screen keyboard and return to your application.

CHAPTER 3

Interface Conventions: Finding Your Way Around

Before we begin our tour of the individual applications, let's explore some of their common details. Whichever of the primary Palm applications you're using, you're bound to encounter many of the same interface elements. Just as every application that runs on Windows or Macintosh operating systems uses basically the same interface, every Palm application uses pretty much the same interface, too.

Familiarize yourself with these interface conventions now, and you're well on your way to mastering all the Palm applications.

The interface elements common to most every Palm application are:

- Drop-down menus
- Dialog boxes
- Pick lists and scroll arrows
- Check boxes
- Input boxes and lines
- Command buttons

If you're at all familiar with Windows or Macintosh computers, you'll recognize many of these elements. For the most part, a dialog box in a Palm application serves the same purpose as a dialog box in a Windows or Macintosh application. Of course, a dialog box does different things depending on the task and the application, but the general principle is the same.

It's not our goal to describe each and every dialog box here. Instead, we'll explain the basic concept behind each of the standard interface elements and tell you how to use them. We go into specifics on each of these elements in the chapters on the individual applications.

Drop-Down Menus

Remember the Menu soft button we described in Chapter 1? (It's the one with a list and an arrow on it.) You can use it to access the application Menu Bar. Then from the Menu Bar, you can access the drop-down menus.

Let's take a look at the Menu Bar in action. First, press the Date Book button to launch that application. Now tap on the Menu soft button. You'll notice that there's now a bar across the top of the screen with the words Record, Edit, and Options displayed on it, as in Figure 3.1. These are fairly standard Palm menu choices.

PART

I

Palm Out of the Box:
The Basics

FIGURE 3.1

The Date Book Menu
Bar displayed

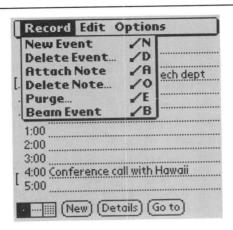

You'll also notice that the word Record is highlighted (this is indicated by the black bar over the word—another standard Palm interface convention) and that there's a small box with six choices directly underneath it. That's the drop-down menu for Record.

To choose any of the items in a drop-down menu, you simply tap on it. Similarly, to choose one of the other items on the Menu Bar, you tap on it. This will bring up its drop-down menu.

Go ahead and try it now. Tap on Options on the Menu Bar to see its drop-down menu.

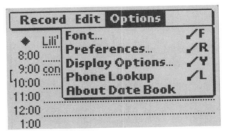

 NOTE If you tap the Menu button and nothing happens, don't panic. Not every application offers menus.

Dialog Boxes

Dialog boxes come in many different shapes and sizes. They range from the very simple, which may only ask that you make a single selection and tap OK (as in Figure 3.2), to the complex, which may require you to set several options before moving on. Complex dialog boxes, such as the one depicted in Figure 3.3, typically fill the entire display area, so you may not immediately recognize that you're dealing with a dialog box.

FIGURE 3.2

A simple dialog box

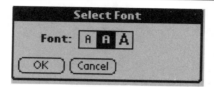

FIGURE 3.3

A complex dialog box, with many options

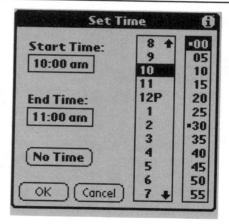

Whatever their size or complexity, all dialog boxes will ask you to tap OK to accept the selections you've made or to tap Cancel if you've changed your mind. Until you choose one of these options, that dialog box isn't going anywhere—dialog boxes are stubborn that way.

Let's try bringing up a dialog box to see what it looks like (and to provide a neat segue to the next element of the interface):

1. With the Date Book open, tap on the Menu soft button. Record will be highlighted on the Menu Bar.

2. In the Record drop-down menu, tap on New Event. This will bring up the Set Time dialog box (see Figure 3.3).

From here, you would ordinarily make some choices for the Start and End Time (or you can choose No Time if you're feeling indecisive). But don't tap OK or Cancel just yet—we want to keep that dialog box on screen so we can explain some of the other interface conventions used there.

Pick Lists and Scroll Arrows

Pick lists and scroll arrows often go hand-in-hand. Both allow you to view your extra long listings on the Palm's petite display area.

Let's go back to the Set Time dialog box in Figure 3.3. Notice the columns of numbers (representing hours and minutes) along the right side of the display. These columns are pick lists. Tap on a number in the hour pick list, and that number appears in the Start Time box or End Time box (we'll explain those boxes later in the chapter).

That's how pick lists work—you tap on something and it's selected. Pretty simple, huh? Remember choosing a country when you first set up your Palm? You made your selection from another form of pick list.

 TIP Sometimes, you'll need to act to make a pick list appear. For instance, take a look at that General Preferences screen again. See the downward facing arrow next to System Sound? Tap on it, and you'll get a pick list of choices. Tap on one of the choices to select it or tap anywhere else on the screen if you change your mind. Either way, the pick list will disappear.

Now take a look at the top and bottom of the hours pick list. See the little arrows? Those are the scroll arrows. If you want to set a date that starts before 8:00 AM (though we can't understand why anyone would ever do such a thing), tap the up arrow until you see the early morning hours in the hour pick list. Want to set up a late night rendezvous? Tap the down arrow to get to the post-dinnertime hours.

Scroll arrows appear in other areas of the interface (not just in pick lists), but they always serve as a means for getting to information that can't be displayed all at once. For example, if you have a memo that fills more than one screen, you'll see scroll arrows connected by a bar (known as the scroll bar) along the right side of the display. Just tap the down arrow to move to the next page, or tap on the up arrow to return to the previous page. In the lower-right corner of some screens, such as the Graffiti help screens, you may see a pair of arrows—one facing up and the other down. These are also scroll arrows. Guess which one you tap to move back (or up) a screen, and which one you tap to move forward (or down) a screen?

Check Boxes

Guess what you do with a check box? Tap in it to check or uncheck it, of course. Check boxes offer basically a yes/no proposition. You may be able to choose no, maybe, possibly, or only on Tuesdays with a check box. Sometimes, when you turn on a check box by checking it, you'll be presented with further choices, but that's as wild as a check box gets.

There aren't any check boxes in the Set Time dialog box, so let's choose another menu item to look at:

1. With the Date Book open, tap the Menu soft button.

2. Tap Options on the Menu Bar.

3. Next, tap Preferences from the Options drop-down menu to display the Preferences dialog box. You can see what it looks like in Figure 3.4

Notice the empty box next to Alarm Preset. That's a check box that hasn't yet been checked. Tap in it with the stylus and a checkmark will appear.

You'll notice that when you put a checkmark in that box, a new option appears next to the words Alarm Preset. That brings us to our next interface elements: Input Boxes and Lines.

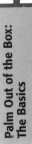

FIGURE 3.4

*The checked box next
to Alarm Preset shows
that it's selected.*

Input Boxes and Lines

Sometimes, you'll need to make more complex choices than just yes or no. At times
like this, you'll be faced with one of three elements: a box with a solid outline, a box
with a dotted outline, or a dotted line (don't sign on it just yet!). Which element you
see will depend on what type of input is required from you.

A solid outline box (as in the Start and End Time boxes of the Set Time dialog box
displayed in Figure 3.3) means that you can either use Graffiti to enter your selection
or tap on it in a pick list.

A dotted outline on an input box (as in the Set Time and Set Date options on the
Preferences dialog box displayed in Figure 3.5) indicates that there's another dialog
box of choices waiting to be revealed after you tap this box.

FIGURE 3.5

*The dotted box, wait-
ing for your tap*

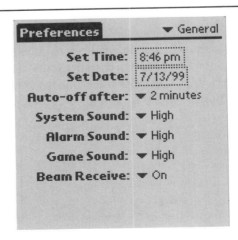

Tap inside the box, and another screen will appear from which you'll need to make another choice—usually by tapping.

To see what we mean:

1. Tap on the Applications soft button to bring up the Application Launcher.

2. Tap on the Prefs icon (the icons in the Application Launcher are arranged alphabetically, so look under P) to bring up the Preferences screen.

3. Tap inside the dotted outline box next to Set Time (you'll see a time displayed in that box already). This will bring up the Set Time dialog box, which you can see in Figure 3.6.

4. If you want to change the time, tap on the up and down arrows to change the hour and minutes. Then tap on OK to return to the Preferences screen.

5. If the time displayed is correct, tap on Cancel to return to the Preferences screen.

Dotted lines indicate that you need to provide some input, much as dotted outline boxes do. But when you see a dotted line (as in Figure 3.7), you can't just tap to make a selection. Rather, you must enter some text using either Graffiti or the on-screen keyboard (both of which we described in Chapter 2).

FIGURE 3.7

*When you see a dot-
ted line, it's time to
start writing.*

Your Palm can make a lot of choices easier for you, but it can't read minds. So brush up on your Graffiti.

Command Buttons

The last element common to every application is the command button. These aren't commands of the Sit, Stay variety—your Palm would never dream of telling you what to do. Rather, you get to tell your organizer what you want. For example, you tap OK or Done to accept the information you've just entered and move on. Or, tap Cancel if you change your mind.

Take another look at Figure 3.7. See the little ovals with the words Done, Details, and Note written inside them? Those are all command buttons. You would tap Done to tell the Address Book that you're finished with this screen. Or you could tap Details to make more choices, or Note to add a note to the Address Book entry.

Command buttons always appear as little lozenges and require just a simple tap to be invoked.

That about sums up the common interface elements. Now you're ready to tackle the applications.

CHAPTER **4**

Personalizing Your Palm

Sure, once you've bought and paid for your organizer, it's technically yours, but until you set it up to function just the way you like, it may as well belong to a stranger. Put your own special imprimatur on your Palm by setting all of its many preferences and watch it go from being "the organizer" to "my Palm."

It's really very simple to personalize a Palm—just tap to your little heart's content. But don't feel obliged to try what seems to be an infinite number of choices all in one sitting.

 TIP If you don't see an icon for the Preferences application in the Application Launcher, don't panic. Do you see the downward facing arrow in the upper-right corner of the screen, with a word next to it? This is the Category menu, which is used for organizing applications. Tap on it to see your choices; then tap on All to display icons for all the applications installed on your organizer.

Most personalizing is done through the Preferences application. To access it:

1. Tap on the Application Launcher soft button (the one that looks like a house) to go to the Applications screen.

2. Tap on the Preferences icon to start configuring options.

Not all the settings you can configure will be displayed immediately. By default, the Preferences application opens to General Preferences. To see the other categories of preferences you can configure, tap on the category drop-down arrow in the top-right corner of your screen. You can see all your choices here.

We'll start with the General Preferences and move on to the more complex settings you can choose.

Setting General Preferences

As the name of this category implies, the options you can set here are pretty general. For the most part, the choices you make here apply to everything you do in the Palm organizer. Think of the general preferences as operating system preferences. Your choices here (which you can see in Figure 4.1) are:

- Set Time
- Set Date
- Auto-off After
- System Sound
- Alarm Sound
- Game Sound
- Beam Receive

FIGURE 4.1

*Set your general
preferences.*

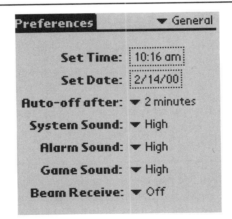

Set Time and Date

The Set Time and Set Date functions should be familiar to you—we covered them in our discussion of setting up your organizer, way back in Chapter 1. Setting these functions through the General Preferences screen works exactly the same way it does when you set these options through the Start Up screens. So, we won't go into detail here.

Just tap in the dotted box next to Set Time or Set Date and follow the steps we provided in Chapter 1 to adjust these options.

Setting the time and date is important because without them your Palm will never know what day to go to when you tap Today in the Date Book, and any alarms you set will be useless.

Auto-off After

The Auto-off After option controls the Palm organizer's auto-shutoff feature. This shuts down your Palm if it is inactive for a specific period of time. Auto-off After lets you choose just how much time must elapse after your last screen tap or button press before the organizer will shut itself down. Auto-off After is a great tool for absent-minded types; it can help you conserve battery power and let your Palm get some rest.

To set Auto-off After:

1. From the General Preferences screen, tap the Auto-off pick list (the arrow next to the words Auto-off After).

2. From the list that opens, tap on the amount of time you want for an auto-off delay. Your choices are 1 minute, 2 minutes, or 3 minutes.

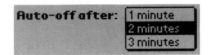

The pick list will close, and you'll return to the General Preferences screen where you can continue configuring options.

TIP   If you find that you need time to think while composing a note, or you read screens of text so slowly that the organizer shuts down before you're done, choose the 3-minute option for auto-off. For most users, the 2-minute setting works just fine. And don't worry if your Palm shuts down while you're in the middle of composing a note; none of your information will be lost. The Palm automatically saves your data as you enter it, so an abrupt shutdown isn't catastrophic. When you power up your Palm again, it will pick up right where you left off.

System Sound, Alarm Sound, Game Sound

Your Palm organizer can make a handful of different sounds—not bad when you consider that it only plays four notes.

System sounds comprise the little clicks you hear when you tap a command button or the little chime tones you hear when you HotSync. Game sounds are the chirps you hear when you torpedo the enemy in SubHunt or the sad song you hear when your ship gets sunk. Alarm sounds are what you hear when the Date Book is reminding you of an event.

You have the same choices for all these sounds: Off, Low, Medium, and High. Off silences all sounds of that type, while the other options refer to the sound's volume. Though you set each of the sound levels individually, they work the same way:

1. From the General Preferences screen, tap the down arrow next to the type of sound you want to configure (System, Alarm, or Game).

2. Tap on the option you prefer from the pick list that pops up.

The pick list will close, and you'll return to the General Preferences screen where you can continue configuring options. If you change your mind, just tap anywhere on the screen besides the pick list and it will close without changing your selection.

 TIP If you only want to receive a visual warning when an alarm sounds, set Alarm Sounds to Off.

Beam Receive

You may recall that in our discussions of the various applications, as well as the physical layout of the Palm organizer, we referred to its IR port and ability to send information through the airwaves to another Palm organizer. And, if you were really paying attention, you'll remember that this is called beaming.

Well, the Beam Receive option lets you choose whether or not you will accept information beamed to your organizer. You have two choices here: On and Off. Turning off the Beam Receive option means you will not receive anything beamed to you; you can't decide to accept business cards but not applications, for example. It's all or nothing. On the plus side, turning off this option saves you a tiny bit of battery power.

To configure the Beam Receive settings:

1. From the General Preferences screen, tap the down arrow next to the words Beam Receive.

2. Tap on either On or Off from the pick list that pops up.

The pick list will close, and you'll return to the General Preferences screen, where you can continue configuring options or move on to another category of preferences.

 TIP We don't see the point in turning Beam Receive off. Since Palm organizers need to be within about three feet of each other to complete a beaming transaction, you'll know when someone is sending you something. You can always just say no at that point. It's easier than having to go into Preferences and turn the option on, should you want to receive the information they're beaming.

Setting Button Preferences

By now you've probably guessed that by setting button preferences you can do things like launch the Expense application when you press the Address Book button (though we're not sure why you'd want to do that). But you may not have realized that you can also set your button preferences to configure what happens when you tap on the Calculator soft button, what happens when you press the HotSync button on the cradle or optional Palm modem, what happens when you raise the antenna on your Palm VII, and what happens when you write a full-screen Pen stroke. You can see all these choices in Figure 4.2.

FIGURE 4.2

Reassign the applications buttons.

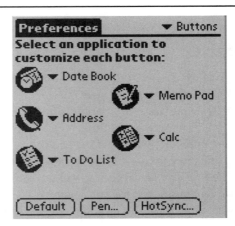

Reassigning the Applications Buttons

When you first start working with your Palm organizer, the standard button settings will seem just fine. But as you start to develop your own usage patterns, you may find that you really don't ever use the Memo Pad, but do use the Mail application all the time. That's when it's time to start setting your button preferences.

To reassign the Applications buttons, from the Button Preferences screen:

1. Tap on the down arrow next to the picture of the button you want to reassign. You can reassign any of the hard buttons or the Calculator soft button.

This will open a pick list of all the applications installed on your organizer.

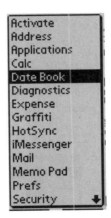

2. Tap on the application you want to assign to the button.

The pick list will close, and you'll return to the Button Preferences screen where you can continue reassigning buttons.

NOTE Don't worry if none of the basic applications are assigned to hard buttons. You can always access these applications using the Application Launcher.

Reassigning the Antenna Action

If you have a Palm VII, you'll see one other picture on the Button Preferences screen: a picture of a Palm VII with its antenna raised. By default, raising the antenna opens the Application Launcher to the wireless category. But, you can reconfigure this feature the same way you reassigned the buttons.

> ⚠ **TIP** If you've mucked up your button reassignments terribly, and want to start from scratch, just tap the Default button to restore your Palm's original button assignments.

Setting the Pen Stroke

You've already learned the basic Graffiti writing strokes, but did you know that there's a special Pen stroke known as the Full-Screen Pen Stroke or the Power Pen Stroke? Rather than translating to a letter on-screen, this stroke can be used to perform an action.

To try out the Power Pen Stroke, drag your stylus from somewhere in the Graffiti writing area up to the top of the screen. By default, this will launch the Graffiti Help application. But, you can change what happens when you write a Power Pen Stroke.

To reconfigure the Full-Screen Pen Stroke, from the Button Preferences screen:

1. Tap on the Pen command button. This will bring up the Pen Preferences screen, which you can see in Figure 4.3.

FIGURE 4.3

Set your Pen options

2. Tap on the down arrow next to the words Graffiti Help to see your options.

3. From the pick list, choose the operation you want to assign to the Pen. Your choices are: Backlight (turns it on or off); Keyboard (launches the on-screen keyboard); Turn Off & Lock (shuts and locks the organizer); or Beam Data (beams the current record to another Palm organizer).

4. Tap OK to accept the action you've just selected and return to the Button Preferences screen.

Configuring the HotSync Button

Your final option from the Button Preferences screen is setting the operation that launches when you press the HotSync button on the Palm cradle or on an optional modem.

By default, pressing either of these buttons will launch a HotSync operation. (For more on HotSyncing, see Chapter 9.) However, you can use either of these buttons to launch any of the applications installed on your organizer.

To change HotSync button preferences, from the Button Preferences screen:

1. Tap on the HotSync command button. This will open the HotSync Buttons screen, which you can see in Figure 4.4.

FIGURE 4.4

Reconfigure the HotSync buttons.

2. Tap the down arrow next to the button you want to reassign. This will open a pick list of all the applications installed on your organizer.

3. Tap on the application you want to assign to the HotSync button. The pick list will close, and you'll return to the HotSync Buttons screen.

4. Tap OK to accept this assignment and return to the Button Preferences screen.

 TIP You can still use the Application Launcher to access the HotSync application.

Setting Digitizer Preferences

Should you find that your screen taps aren't registering properly, your Graffiti strokes never create the proper letters, or you've had to perform a hard reset, it's time to recalibrate your digitizer. You do that through the Digitizer Preferences screen.

You calibrated the digitizer when you first started your Palm organizer, so you already know the procedure. Just follow the instructions and tap where the Xs appear.

If you need more help, turn back to Chapter 1.

 TIP   Don't choose Digitizer from the Preferences category drop-down list unless you really want to recalibrate your screen. You only need to recalibrate if your screen taps or Graffiti strokes aren't being read properly. Once the application launches, you have to finish the calibration process. It only takes a second, but why bother, if you don't need to?

Setting Format Preferences

You know where you live and how the date and time are usually formatted in your country. Why not let your Palm organizer in on the secret? You can do that through the Format Preferences screen.

The Format Preferences screen lets you set your default country, which then configures how the date, time, start day for your week, and numbers are displayed according to the standard conventions of the country you selected. For example, here in the U.S., the week starts on a Sunday; time is expressed using a 12-hour clock with an AM or PM (5:30 AM, or for those in the military, 0-dark-30); dates are displayed as month/day/year (2/14/00); and we use commas to separate thousands (10,000). In Europe, however, the week starts on a Monday; time is expressed using a 24-hour clock (05:30); dates are displayed as day/month/year (14/2/00); and thousands are separated by periods (10.000).

All of the Palm applications use the country default settings. However, you can customize any of the format preferences so the applications display information however you prefer. You can see all your choices in Figure 4.5.

FIGURE 4.5

Format preferences

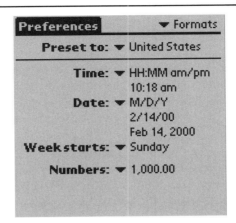

Let's start by setting the default country. To do this, from the Format Preferences screen:

1. Tap on the down arrow next to the words Preset To. This will open a long pick list of countries.

2. Scroll through the list until you find the country you want, then tap on its name.

This will return you to the Formats Preferences screen, where the settings for Time, Date, Week Starts, and Numbers will have changed to reflect the conventions of the country you selected. To change any of these display options:

1. Tap on the down arrow next to the format you want to change. We'll choose Date, for now. This will bring up a pick list of Date format choices.

2. Tap on the format you prefer. The pick list will close, and you'll return to the Format Preferences screen.

3. Follow these steps to change the Time, Week Starts (you can choose Sunday or Monday), and Numbers.

The formats you choose will be applied in all the Palm applications.

Configuring the Modem

If you want to surf the Web or send e-mail with your Palm organizer, you're going to need to buy an optional modem. Unless, of course, you have a Palm VII, which can connect to the Internet straight out of the box. It doesn't actually surf the Web, but we'll explain that in Chapter 13.

In addition, we'll explain everything you need to set up and use a modem with your Palm organizer in Chapter 11. As with any modem, you'll need to do some configuring. For that, you'll use the Modem Preferences screen. Until you actually have a modem in hand, though, there's no reason to mess with the modem preferences; they won't affect the operation of any other aspect of your organizer. And, preferences being such a personal thing, what you set for one modem may not be to your liking for another.

Setting Network Preferences

Like modem preferences, network preferences only come into play when you have a modem connected to your Palm organizer. When configured to work with a modem, network preferences make it possible to use the Palm's built-in TCP/IP (communication) software to connect to the Internet Service Provider of your choice or to dial in to a remote access server.

The TCP/IP software is a built-in part of the operating system. You configure it through the Preferences application. Just choose Network from the category drop-down list in the upper-right corner of the Preferences screen to get to the Network Preferences screen. TCP/IP stands for Transmission Control Protocol/Internet Protocol—the communications protocols suite used to connect to the Internet. Because this is the de facto standard of the Internet, virtually every piece of hardware or software that works to help get you online supports these protocols. They do all the hard stuff, so you don't have to figure out a whole bunch of settings.

We'll explain how to configure network preferences and how they interact with Modem Preferences in detail in Chapter 11.

Configuring the Owner

We're sure that by now, you're very proud of your Palm organizer and want the world to know it's yours. If that's the case, you'll be thrilled with Owner Preferences.

Owner Preferences don't really work the same way the other Preferences applications do. You won't find drop-down menus or pick lists of options here. Instead, Owner Preferences provides a place for you to enter your name, company name, phone number, and any other information you want attached to your organizer. Think of the owner preferences as the Palm equivalent of a luggage tag.

To enter your Owner Preferences, from the Preferences application screen:

1. Tap on the Preferences category arrow in the upper-right corner of any of the Preferences screens, and choose Owner from the drop-down list, which brings up the Owner Preferences screen.

2. Enter your information using either Graffiti or the on-screen keyboard. If you enter more information than can fit on one screen, a scroll bar will appear along the right side of the screen. As with the Memo Pad, you are limited to 4K for your owner preferences, or roughly 14 screens of text.

So why would you bother entering owner information? Well, for the same reason you put a tag on your suitcase; so you can help your organizer find its way back to you should you lose or misplace it. You can also safeguard this information so it can't be altered by anyone but you. To do this, assign a password to the organizer using the Security application. (We explain how to use this application in Chapter 7.) With a password in place, the Owner Preferences information is locked and you'll see an Unlock button at the bottom of the screen (as in Figure 4.6).

FIGURE 4.6

*Locked owner
preferences*

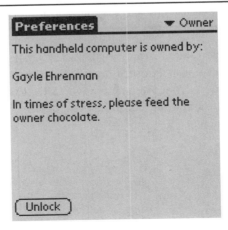

When the Owner Preferences are locked, they can't be changed. If you want to edit your owner preferences:

1. Tap the Unlock command button at the bottom of the Owner Preferences screen.

2. Enter the password that you assigned using the Security application.

3. Tap OK to close the password screen and return to the Owner Preferences screen. You can now edit the Owned By text the same way you would change text in any other application.

Setting Shortcuts

Now that you've been using your Palm organizer for a little while, you've probably noticed that there are a handful of words you enter over and over again. Don't know about you, but we rarely make it through a day without entering "meeting" in the Date Book.

Fortunately, the Palm has a handy little feature that makes it simpler and quicker to enter your frequently used words. This little lifesaver is called ShortCuts. As we explained in Chapter 2, *Mastering Graffiti*, ShortCuts are essentially abbreviations that let you enter just a special Graffiti stroke and a couple of letters to get a complete word or a phrase up to 40 characters. Your organizer comes with a few preconfigured ShortCuts that you can use as is or edit to meet your needs. Or, you can create your own ShortCuts as you need them.

 NOTE You can use ShortCuts in any of the main Palm applications, but you can only edit the existing ones and create new ones through ShortCuts Preferences.

Before you start customizing ShortCuts, take a look at the preconfigured ones. To access the list, just choose ShortCuts from the Preferences category list. As you can see in Figure 4.7, the Palm comes with ShortCuts set up for Breakfast, Dinner, Date Stamp, Date and Time Stamp, Lunch, Meeting, and Time Stamp.

Palm Out of the Box:
The Basics

FIGURE 4.7
The ShortCuts

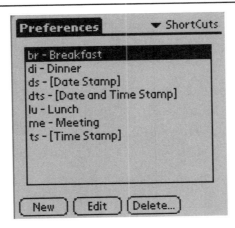

We explained how to use these existing ShortCuts in Chapter 2, so we won't rehash that subject here. Instead, let's get into creating your own ShortCuts. First, take a look at that list in Figure 4.7. Notice that each ShortCut in the list has a two- or three-letter abbreviation, which is the name of the ShortCut, followed by a word or two. The whole word is what appears when you enter the ShortCut using Graffiti. Any ShortCuts you create must also have these elements.

Let's create a ShortCut for the word Appointment. With the ShortCuts screen open:

1. Tap on the New command button. You'll see a ShortCut entry screen, as in Figure 4.8.

FIGURE 4.8
ShortCut entry

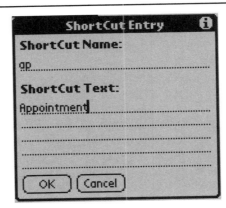

2. Tap on the ShortCut Name line and start entering the letters you want to use for your ShortCut abbreviation. You can either use Graffiti or the on-screen keyboard. We'll use the letters ap for appointment.

3. Tap on the ShortCut Text line and enter the word you want to appear when you use this ShortCut. Remember to use a Cap Shift if you want the first letter of your word to be capitalized. For this example, enter Appointment.

4. Enter a space after the last word in your ShortCut text, so Graffiti will automatically add one after the word.

5. Tap OK to accept this ShortCut and return to the ShortCuts Preferences screen.

You'll see the ShortCut you just created on the list, as in Figure 4.9.

FIGURE 4.9

The new list of ShortCuts

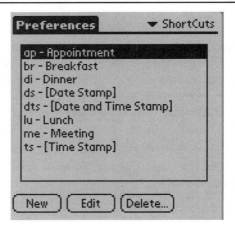

If you need to make a change to a ShortCut, with the ShortCut list displayed on screen:

1. Tap on the ShortCut you want to alter. A black bar appears across it to let you know it's selected.

2. Tap on the Edit command button. This opens the ShortCut entry screen.

3. Make whatever changes you want using either Graffiti or the on-screen keyboard.

4. Tap OK to accept your changes, close this screen, and return to the ShortCuts list.

Of course, you can also delete ShortCuts. To do this, with the ShortCut list displayed on screen:

1. Tap on the ShortCut you want to delete. A black bar appears across it to let you know it's selected.

2. Tap on the Delete command button to open a Delete confirmation box.

3. Tap OK if you really want to get rid of that ShortCut. This closes the dialog box and returns you to the ShortCuts list, where the ShortCut you just deleted will be gone.

TIP Don't worry if you accidentally delete one of the preconfigured ShortCuts. You can create them all again. For the time and date stamp ShortCuts, instead of writing Time Stamp, Date Stamp, or Date and Time Stamp as the ShortCut text, you enter @TS, @DS or @DTS. Make sure to use capital letters, and your ShortCut will come out just fine.

Configuring Wireless Operations

You'll only see this category listed under Preferences if you have a Palm VII organizer. And even then, you don't get many options.

Choose Wireless from the Preferences category drop-down menu and you'll see all your choices, as in Figure 4.10.

FIGURE 4.10

Wireless options

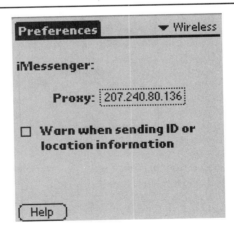

Next to iMessenger, you'll see your address for the Palm.Net network. This will be the name you selected when you activated the service. You can't change this name here. We'll explain your options for working with the Palm.Net service in Chapter 13.

In the box next to Proxy, you'll see a string of numbers representing the IP address for the Palm.Net proxy server. Unless you want to dial in to a different server, like the one for your company's network, and you have that specific IP address, do not touch this setting. If you want to use your Palm.Net service for Web clipping or e-mail, your Palm VII needs to know its Proxy server address (it's like a phone number for Internet connections).

 NOTE Explaining how Internet communications work is really beyond the scope of this book. But, we're sure there are some of you aching to know what a Proxy server is, so here's a quick definition. A Proxy server sits out there on the Internet somewhere—in between a client application (in this case iMessenger or a PQA) and a server—where the information resides. The Proxy server receives the request from your Palm VII and sees if it can fulfill the request. If the Proxy server can't fulfill the request, it sends the request on to the appropriate server. In most cases, a Proxy server speeds up your Internet interactions.

If for some reason, you need to change this address:

1. Tap in the box next to the word Proxy. This will bring up the Edit Proxy dialog box, as in Figure 4.11.

FIGURE 4.11

Editing the Proxy server address

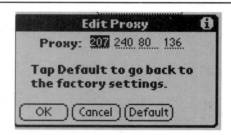

2. Select the numbers you want to change and then enter the new address using either Graffiti or the on-screen keyboard. The dots that separate the address segments stay in place—they're an intrinsic part of the address.

3. When you're satisfied with the address, tap OK to accept it, close this dialog, and return to the Wireless Preferences screen.

 TIP Don't panic if you just couldn't stop yourself from monkeying with the Proxy server address and now can't remember what it should be. Tap on the Default command button and the address will be reset to that of the Palm.Net Proxy server. And you'll never have to admit your foolishness to anyone.

PART II

The Applications

LEARN TO:

- **Use the Four Basic Applications**

- **Use the Secondary Applications**

- **Beam Data**

- **HotSync to the Windows and Macintosh**

- **Navigate the Palm Desktop**

# CHAPTER 5

Appointments and People: Mastering the Date Book and the Address Book

I n this chapter you'll learn about two of the most important applications your Palm has to offer: the Date Book and the Address Book.

The Date Book provides a handy place to keep track of all your very important business meetings, hot dates, special events, and assorted other appointments you really shouldn't forget (like that trip to the periodontist you've been putting off). We'll explain how to add an appointment, reschedule it, reschedule it yet again, delete it, and start all over—all without breaking a sweat.

The Address Book lets you keep track of the people you know. In this chapter we'll explain how to add people to your Address Book, sort them, get rid of the folks you never want to talk to again, customize your entries, create your own electronic business card, and lots more.

The Date Book

The Palm Date Book offers more flexibility and interactivity than a paper calendar or a desktop PIM. Can a paper calendar remind you about an upcoming meeting, or display all your appointments for a day, a week, or a month, and then go back to the day view again? Of course not. A desktop PIM, while every bit as capable as the Palm Date Book, just won't fit in your pocket, no matter how hard you try.

 NOTE The Palm Date Book thinks of every entry as an event. So whether you're taking your two-door in for a tune-up, your wiener dog in for a wash, or whether you're breakfasting with a Baron, it's an event—at least as far as the Date Book is concerned.

The Views

Let's start our discussion of the Date Book with a look at how it displays information. With the Date Book, you get three primary Views (or ways to see your calendar). The Views are:

- Day View
- Week View
- Month View

There's also a year view, but that one's pretty self-explanatory.

These views correspond to those Day-At-A-Glance, Week-At-A-Glance, Month-At-A-Glance pocket-sized paper organizer books. In those organizers, as in the Palm Date Book, the rule is that the longer the period of time you're displaying, the less detail you can see at any given time.

When you press the Date Book button, the calendar automatically opens to the Day View, which you can see in Figure 5.1.

FIGURE 5.1

Today's schedule

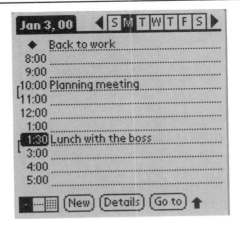

This View lets you see just what's on your agenda for today or any other single day you select. Day View displays the most information and is the one you use to enter new appointments and make changes to existing ones. For these reasons, Day View is the view you'll use most often—that's why it's the default.

 TIP To see a different day in Day View, tap on the letter for that day (for example, M for Monday) on the bar at the top of the screen.

Week View shows a week's worth of appointments at a time. In this view, appointments are depicted as shaded blocks of time, as you can see in Figure 5.2. You can't see any details about an appointment, but you can see when it's scheduled for.

FIGURE 5.2

*What's on tap
this week?*

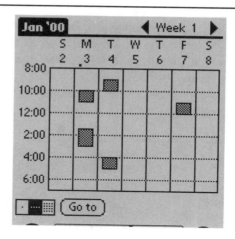

Tap on a shaded block, and a box with the date, time, and name of the appointment pops up at the top of the display. You can add an event in Week View by tapping on an open block of time on the grid. This will take you to Day View, where you can add, edit, and delete events to your heart's content.

Week View offers one neat thing that none of the other views do: Drag-and-Drop editing. This lets you just drag an appointment that needs to be rescheduled to its new date and time. We explain how to do this in greater detail later in this chapter.

 TIP There are two ways to navigate to another week, while in Week View: You can tap the scroll arrows at the top of the screen until the week you want is displayed, or you can tap the Go to command button and then tap on the day you want from the pop-up calendar.

Week View isn't the most useful tool for scheduling events, but it can help you get a quick idea of how hectic your week is and visualize just when you have a free block of time.

Month View provides even less information about your events than Week View. As you can see in Figure 5.3, Month View presents a typical calendar grid.

FIGURE 5.3

Month View

Since that's a lot of information to fit on the Palm's small screen, the boxes for each day in a month are pretty tiny. So, any events you have scheduled are depicted as black dots; multiple dots mean multiple events. A dot in the upper-right corner of the box indicates a morning event, while one in the lower-right corner is an afternoon event; a dot in between those two indicates an event set for the middle of the day. If you see a + sign in the bottom-left corner of the box, that indicates an untimed event. To see what a dot represents, tap once in the box for the day it's scheduled, and the Day View opens up. From there, you can see all the details of an event and make any changes you like.

TIP There are two ways to change the month displayed in Month View: you can tap on the scroll arrows at the top of the screen, or you can tap the Go to command button and then choose a month from the pop-up calendar.

Since you have three different ways to look at your Date Book, you need a simple way to change from one view to another. Fortunately, the Palm organizer provides two different techniques for surfing through views: You can push the Date Book hard button or you can tap the Change View icons on-screen.

As you've already noticed, pushing the Date Book button *once* starts up your Palm and opens the Date Book to Day View. Push the button a *second time*, with the Date Book already open, and the display changes to Week View. Push that button a *third time,* and you'll see the Month View. Push the button one last time, and you return to Day View.

If you don't have the patience for a scenic journey through the Date Book views, you can tap on the Change View icons at the bottom-left corner of the Date Book screen to go directly to the view of your choice. Tap on the box with a single dot for Day View, the box with a row of four dots for Week View, or the box that's just full of dots for Month View.

These icons always appear in the same place on the Date Book display, no matter which view you're looking at. They offer the quickest way to navigate from view to view, but require you to first turn on your Palm and switch over to the Date Book before you can use them.

When we're just trying to quickly check on an event, we find it easier to just keep pressing the Date Book button to change views. This way, we don't even have to take the stylus out of its cozy slot.

Adding Events

You'd never guess judging by its compact size that the Palm is a very versatile device. Virtually anything you can do with it can be done at least two different ways.

Adding events to the Date Book is no different. You can add events the quick way or the complete way, which is only slightly less quick than the quick way.

The quick way really just lets you pick a time for your event and give it a name or brief description (Lunch with the boss). To attach a note to an event, set an alarm, or fine-tune its time (10:20 start, instead of 10:00), you'll need to use the complete approach. Or you can use a combination of the two. For example, you can get an appointment on the calendar the minute it's set using the quick way, and then adjust or edit it using the complete approach when you have more time.

We'll explain how to use both methods in the following sections.

 NOTE Any of the directions for using the Date Book assume that you have it already open to Day View, unless otherwise specified.

The Quick Way

To enter an event the quick way:

1. Tap on the dotted line next to the time your event starts.

2. Enter a name for your event using Graffiti, the on-screen keyboard, or, to go really quick, a shortcut. (For more on entering text, see Chapter 2.)

That's it. Your event will appear in the appropriate time slot.

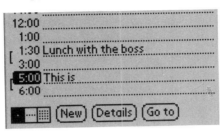

When you enter an event the quick way, you don't get to specify an end time. By default, all events entered the quick way are assigned a duration of one hour. If you want a longer or shorter event, you'll have to make some changes using the complete method, which we explain next.

The Complete Way

If your event can't possibly be completed in an hour or requires much more information than a simple name, the complete way is for you.

To enter an event the complete way:

1. Tap the New command button at the bottom left of the display.

NOTE Alternately, you can tap the Menu soft button, then choose Record ➤ New Event from the Menu Bar. Or, using Graffiti, you can enter the command character and N.

This will bring up the Set Time dialog box, which you can see in Figure 5.4.

2. Pick a Start Time for your event by tapping on the appropriate hour and minutes in the pick list, or write the time using Graffiti.

FIGURE 5.4

*The Set Time
dialog box*

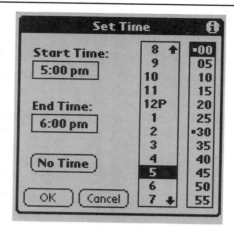

3. Tap in the box next to End Time, then tap on the appropriate hour and minutes in the pick list, or write the time using Graffiti to set the ending time for your event.

4. Tap OK to accept the time you selected.

This will take you back to the Day View, where the cursor will be blinking on the line next to the start time of your event. Enter a name for your event the same way just as you would in the quick way and you're done.

You'll notice that there is a bracket to the left of the start time of your event (see Figure 5.1), which connects to the end time you selected. This is a tool to help you quickly see how long an appointment lasts.

TIP   There's a quicker, yet still complete way to enter a timed event: Start writing the Start Time for your event using Graffiti (remember to write on the numbers side of the Graffiti writing area), and the Set Time dialog box will open automatically with the time you wrote selected. You can finish entering your event the way you normally would, using the complete way.

Untimed Events

Not every event needs a start time. A birthday, for instance, happens all day, not just at a particular hour. The Date Book gives you two ways to set up an event with no time attached.

In the Set Time dialog box, you may have noticed a No Time command button. This button offers the long way to add an untimed event. To use this approach:

1. From Day View, tap the New button. This will bring up the Set Time dialog box.

2. Tap on No Time.

3. Tap OK.

   This will take you back to Day View. Look at the first line of the display; you'll notice a white diamond in a black square where the time would ordinarily be and the blinking cursor just after it.

   The diamond indicates an event with no start or end time—an untimed event, in Palm-speak.

4. Enter a name for your event, and you're done.

Of course, there's a quicker way to enter an untimed event. To take the quick route, with the Date Book in Day View, start entering a name for your event using Graffiti.

 WARNING Do not tap anywhere on the Day View screen before you start writing, or you won't get an untimed event.

The event will appear on the first line of the Day View display, with the diamond icon next to it, same as if you had used the long way.

 NOTE When creating an untimed event the quick way, you must use Graffiti. The on-screen keyboard can't be activated until you choose a time for an event—which rules out using it to create an untimed event, now doesn't it?

Editing an Event

Appointments were made to be broken—or at least postponed. Luckily, the Date Book provides several different ways to make changes to an event.

You can easily change the date, time, duration, and name of an event. So, if that 10-minute teleconference on Tuesday suddenly becomes a three-hour town hall meeting on Thursday, it's easy to fix in the Date Book—if not in real life. No eraser, White Out, or red pens required.

As with entering an event, there are several ways to change one as well. These approaches range from easy to slightly less easy. Most editing, as with entering events, needs to be done from the Day View. We'll address any exceptions as they crop up.

Changing the Name

If you realize there's a typo in an event's description, or you need to add another name to your list of meeting participants, just call on your knowledge of Graffiti and your trusty stylus to make the change.

To add to an event name:

1. Tap within the existing text at the point you'd like the new text to appear.

2. Start writing in the Graffiti box, or tapping on the on-screen keyboard to enter the new information.

That's all there is to that.

To delete part of an event name—or the whole name, for that matter:

1. Select the text you want to replace. (To select, tap your stylus at the beginning or end of the word you want to select, and drag across. A black bar will appear to show it's selected.)

2. Draw the Graffiti character for backspace (a dash drawn from right to left), or tap the Menu soft button, and then choose Edit ➤ Cut.

Either way, the outdated text will disappear. You can just start typing to add a new name.

Changing the Date and Time

Though names of events sometimes change, their date and time tend to change more often. True to the flexibility of the Palm, there are multiple ways to handle this.

Remember when we said that you can drag-and-drop events while in Week View? When you need to change the date of an event, this capability comes in really handy.

To change the date and time of an event while in Week View:

1. Press the stylus down on the event you want to change, and hold it there.

A box with the event details will appear, so you can be sure you selected the right event.

2. Drag the stylus along the display, without lifting it off the screen, to the new date and time for the event.

3. When you're satisfied with the new time slot for the event, just lift your stylus off the screen, and the event will stay where you put it. Good event!

Unfortunately, drag-and-drop doesn't work in the Day or Month Views. There is absolutely no way to edit an event in Month View. In Day View, you can reschedule an appointment by cutting and pasting it to a new day and time slot or by entering the new information in the Event Details dialog box.

To cut and paste an event to a new time slot, from Day View:

1. Select the name of the event you want to reschedule.

2. Tap the Menu soft button, then choose Edit ➤ Cut (see Figure 5.5).

FIGURE 5.5

Use the menus to Cut and Paste an event.

3. Tap on the dotted line next to the new time slot for the event, and again tap the Menu button, and choose Edit ➤ Paste.

NOTE Alternately, you could use the Graffiti commands, which are / (written from bottom left to top right), X, and / P, for cut and paste respectively.

The event will appear in its new time slot.

If you want to change the day for an event as well as the time, you can still cut and paste. Just remember to switch to the new day before pasting the event back in to the Date Book.

The other alternative is to reschedule an event using the Event Details dialog box. If you're not comfortable selecting text, this method will work perfectly for you. Even if you're a whiz with a stylus, you may like the one-stop editing control this dialog box provides.

To reschedule an event using the Event details dialog box:

1. Tap on the name of the event you want to reschedule.

2. Tap on the Details command button to bring up the Event Details dialog box, which you can see in Figure 5.6.

FIGURE 5.6

You can reschedule an event using the Event Details dialog box.

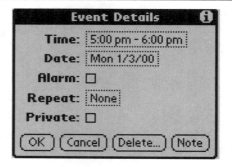

3. Tap in the Time box to change the start and end times of your event. This will bring up the Set Time dialog box.

4. From the Set Time dialog, tap in the boxes next to either Start or End Time to pick a new time from the list. When you've selected a new start and end time, tap OK to return to the Event Details screen.

5. Tap OK to return to Day View.

There are a few other things you can do through the Event Details dialog box. We'll discuss those next.

Adding Alarms

Chances are, you use an alarm clock to wake yourself up in the morning, so why not set an alarm to wake you from your stupor and remind you when it's time for an important meeting?

The Palm organizer lets you set an alarm for any event and even determine how long before the event you want to be alerted, how many times the alarm should sound, and what that alarm should sound like. We'll explain how to change the alarm sound and frequency a little later in this chapter.

For now, let's just look at how to set an alarm. From the Day View:

1. Tap on the name of the event you want to be alerted about.

2. Tap on the Details command button to bring up the Event Details dialog box.

3. Tap in the Alarm checkbox. A checkmark will appear, along with a pull-down list for selecting how long before the event you want to be reminded (see Figure 5.7). The default reminder time is 5 minutes.

Setting an alarm

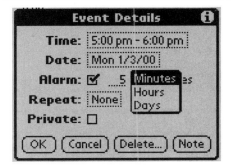

4. To change the reminder time, tap the down arrow next to Minutes to change to Hours or Days.

5. Select the number 5 and enter a new number using Graffiti or the on-screen keyboard.

6. Tap OK when you're satisfied with the configuration of your alarm. This will take you back to Day View.

When the alarm you set goes off, a Reminder screen pops up, showing the description, date, and time of your event. You can see this screen in Figure 5.8. You'll need to tap OK in this screen to dismiss it and keep working.

If you've set an alarm for a timed event, the Palm will turn itself on just to deliver its alert message. You can set alerts for untimed events, too, but the Palm doesn't sound a warning for them and it won't turn itself on just to display a reminder. You'll see the reminder whenever you get around to powering up your Palm, though.

FIGURE 5.8

*Remember your
appointment.*

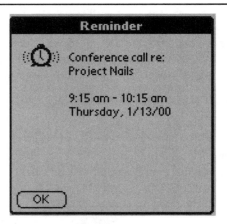

TIP You can set your Palm to only deliver visual warnings, without the sound cues. For directions, see "System Sound, Alarm Sound, Game Sound" in Chapter 4.

Changing an Event into a Recurring Event

You know that meeting your dread? The one that happens every Friday at 4:00 PM? You don't have to add it to the Date Book 52 times. You can add it once as a recurring event.

You set up a recurring event using the Event Details dialog box, accessible through Day View.

First, add the event using either the quick or the complete methods we described earlier in this chapter. To make the event into a recurring event, follow these steps:

1. Tap on the name of the event on the Day View calendar to select it.

2. Tap on the Details command button.

3. In the Event Details dialog box, you'll see the Repeat option, with None displayed in the dotted box next to it. Tap in this box to bring up the Change Repeat screen.

4. Tap on Day, Week, Month, or Year, depending on how often you want the event to recur.

The choice you make here will determine what options you're presented with next. For example, when you choose Day, you can select how many days will pass between recurrences of the event and when the event should stop recurring. You can see these choices in Figure 5.9.

FIGURE 5.9

A daily recurrence

When you set an event to recur every week, you also get to pick what day the event takes place on (see Figure 5.10).

FIGURE 5.10

Weekly recurrence

PART

II

The Applications

With an event that recurs once a month, you can decide whether the event should take place on a particular day every month (like the 3rd Wednesday of the month) or date (like the 21st of every month). You can see these options in Figure 5.11.

FIGURE 5.11

Monthly recurrence

 NOTE It may look like the Date Book treats each instance of a recurring event as a separate entity, but if you make a change to one instance (or delete it), you'll be asked if you want to make the same change to every occurrence of the event. You can change just this week's meeting from 4:00 PM to 2:00 PM, or you can change the time for the meeting for all eternity.

Adding a Note

Sometimes, you can't fit all the information you need for a meeting in its name. For times like these, you really need a note. Fortunately, it's easy to create a note and link it to an appointment.

You can attach a note to an event using the Event Details dialog box or by selecting Record ➤ Attach Note. You can even do it entirely through Graffiti, by writing the Graffiti command character followed by A.

To attach a Note to an event using the Event Details dialog box, start in Day View, and then:

1. Tap the Details command button to bring up the Event Details dialog box.

2. Tap the Note command button. This will open a new note with the name of your event in its title bar.

3. Enter text into the note using Graffiti or the on-screen keyboard.

4. Tap Done when your note is complete.

This will take you back to the Day View. Take a look at the event you were just working with. See the picture of the dog-eared sheet of paper to the right of the event's name? That tells you it has a note attached. To view the note, just tap on the little picture, and the note opens up.

Private Events

There's one last thing you can do to an event through the Event Details Dialog box: Make an event private. To do this, just tap the Private checkbox in the Event Details dialog box.

 TIP Making an event private doesn't make it invisible or hide it from view—unless you've set your Palm organizer to Hide Private Records. You do this through the Security application, which we cover in Chapter 7.

Performing a Phone Lookup

One of the best things about the Palm organizer is the way its applications work together. The Phone Lookup feature is one of the best examples of that synergy.

Here's how Phone Lookup works: Suppose you have a meeting schedule with your co-author, whom you know is listed in your Address Book. You can perform a Phone Lookup to find that co-author's name and number in the Address Book and have it automatically tacked on to the event in your Date Book. This way, you have all the information you need to confirm that meeting in one place. Pretty slick, huh?

To perform a Phone Lookup, you need to be in Day View. From there:

1. Tap on the name of the event to which you want to add a contact name and phone number.

2. Tap on the Menu soft button, then choose Options ➣ Phone Lookup. (Or, you can write a command stroke then L using Graffiti.)

This will bring up the Phone Lookup screen (which is really your Address Book). You can see it in Figure 5.12.

3. From the Phone Lookup screen, select the name you want to tack on to your event—or just start entering the first few letters of the name you want using Graffiti. The name should be selected in the Phone Lookup list.

4. Tap the Add button, and the name and number will appear as part of your event's name.

You're back in Day View, and there it all is.

FIGURE 5.12

Phone Lookup

Setting Preferences

You have a number of options for how the Date Book looks and behaves. You can make all of these choices by going to Options ➤ Preferences. This will bring up the Preferences dialog box (see Figure 5.13).

FIGURE 5.13

The Preferences dialog box

The Preferences dialog box lets you:

- Set the Start and End times for your day

- Configure the Alarm Preset (which determines the default time value for an alarm)
- Choose an alarm sound (try them out; they're entertaining)
- Determine how many times you want to be reminded about an event, and how often the reminder should sound

These are all simple scroll and tap choices that are otherwise set at default values. You can override the Start and End time by adding an event that falls outside those hours. For example, your default end time may be 8:00 PM, but when you schedule a 10:00 PM event, it will be displayed in Daily View.

Similarly, your Alarm Present may call for an alert five minutes before an event, but you can choose a different time frame when setting up the alarm for a specific appointment.

Setting Display Options

The Options menu is also where you go to configure what information the Date Book displays. Choose Options ➤ Display Options to set up the look you want for Day and Month Views.

From the Display Options dialog box (show in Figure 5.14), you can choose to:

- Show Time Bars, which let you see the duration of an event in Day View
- Compress Day View, which eliminates blocks of empty hours between events
- Show Timed and Untimed Events in Month View
- Show Daily Repeating Events in Month View

PART

II

The Applications

FIGURE 5.14

Set the Display Options.

These are all check box options. Tap to turn them on; tap again to turn them off. You have to admire the simplicity of it all!

Choosing a Font

There's one other way to change the look of the Date Book: by changing the Font. To do this, choose Options ➤ Font. In the Font dialog box that opens up (which you can see in Figure 5.15), tap on the letter that looks best to you.

FIGURE 5.15

Tap to choose a Font

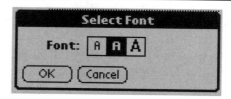

This will change all the listings in your Date Book to this font. Tap OK when you're satisfied with your choice.

If you're used to the zillions of font choices on a desktop PC, this might be a bit disappointing to you. But, the three choices you're given are all optimized for display on the Palm's tiny screen, so you can't go wrong whichever you choose. Standard desktop fonts could never look as good. You'll just have to accept that sometimes less really is more.

Deleting an Event

Sometimes, in spite of your best intentions, an event gets cancelled. When this happens, it's time to cut your losses and delete the defunct entry.

You delete events from Day View. To get rid of an event:

1. Tap on the name of the event you want to remove.

2. Tap the Details command button to bring up the Event Details dialog box.

3. Tap the Delete button.

This will bring up a confirmation message that reads "Delete Selected Event?"

4. Tap OK.

Voila! The event is gone, and you're back in Day View.

Of course, there's another way to get rid of an event, which we show in Figure 5.16.

FIGURE 5.16

Delete an event.

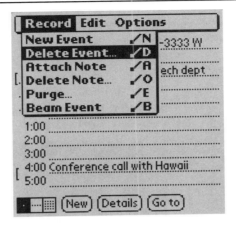

1. Tap on the name of the event you want to remove.
2. Tap on the Menu soft button to bring up the Menu Bar.
3. Choose Record ➤ Delete Event.

You'll see that same nagging confirmation message.

4. Tap OK for the same result—that's one fewer event on your schedule!

 TIP If you think you may ever want to recall this defunct event, check the Save Archive Copy On PC box in the confirmation message window. This will save a copy on your desktop, the next time you HotSync. We explain more about using archives in Chapter 10.

Purging Your Date Book

While we're on the subject of cleaning house, consider this: Do you really need to know what time last October you saw the dermatologist? We thought not. So why not get rid of all those over-and-done-with events, and stop living in the past?

Sure, each event only takes up a tiny bit of your Palm's memory, but all those tiny bits add up over time. Thousands of doctor appointments later, there's no room on your Palm for that new application you just downloaded.

PART

II

The Applications

The solution is to purge old events. Trust us, this is one purge that will make you feel better. You can choose how old an event must be before it's purged, and whether or not to save a copy of all these purged events in an archive file on your PC (where space is usually plentiful). We explain archiving in greater detail in Chapter 10.

If you want to purge your Date Book, you must be in Day View. From there, choose Record ➤ Purge. From the resulting dialog box, you can decide to purge events that are one, two, three weeks, or a month old, and whether or not to archive these events. Then, tap OK, and kiss those old events goodbye.

Now, you're a master of the Date Book. It's time to move on to the Address Book.

The Address Book

Before we adopted the Palm as our organizer of choice, we used a very common method for keeping track of names and numbers—the yellow sticky approach. You know how it works: You write a phone number (and, maybe if you're smart, a name) on the smallest yellow sticky pad you can find, and stick the tag on the edge of your monitor. Then you hope. Hope that it doesn't fall off, get swept away with a feather duster, or just vanish. Maybe, if you're very lucky, you'll be able to find the number when you need it. But what are the odds of that happening?

Now, with the Palm organizer in hand, we are models of efficiency. We can recall any telephone number in our possession with the press of a button. We've categorized everyone we know (not much different than in real life), so we don't need to sort through the veterinarian, the dry cleaner, assorted aunts, uncles, and acquaintances, just to find our editor's number. She's categorized as Business, while all those other folks are Personal. That makes it easy and efficient to find just whom we're looking for at any given time.

Knowing the Views

Like the Date Book, the Address Book has multiple views. Instead of providing a Day, Week, and Month View, Address Book gives you an Address List View and an Address View. Keep reading for more details on each.

The Address List

The Address List is what you see by default when you press the Address Book hard button. As you can see in Figure 5.17, the Address List shows exactly what you'd expect: a list of every name and number you've entered into the Address Book. That list may run one screen, two screens, or even longer. Its length will be determined by how many people you know and how diligent you are about adding names to the Address Book.

FIGURE 5.17

The Address List

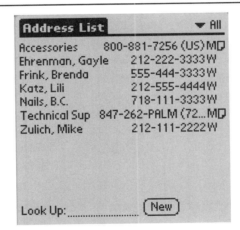

The Applications

If your list runs more than one screen, you'll see scroll arrows in the bottom right corner of the display. Tap on these to move up or down through the list. Alternately, you can use the Scroll Button at the bottom of the device to navigate the Address List.

You can decide what information gets displayed in this list. We'll explain how to set Address List options later in this chapter.

Tap on a name in the Address List and you'll see the Address View.

Address View

Where the Address List provides a quick view of all the entries in your Address Book, the Address View provides full details on just one entry at a time.

Think of the Address List as the big picture and the Address View as the close-up. You can see what Address View looks like in Figure 5.18.

From Address View you can access everything from an e-mail address to a street address. It's also the view you start from to edit an entry (or record, in Palm-speak). From this view, you can also attach a note to a record, delete a record, beam it, or turn it into a business card.

FIGURE 5.18

Address View

When you're finished doing all these great things, or when you're through with looking at a record in Address View, tap Done to return to the Address List.

That's basically all there is to navigating the Address Book. Let's start entering some names and numbers.

Creating Address Records

Creating Address Records is just a fancy way of saying "adding people to your Address Book." Whatever you call it, it's really a very simple process that closely maps to the way you enter information in a paper address book or a desktop PIM.

Every name you enter is considered its very own record. You can enter the same name as many times as you want (but why would you do that?), and each entry will be a new record. The Address Book won't stop you from creating duplicate records, so you're on your own there.

 NOTE All procedures in the remainder of this chapter start from the Address List. To get to that point, just press the Address Book hard button or tap on the Address Book icon in the Application Launcher.

To create an Address Book entry:

1. Tap on the New command button at the bottom of the Address List screen.

This will bring up the Address Edit dialog box, which you can see in Figure 5.19.

FIGURE 5.19

The Address Edit dialog box

2. Last Name will be highlighted to show that it is the active line. Enter the last name of your entry using either Graffiti or the on-screen keyboard.

The letters you enter will appear on the Last Name line.

 TIP Though you might be inclined to write directly on that last name line—don't. You can only write Graffiti in the box at the bottom of the screen.

---

3. When you're done entering a last name, tap anywhere on the line next to First Name, and enter a first name for your contact the same way you did the Last Name.

4. Continue this process to enter a title and company for your contact.

5. Tap on the line next to Work to add a work phone number. Remember to write numbers on the number side of the Graffiti writing area.

6. Follow step 5 to enter a home phone number, fax number, and e-mail address. Skip the Other line for now; we'll come back to that.

7. To enter a street address, you may need to scroll to the next screen. To do this, press on the down Scroll Button or tap the down arrow in the lower-right corner of the screen.

8. When the next page of the Address form is displayed, enter the mailing address the same way you entered other information.

   You'll see everything you entered on the appropriate lines.

9. When you're finished entering information, tap Done to close the Address View and return to the Address List.

If you want to find out what's up with that Other option and the arrows next to some of the rows, keep reading.

As we explained in Chapter 3, when you see a downward facing arrow, it means there's a drop-down menu lurking within.

Tap on the arrow next to Other in the Address Edit view to see what other choices you have. A drop-down menu with all the types of information that can be entered on that line will appear, as in Figure 5.20.

FIGURE 5.20

The Other options

If you want to add a Pager number for this entry, tap on Pager to select it. Pager will replace Other on the Address Edit screen.

There are some other options for fine-tuning how your Address Book entries are displayed in the Address List. We'll look at those next.

Setting the Details

By default, the Address List displays the Last Name, First Name, and Work phone for all records. You can change this for an individual record or for every record in your Address Book. We'll get to the setting of global Address Book preferences later in the chapter. For now, let's just look at how an individual record is displayed.

Using Show In List

The changes we explained in the previous section affect how a record looks in Address View. But, you can also change how it looks in the Address List. To do that:

1. Tap on a name in the Address List to open it in Address View.

2. Tap on the Edit command button at the bottom of the screen.

    This will bring up the Address Edit dialog box.

3. Tap on the Details command button at the bottom of the screen.

    This will open the Address Entry Details dialog box, as in Figure 5.21.

FIGURE 5.21

The Address Entry Details dialog box

You'll notice the Show In List option, with an arrow next to it. This indicates a pull-down menu of choices.

4. Tap on that arrow to see what other options you have for displaying information in the Address List.

    Your choices are: Work, Home, Fax, Other, E-Mail.

5. Tap on whichever piece of information you want displayed alongside the name in the Address List.

6. Tap OK to close this dialog box and return to the Address Edit screen.

7. Tap Done to close the Address View and return to the Address List.

Picking a Category

You probably noticed a couple of other choices in the Address Entry Details dialog box. One of the most important of these is Category.

Categories give you an easy way to sort Address records. The more records you have, the more useful categories become. When you only have 10 listings in your Address Book, it's no big deal to scroll through the list to find the number you need. But when you have more listings than can be displayed on a single screen, categories are an invaluable organizational tool.

Don't wait until the entries start piling up: Assign a Category to each record as you enter it.

To assign a Category:

1. Tap on a name in the Address List to open it in Address View.

2. Tap on the Edit command button at the bottom of the screen.

This will bring up the Address Edit dialog box.

3. From the Address Edit screen, tap on the arrow in the upper-right corner to see the pull-down list of Categories to choose from.

4. Tap on a Category on that list to assign it to the open Address record.

 NOTE You can also assign categories the long way: With the Address Edit dialog box open, tap on the Details command button, to open the Address Entry Details dialog box, then tap on the Category drop-down menu to select a Category. Tap on OK when you're done.

Making a Record Private

There's one last option you can set in the Address Entry Details dialog box: to make a record private.

To do this, just tap the Private check box in the Address Entry Details dialog box. A checkmark will appear to show you the choice is active. Tap OK to close this dialog box and return to Address Edit View.

 TIP Making an event private doesn't make it invisible or hide it from view—unless you've set your Palm organizer to Hide Private Records. You do this through the Security application, which we cover in Chapter 7.

Attaching a Note to a Record

Notes are clingy little things. While they can exist quite well on their own, they're at their most useful when they're attached to another type of Palm record. Earlier in this chapter, we explained how to attach a note to a calendar entry; now we'll explain how to attach a note to an Address Book record.

The basic principle and purpose are the same, no matter which application you're working in. You create an Address Book record that needs a little extra information, then create a note, and finally, introduce them to each other.

You don't have to create and attach the note at the same time you create the Address Book record. You can wait till the need arises—perhaps when you've finally asked for directions to your friend's house—and then stuff that information into a note. The one thing you can't do is take an existing note created through the Memo Pad and then link that to an Address Book record. If you want information to travel with a name and number, you must add your note through the Note function in the Address Book.

To add a note to an Address Book record:

1. Tap on a name in the Address List to open it in Address View.

2. Tap on the Edit command button at the bottom of the screen.

   This will bring up the Address Edit dialog box.

3. Tap the Note command button. This will open a new note with the name of your Address Book record in its title bar.

4. Enter text into the note using Graffiti or the on-screen keyboard.

5. Tap Done when your note is complete.

This will return you to the Address Edit dialog box. Tap Done to return to the Address List. Now take a look at the Address Book record you were just working with. See the picture of the dog-eared sheet of paper to the right of the event's name? That tells you it has a note attached. To view the note, just tap on the little picture, and the note opens up. Tap Done when you're finished reading (or editing it), and you're right back to the Address List.

Alternately, if you open an Address Book record to Address View, you can see the note you attached at the bottom of the screen.

NOTE   You can also attach a note to an Address Book record by using the Menu. Follow step 1 above, then tap on the Menu button. Choose Record ➢ Attach Note. Then follow steps 4 and 5 above to complete the action.

PART

II

The Applications

Of course, anything you can create can also be deleted. To delete a note that's attached to an Address Book record:

1. Tap on the note you want to delete in the Address List to open it in Note View.

2. Tap on the Delete command button at the bottom of the screen.

This will bring up the Delete Note dialog box.

3. Tap Yes to confirm the deletion. The dialog box will close, and you'll be back in the Address List. Notice that the icon for a note is no longer part of that particular record.

Creating a Business Card

You already know how useful your little cardboard business card is. Imagine having a business card that is always with you and that you can give out infinitely, with no worry of running out. Your Palm Address Book gives you a way to create an electronic business card that you can easily exchange with other Palm users. You'll know you're hooked on your Palm organizer when you've beamed your business card. It's the ultimate in Palm-chic.

To create your Palm business card:

1. Create an Address Book record with your own information, following the steps in the Creating Address Records section of this chapter.

2. Tap on the record that you just created in the Address List to open it in Address View.

3. Tap on the Menu soft button to open the Menu Bar.

4. Choose Record ➤ Select Business Card.

5. Tap on Yes in the Select Business Card dialog box, as seen in Figure 5.22.

This will return you to the Address View, where you'll see a tabbed address card at the top of the screen, next to Address View. (You can see this icon in Figure 5.18, earlier in this chapter.) This lets you know that this record has been designated as your business card.

FIGURE 5.22

Just say yes to an electronic business card.

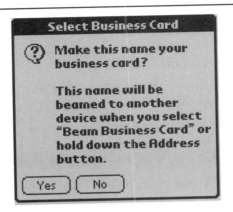

 TIP Though in the paper world you can have many business cards, your Palm organizer only lets you designate one Address Book record as your business card. There's no deselect option for business cards, either. If you change your mind, just select a new record as your business card and the previous choice just goes back to being a plain, old record.

You exchange business cards with other Palm users by using the organizer's IR capabilities. The process is called beaming. We explain how to beam business cards, as well as a host of other Palm goodies, in Chapter 8.

Editing and Deleting Records

If there's one constant in life, it's change. And the more people you add to your Address Book, the more you need to get used to change. Don't know about you, but the folks we know seem to continually change jobs, addresses, and job titles. If it can be changed, they change it.

With the Palm Address Book, it's no big deal. A couple of taps and some Graffiti strokes later, and that formerly out-of-date Address Book entry is now au courant.

Editing an Address Book record is a lot like creating one, only you start with data on the page.

To edit an Address Book record:

1. Select the text to copy, then tap on the record you want to change in the Address List to open it in Address View.

2. Tap on the Edit command button at the bottom of the screen.

This will bring up the Address Edit dialog box.

3. Make any change you want to the record using Graffiti or the on-screen keyboard, following the same process we outlined in the Creating Address Records section earlier in this chapter.

4. Tap Done when you're satisfied with your changes. This will return you to the Address List.

You can also cut, copy, and paste text from one line in an Address Book record to another, or from one Address Book record to another. To do this, open the record you want to cut or copy from in Address Edit mode, then:

1. Tap the Menu soft button, then choose Edit ➤ Cut from the Menu Bar.

2. Tap on the dotted line next to the line you want to add the text to, tap the Menu button again, and choose Edit ➤ Paste.

 NOTE Alternately, you could use the Graffiti commands, which are / (written from bottom left to top right) X and / P, for cut and paste respectively.

The text will appear on its new line.

3. Tap Done when you're satisfied with your changes. This will return you to the Address List.

If merely altering a record isn't enough, and you need to trash it outright, follow these steps to delete a record the quick way:

1. Tap on the record you want to delete in the Address List to open it in Address View.

2. Tap the Menu soft button to open the Menu Bar.

3. Choose Record ➤ Delete Address.

4. Tap the check box next to the Save Archive Copy On PC option, if you think you might ever want this record again.

5. Tap OK in the Delete Address dialog box to confirm the deletion and return to the Address List. The offending record will be gone, gone, gone.

There's also a long way to delete an Address Book record:

1. Tap on the record you want to delete in the Address List to open it in Address View.

2. Tap on the Edit command button at the bottom of the screen.

This will bring up the Address Edit dialog box.

3. Tap on the Details command button at the bottom of the screen.

This will open the Address Entry Details dialog box.

4. Tap on the Delete command button.

5. Tap the check box next to the Save Archive Copy On PC option, if you think you might ever want this record again.

6. Tap OK in the Delete Address dialog box to confirm the deletion and return to the Address List. The offending record is just as gone as if you'd deleted it the quick way. Any notes you may have had attached will be gone, too.

Customizing Your Records

To make your Address Book records even more useful, you can customize them a bit so they work more the way you do.

You can create your own categories, reorganize the order of some of the information in individual records, and create custom fields to display whatever information you find useful. Hey, it's your Address Book; make it work for you.

Creating New Categories

The Palm Address Book comes with five categories:

- All
- Business
- Personal
- QuickList
- Unfiled

By default, all Address Book records you create go into the Unfiled category. You can easily move them into one of the other categories by following the steps we outlined in the Creating Address Records section of this chapter.

The All category displays every record in your Address Book, whether you've categorized it or not.

PART

II

The Applications

The QuickList serves as a file box for the records you use most often, but it's really no different than any of the other categories.

If these five categories aren't specific enough for you, you can add your own categories or change the names of the existing ones—except for All and Unfiled, which can't be edited.

To create your own categories:

1. From the Address List, tap on the arrow next to the name of the category currently being displayed.

   This will open the Category pull-down list.

2. Tap on Edit Categories at the bottom of the pull-down list to open the Edit Categories screen.

3. Tap on the New command button at the bottom of the screen.

   This will open the Edit Categories dialog box, which you can see in Figure 5.23.

FIGURE 5.23

*Add a new
category here.*

4. Enter a name for your new category using Graffiti or the on-screen keyboard.

5. Tap OK to close this dialog box and return to the Edit Categories screen.

Either add another category following steps 3, 4, and 5, or tap OK to return to the Address List. If you just want to change the name of one of the existing categories, say from Business to Customers, follow steps 1-2 above, then:

1. Tap on the name of an existing category to select it. It will be covered with a black bar to show it's selected.

2. Tap on the Rename command button at the bottom of the screen to open the Edit Categories dialog box.

   The name of the category you selected will appear, with a bar over it, in the Edit categories dialog box.

3. Add a new name for this category using either Graffiti or the on-screen keyboard.

4. Tap OK to return to the Edit Categories screen.

5. Either edit another category following steps 1-4, or tap OK to return to the Address List.

Any records you previously assigned to the category you just renamed will now appear under the new category name. You can add new records to this (or any categories you create) the usual way.

If you delete a category that has records assigned to it, those records won't disappear. They'll just get shoved into the Unfiled category, which serves as a dumping ground for homeless records.

Setting Custom Fields

There are plenty of lines to add most of the information you need to an Address Book record. But what if you want to add a tidbit that there isn't a handy place for? Like a birthday or the name of someone's executive assistant. Just make your own entry line. That's what those Custom lines in the Address Book record are for.

To create a Custom Field (or line, which is the same thing):

1. From the Address List, tap on the Menu soft button to open the Menu Bar.

2. Choose Options ➤ Rename Custom Fields. This will open the Rename Custom Fields dialog box, which you can see in Figure 5.24.

   You'll notice Custom 1, Custom 2, Custom 3, and Custom 4 on the text entry lines.

FIGURE 5.24

Add a spot for special information.

3. Select the Custom listing you want to change. A black bar will appear over it to show the text is selected.

4. Enter a new name for the field using either Graffiti or the on-screen keyboard.

PART

II

The Applications

This name will appear in place of the old field name in the Rename Custom Fields dialog box.

5. Tap OK to accept this new name and return to the Address List.

This new field will appear on all your Address records—the new ones, as well as those you've already created.

Reordering Information

There is one last way you can customize Address Book records: by changing the order of some of the fields.

To change the order of information in an Address Book record, you use the Other field in Address Edit view. We introduced this field way back in the section on Creating Address Records, so flip back to that section and take a look at Figure 5.20 to refresh your memory.

As we mentioned previously, you can change the Other field in an Address record to display a variety of different types of information. Tap on the down arrow next to Other to see the drop-down list of choices. They are: Work, Home, Fax, Other, E-Mail, Main, Pager, and Mobile. Tap one of these options, and it replaces Other in the Address record.

You can also use these menus to change the order of some of the information in your record. For example, you can swap the Home line for the Work line, so the home phone number appears in the list first. Since you can only switch lines with the arrow next to them, some items will need to stay where they are.

To change the order of fields (in this case, we'll swap Work and Home):

1. Tap on the record you want to reorder in the Address List to open it in Address View. (You can also do this to a new record, as you're creating it).

2. Tap on the Edit command button at the bottom of the screen.

This will bring up the Address Edit dialog box.

 NOTE Notice the downward arrows next to Work, Home, Fax, Other, and E-mail. This indicates that there's a drop-down list of options available for each of these fields.

3. Tap the arrow next to Work.

You'll see the same pull-down list we saw next to Other.

4. Tap on Home on the drop-down list.

Home will appear on the record in place of Work. It will also appear in its original spot, on the next line. You probably don't need to enter two Home phone numbers, so we'll change that one to Work.

5. Tap on the arrow next to the second Home field.

You'll see that same drop-down list yet again.

6. Tap on Work on that drop-down list.

The second Home field changes to Work. You've successfully swapped the order of these two fields. You can do the same thing with other fields that have arrows next to them, if you like.

When you reorder information in a record, as we just did, the change only affects the record you were working in. New records you add and your existing records maintain the usual order of information. Unfortunately, there's no way to make this a global change that applies to the entire Address Book. Maybe someday.

Using the Records You Created

By now, you know how to create Address Book records, customize them, and categorize them. That means its time for us to explain some of the ways to find just the record you want, quickly and easily.

Sure, you can scroll through the entire Address List to find the name you need, but there are quicker ways: using the Look Up feature and sorting by category.

Using Look Up

At the bottom of the Address List, you'll notice the words "Look Up," followed by a text entry line.

This feature lets you quickly find a name in your Address Book, without scrolling. To use Look Up:

1. From the Address List View, start writing the first couple of letters of the name you're looking for using either Graffiti or the on-screen keyboard.

   The Address List will scroll to the name that most closely matches what you entered. The first likely match will have a black bar over it to show it's selected.

2. Tap on the selected name to display its record in Address View.

 TIP Look Up only searches through the category currently being displayed in the Address List. So, if the name you want is in Business and you have Personal displayed, you may not get a match.

The more names you have in your Address Book, the more you'll come to rely on Look Up. Still, it has a few limitations:

- It can only recognize words, so you can't enter a phone number and get a match.

- It can only recognize the beginning of last names, so you can't enter Smi and expect Look Up to find Mr. Firesmith or Mrs. Smith Parker.

- It always takes you to the first listing that matches what you entered, so if you have five listings for Smith, Look Up will always choose the first one. You'll have to scroll from there.

Hey, we never said Look Up was perfect, just extremely useful.

Sorting by Categories

In the section on Creating Address Records, we explained how to assign categories to Address Book records. If you haven't done that yet, go back and categorize all your entries now. Go on, we'll wait.

OK, now that you're back, we'll explain why categorizing is so important and show you how to navigate through categories.

Once you have more than 10 or 15 names in your Address Book, navigating by scrolling becomes impractical. The Look Up feature knocks considerable time off the search for a name, but you can make Look Up even more powerful by categorizing your records.

Look Up only searches through the category currently being displayed in the Address List. So, if you have All displayed (or Unfiled, if you haven't done any categorizing), it has considerably more records to search through than if you have a single category up on-screen.

If you can't remember the name of that new customer, Look Up can't help you. But, if you categorized the record in Customers, you could flip over to that category and do a quick scroll to find the record. It's not perfect, but under the circumstances, it's the quickest approach you've got.

There are two ways to change the category displayed in the Address Book. We'll call them the scenic route and the direct route.

To change the category displayed in the Address List via the scenic route:

1. Push the Address Book hard button to open the Address Book to the Address List.

   The last category you were looking at will be displayed. Let's assume for this discussion that it was All.

2. Push the Address Book button again to display the next category. In this case, it would be Personal.

3. Keep pressing the Address Book button to cycle through all the categories.

To change categories via the direct route:

1. From the Address List, tap on the arrow next to the category name in the upper-right corner of the display.

   This will open the category drop-down menu.

2. Tap on the name of the category you want to display.

The Address List will change to show only the records you've assigned to that category.

Pretty simple, isn't it?

Setting Address Book Preferences

There are a few more things you can do in the Address Book to make it more uniquely yours. You can change the font the Address Book uses for both the Address List and the individual records.

To change the font for the Address List:

1. With the Address List open, choose Options ➤ Font from the Menu.

2. In the Font dialog box that opens up, tap on the letter style that looks best to you.

This will change all the listings in the Address List to this font. Tap OK when you're satisfied with your choice.

 TIP The font you choose for the Address List will also be the font used for the first and last name of each record or the company and last name of each record, depending on what you've chosen to display in the list.

To change the font for all your Address records (you can't change just one, or part of one):

1. Tap on any record in the Address List to open it in Address View.

2. Tap on the Menu button to bring up the Menu bar.

3. Choose Options ➢ Font.

This will open up the Font dialog box.

4. Tap on the font that looks best to you.

This will change all your Address Book records to the font you selected.

5. Tap OK when you're satisfied with your choice.

This will close the Font dialog box and return you to Address View.

All of the other Address Book preferences are set from the Address Book Preferences dialog box. To access this box:

1. From the Address List, tap on the Menu button to bring up the Menu bar.

2. Choose Options ➢ Preferences.

This will open the Address Book Preferences dialog box, which you can see in Figure 5.25.

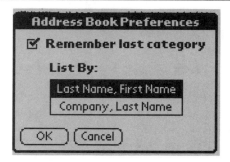

FIGURE 5.25

Choose how to organize your Address List.

You have just three choices here:

• Remember last category

• List By Last Name, First Name

• List By Company, Last Name

When you tap in the Remember Last Name check box to select this option, the Address Book will automatically open to the last category you had displayed—even if you switch applications. If you don't check this box, the Address Book will always open to the All category.

The List By options let you decide what gets displayed in the Address List. This choice applies across all your categories; there's no way to change List By options for just a single category. You can decide to view records by Last Name, First Name or Company, Last Name.

Company, Last Name is useful if you have lots of business contacts and care more about finding a particular company than a person. If you have lots of personal contacts, though, this option will give you lots of empty space in the Address List where that company name should go. In this case, the Last Name, First Name choice is the better one.

PART

II

The Applications

CHAPTER **6**

Lists and Notes: Mastering the To Do List and the Memo Pad

Throw out your little yellow sticky pads! Liberate your scrap paper! With a Palm organizer in your pocket, you no longer need those inferior tools for creating lists of tasks you have to complete or notes from that important phone call with the client. Creating and organizing To Do Lists and Memos are two things that the Palm organizer excels at. If you can put it into words, the Palm can help you keep track of it.

The To Do List

What can we say about To Do Lists that you don't already know? They're always full; you never have enough time to finish everything on them; and invariably, the list will just vanish on a daily basis—at the least convenient time possible.

The Palm To Do List can't help with the too many tasks/too little time problem, but it's guaranteed not to get lost just when you need it most.

The To Do List does just what you'd expect: it provides a convenient place to jot down all the tasks you need to get accomplished but are likely to forget.

The To Do List is more than just a static list; it's an organizational tool, too. You can assign categories to your To Dos, so on Saturday you don't have to look at all that stuff waiting for you on Monday morning. You can also sort To Dos by their order of importance, so "Finish sales report" appears before "Buy chocolate ice cream" on your list (or not, depending on how bad the day has been). And best of all, the To Do List remembers what tasks you didn't finish today, and automatically carries them over to tomorrow—or to next month, if it takes you that long to finish the job.

Let's jump right in to that To Do List. It won't fill itself, after all.

Creating a To Do

Press the To Do List hard button to go straight to the To Do List. You don't get a choice of views here, as with the other applications. There's a list, and that's it.

Amazingly enough, there will be items on the list the very first time you launch it. The fine folks at Palm Computing have thoughtfully provided some reminders so you wouldn't be lulled into thinking that your To Do List could ever possibly be empty. You weren't foolish enough to imagine such a thing, were you?

You can stall all you want on completing their assigned tasks, but it's time to start adding your own tasks. You have two methods to choose from when adding a To Do: the super quick way and the slightly less quick way.

The super quick way to add a To Do is so quick, it only has two steps:

1. Press the To Do List hard button to open the To Do List.

2. Start entering text in the Graffiti writing area.

The To Do List will recognize that you're adding a new item to the list, and automatically start entering your To Do on the first available line. You can see the To Do List with a new entry in progress in Figure 6.1.

 NOTE This method won't work with the on-screen keyboard. It's a Graffiti-only technique.

FIGURE 6.1

What a To Do!

PART

II

The Applications

 NOTE All the rest of the step-by-step instructions in this chapter will assume that the To Do List is already open.

The slightly less quick approach really isn't much slower than the super quick way. To add a To Do:

1. Tap the New command button at the bottom left of the screen.

   You'll see a new dotted line at the bottom of the To Do List. The cursor will be blinking at the start of the line to show that it's ready for your input.

2. Enter your To Do using either Graffiti or the on-screen keyboard.

3. Tap anywhere on the screen (except the line where your new To Do goes) to let the To Do List know you're finished entering text.

If you have a To Do that involves a name and phone number that are already entered into your Address Book, Phone Lookup can locate them and paste them into your To Do item.

To perform a Phone Lookup:

1. With the To Do List open, tap on the To Do item you want to add a name and number to.

 TIP Be sure to tap at the exact place in the To Do where you want the name and number to appear. For example, after the word Call.

A black highlight bar will appear over the To Do's priority, to show you that it's been selected.

2. Tap on the Menu soft button, then choose Options ➤ Phone Lookup. (Or, you can write a command stroke, and then write L using Graffiti.)

This will bring up the Phone Lookup screen (which is really your Address Book). You can see it in Figure 6.2.

3. From the Phone Lookup screen, select the name you want to tack on to your To Do.

4. Tap the Add button, and the name and number will appear as part of your To Do.

 TIP Here's a really quick way to add a name to your To Do: Enter part or all of the name you want to include using either Graffiti or the on-screen keyboard. Select the text (drag your stylus across it), tap the Menu button, then choose Options ➤ Phone Lookup from the Menu bar. If Lookup comes up with a direct hit, it will automatically paste the name and number into your To Do. If it comes up with multiple possible matches, the Address List will pop up, and you can choose the correct name by tapping on it.

This takes you back to the To Do List; the name and number are there for all to see. That's all there is to that To Do. Of course, there are some choices you can make to organize that lumbering list. We'll explore those next.

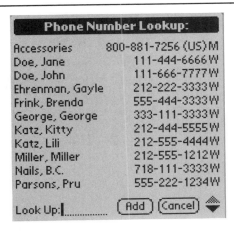

FIGURE 6.2

*Lookup a name and
add it to your To Do.*

PART

II

The Applications

Organizing Your To Dos

There are basically two ways to organize your To Do List items: by assigning categories
to them and by assigning priorities to them.

You assign categories to your To Dos to remind yourself what type of task that To
Do is—a business task, a personal task, etc. Priority lets you decide just how important
a task is—priority 1–5.

Of course, you can assign both a category and a priority to a To Do, so your personal tasks can be every bit as important as your business tasks.

To help you organize, prioritize, and visualize your very busy day, you can also
assign a due date to a To Do. So now, you can have a Priority 1 Business To Do due to
be completed tomorrow. Pretty efficient, isn't it?

Categorizing To Dos

To assign categories to To Do items:

1. Tap on a To Do item on the list to select it.

   You'll see a black highlight bar over the completion check box and priority to
   the left of the description of the task. This lets you know which item is selected.

2. Tap on the Details command button at the bottom of the screen.

   This will open the To Do Item Details dialog box, which you can see in Figure 6.3.

FIGURE 6.3

Pick a category from the To Do Items Details dialog box.

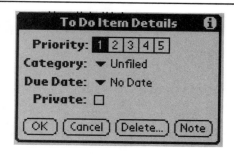

3. Tap on the down arrow next to Category to open the drop-down list of available categories.

4. Tap on the Category you want to assign to this task.

5. Tap OK to accept your choice and return to the To Do List.

The next To Do you add to the list will automatically be assigned the same category as the last one you created. You can follow the steps above to assign it to a different category.

 NOTE You may have noticed that the last item on the category pull-down list is Edit Categories. This is used to rename existing categories and create new ones. We'll walk you through that process later in this chapter.

Setting Priorities

Notice that number just to the left of each of your To Dos? That's the priority. Your choices are 1 (most important) to 5 (whenever I get around to it). By default, the To Do List gives a new To Do the same priority you selected for your last addition to the list. So, if you gave "Pick up dry cleaning" a priority of 4, whatever you enter next will automatically be ranked a 4 (even if it has a good beat and is easy to dance to).

It's very easy to change the priority of a To Do. Here's how:

1. Tap on the priority number for the To Do you want to change.

A drop-down menu will appear, listing 1–5.

2. Tap on the new priority you want to assign to the item.

That number will appear next to the description of your To Do.

Of course, there's another way to change the priority (it wouldn't be true to the Palm way if there wasn't). Here's the alternate approach:

1. Tap on the To Do List item you want to reprioritize to select it.

2. Tap the Details command button.

The To Do Item Details dialog box will open.

3. Tap on the number of the priority you want to assign to the item.

4. Tap OK to accept your choice and return to the To Do List.

The new priority number will appear next to the description of your To Do List item.

Both methods work equally well. We're partial to the first approach because it's quicker, and we like to do as much on a single screen as possible.

Assigning a Due Date

What's a To Do without a due date—actually it's just a "To." Now that will never do! Bad puns aside, we're very deadline driven (just ask our editor) and like to know what is the absolute latest date we can finish something without getting into trouble. That's what we call a due date.

Your choices for assigning a due date to an item are the same as for assigning a priority. You can either carry out the action on the To Do List screen or through the To Do Item Details dialog box.

 NOTE By default, the To Do List does not show due dates on screen. You will not be able to assign due dates on the To Do List screen until you enable their display (the dialog box method will still work). We explain how to turn on this display option in the section on Setting To Do List Preferences.

To assign a due date from the To Do List screen:

1. Tap on the date at the far right of the To Do List item to which you want to give a due date. (You may see a dash instead of a date; if so, just tap on the dash.)

PART

II

The Applications

This will bring up a menu of due date options: Today, Tomorrow, One Week Later, No Date, and Choose Date.

2. Tap on Choose Date to bring up the Due Date calendar.

   You navigate this calendar the same way you do the Date Book calendar.

3. Tap on the month and date you want to apply.

   This will return you to the To Do List, where you'll see a new Due Date assigned to your item.

You could just have tapped on Today or Tomorrow to choose one of those as your due date. If you set Today's Date when you first configured your Palm organizer, these options will be accurate. If you skipped that step, go back to Chapter 1 and take care of it now.

You can also assign a Due Date to an item using the To Do Item Detail dialog box. Follow the steps for assigning a priority to a task, and you're most of the way there. Instead of tapping on priority in that dialog box, tap on the down arrow next to Due Date and pick a date from the list. Your choices are the same here as they are when you access the list from the To Do List screen.

We're partial to the on-screen approach, because it just seems quicker and more direct. If you need to set the priority and due date, as well as mark a record private all at the same time, the dialog box method is the way to go.

Working with To Dos

There are some other things you can do with your To Dos. You can:

- Mark them private
- Edit and delete them
- Mark them done
- Attach notes to them
- Get rid of the really old ones
- Beam them to other Palm users

Many of these concepts work the same way they did in the Date Book and Address Book. So, if you read those sections, the following may sound familiar.

Marking a To Do Private

The To Do Item Details dialog box is where you go to mark a To Do item as private. In fact, there's no other way to carry out this task, except through the dialog box. (We knew it existed for a reason!) Marking a To Do private works the same way it did in the Date Book and the Address Book.

To mark a To Do private:

1. With the To Do List open, tap on the name of the item you want to mark private.

2. Tap on the Details command button to open the To Do Item Details dialog box.

3. Tap in the check box next to Private.

A checkmark will appear to show this option is selected.

4. Tap OK to accept this choice, close the dialog box, and return to the To Do List.

Remember, though, that unless you've chosen to Hide Private Records in the Security application, you'll still see your private To Do in the To Do List. For more on hiding private records, see Chapter 7.

Editing And Deleting a To Do

Anything you can enter in to your Palm organizer, you can also change. To Dos are no exception. To change the priority or category of a To Do, just follow the same steps you used when first setting those options.

To change the description of a To Do, you have a few choices:

- If you want to undo what you just did when entering or editing, choose Edit ➤ Undo from the Menu Bar.

- If you just want to add to the description, tap at the point you want to new text to appear, and start entering more text using either Graffiti or the on-screen keyboard.

- If you want to delete part of the text (but not the category or priority), select the text you want to replace by tapping and dragging the stylus across it. Then either cut it by choosing Edit ➤ Cut from the Menu Bar, or by just entering new text to replace what is highlighted.

- If you want to delete all the text of a To Do yet maintain the detail information, either select all the text using the method described above, or choose Edit ➤ Select All from the Menu Bar.

If you want to delete an entire To Do:

1. With the To Do List open, tap on the name of the item you want to delete.

PART

II

The Applications

2. Do either of the following:

- Tap on the Menu soft button to bring up the Menu Bar. Choose Record ➤ Delete Item.

or

- Tap on the Details command button to bring up the To Do Item dialog box, and then tap on Delete.

3. Tap OK in the dialog box after checking the Save Archive On PC check box, if you think you may need this To Do at some future time.

Either way, the To Do will be gone from the list.

Marking a To Do Done

Perhaps the very best thing you can do with a To Do is complete it. When this happens, just tap in that little empty check box next to the priority you assigned, and voilá, it's done. Depending on how you've set up your To Do List preferences, you'll either see a checkmark in that box (as in Figure 6.4), or the item will simply disappear from your list. We explain how to set To Do List preferences later in this chapter.

FIGURE 6.4

They're all done, but one.

Attaching Notes to To Dos

To Dos are wonderful, but there is a limit to how long they can be. No To Do can run longer than a single screen or roughly 12 lines or about 255 characters. So, what do you do when you need to buy 15 items at the supermarket—create 15 separate To Do entries? No way. Just create one To Do item that has the name "Go shopping" and attach a note to it, which lists everything you need to buy.

Assuming you didn't read that last section and giddily mark every item on your list done, let's select a To Do from the list and attach a note to it. Here's how:

1. With the To Do List open, tap on the name of the item to which you want to attach a note.

2. Tap on the Menu soft button to bring up the Menu Bar.

3. Choose Record ➤ Attach Note.

   You'll see a Note screen, with the name of your To Do in the title bar at the top of the screen, as in Figure 6.5.

PART

II

The Applications

FIGURE 6.5

A new note

4. Start entering the text for your note using either Graffiti or the on-screen keyboard.

5. Tap the Done command button when you're satisfied with the contents of the note. This will return you to the To Do List.

 NOTE   You can also use the To Do Item Details dialog box to attach a note. Just select the To Do to which you want to add a note, tap on the Details command button, and then tap the Note button in the To Do Item Details dialog box. Follow steps 4 and 5 above.

When you're back at the To Do List, you'll see a picture of a dog-eared piece of paper next to the due date of the To Do, which indicates there's a note attached to this item. Just tap on this picture to open the note for reading, editing, or deleting (tap on the Delete command button with the note open, and then tap on Yes in the Delete Note dialog box).

Purging Old To Dos

Once a To Do is done, what good is it? Why not clear out some space on your Palm organizer for some new To Dos—or maybe even a game? Just purge all the To Dos you've marked as completed and reclaim some of that memory.

To purge To Dos:

1. With the To Do List open, tap on the Menu soft button.

   This will bring up the Menu Bar.

2. Choose Record ➣ Purge, as shown in Figure 6.6.

   This will bring up the Purge dialog box.

3. If you think you might ever want a record of those old To Dos, tap in the Save Archive Copy On PC check box.

   A checkmark will appear in the box to show that this option is selected.

4. Tap OK to delete all the completed To Dos from your Palm organizer once and for all.

 NOTE We explain how to retrieve items you've archived in Chapter 10.

FIGURE 6.6

*Get rid of those old
To Dos.*

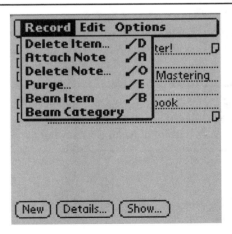

Beaming To Dos

You can knock To Do items off your list one other way: by assigning them to someone else. You can do this by beaming a To Do (or a whole category of To Dos) to another Palm user. It's a simple process that we explain in detail in Chapter 8.

Beaming won't actually remove the item from your To Do List, but if someone else is taking care of that task, it's not your problem any more.

Working with Categories

Earlier in this chapter, we explained how to assign a category to your To Dos. Now we'll explain how to work with those categories. You can sort To Dos by category, rename existing categories, and create some new ones, as well.

Sorting To Dos by Category

There's really no point to assigning To Dos to categories if you always leave the list open to the All category. The fastest way to find a To Do is to look in the category it's been assigned to.

To change the category your To Do List displays, just tap on the down arrow next to the category in the upper-right corner of the To Do List screen. Next, tap on the category you want to see from the drop-down list that appears. The To Do List will change to show only the items you've assigned to that category.

So, on Saturday, when you're trying to figure out what errands you need to run, you can tap your way over to the Personal category and see only your Saturday To Dos. This way you won't be reminded of that report that's due on Monday, which you haven't finished yet.

Customizing Categories

Your Palm organizer comes complete with four To Do List categories: All, Business, Personal, and Unfiled. All displays every item entered into your To Do List. Unfiled is where all the items you haven't assigned categories to go. Business and Personal stay empty until you assign work- and life-related To Dos to them. These category names may be the same as those used by the other Palm applications, but the categories don't carry over from one application to the next. The Business category in the To Do List will not contain any Date Book items you classified as Business. And, should you decide to create custom categories, they'll be available only in the application you create them in.

If these categories don't meet your needs, if, for example, you'd like to have a category for a specific project, you can create your own category or rename one of the existing ones. You can also delete a category you're no longer using.

All of these actions can be carried out from the Category pull-down list we used to change the category displayed by the To Do List. To customize your categories:

1. With the To Do List open, tap on the down arrow next to the category in the upper-right corner of the screen.

   This will open the drop-down list of categories.

2. Tap on Edit Categories.

   This will open the Edit Categories dialog box, which you can see in Figure 6.7.

FIGURE 6.7

Start here to rename a category or add a new one.

To rename one of the existing categories, say from Business to Customers, follow steps 1-2 above, then:

3. Tap on the name of an existing category to select it. It will be covered with a black bar to show it's selected.

4. Tap on the Rename command button at the bottom of the screen to open the smaller Edit Categories dialog box. (You can see this box in Figure 6.8.)

   The name of the category you selected will appear, with a bar over it, in this box.

5. Add a new name for this category using either Graffiti or the on-screen keyboard.

6. Tap OK to return to the Edit Categories screen.

7. Either rename another category following steps 3, 4, 5, and 6 or tap OK to return to the Address List.

Any To Dos you previously assigned to the category you just renamed will now appear under the new category name. You can add new To Dos to this (or any categories you create) the usual way.

FIGURE 6.8

A category's name means everything.

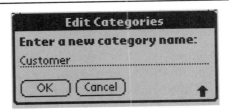

If you want to create a brand new category, follow steps 1 and 2 to access the Edit Categories dialog box, then:

3. Tap on the New command button at the bottom of the screen.

This will open another, smaller Edit Categories dialog box (we wish they'd give these things distinct names).

4. Enter a name for your new category using Graffiti or the on-screen keyboard.

5. Tap OK to close this dialog box and return to the Edit Categories screen.

6. Either add another category following steps 3, 4, and 5, or tap OK to return to the To Do List.

Your new categories will appear in the same drop-down list as the existing categories. Start adding To Dos whenever you're ready.

 NOTE You can also customize your categories through the Category drop-down list in the To Do Item Details dialog box. Just tap on Edit Categories at the bottom of this list, and follow the steps we've outlined above.

Just as you can create new categories, you can delete existing ones (except for All and Unfiled, which are untouchable). To delete a category:

1. With the To Do List open, tap on the down arrow next to the category in the upper-right corner of the screen.

This will open the drop-down list of categories.

2. Tap on Edit Categories.

PART

II

The Applications

3. Tap on the name of an existing category to select it. It will be covered with a black bar to show it's selected.

4. Tap on the Delete command button at the bottom of the screen.

This will bring up the Remove Category dialog box if you have To Do list items filed in this category. Otherwise, the category will just be deleted.

5. Tap Yes to complete the deletion.

This will return you to the Edit Categories screen. Tap on the OK command button to return to the To Do List. Any To Dos you had previously assigned to that category will be moved into Unfiled. If you want to get rid of them as well as the category they once belonged to, you'll have to delete the To Dos individually.

If you delete a category, all the To Do items you had assigned to the now defunct category will be shuttled into the Unfiled category, so you can refile them.

Setting To Do List Preferences

The information that gets displayed in your To Do List is largely up to you. You can pick and choose how much, or how little, your To Do List shows by setting To Do List Preferences.

To set these Preferences:

1. With the To Do List open, tap on the Show command button at the bottom of the screen.

This will open the To Do Preferences dialog box, which you can see in Figure 6.9.

2. Tap the downward arrow next to Sort By to change the way To Do items are sorted. As you can see in Figure 6.10, you can choose from:

- Priority, Due Date
- Due Date, Priority
- Category, Priority
- Category, Due Date

These items let you determine what order To Do List items appear on-screen. Priority, Due Date, for example, will order the list so all items that are Priority 1 appear at the top of the list; if there are multiple items with that priority, the Due Date will serve as the next qualifier. So, Priority 1 items with a due date of today will appear before Priority 1 items with a due date of next week, and before Priority 2 items, etc. The other Sort By options work the same way, sorting by two qualifiers each.

THE TO DO LIST

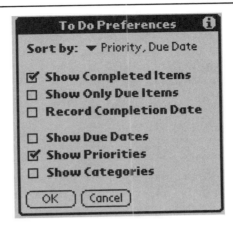

Choose how to sort
your To Dos

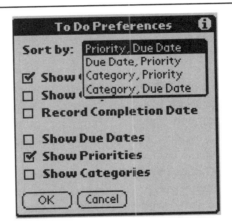

PART

II

The Applications

Let's set some other preferences now. Tap the check boxes next to the items you want
to display. Your choices are:

Show Completed Items   Puts a checkmark next to an item you've
marked completed, but leaves it on the To Do List.

Show Only Due Items   Displays only items with no due date or a due
date of today, or items that are overdue.

Record Completion Date   Changes the due date to the date you mark
the task complete.

Show Due Dates   Shows the date you want a task done by.

Show Priorities   Shows the priority you assigned next to the description of the To Do.

Show Categories   Attaches the category name you've assigned the To Do next to its due date.

Check or uncheck these items until the To Do List looks the way you like it. No change is permanent, so experiment.

 TIP   There isn't that much room on the Palm screen, so don't select everything you can display on the To Do List. It won't all fit and still be readable.

You can now consider yourself a master of the To Do List. It's time to move on to another application.

The Memo Pad

Got something important you need to jot down, but it doesn't fit in the Date Book, Address Book, or the To Do List? Then the Memo Pad is what you want.

The Memo Pad is the Palm's version of a notebook—it gives you a blank page where you can write down anything that you want to keep handy: notes for a meeting, a travel itinerary, or ideas for your book. All these things will fit quite comfortably in the Memo Pad.

We know plenty of folks who use the Memo Pad as a temporary storage site, entering information there quickly, then cutting and pasting it into the Date Book or Address Book as time permits. There's nothing wrong with using the Memo Pad as an electronic in-box, as long as you remember to move all those bits of information over to a more suitable location. Otherwise, all the other Palm applications will get very lonely. More importantly, you'll have a tough time finding anything if your Memo Pad is stuffed with hundreds of unrelated snippets.

Right out of the box, the Memo Pad accepts only text: letters and numbers written using either Graffiti or the on-screen keyboard. You can't use it to draw diagrams, charts, or maps. Also, the Memo Pad puts a limit on the length of every memo. It holds you to 4K per memo. That may not sound like much, but it translates to roughly 14 full screens of text. That isn't enough space to write a book chapter (even if it is about the Memo Pad), but we've found that it's large enough for the type of jotting we do on the Palm organizer. Quite frankly, we can't see doing that much writing using either Graffiti or the on-screen keyboard. For anything that long, we'd write it using the Palm Desktop software, then just HotSync it over. For more on the Palm Desktop, see Chapter 10. We explain everything you need to know about HotSyncing in Chapter 9.

If you feel like the limitations of the Memo Pad are holding you back, you'll be pleased to know that there are some clever folks who have found ways to make the Memo Pad accept drawings and longer blocks of text. We'll tell you about some of those add-on software tools in Chapters 17 and 19.

Don't go flipping over to another chapter just yet. We're about to start explaining what the Memo Pad can do without outside assistance—except for some help from you, of course.

Navigating through the Memo List

When you open the Memo Pad, either by pushing the Memo Pad hard button or by tapping on the Memo Pad icon in the Application Launcher, you'll see the Memo List. Figure 6.11 shows you what it looks like.

FIGURE 6.11

A list of important memos

Even if this is the first time you're using the Memo Pad, you won't just see an empty list. The folks at Palm Computing were thoughtful enough to provide a few memos to get you started. They're actually quite helpful—the memos and the folks at Palm Computing, that is.

Each memo on the list has the same elements. It has a number and a description (or name). The number indicates nothing more than where this memo falls in the category currently being displayed. By default, the Memo Pad numbers memos sequentially, so if you already have 10 memos within a category and add one more, it will be assigned the number 11. As with anything in the Palm organizer, you can change that by manually sorting your Memo Pad entries. We'll explain how to do that later in this chapter.

You can also sort your memos alphabetically, so that any memo you create will be assigned a number according to where it fits in the category list being displayed. So, if the first letter of the description for the first memo on your Business list starts with "w" and the next memo you create has a description that starts with "a," that new memo will take over the number one spot on the list. All the other memos will be bumped down a spot.

That was a long-winded explanation, wasn't it? The whole numbering and sorting thing sounds way more complicated and time consuming than it really is. We'll explain sort order later in this chapter. For now, just know that the numbering happens instantaneously and the Palm can handle the whole thing without any help from you.

Now, back to the other part of the memo displayed in the Memo List: the description. This description or name (we'll use the two words interchangeably) is taken from the first line of a memo. So, if you want your memo to have a proper title, like Shopping List, take care with what you write on that first line. Don't just start in writing your memo, otherwise you'll wind up with a memo named Eggs. And one last thing about naming memos: you don't have to put anything on the first line of a Memo, but this makes for a Memo without a name. All you'll see in the Memo List is a number and a blank space where the memo's name should be. How will you ever know what the memo is about if you don't give it a name?

Adding a Memo

Now that we've explained the parts of a memo, let's take a look at the process for creating one. If you've been following along with the procedures for creating new records in any of the other applications, you won't be surprised to find out that there are two ways to create a new memo.

As in the To Do List, you can simply launch the Memo Pad and start entering text using Graffiti—the on-screen keyboard doesn't work at this point. The application will flip to a new Memo screen and accept whatever text you enter. When you're satisfied with the contents of your memo, you just tap Done to return to the Memo List. You can see the Memo screen in Figure 6.12.

FIGURE 6.12

*Start writing to fill the
Memo screen*

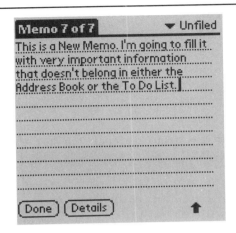

There's another way to start a new memo:

1. Tap on the New command button at the bottom left of the Memo List.

   This will open a new Memo screen (which will show you what number the memo will be assigned along the top of the screen).

2. Enter the text you want in the memo using either Graffiti or the on-screen keyboard.

3. Tap done when you're finished writing. This will take you back to the Memo List.

 TIP   You don't need to worry about scrolling when you write memos that run longer than a single screen. The Memo Pad will keep advancing the memo so you always see a blank line to write on. You will have to scroll for yourself, though, when you come back to read this magnum opus.

Working with Memos

Creating memos is only the beginning of what you can do with the Memo Pad. You can do many of the same things here that you can do in the other Palm organizer applications, including reading and editing the records you create, categorizing them, customizing them, adding phone numbers to them, and sorting them for easy retrieval. That's a lot of stuff for one little memo to handle.

Reading and Editing a Memo

At some point, you'll want to read, and possibly edit, the memos you've created. Why bother writing stuff down if you never look at it again? And heck, Hemingway believed (and this is a very loose paraphrase here) that the first draft of anything was useless. We're certain he used much stronger language, but we'd like this book to maintain a G rating. So read, reread, and edit away.

To read a Memo:

1. With the Memo List open, tap on the name of the memo you want to read.

This will open the memo in Memo View.

2. Read. (You're on your own for how to do that.) Use the scroll bar along the right side of the screen or the Scroll buttons to see any parts of the memo that don't fit on the screen.

3. When you're finished reading the memo, tap Done to close it and return to the Memo List.

Suppose you start reading a memo and suddenly realize that you left out some important information. That's easy to fix. To add text to an existing memo:

1. Open the memo you want to amend following step 1 in the directions for reading a memo.

This will open the memo in Memo View.

2. Tap in the place in the memo where you want to add new text.

An insertion point (represented by a blinking vertical line) will appear at the place where you tapped.

3. Add whatever text you like using either Graffiti or the on-screen keyboard.

4. When you're finished adding to the memo, tap Done to close it and return to the Memo List.

Suppose you realize that the second step in the recipe you've written out really isn't quite right. You can replace some of that existing text easily. There are two ways to do this; we're running out of clever names for methods, so we'll just call them the selection method and the menu method.

To replace text using the selection method:

1. Open the memo you want to amend following step 1 in the directions for reading a memo.

This will open the memo in Memo View.

2. Select the text you want to move or replace by tapping on it and dragging the cursor across the screen. (If you've forgotten how to select text, turn back to Chapter 2.)

A black highlight bar will appear over the text you selected.

3. Enter new text using either Graffiti or the on-screen keyboard.

The new text will appear in place of the text that you selected.

4. When you're finished replacing text in the memo, tap Done to close it and return to the Memo List.

If you'd prefer to use the Menu method, follow steps 1 and 2 in the selection method, then:

3. Tap on the Menu soft button to open the Menu Bar.

4. Choose Edit ➤ Cut to remove the text you have highlighted.

The text will disappear.

5. If you want to add the text somewhere else in the memo, tap on the screen at the point you want to add the text.

You'll see an insertion point.

6. Tap the Menu soft button to open the Menu Bar.

7. Choose Edit ➤ Paste to insert the text you previously cut into its new place in the memo.

8. When you're finished moving text in the memo, tap Done to close it and return to the Memo List.

 NOTE If you want to have the same text appear in two different places in a memo (or even in two different memos) follow the steps in the Menu method, but choose Edit ➤ Copy instead of Edit ➤ Cut. If you're pasting the text into a different memo, remember to open that menu before choosing Edit ➤ Paste.

If you need to get rid of the full text of a memo, you can tap the Menu soft button, then choose Edit ➤ Select All from the Menu Bar. All of the text will be highlighted. You can replace this selected text using either of the methods we described above.

Frankly, we don't see the point in replacing all that text. It's easier to just delete the offending memo and start over. Stick with us, and we'll explain how to delete a memo in the next section.

Deleting a Memo

While we're on the subject of memos you don't want anymore, let's discuss the two ways you can get rid of them.

First, let's look at the really quick way:

1. With the Memo List open, tap on the name of the memo you want to delete.

   This will open the Memo View.

2. Tap on the Menu soft button.

   This will bring up the Menu Bar.

3. From the Menu Bar, choose Record ➤ Delete Memo.

   This will bring up the Delete Memo dialog box.

4. Tap the check box next to the option Save Archive Copy On PC, if you think you might ever want access to this record again.

5. Tap OK in the Delete Memo dialog box to confirm the deletion and return to the Memo List. The offending memo will vanish without a trace.

There's also a long way to delete a memo:

1. With the Memo List open, tap on the name of the memo you want to delete.

   This will open the Memo View.

2. Tap on the Edit command button at the bottom of the screen.

   This will bring up the Address Edit dialog box.

3. Tap on the Details command button at the bottom of the screen.

   This will open the Memo Details dialog box.

4. Tap on the Delete command button.

   This will open the Delete Memo dialog box.

5. Tap the check box next to the option Save Archive Copy On PC, if you think you might ever want to access this memo again.

6. Tap OK in the Delete Memo dialog box to confirm the deletion and return to the Memo List. The offending memo is just as gone as if you'd deleted it the quick way.

We're really not sure why you'd want to use the long way to delete, unless you just want to prolong the process as much as possible. The quick way works just fine for us.

Categorizing a Memo

As you were creating that first memo, you may have noticed the Details command button at the bottom of the screen. This button is used to categorize a memo (and to mark it private, which we'll explain a little later).

There are two ways to assign a category to a memo—the quick way, and the not-so-quick way.

To assign a category to a memo the quick way:

1. With the Memo List open, tap on the name of the memo you want to categorize.

This will open the memo in Memo View.

2. Tap on the arrow next to the currently assigned category located in the upper-right corner of the screen. If you haven't done any categorizing yet, this will probably say Unfiled.

Tapping on this arrow will open a drop-down list of categories. You can see this list in Figure 6.13. Tap the new category. The list will close, and the category you selected will appear in the upper-right corner of the screen.

3. Tap Done to close this memo and return to the Memo List.

The Applications

FIGURE 6.13

Pick a category from the drop-down list.

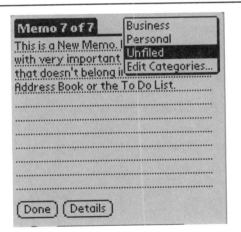

To assign a category to a memo the not-so-quick way:

1. With the Memo List open, tap on the name of the memo you want to categorize.

This will open the memo in Memo View.

2. Tap on the Details command button to open the Memo Details dialog box.

3. Tap on the arrow next to the word Category to access the drop-down list of memo categories. (You can see this list in Figure 6.14.)

FIGURE 6.14

The category list looks the same, no matter how you access it.

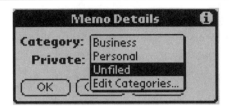

4. Tap on the category you want to select.

The category drop-down list will close.

5. Tap on OK to close this dialog box and return to the Memo View.

6. Tap Done to close this memo and return to the Memo List.

So why would you want to go through all these extra steps when you can get the same results with just two taps? There's only one reason we can think of: if you want to mark a memo Private at the same time you're categorizing it. You need to open the Memo Details dialog box to mark a memo private, so while you're there, you may as well categorize it. If you're not into privacy, stick to the quick way to categorize a memo.

Marking a Memo Private

As we mentioned earlier, the Memo Details dialog box is where you go to mark a memo private. This works the same way it did in the Date Book, the Address Book, and the To Do List.

To mark a memo private:

1. With the Memo List open, tap on the name of the memo you want to mark Private.

This will open the memo in Memo View.

2. Tap on the Details command button to open the Memo Details dialog box.

3. Tap in the check box next to the word Private.

A checkmark will appear to show this option is selected.

4. Tap OK to accept this choice, close the dialog box, and return to Memo View.

Remember, though, that unless you've chosen to Hide Private Records in the Security application, you'll still see your private memo in the Memo List. For more on hiding private records, see Chapter 7.

Viewing Memos by Category

We already walked you through the process of assigning categories to your memos, but there's really no point to categorizing if you're always going to look at the full Memo List.

When those old memos start piling up, it gets really tough to find what you're looking for—unless you view your memos by category. To do this:

1. With the Memo List open, tap on the down arrow next to the currently displayed category located in the upper-right corner of the screen. If you haven't changed views at all, it will probably say All.

   This will bring up a drop-down list of categories.

2. Tap on the name of the category you want to view.

The Memo List will change to show only the memos you've assigned to that category.

 TIP If you want to scroll through all the categories in the Memo Pad (or the Address Book or the To Do List), press the appropriate application hard button repeatedly. The application will cycle through all its categories, much the way pressing the Date Book hard button repeatedly cycles through all the calendar views.

Creating a Category of Your Own

By default, the Memo List has four categories: All, Business, Personal, and Unfiled. You can easily add your own categories and rename the existing ones (except for All and Unfiled, which can't be altered).

To rename existing categories and add some of your own:

1. With the Memo List open, tap on the down arrow next to the currently displayed category, located in the upper-right corner of the screen. If you haven't changed views at all, it will probably say All.

   This will bring up a drop-down list of categories.

2. Tap on Edit Categories, the last item on the list.

   This will bring up the Edit Categories dialog box, which you can see in Figure 6.15.

PART

II

The Applications

FIGURE 6.15

*Add a new category
or rename an
existing one.*

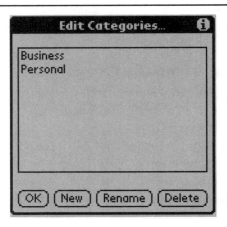

3. Tap on the New command button at the bottom of the screen.

   This will open another, smaller Edit Categories dialog box.

4. Enter a name for your new category using Graffiti or the on-screen keyboard.

5. Tap OK to close this dialog box and return to the Edit Categories screen.

6. Either add another category following steps 4 and 5, or tap OK to return to the Memo List.

If you just want to change the name of one of the existing categories, say from Business to Customers, follow steps 1 and 2 above, then:

3. Tap on the name of an existing category to select it. It will be covered with a black bar to show it's selected.

4. Tap on the Rename command button at the bottom of the screen to open the smaller Edit Categories dialog box.

   The name of the category you selected will appear, with a bar over it, in this box.

5. Add a new name for this category using either Graffiti or the on-screen keyboard.

6. Tap OK to return to the Edit Categories screen.

7. Either rename another category following steps 1–4, or tap OK to return to the Address List.

Any records you previously assigned to the category you just renamed will now appear under the new category name. You can add new records to this (or any categories you create) the usual way.

Adding a Phone Number to a Memo

As we mentioned in Chapter 5, the Palm provides a neat feature for using information you've entered in the Address Book in the other applications. It's called the Phone Lookup.

If you have a memo that you'd like to add a name and number to, and you have that information already entered into your Address Book, Phone Lookup can locate it and paste it into your memo.

To perform a Phone Lookup:

1. With the Memo List open, tap on the name of the memo to which you want to add a name and number.

   This will open the memo in Memo View.

2. Tap on the Menu soft button, then choose Options ➤ Phone Lookup. (Or, you can write a command stroke then L using Graffiti.)

   This will bring up the Phone Lookup screen (which is really your Address Book). You can see it in Figure 6.16.

3. From the Phone Lookup screen, select the name you want to tack on to your event.

4. Tap the Add button, and the name and number will appear as part of your event's name.

   You're back in Memo View, and there it all is.

Alternately, you can enter part of a name (or the whole name) you want to add to your Memo, select it, then perform a Phone Lookup. If Lookup finds a direct match, it will automatically add the name and number to your memo. If it finds a partial match, it will open the Phone Lookup screen, and you'll have to pick the right name yourself.

PART

II

The Applications

FIGURE 6.16

Phone Lookup

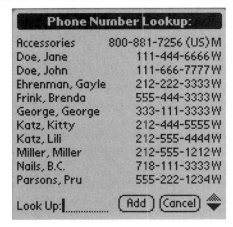

Changing the Appearance of a Memo

If you're having trouble reading your memos, you'll want to try changing the fonts (and maybe getting your eyes checked). You can change the font used for the Memo List and for all your memos. You can't change the font on an individual memo, though. It's all or nothing.

To change the font used for the Memo List:

1. With the Memo List open, tap on the Menu soft button.

This will bring up the Menu Bar.

2. From the Menu Bar, choose Options ➤ Font.

3. Tap on the letter that looks best to you.

4. Tap OK to accept your selection and return to the Memo List.

The look of the list will reflect your font selection.

To change the font used by all your memos:

1. With the Memo List open, tap on the name of any memo.

This will open the memo in Memo View.

2. Follow steps 2-4 above.

The look of your memo will reflect your font selection.

Any new memos you create will use the font you just selected, until you change it again for all the memos.

Sorting Your Memos

You've already been industrious and assigned categories to all your memos. And you've even chosen to view those categories. That's one way to organize your memos, but you can take it a step further and determine what order memos appear in within a category. You can choose to sort memos manually or alphabetically.

As we discussed at the beginning of this chapter, the Memo List sorts memos manually by default, so they appear on the list in the order you created them. We'll explain how to change this order in just a little bit. Sorting memos alphabetically arranges them in alphabetical order—no surprise there.

 TIP Since the Memo List uses the first word of the first line of a memo as the basis of its alphabetizing, it's easy to get a memo to the top of the list—just start it with a zero, punctuation character, or if you're partial to letters, AAA. Works just like the Yellow Pages.

To change the sort order of the Memo List:

1. With the Memo List open, tap on the Menu soft button.

   This will bring up the Menu Bar.

2. Choose Options ➤ Preferences.

   This will open the Memo Preferences dialog box, which you can see in Figure 6.17. You'll see the word Manual next to Sort By:.

3. Tap on the word Manual (or the arrow next to it) to see your sort choices.

4. Tap on the sort method you prefer: Manual or Alphabetic.

5. Tap OK to accept you choice and return to the Memo List.

Choose a sort method.

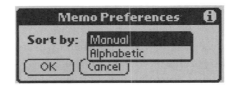

If you chose to sort alphabetically, you'll next see the warning message that appears in Figure 6.18. This lets you know that any manual sorting you've done previously is about to be blown away. Tap on Yes if you can live with this. After you do, the Memo List will be sorted alphabetically.

Say Yes to the alphabet.

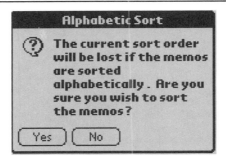

If you chose to sort manually, you can further customize the order messages appear in the Memo List by dragging them to the place in the list where you want them to appear.

To manually reorder your Memos:

1. With the Memo List open, tap and hold the stylus down on the memo you want to move.

   You'll see a black highlight bar over the name of the memo, which shows you it's selected.

2. Drag the memo to the place on the list where you want it to appear.

   You'll see a dotted line on the Memo List, which indicates where the memo will be inserted.

3. Lift your stylus off the screen when you're happy with the memo's placement.

   The memo will now appear in its new order.

Beaming Memos

There's one last thing you can do with memos: share them and their categories with other Palm users. This is accomplished by beaming them to other Palm folks, who may want to partake of your fine prose.

It's a simple process that we explain in detail in Chapter 8. But be patient! First, you need to learn how to work all the secondary programs installed on your Palm organizer. We'll cover those applications in Chapter 7.

CHAPTER **7**

Mastering the Secondary Applications

I f you're like most Palm organizer users, you'll spend the bulk of your time working in the Date Book, Address Book, To Do List, and Memo Pad—the four main applications preinstalled on your Palm. However, there are a handful of other, less glamorous applications that may not warrant their own hard buttons, but are every bit as useful as the big four. You may not use these applications multiple times a day, or even once a day, but it pays to master them, because when you need them, you really need them.

The co-starring applications common to all Palm organizers are:

- Calculator
- Security
- Expense
- Mail
- Graffiti
- HotSync
- Preferences
- Welcome

On a Palm VII organizer, you will also see icons for Activate, Diagnostics, iMessenger, Palm.Net, and a host of PQAs in the Application Launcher. The PQAs (Palm Query Applications, which the Palm VII uses to interact with the Internet) are add-on applications, so we'll explain them later on, in Chapter 13. We'll explain how to use these Palm VII applications at the end of this chapter. You can see all the co-starring applications in Figure 7.1.

FIGURE 7.1

A glimpse at some of the applications installed on your organizer

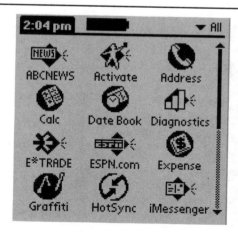

Whether they're specific to the Palm VII or common to all the Palm organizers, you access all these secondary applications the same way: by tapping an icon in the Application Launcher. As a reminder, to get to the Application Launcher, tap on the soft button that looks like a house (it's the top-left soft button).

 TIP If you don't see all these applications in the Application Launcher, don't panic. You may be viewing a particular category, like System, which doesn't include every secondary application installed on your organizer. To see them all, tap on the down arrow in the upper-right corner of the Application Launcher screen, then tap on All from the drop-down menu. Your screen will now be filled with icons for every application installed on your Palm organizer, including the ones you normally launch using the buttons.

Once you're looking at the full array of icons in the Application Launcher, simply scroll to the one you want, using either the scroll bars on the right side of the screen or the Scroll button.

 TIP The quickest way to find the application you're looking for is to use Graffiti. Enter the first letter of an application's name in the Graffiti writing area, and the Application Launcher will scroll to the first application that corresponds with the letter you entered.

Now let's look at these co-starring applications one at a time, and explore some of their unique capabilities.

The Calculator

For most people, the Calculator is both the most familiar and easiest to use of the Palm applications. That's because it looks just like every other basic calculator you've ever seen. See for yourself in Figure 7.2.

It also works pretty much the same as every other calculator, with a couple of exceptions. These are the two unique features of the Palm Calculator: Recent Calculations and Memory. We'll explain those features in just a bit. First, let's address the basics of the Palm Calculator.

PART

II

The Applications

FIGURE 7.2

*The very basic Palm
Calculator*

This Calculator can't do any specialized or higher mathematical calculating. Like one of the authors of this book (that would be the one without the engineering degree), its mathematical abilities cover just the basics: addition, subtraction, multiplication, division, and percentages (yes, we know this is really just another form of multiplication). Square roots, trigonometric functions…the Palm Calculator, like the aforementioned author, was absent when they taught those. If you really need to compute such things, there are specialized calculators available for your Palm. See Chapter 16 for more about those.

For those who believe that it's best to stick to basics, the Palm Calculator will do just fine. It really couldn't be simpler to use. To figure out what $(700-135) \times 14\%$ equals, just tap on the appropriate on-screen buttons. The Calculator's buttons are big enough to use your fingers instead of the stylus. If you choose this route, please wash your hands first. There's nothing worse than pizza grease on a Palm screen. Oh, and in case you were wondering, the answer is 79.1.

We trust that you found all the keys for that above example without any difficulty. But you may have been wondering what those other keys, like +/-, CE, C, MC, MR, and M+ do. Well, since you asked so nicely, we'll just have to explain.

The +/- key is used to turn a positive number into a negative one, or vice versa. Try it out by entering 50, then tapping +/- once. You'll see a negative sign in front of the 50. Tap it again, and the number goes back to being a positive.

The CE key clears your most recent entry. So, if you tapped in 51 when you really meant 50, tap CE to clear out the mistake. The rest of your calculation will still be in tact.

When you're completely done with a calculation, tap on C. This will wipe the slate clean, erasing everything you've done so far so you can start with a fresh calculation.

MC, MR, and M+ are all used for one of the Palm Calculator's special tricks—its Memory. This lets you store a value, which could be a single number or the result of a string of calculations, in Memory. To try this out:

1. Tap in 500, then tap the M+ button. That will add 500 to Memory.

2. Clear the display by tapping C.

3. Now, tap in 100 + MR. You'll see 600 in the display. That's because the MR button recalls whatever value you had stored in Memory. MC clears out the Memory.

When you have a value stored in memory, you'll see a lowercase m in the upper-left corner of the Calculator display. You can see this in Figure 7.3.

FIGURE 7.3

*Memories of
numbers past*

PART

II

The Applications

This Memory stuff all works pretty much the same way it does in a non-Palm calculator. But the Palm Calculator can do one thing those one-trick ponies can't—show you all your recent calculations.

After you've performed a few highly involved mathematical processes, or just checked the waiter's addition on your dinner tab and figured out a 15% tip, tap on the Menu soft button. From the Menu bar, choose Options ➤ Recent Calculations (or enter the command stroke followed by I using Graffiti). This will show you just what it claims: a list of your recent calculations, as in Figure 7.4.

The Recent Calculations list isn't as good as a paper adding machine tape, since it can only show the last three or so calculations you performed. But, it does provide a handy way to double-check your math. You only get one screen's worth of calculations, though, so in a lengthy chain of calculation, check often to confirm that you're on the right track.

FIGURE 7.4

Recent Calculations

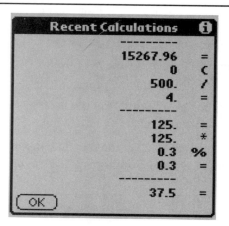

Security

Palm Security can't compare to having a burly man tasked with keeping you safe at any cost, but it can give you a way to keep your precious Palm organizer data from prying eyes. Palm Security is actually rather focused. It does just three things: it lets you hide or show private records, set a password for your organizer, and turn off and lock your organizer. You can see all these choices in Figure 7.5.

FIGURE 7.5

Security in an insecure world

Hiding Records

We discussed how to hide or show private records in our discussions of marking records private in the Date Book, Address Book, To Do List, and Memo Pad (Chapters 5 and 6). We explained that though you may choose to mark records private, they would still be visible in your applications—unless you chose to hide private records in the Security application. Well, now's your chance to make all those private records truly disappear from sight.

To hide your private records:

1. From the Security application, just tap on Hide. It's right next to Show, which is your other choice for Private Records.

2. Next, you'll see a confirmation dialog box (as in Figure 7.6), which explains that by choosing Hide, any records you marked as private will be hidden.

3. Tap Hide again here if you're certain of your choice. This will return you to the Security application's main screen.

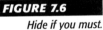

FIGURE 7.6

Hide if you must.

A black box will appear around Hide to show that this choice is active. Now, if you go back to look at records that you previously marked Private, you won't be able to find them. They still exist, but now they're invisible.

If you want to see those hidden, private records, you have two choices: Either follow the steps above, but tap Show instead of Hide, or enter a password. Of course, you first have to set the password before you can use it to make a hidden record reappear. So, let's set a password.

Setting a Password

You can only create one password for your Palm organizer, but you can use it to safeguard just the private records on your device or the entire device.

To set a password:

1. From the Security application, tap in the entry box next to the word Password. By default, you'll see Unassigned in this box.

2. This will bring up the Password dialog box, as in Figure 7.7.

3. Enter a password using either Graffiti or the on-screen keyboard.

4. Tap OK to accept your password.

5. This will open a confirmation dialog box.

6. Re-enter the password you just selected.

7. Tap OK to accept the password and return to the Security application.

FIGURE 7.7

Enter a password here.

The word Assigned will now appear where the word Unassigned previously appeared.

 TIP Palm organizer passwords are not case sensitive. So don't bother capitalizing any letters—uppercase or lower, it's all the same to the Palm.

If you want to show private records you've previously hidden, and you have a password assigned, you'll need to enter the password to make those records visible again. It's a simple process: Just tap on Show Private Records, then enter your password when prompted.

If you didn't assign a password, simply tap Show Private Records to make them reappear.

 TIP If you forget your password, you can choose Forgotten Password from the Security screen to wipe it out. Unfortunately, this will not only delete your password, but all your private records with it. So, REMEMBER YOUR PASSWORD.

Lock Down Your Palm

The password that you just set can also be used to safeguard your Palm—should it fall into the wrong hands. To invoke this option, from the Security application:

1. Assign a password, following the steps above.
2. Tap on the Turn Off & Lock Device command button.
3. This will bring up a confirmation dialog box, as in Figure 7.8.
4. Tap the Off & Lock command button to confirm the action.

PART

II

The Applications

FIGURE 7.8

Confirm the lock-down.

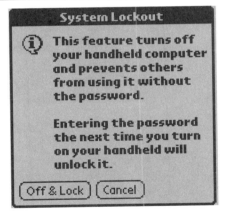

Your Palm organizer will turn itself off.

The next time you hit the power switch on your Palm organizer, you'll have to enter your password in the System Lockout dialog box (as in Figure 7.9) before you can access any of the data or applications on your device.

Turn Off & Lock only works once. If you want to use it next time you're ready to retire your Palm organizer, you'll have to activate it again.

 WARNING Don't lock down your Palm organizer unless you're certain you can remember the password. Though there's a Forgotten Password option in the Security application, there's no way to get to it if you've locked down your device and can't recall the password to activate it. If you've locked down your device and forgotten the password, your only option is to perform a Hard Reset (we explain how in Appendix B). A Hard Reset will erase your password, but it will erase all your data as well. So, for heaven's sake, REMEMBER YOUR PASSWORD.

FIGURE 7.9

*No Password,
no Palm*

 TIP One last reason to REMEMBER YOUR PASSWORD: You can't delete a Password or change it if you can't remember it. If you've given up on all this cloak-and-dagger stuff, tap on Assigned (next to Password), enter your current password, and then tap on the Delete command button. If you want to change your password, enter a new password in this dialog box instead.

A couple of last points on locking down your Palm organizer: This is really only useful if you're trying to safeguard your data from busybodies and kids. Busybodies, like that weasel of a sales rep trying to steal your account, won't be able to filch your contact info. And Junior won't be able to accidentally wipe out next week's schedule. But Turn Off & Lock won't do you much good should Junior decide to drop your Palm in a bowl full of Cheerios.

And if you think Turn Off & Lock will make a would-be Palm thief change his mind, think again. Yanking the batteries out of the device for a couple of minutes will take care of that pesky password. Any thief smart enough to know a Palm is worth stealing will know about the battery trick.

Expense

Forget about coming home from a business trip with your pockets crammed with random receipts. Do you really look forward to the hours of fun it takes to turn those receipts (and all the ones you lost) into a coherent expense report? Unless you're really a glutton for punishment, forget the paper and pencil approach and try out the Palm Expense application. It offers a convenient, easy way to track expenditures, and it lets you pass this information on to an Excel spreadsheet, so you can generate an expense report painlessly.

If you don't have Microsoft Excel installed on your desktop PC, stop right here. There's really no way to get the information in the Palm Expense application out without exporting it to an Excel spreadsheet.

 NOTE Unfortunately, Microsoft Excel is an application you have to buy as part of the Microsoft Office suite. If you have a relatively new PC, it may have come preinstalled, otherwise you're looking at a major financial investment.

With that caveat out of the way, here's what you can do with Expense. You can:

- Record the date, type, and amount of an expense.
- List a vendor and city for an item.
- List people present when the expense was incurred.
- Sort expense items by category.
- Specify a payment method for an item.
- Attach a note to an expense item.

This may seem like a robust list of options, but the Expense application is actually one of the weakest links in the Palm world. It offers little in the way of customization and not much flexibility either—two things we've grown accustomed to with other Palm applications. Still, we admit to using Expense—it's better than nothing.

Entering an Expense

Entering an item (what Expense calls a record) is quite simple. From the Application Launcher, tap on the Expense icon. You'll see the Expense list screen, as in Figure 7.10.

FIGURE 7.10

The Expense tracker

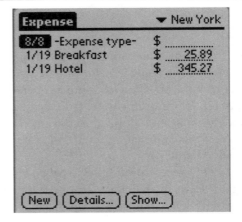

From this screen:

1. Tap on the New command button. An entry line for your first Expense item will appear, filled in with the current date, the words Expense Type, and a blank space where you enter the amount of your item.

2. The cursor will be blinking in the amount line, so go ahead and enter the amount first, using either Graffiti or the on-screen keyboard.

TIP You can also add a new Expense item by simply starting to write in the numbers side of the Graffiti writing area. A new item line will automatically open. Or, write the first letter of the type of expense (T for Taxi, for example), and a new item of that type will be created; then you just have to add an amount.

3. When you're done entering an amount, tap on the words Expense Type.

4. This will bring up a list of 28 types of expenses (as in Figure 7.11).

5. Tap on the one that most closely matches the nature of your expense, Taxi or Dinner, for example. This expense type will appear in the expense list. If none of the choices is a perfect match, you'll have to go with Other; Expense doesn't let you rename existing expense types or add your own.

PART

II

The Applications

FIGURE 7.11

What did you spend the money on?

 TIP   You must pick an expense type, or the item will not be saved.

5. To change the date of an expense item, just tap on the date. This will bring up a calendar. Tap on the appropriate date from there.

Adding Details

With a basic expense item created, it's time to add the details that the bean counters will want when you create your expense report.

To add more information:

1. Tap on the item you want to beef-up.
2. Tap on the Details command button at the bottom of the Expense list screen.
3. This will open the Receipt Details dialog box, which you can see in Figure 7.12.

FIGURE 7.12

Add details to an Expense.

4. To assign the item to a category, tap on the word Unfiled (next to Category). This will bring up a list of categories you can choose from and an Edit Categories option for creating your own categories.

5. This works exactly the same way as categorizing any other type of Palm record. If you're not sure what to do, take a look at the section on categorizing records in Chapters 5 and 6.

6. If you want to change the type of expense, tap on the down arrow next to Type to pick another choice from the list.

7. Tap on the word Unfiled next to Payment to choose a payment option.

8. This will bring up a list of methods for paying an expense, including choices for American Express, Visa, MasterCard, Cash, Check, and Prepaid. There's even a generic Credit Card option, if those don't suit you.

9. Tap on the dollar sign next to Currency if the price of the item was determined in a currency other than US dollars. There's an Edit Currencies option that lets you add another type to the dollars; British pounds and German Deutsche Marks appear in this list by default. We'll discuss customizing the currency list a little later in this chapter.

10. Tap on the text entry line next to the word Vendor to add the name of the company associated with this expense (for example, if you took a client to Windows on the World for lunch, you'd enter the name of that restaurant on the Vendor line). Enter the name using Graffiti or the on-screen keyboard.

11. Tap on the text entry line next to the word City to add the name of the city where you spent this money (in our above example, that would be New York

since that's where Windows on the World is located). Enter the name using Graffiti or the on-screen keyboard.

12. To add information on who you took to lunch, tap on the word Who next to Attendees.

13. This will open a Memo Pad screen with the word Attendees on top. You can Lookup people in your Address Book to add them to this Expense item, or enter their names using Graffiti or the on-screen keyboard. Both methods work the same as they do when using the standard Memo Pad. If you're not sure how to do this, see Chapter 6.

 TIP   Lookup will only present you with the names of people whose Address Book listing includes a company name.

14. Tap Done when you're finished entering Attendees to your item.

This will return you to the Receipt Details screen.

15. If you want to add a Note to your item, perhaps to detail what was discussed at that extravagant lunch, tap on the Note command button at the bottom-right corner of the screen.

16. This will bring up a Note screen that lists the type of item it's attached to at the top. Enter information using Graffiti or the on-screen keyboard, and tap Done when you're satisfied. This will return you to the Receipt Details screen.

17. Tap OK to accept all the details you've added and return to the Expense list.

 TIP   You don't need to restrict the information in the Attendees screen to just names and numbers. Add whatever you like here, rather than attaching a note to the Expense item. It's an easy way to have some information on what you discussed at a business lunch close at hand.

Choosing a Currency

As we mentioned previously, by default, Expense shows all amounts in US dollars. You can change the default by:

1. With the Expense list open, tap on the Menu soft button, then choose Options ➤ Preferences from the Menu Bar.

2. In the Preferences dialog box (which you can see in Figure 7.13), tap on the dollar sign next to the words Default Currency.

3. This will bring up the standard currency list, as well as an option to Edit currencies. Tap on this last choice to open the Edit Currencies dialog box, as in Figure 7.14.

4. Tap on any of the currencies listed or on one of the unassigned slots (marked None) to bring up a list of countries.

5. Tap on the one with the currency of your choice. The symbol for that country's currency will now appear in your currency list.

6. Tap OK to return to the Preferences dialog box.

7. Now, from the Preferences dialog box, tap on the dollar sign next to Default Currency again to choose the symbol for the currency you want to choose as your default (perhaps Yen, if your travels take you to Japan on a regular basis).

If none of the selections on the currency list suits your needs, you can create a custom currency. To do this:

1. With the Expense list open, tap on the Menu soft button, then choose Options ➤ Custom Currencies from the Menu Bar.

2. This will open the Custom Currencies dialog box, as in Figure 7.15.

3. Tap on Country 1 to add your first new country.

4. From the Currency Properties dialog box, enter a name and symbol for your currency using Graffiti or the on-screen keyboard.

5. Tap on OK when you're done to return to the Custom Currencies screen.

6. Add another country following these same steps, or tap on OK to accept your changes and return to the Expense list.

PART

II

The Applications

FIGURE 7.15

Create a currency of your very own.

You can use a Custom Currency as your default by following the steps for picking a default currency, outlined earlier.

Sorting by Category

If you assigned categories to your Expense items, you can sort them by Category just as you could for any application. The steps are the same here as in the applications discussed in Chapters 5 and 6. Flip back to one of those chapters if you need a refresher course in sorting by Category.

Display Options

There's one last option when working with Expense items—you can decide what to show in the Expense list. With that list open, tap on the Show command button to open the Show Options dialog box (which you can see in Figure 7.16).

Here, you can choose to sort expenses by date or type; to display mileage entries in miles or kilometers; and to show or hide the currency symbol. The first two options are simple pick lists; just tap on the choice you want to change, then pick from the list. Show currency is a check box—tap to turn the option on; tap again to turn it off.

Transferring Data to Excel

To get the data you just entered out of Expense and into a spreadsheet, you must have Microsoft Excel 5.0 or later and the Palm Desktop software installed on your desktop PC. You can view and print your Expense data in an Excel spreadsheet using the Palm Desktop software.

The information transfers through the Palm Desktop software using the supplied expense report templates and requires you to perform a HotSync. We'll explain the process in greater detail in Chapter 9.

Mail

Mail is one of the most underrated of the Palm applications. Like Expense, it requires a connection to your desktop PC to work most of its magic. But, unlike Expense, Mail can both send information to the desktop and receive information back from it. That makes Mail a two-way application where Expense is a one-way street.

Mail isn't a full-fledged e-mail application. It can't send or receive mail on its own. Instead, Mail is a helper application that works in conjunction with your standard e-mail program to pass messages back and forth between your desktop PC and your Palm organizer.

We'll go into the particulars of using Mail in Chapter 12. For now, let's just say that to use Mail, you need a supported e-mail client on your desktop PC, an Internet connection, and the Palm Desktop software. With these pieces in place, you can use Mail to read, send, and delete e-mail messages.

Mail looks very much like a standard e-mail client, providing you with an Inbox and an Outbox, as you can see in Figure 7.17.

FIGURE 7.17

What's waiting in the Outbox?

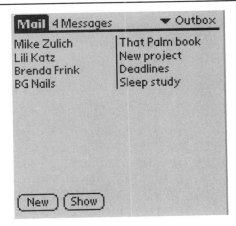

Tapping on a message opens it for reading, as in Figure 7.18.

FIGURE 7.18

Read your Mail.

NOTE The Mail application is entirely separate from the iMessenger application on the Palm VII. Where Mail is a helper application, iMessenger is a standalone wireless messaging client. You can read more about using iMessenger in Chapter 13.

Graffiti

If you just can't get the hang of the Graffiti language, try out the Graffiti trainer that comes pre-installed on your Palm organizer. From the Application Launcher, just tap on the icon that looks like the Graffiti stroke for the letter N to launch this application. You can see what the Graffiti trainer looks like in Figure 7.19.

FIGURE 7.19

Learn your letters.

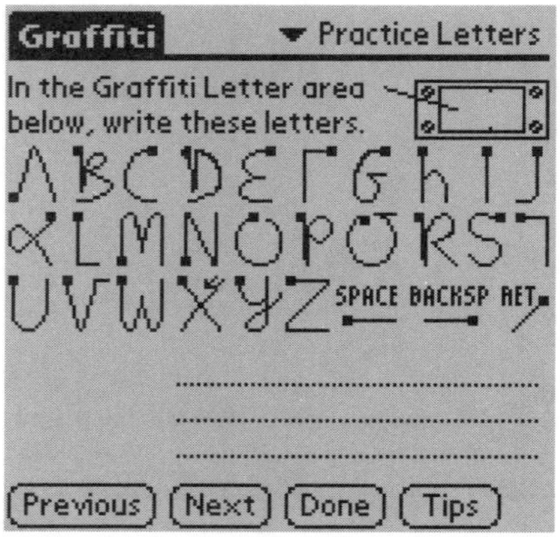

From here, you can get a quick tutorial on all things Graffiti, from where to write to how to form characters.

To use the Graffiti trainer for practicing your strokes:

1. Tap on the Try It! Command button located at the bottom left of the screen to enter the practice area.

2. Here you will see detailed information about using Graffiti.

3. Tap on the Next command button to practice writing capital letters.

4. Here you can try writing all the letters of the alphabet.

There are also screens that can help you get the hang of writing numbers using Graffiti, as well as provide direction on using the on-screen keyboard.

NOTE For more on using Graffiti, see Chapter 2.

HotSync

If you ever intend to move data from your Palm organizer to your desktop PC (or vice versa), you'll need to get familiar with HotSync.

We'll discuss how to use this application in-depth in Chapter 9. For now, we'll just offer a basic introduction to what HotSync is and how you use it.

HotSync is the technology that the Palm organizer uses to "speak" to your desktop PC. It essentially grabs the data from your Palm and pushes it across to the Palm Desktop software.

You get to make some choices for how HotSync works, such as which applications get synced with the Palm Desktop and whether you sync using the cradle (this process is called a Local HotSync) or via a modem (called a Modem HotSync).

To launch the HotSync application from the Application Launcher, just tap on the HotSync icon—it's the circle with the facing arrows. Next, you'll see the HotSync screen, as in Figure 7.20.

FIGURE 7.20

Choose your HotSync.

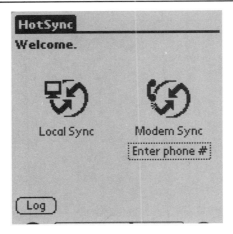

If you've already configured all your settings for a Local HotSync, just drop your Palm organizer in its cradle and press the HotSync button on the front of the cradle (it looks a lot like the HotSync icon).

PART II
The Applications

This will automatically launch the HotSync operation and initiate a sync call to your desktop PC. The rest is data backup history.

 WARNING Have we reminded you lately to HotSync your Palm? Do it now—before disaster strikes. If you don't know how, turn to Chapter 9 for all the details.

Preferences

The Preferences application allows you to set preferences for what you want your Palm organizer to do. You may remember Preferences from Chapter 1, where we showed you how to set the date and time. Yup, that was the Preferences application that let you do that.

Preferences can handle a whole lot more; in fact, it's the application you'll use to configure or reconfigure any of the operating system parameters. You use Preferences to control everything from the sounds your Palm makes when an alarm goes off, to what applications run when you press the hard buttons, to what Internet service your Palm uses when dialing out over a modem. You can see the full list of Preferences in Figure 7.21.

FIGURE 7.21

What do you prefer?

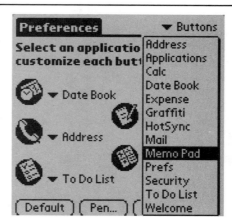

For a refresher in configuring your Preferences, turn back to Chapter 4.

Welcome

The Welcome application should seem familiar to you. It's the one that launched the very first time you powered up your Palm organizer. We also explained how to work through Welcome way back in Chapter 1. In case you've forgotten what we're talking about, take a look at Figure 7.22.

FIGURE 7.22

You're always Welcome.

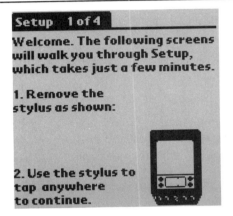

The Welcome application walks you through the process of setting up your Palm organizer, from setting screen parameters to setting the date and time. If you didn't finish the whole shebang the first time around, you can always tap on the Welcome icon (it's the one with the open door) in the Application Launcher to complete the set-up process. Of course, you can just set up your Palm organizer the grown-up way—using the Preferences application.

And, yes, you can delete Welcome once you feel like a Palm owner, instead of a perpetual visitor. We'll explain how in Chapter 9.

 WARNING   Once you start setting up your organizer through the Welcome application, you can't stop. You have to finish the full setup process, before Welcome will go away.

The Palm VII Applications

In addition to all the applications we've described so far, the Palm VII offers four unique applications of its very own. These are:

- Activate
- Diagnostics
- iMessenger
- Palm.Net

All of these applications appear only on the Palm VII because they're used for some aspect of wireless connectivity—which is a Palm VII-only feature.

Activate

Activate is used to set up your Palm.Net account. Palm.Net is the network the Palm VII uses for wireless e-mail and Web clipping (the Palm VII's answer to plain old Web browsing). We'll explain Web clipping in greater detail in Chapter 13.

 NOTE Activate is a very different type of Palm application for one very good reason: You only use it once, and then it won't run again. Don't worry; you won't need to run it again.

When you first get a Palm VII, you'll need to decide what Palm.Net service plan you want to purchase (there are only a couple of choices, and they're fully explained in a special Palm.Net brochure that comes with your Palm VII). Then, after waiting a little over an hour (after first putting batteries in your Palm) for the wireless transmitter to charge up, you'll be ready to set up your Palm.Net service. That's where Activate comes in.

To use Activate, you simply raise the antenna on your Palm VII and follow the on-screen instructions. Alternately, you can tap on the Activate icon and then raise the antenna to get started with wireless communications.

Be sure to have your credit card handy when you're ready to activate your Palm.Net account. You're going to have to enter a credit card number (you didn't think Palm.Net was free, did you?), your name, company name, billing address, phone number, current desktop e-mail address, and choice of service plan.

Just follow the on-screen instructions and enter the required information using Graffiti or the on-screen keyboard.

TIP Don't be concerned about sending all that private information out through the air-waves. The Palm VII uses some pretty sophisticated encryption technology to render sensitive information unreadable by anyone but the party it's meant for. For all you geeks out there, the encryption scheme is called elliptic curve cryptography, and it's from a company called Certicom. You can find out more about encryption at www.certicom.com.

As part of the activation process, you'll also be asked to choose a username and password. Activation will make a few suggestions for a username, in case you're drawing a blank. You're free to choose one of these or create one of your own; the only restriction is that the name must be no shorter than 4 characters and no longer than 15 characters.

This username will become your Palm.Net e-mail address. For example, if your username is JaneDoe, your Palm.Net e-mail address will be JaneDoe@palm.net.

 NOTE We would have shown you what the whole activation process looks like, but in our rush to start communicating wirelessly, we didn't take the time to shoot screenshots. We couldn't go back and start over, because once you activate your Palm.Net service, it stays activated unless you perform a hard reset on your organizer.

 TIP Be sure to write down the username and password that you selected. You can record them in the Memo Pad, but we'd also advise keeping a copy off your Palm organizer (just in case). You'll need your username and password to get information on your Palm.Net usage.

Diagnostics

Once you've activated your Palm.Net service, it's time to start communicating via the airwaves. You have to admit that using your Palm VII for wireless communication is incredibly cool (that's the point of this device, isn't it?), but it can be a tiny bit tricky.

Wireless communication relies on radio signals. And these can be strong or weak, depending on how clear a path the signal has from where you're located to where the transmitter is located. Reception can be affected by all kinds of objects blocking the path of the signal. And when you have poor reception, your Palm has to work harder to try to maintain a connection to the network. This can sap your batteries in a hurry.

Fortunately, as long as you're in an area that offers Palm.Net coverage (more about that in the Palm.Net section later in this chapter), improving your reception is usually a matter of adjusting the Palm VII antenna and moving your physical location.

You can see if moving ten feet to your left has had any effect on reception by using the Diagnostics application.

To check signal strength:

1. Raise the antenna on your Palm VII.

2. Tap on the icon for the Diagnostics application in the Application Launcher. It's the icon that looks like a vertical bar chart.

3. Wait a couple of seconds while Diagnostics transmits some radio waves and measure how well they're getting through.

In a couple of seconds (or less), you'll see vertical bars depicting the strength of your Palm VII's signal. The more bars you see, the stronger the signal. Diagnostics will also show you the signal strength as a percentage. The higher the number the better. You can see what this screen looks like in Figure 7.23.

FIGURE 7.23

How strong is your signal?

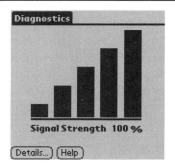

If you're out of range for Palm.Net service, or the radio waves just can't get through (as is often the case in our garden apartment), you'll see an error message telling you that the signal is too weak in your area or you are outside the Palm.Net coverage area. If you had coverage from the same location yesterday, just try moving to an open window and see what happens. Chances are good you'll pick up a signal.

 TIP You can monitor your signal strength while you're using a query application or iMessenger. A tiny version of the Diagnostics bar chart appears in the upper-right corner of the screen anytime you perform a wireless transaction.

You may have noticed a Details command button on the bottom of the Diagnostics screen. Tapping on this button will open a list of some very technical information about your Palm VII and its wireless features.

Some of the things you can find out here include:

- Palm.Net service activation: This is strictly a Yes or No situation—either your service has been activated or it hasn't.

- Signal strength: Measures the strength of your wireless transmission as a percentage.

- Software version: Tells you what version of the Palm operating system your organizer is running.

- Strength of your AAA batteries: Tells you how much voltage is left in your batteries.

- Transmitter Charge: Shows you the voltage remaining in the transmitter.

- Scheduled Charge: Indicates when the transmitter is scheduled to be recharged. The choices here are:

    - Not Scheduled (transmitter has adequate power)

    - Today or Tomorrow, with a time (your transmitter will be charged at the designated time)

    - Charging (the organizer is recharging the transmitter)

    - Charging suspended (transmitter can't be recharged because there are already too many demands on the organizer's power—probably because you have the backlight on)

- Base Station: Tells you which tower in the wireless network you have made a connection with; the tower will usually be located within a 20 mile radius of your current location.

- MSN: This is your Palm VII's manufacturer-assigned, unique serial number, which is also printed on the back of your organizer. It identifies the wireless transmitter inside your device, which a support technician may ask you for if you request help.

IMessenger

IMessenger is the Palm VII's wireless mail application. You use it to send and receive mail using the Palm.Net service.

PART

II

The Applications

Take a look at iMessenger in Figure 7.24. Looks a lot like Mail, doesn't it? Like Mail, iMessenger offers folders labeled Inbox, Outbox, Deleted, Filed, and Draft. Reading and creating messages also work pretty much the same way in the two applications.

Tap on the iMessenger icon in the Application Launcher (it's the one with a snail-mail letter superimposed over a black diamond) to see what we mean.

FIGURE 7.24

An iMessenger mail box

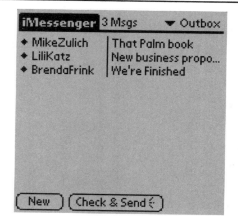

The primary difference between the two applications is that iMessenger works directly with your Palm.Net account, with no desktop PC required. You can send and receive e-mail straight from iMessenger, without having to HotSync to your desktop PC. In contrast, the Mail application only offers a way to manage mail from a standard, desktop PC-based e-mail account on your Palm organizer. It can't connect to an online service by itself, download messages, or send them out to a service provider. It's just a helper application.

We'll explain how to use iMessenger in more detail in Chapter 13.

Palm.Net

As we've already discussed, Palm.Net is the network service your Palm VII uses to access the Internet, both for working with e-mail using iMessenger and for doing Web clipping (the Palm VII's answer to Web surfing). So what's that Palm.Net icon doing in the Application Launcher? It's there to help you monitor the status of your Palm.Net account.

To check up on your account:

1. Tap on the Palm.Net icon (it's the one with the Palm device superimposed over a black diamond) in the Application Launcher, to open to the Palm.Net screen. You can see what this screen looks like in Figure 7.25.

FIGURE 7.25

How's your account doing?

PART

II

The Applications

2. Tap on My Account to go to the My Account page, which you can see in Figure 7.26.

FIGURE 7.26

Enter your username to find out how much you're spending.

3. Enter your Palm.Net username and password on the appropriate lines using Graffiti or the on-screen keyboard.

4. Tap on the Submit command button. The key next to the word Submit tells you that the information you just entered will be encrypted before it is sent, to ensure its safety.

5. At this point, your Palm VII will contact the Palm.Net service. A couple of seconds later, it will return with details on what service plan you've selected, when your billing cycle begins and ends, how many KB your plan includes, how many KB you've used, and what your total estimated charges are for that billing cycle.

6. When you're done reading this information, tap on the back arrow at the top of the screen to return to the My Account login screen.

7. Tap the back arrow again to return to the opening Palm.Net screen.

 NOTE Does tapping on those back arrows remind you of using a Web browser? It should. The Palm.Net application is a PQA (Palm Query Application), what the Palm VII uses for viewing Web content. We'll discuss PQAs in more detail in Chapter 13.

You can also use the Palm.Net application to access a database of Customer Support information. To do this:

1. From the opening Palm.Net screen, tap on the Customer Support option.

2. This will take you to a screen full of Customer Support options, which you can see in Figure 7.27. Here, you can get information on billing, query applications, iMessenger, as well as reception tips and a glossary of wireless terms.

FIGURE 7.27

When in doubt, ask customer support.

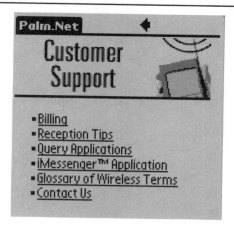

3. Tap on whatever subject you'd like more information on.

4. A screen full of information on that subject will be displayed.

Customer Support doesn't require an active connection to Palm.Net to operate. All its information is stored on your Palm VII. It works like a FAQ on a Web site—there's a series of descriptions of the most common questions about wireless service, and that's it. For any problems you're having, you'll have to go straight to real, live technical support folks.

 NOTE When you're away from your Palm VII, you can get all the account information and customer service support you need from the Palm.Net Web site (www.palm.net). There's also a host of new information here that isn't accessible from your organizer. And, if you forget your password, you'll need to visit the Web site to reset it.

PART

II

The Applications

CHAPTER **8**

Beaming by the Numbers

Remember that IR port on your Palm organizer that we mentioned way back in Chapter 1? The suspense is over. We're finally going to tell you how to use it.

For those of you who have no idea what we're talking about, here's a quick refresher. Every model of Palm includes an infrared (IR) port. From the outside of your Palm, all you see is a shiny black plastic window along the device's top edge. But, inside the device lies a proprietary IR transceiver that makes it possible to send and receive information wirelessly from one Palm organizer to another. This process, which uses infrared light, is known in the Palm world as beaming.

You can beam from any IR-equipped Palm to any other. Say, from a Palm III to a Palm V, or vice versa. All Palms speak the same beaming language.

 NOTE   You're probably thinking, "Hey, my notebook PC/printer/Windows CE device has an IR port. I can beam stuff from my Palm to one of those devices." The sad truth is that you can't—at least not without some third-party applications. Most devices, like notebook PCs, use an industry-standard form of IR, called IRDA, so they can speak to each other. The Palm, on the other hand, uses proprietary technology, so it doesn't speak the same dialect of IR as those other devices.

Out of the box, your Palm can beam data, such as Address Book records, categories, and some applications from one organizer to another. There are a few of things you need to know to beam successfully.

- Data from the four main applications is beamable, but you can't beam information from Expense, Calculator, PQAs and many third-party applications.

- Not all applications are beamable. Any application that came preinstalled on your organizer is locked and can't be beamed to another organizer. Applications you install yourself can generally be beamed to another Palm user.

- You can't beam something to another Palm user without their consent. Their organizer must be powered on and they must choose to receive whatever you're beaming. Think of it as going to visit someone: You can ring the bell until your finger falls off, but unless they answer the door, you're not getting into the house.

- The sending and receiving Palm organizers must be facing each other, with a clear line of sight between their IR ports.

- The organizers must be no more than 3 feet apart, and no closer than 4 inches for the beaming to succeed.

 TIP In order to either send or receive beamed data or applications, you must have the Beam Receive option turned on in the Preferences application. Turn back to Chapter 4 if you're not sure how to activate this option.

Beaming and Receiving Applications

Your Palm can indeed beam whole applications to another Palm. There are two restrictions: The application must be beam-enabled (that's a choice the application developer gets to make) and must be stored in the Palm's RAM. Applications such as the Address Book, Date Book, Memo Pad, and To Do List are stored in the Palm's ROM, just like the Palm operating system. This means you can't delete them, beam them, or otherwise touch them.

To beam an application:

1. Open the Application Launcher

2. Tap on the Menu soft button to open the Menu Bar. By default, you'll see the App drop-down menu, as in Figure 8.1.

PART

II

The Applications

FIGURE 8.1

The Application drop-down menu

3. Tap on Beam to open the Application Beam dialog box (see Figure 8.2).

FIGURE 8.2

*Pick an application
to beam.*

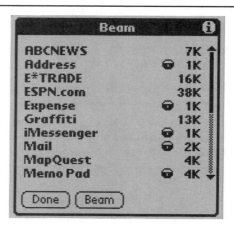

This screen displays the names of all the applications installed on your organizer, as well as their size. But just because they're all here doesn't mean you can beam them all.

Take a closer look at Figure 8.2 above and you'll notice a lock next to the size of some of the applications. You'll see the lock next to the Address Book, for example. This means that application is locked in to the organizer and can't be beamed. Any application without a lock next to its size can be transmitted to another Palm organizer. You'll also want to consider the size of an application before you decide to beam it. The smaller the application in kilobytes, the quicker it will beam. Most Palm applications are small enough to beam in a matter of seconds, but make sure you know what you're getting yourself into.

To beam one of the unlocked applications, from the Application Beam screen:

1. Tap on the name of the application you want to send. For this example, we'll choose the MapQuest PQA. You'll see a black bar across the name of the application to show it's selected, as in Figure 8.3.

FIGURE 8.3

*The application is
ready for beaming.*

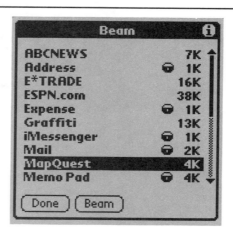

2. Tap on the Beam command button.

3. When you see the Beam status dialog box, point the IR port of your Palm directly at the IR port of the receiving unit.

4. When the Beam status dialog box tells you the transmission is complete, you can continue using your organizer.

Receiving a beamed application is even easier. Just have your organizer powered on and pointed at the sending Palm device. After that device has initiated the beam, you'll see a dialog box that says, "Do you want to accept MineHunt (or whatever application is being beamed)?" Just tap on the Yes command button to accept or No if you don't want the application.

Once you accept, the application may not turn up in the Application Launcher right away. But move to another application, then return to the Application Launcher, and the newly beamed application should be there, filed in the Unfiled category. Feel free to move it wherever you like, and start playing.

 TIP Having trouble beaming from a Palm VII to any of the Palm III models? It's probably because you're not lining up the IR ports exactly right. On the Palm VII, the IR port lies along the top edge near the front of the device; on the Palm IIIs, it's near the back of the device. So either tilt your Palm VII down or your Palm IIIup , and you should be in business. Oh, and try removing the flip-up cover from the III—it often blocks the IR port's line of sight.

Beaming and Receiving Records

Just as you can beam whole applications to another Palm organizer user, you can get more specific and beam a particular record.

This is probably the most common use for the beaming technology—to send a specific appointment, To Do List item, or Address Book entry to another Palm user.

Of all the types of records you can beam, the one you'll send most often is your business card. You may recall from Chapter 5 that you can create your own digital business card using the Palm Address Book. Once you've done that, you can just beam your business card to another Palm user when you link up at a trade show, business meeting, or Silicon Valley cocktail party. Much more au courant than passing out little bits of cardboard, don't you think?

PART

II

The Applications

Beaming and Receiving a Business Card

If you haven't yet created a business card, do so now. You're not a full-fledged member of the Palm club until you have! Just follow the steps in Chapter 5. (Here's a quick recap: Create an Address Book record with your own information. Choose Record ➤ Select Business Card from the Menu Bar. This record will now officially be your business card.)

To beam your business card:

1. Open the Address Book.

2. Tap on the Menu soft button to bring up the Menu Bar.

3. Choose Record ➤ Beam Business Card (see Figure 8.4).

FIGURE 8.4

Beam that business card.

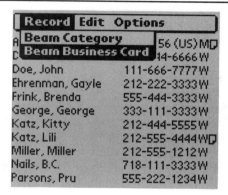

4. When you see the Beam status dialog box, point the IR port of your Palm directly at the IR port of the receiving unit.

5. When the Beam status dialog box tells you the transmission is complete, you can continue using your organizer.

TIP There's an even quicker way to beam a business card: Just press and hold the Address Book button down for one second, and the beaming will begin.

Though you may subscribe to the theory that it's better to give than to receive, chances are that right after you beam you business card to someone, they'll want to beam their card back to you. And of course, you'll have no choice but to accept the beam—because it would just be plain rude not to reciprocate.

Receiving is even easier than beaming. When the dialog box reading "Do you want to accept (their business card name here)?" appears, just tap on the Yes command button, and that record is added to your Address Book. The record will also automatically open so you can see what kind of lovely gift you've just received.

 TIP If you're trying to beam to another user, but your Palm returns a message after a few seconds that it could not find a receiving computer, chances are that either you and your buddy aren't aiming your devices straight, or that Beam Receive has been turned off on the receiving unit. Have your intended recipient check to make sure Beam Receive is turned on in the Preferences application and then try again.

Beaming Other Types of Records

You can just as easily send a different Address Book record or a To Do List item as you can a business card.

 TIP Beaming just sends a copy of the record, application, or category to the receiving Palm organizer. Whatever you beam remains on your system until you manually delete it.

To send any other type of record:

1. Open the application you want to beam from.
2. Tap on the record you want to beam.
3. Tap on the Menu soft button to open the Menu Bar.
4. From the Menu Bar, choose Record ≻ Beam Item (for the To Do list; in the Address Book the menu option is Beam Address; in the Memo Pad, it's Beam Memo; in the Date Book, it's Beam Event—whatever you call it, you're still beaming a single data record). You can also enter the ShortCut character and B using Graffiti. You can see this menu in Figure 8.5.

Beam the item of your choice.

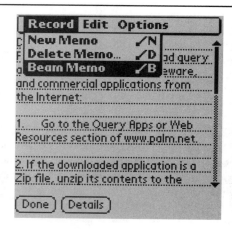

5. When you see the Beam status dialog box, point the IR port of your Palm directly at the IR port of the receiving unit.

6. When the Beam status dialog tells you the transmission is complete, you can continue using your organizer.

NOTE These steps work for beaming To Do List items and Date Book entries. To beam an Address Book entry or a Memo Pad record, you'll need to tap on the name of the record from the list to open it. With the record open, you can then follow the rest of the steps to beam it away.

Receiving any record works exactly the same way as receiving a business card or an application, so we won't explain the process again here. Just tap on Yes and get on with your life.

Beaming and Receiving Categories

Sometimes, a single record isn't enough. Picture this: You're working on a project, code-named Bengal, and have lots of To Do List items associated with the project (and they're all appropriately categorized, of course). Suddenly, you get promoted and can delegate all the mundane stuff to your brand new assistant. Rather than write out an entirely new To Do List for him, why not just beam all your Project Bengal To Dos to his Palm organizer? It's just as easy to beam an entire category as it is to beam a single item—assuming you've been a good little Palm user who's been categorizing records as you enter them.

To beam a category:

1. Make sure the category you want to beam is displayed on screen. If it's not, just select it from the Category drop-down menu in the top right of the screen.

2. Tap on the Menu soft button to bring up the Menu Bar.

3. From the Menu Bar, choose Record ➤ Beam Category to send all the records within that category to the recipient's Palm organizer (see Figure 8.6).

FIGURE 8.6

Beam an entire category.

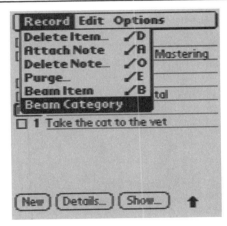

4. When you see the Beam status dialog box, point the IR port of your Palm directly at the IR port of the receiving unit.

5. When the Beam status dialog box tells you the transmission is complete, you can continue using your organizer.

Depending on how many records you have within a category, this process can take anywhere from a couple of seconds to a minute or so.

 TIP You can only beam a category from one application at a time. So, if you want to beam Memos, To Do List items, and Address Book records for Project Bengal to your assistant, you'll need to repeat the Beam category operation in each of those applications.

Guess what you have to do to receive a beamed category? You're absolutely right—just tap on the Yes command button when the dialog box appears asking if you want to receive the category.

What you'll never guess, though, is what happens to all the records within the beamed category. They just get dumped into Unfiled—even if you meticulously created the exact same category name as the one being beamed to you. It doesn't matter what you do on the receiving or sending end. All those carefully categorized records get unceremoniously dumped into Unfiled like yesterday's trash.

This was a shocker to us, too. And it's one reason why we rarely beam whole categories to anyone. It's a pain to have to sort through everything to decide what's a newly beamed record and what you already had lying around. Of course, the fact that we don't have any assistants to farm tedious tasks out to is also a deterrent. But that's just an operational detail.

CHAPTER **9**

HotSyncing: The Palm Elixir of Life

By now, you're probably tired of us nagging you to HotSync. Perhaps you've decided to heed our advice and have turned here for direction. Well, ask and you shall receive.

For those of you who have just turned here out of idle curiosity, we'll start by explaining the vital role the HotSync plays in the world of Palm Computing.

The HotSync is the sole way your Palm organizer communicates with your desktop PC—be it a Windows system or a Macintosh. You'll need to HotSync to back up data from your Palm to your desktop PC and to restore that data in event of a Palm meltdown. You'll need to HotSync to install new applications on your Palm, to retrieve mail from your desktop e-mail system, and to upload information you've entered in the Palm Desktop software.

On a more technical level, the HotSync is a two-way synchronization of records between your Palm and your desktop PC. Any changes you make on your Palm or your desktop PC get updated on both platforms when you HotSync. For an even more technical explanation of HotSyncing, see Chapter 22.

The primary way to HotSync, and the technique you'll likely use most often, is the Local HotSync. This technique uses the Palm Cradle, your desktop PC, and your Palm organizer. We'll explain everything you need to know to effortlessly perform a Local HotSync in this chapter.

The Four Faces of HotSync

The Palm organizer offers four different ways to HotSync. Here's a rundown on what each method entails, when to choose it, and where you can find more information on its execution.

Local HotSync—This technique, which we'll discuss at length in this chapter, uses the Palm cradle connected to a serial port on your desktop PC. This approach works best when you are working at your desktop PC. It's also a must for your first HotSync operation.

Modem HotSync—This HotSync uses a modem connected to your Palm organizer, and another connected to your desktop PC. The two modems communicate with each other to complete the HotSync. This approach is useful for synchronizing data when you're working from a remote location. We explain the ins and outs of Modem HotSyncs in Chapter 11.

Continued

CONTINUED

Direct Network HotSync—This form of HotSync works like a Local HotSync, but lets you connect to a local area network (LAN) or a wide area network (WAN). You should use this approach when you are away from your desktop PC, but at another computer on the same network with a Palm cradle connected to a serial port. Because this form of HotSync requires intervention from a network administrator or IT person, it is beyond the scope of this book. Refer to your Palm Handbook for instructions.

Dial-In Network HotSync—This form of HotSync works like a Modem HotSync, but dials into a server on your network instead of your desktop PC. You can use Dial-In Network HotSync when you are out of the office and have a dial-in account. As with a Direct Network HotSync, this will require setup by a network administrator; we will not be covering this topic. Refer to your Palm Handbook for instructions.

Now that we've gotten all the preliminaries out of the way, let's get ready to HotSync.

Getting Ready to HotSync

Before you can HotSync, there are a few things you need to do. You'll need to plug in the Palm cradle, install and set up the Palm Desktop Software, and set up the HotSync Manager. It may sound like a lot to do, but each process is quick and easy.

 TIP The HotSync process works the same on a Windows PC and a Macintosh PC. But, there are some differences in the desktop software for these two platforms. So, wherever there's a difference, we'll explain the Macintosh procedure in a Tip like this one.

Plugging in the Palm Cradle

Plugging in the Palm cradle is a simple task that involves the plug and an open serial port on your desktop PC. Ideally, you should plug in the cradle before you even install the Palm Desktop software since that software looks for the cradle as part of its installation process.

To plug in the cradle:

1. Locate an unused serial port on your desktop PC. Serial ports are the ports that modems and other peripherals get plugged in to.

2. With your computer turned off, plug the Palm cradle into the port. If your serial port has a 25-pin connector, you may need to use the 9-pin to 25-pin converter included with your Palm organizer.

3. Screw down the connector, so it doesn't come loose.

4. Power on your computer.

 TIP   Macintosh users will need a special adapter, which is not included with the Palm organizer. This adapter connects to the Cradle's 9-pin plug and has a round serial port connector on the other side, so it can be plugged into your Mac's serial port. You can get this adapter from Palm as part of the MacPac, which also includes the Macintosh version of the Palm Desktop software. You can order the MacPac from the Palm Computing Web site (www.palm.com, $9.95) or buy it at a computer or office supply store. The MacPac includes the adapter. If you already have an adapter, or if you have an old version of the MacPac, you can simply download the latest version of the software (version 2 or version 2.1 for Power Mac users) for free from the Palm Web site; the original adapter will still work fine.

That's all there is to plugging in your cradle. Now you're ready to install the Palm Desktop software.

Installing and Setting Up the Palm Desktop Software

We're not going to hold your hand all the way through the installation process for the Palm Desktop software. You're a big computer user now; you can follow on-screen directions, can't you?

OK, we'll get you started on the installation part; but then you're on your own—no matter how much you whine.

To install the Palm Desktop software:

1. Put the Palm software CD (which either came with your device or came with the MacPac) into the CD-ROM drive of your desktop PC.

The Palm Desktop installer will appear (as in Figure 9.1).

FIGURE 9.1

Just click Install, and get on with it.

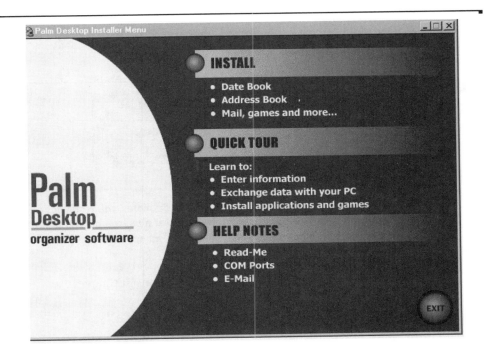

TIP If you downloaded the Mac Desktop software from the Web, first decompress it using StuffIt Expander or some comparable decompression utility. Then, double-click the Palm MacPac Installer icon and follow the on-screen instructions. You'll have the same choices as Windows users.

PART

II

The Applications

2. Click Install.

Follow the rest of the on-screen instructions to complete the installation. Along the way, you'll get to choose whether to install all the software components (a Typical installation) or just some of them (a Custom installation); sync your data to the Palm Desktop Software or to Microsoft Outlook; pick a username (what the Palm Desktop Software and HotSync Manager will know you as—see Figure 9.2); and specify what serial port your organizer is connected to and at what speed (you'll only be given this choice if the Palm can't automatically detect what port your Cradle is connected to). Palm VII users will also have the option to install PQAs from the CD. Don't worry if you don't see all these options. If the install process can detect the information, it won't ask for your input. Every Palm must have its own username. Usernames may have up to 15 characters, and can include spaces. We'd suggest using your own name as your Palm username. It makes life simpler.

FIGURE 9.2

What will you call your Palm?

TIP Mac users: When the installation completes, the HotSync setup application will automatically launch. You will have to enter a username and cradle port at this time.

Your Palm Desktop software is now set up and ready to use. We'll explain how to enter information into the Desktop applications in Chapter 10.

Setting Up HotSync Manager

One of the applications you just installed was the HotSync Manager. HotSync Manager is the application that oversees all HotSync operations. It watches the serial port you plugged the cradle into (as well as the modem, if you're set up for Modem HotSync) and listens for a HotSync command. The command is issued when you press the HotSync button on the cradle. HotSync Manager must be running in order to HotSync your organizer.

Fortunately, by default, the HotSync Manager is set to start automatically when you start your computer. You can see an icon for it in the System Tray of your Windows 95 or 98 desktop, as in Figure 9.3.

FIGURE 9.3

The HotSync icon in the system tray looks just like the HotSync button on the cradle.

You can change how HotSync Manager operates by clicking its icon in the Windows system tray, then choosing Setup from the pop-up menu. This will open the HotSync Manager Setup dialog box, as in Figure 9.4.

FIGURE 9.4

How should HotSync Manager run?

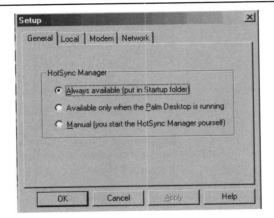

TIP Macintosh users can access the HotSync Manager Setup options by opening the Palm folder, then double-clicking the HotSync icon. You can see this screen in Figure 9.5.

FIGURE 9.5

HotSync Setup on the Mac

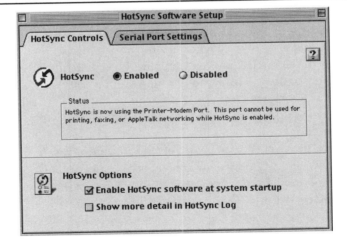

Your choices here are to make the HotSync Manager always available, which is the default setting; to have it only available when the Palm Desktop is running, which means you can only HotSync when the Palm Desktop software is active; or to require a manual start, which means that you launch the HotSync Manager from the Windows Start button Programs menu. We'd advise going with the default setting, unless your Palm cradle has to share a serial port with your modem; in that case, use either of the other two options.

 TIP On the Macintosh, you can choose to Enable the HotSync Manager, which means that you can't use the Printer-Modem Port for anything else; or Disable it to free up that port. You also have the choice to Enable HotSync at system startup, or not. Even if you choose to Enable HotSync at system startup, you will not see any sort of icon for the HotSync Manager in the Macintosh Menu bar. You have to open the HotSync Manager software to see an icon.

To perform a Local HotSync, you really don't have to do any more configuring of the HotSync Manager. By default, it's set for a Local HotSync and it already knows what port your Cradle is attached to.

Now, there's nothing left to do but HotSync away!

HotSyncing to Your Heart's Content

Performing a Local HotSync really couldn't be easier. Just pop your Palm into its cradle and press the HotSync button. That's it, really.

The HotSync Manager, which has been patiently sitting by and waiting for something to do, will leap into action, power up your Palm, and coordinate the process of transferring data from the Palm to your desktop PC, and vice versa. You really don't need to do anything else, but stay out of the way while the HotSync Manager does its thing.

Of course, you can get involved—if you really want to. We'll explain the whys and hows in the "HotSyncing Under Special Circumstances" section of this chapter.

For now, let's explore what actually happens when you HotSync—the first time and every time.

Your Very First HotSync

Whenever you HotSync, the same basic process happens. The HotSync Manager launches, powers up your Palm, compares the data on your organizer and your desktop PC, and updates both devices with the latest data. That's the default mode of operation—synchronizing all the files and applications on your Palm and your desktop PC. You can change these options; we'll explain how later.

For now, let's go the simple route and just do a plain vanilla HotSync. We're assuming here that you've already connected the cradle to your desktop PC, that you have installed the Palm Desktop software, and that HotSync Manager is running. If this is not the case, go back and complete these steps first.

To perform your very first HotSync:

1. Put your Palm organizer in the cradle.

2. Press the HotSync button on the front of the cradle.

3. If you have assigned a password to your organizer, enter it now.

4. Click the username you assigned to your Palm from the Users dialog box. Chances are, at this point, there's only one name on the list. (You can see this dialog box in Figure 9.6).

Guess which username to choose.

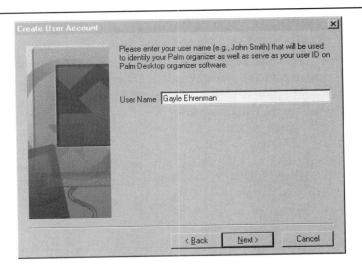

Create User Account

Please enter your user name (e.g., John Smith) that will be used to identify your Palm organizer as well as serve as your user ID on Palm Desktop organizer software.

User Name | Gayle Ehrenman

< Back | Next > | Cancel

5. Click OK to close this dialog box, and continue with the HotSync. You'll see the HotSync Progress dialog box (as in Figure 9.7). This will display what's happening with the HotSync, and automatically close when the HotSync is completed.

FIGURE 9.7

Watch that HotSync fly.

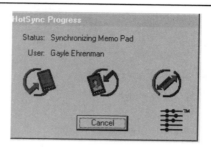

 TIP You only have to pick a username the first time you HotSync your organizer—if you're the only one syncing a Palm to this particular desktop PC.

Subsequent HotSyncs

After that first HotSync, you have even less to do with the whole process. You won't have to pick a username from the list—both HotSync Manager and your Palm now know their identity, and everything is configured to work.

So, just press the HotSync button and get out of the way. Your Palm and the HotSync Manager will take it from here.

You probably noticed that your first HotSync went pretty quickly. That was because there probably wasn't much information to exchange and synchronize. The more information you add to your Palm and the Palm Desktop software, the longer the HotSync will take. A HotSync only synchronizes whatever data has changed since the last time you HotSynced. To keep HotSync times short, sync often; that way there will be fewer changes to process per sync.

 TIP The default HotSync action is to synchronize all data between the Palm and your desktop PC. You can change this action for any or all of your Palm applications. See the section on customizing HotSync operations to find out how.

Installing and Deleting Applications

When you installed the Palm software, you installed one other application besides the HotSync Manager and the Desktop Software. You also installed the Install Tool. This tool doesn't actually install applications; it works with a HotSync to install extra software on your organizer—whether that software is a new PQA for your Palm VII, a game for your Palm IIIx, or a Hack for your Palm V.

 TIP The CD-ROM that comes with your Palm VII contains a number of extra query applications. These get copied into a folder called Add-ons when you install the Desktop software. You add them to your Palm by using the Install Tool.

All of the software you install on your Palm organizer gets stored in its RAM memory. This means that you can easily remove it from your organizer. We'll explain how to delete software after we teach you how to install it.

Installing Software

There are three ways to install software onto your Palm; all require you to first download software (or install it) onto your desktop PC, then use the Install Tool and a Hot-Sync to transfer it onto your Palm.

The three methods to install software are:

- Double-clicking
- Using the Palm Desktop software
- Using the Install Tool directly

 TIP Like all computer files, Palm files have a name followed by a dot and a format suffix, for example palm.prc. The suffixes for Palm files are PRC, PDB, and PQA.

The double-clicking approach is the simplest. Just find the file you want to install on your Palm organizer in the Windows Explorer and double-click its name. The Install Tool will automatically open and show the name of the file you just added, as in Figure 9.8. Just click OK in this dialog box to install the program when you next HotSync.

FIGURE 9.8

*Adding a file to install
the easy way*

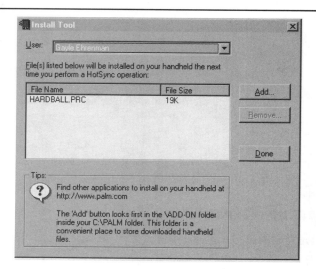

Installing an application through the Palm Desktop software isn't much tougher than using the double-click approach, but it does require a few extra steps. To install an application using the Palm Desktop:

1. Launch the Palm Desktop software by double-clicking its icon from your Windows desktop, or by choosing Palm Desktop from the Palm Desktop folder in the Windows Program folder.

2. Click the Install button along the left side of the Palm Desktop screen (or choose View ➤ Install from the menus along the top of the screen). This will bring up the Install Tool dialog box, with no files listed, as in Figure 9.9.

FIGURE 9.9

The Install dialog, waiting for you to pick a file

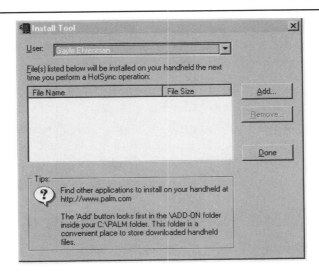

3. Click the Add button (or press Alt+A). This will bring up the Open dialog. By default, it will be set to Look in the Add-on folder.

4. Browse until you find the file you want to install, if it's not in the Add-on folder.

5. When you find the file you want to install, click its name to select it. You'll see a highlight bar across it.

6. Click Open. The Open dialog box will close and the file you selected will now be listed in the Install Tool dialog box.

7. Click Done. You'll see another dialog box (as in Figure 9.10) that reminds you that the application(s) will not be installed until you HotSync.

FIGURE 9.10

Remember to HotSync.

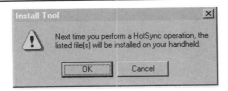

8. Click OK, and this dialog box will close, as will the Install Tool dialog box.

9. Put your Palm in its cradle and push the HotSync button to HotSync and complete the installation.

TIP You can install multiple applications during a single HotSync. Just follow steps 4–6 above for each application you want to install. Then move on to steps 7–9.

The final method to install applications on your Palm organizer is by using the Install Tool directly. To use this approach:

1. Click the Windows Start button, then choose Programs ➤ Palm Desktop ➤ Install Tool. This will open the same exact Install Tool dialog box as you see when working through the Palm Desktop software. You can see it in Figure 9.9.

2. Follow steps 3–9 above to complete the file installation.

Installing Files on a Macintosh

You only get one way to install files from your Mac to your Palm: through the Install Tool. To install files:

1. Open the HotSync Manager (it's located in the Palm folder, along with the Palm Desktop application).

2. Choose HotSync Install (or press ⌘+I). This will open the Install Handheld Files dialog box, which you can see here.

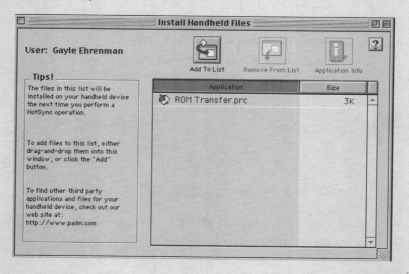

Continued

CONTINUED

3. Click the Add To List icon. This will bring up the Open dialog box, which you can see here.

4. Locate the file you want to install, and click its name to select it.
5. Click Add File. The Open dialog box will close, and you'll see the file you selected listed in the Install Handheld Files dialog box.
6. Close the Install Handheld Files dialog box.
7. Put your Palm in its Cradle and push the HotSync button to complete the installation.

Alternatively, you could just drag and drop a Palm file into the Install Handheld Files dialog box, rather than using the Add to List button.

After you've completed your HotSync, take your Palm out of the cradle and tap on the Application soft button to open the Application Launcher. You should see an icon for your newly installed application. It will be categorized as Unfiled. If you want to move it to another category, such as the Palm.Net category if it's a PQA, from the Application Launcher screen:

1. Tap on the Menu button to open the Menu Bar.
2. From the Menu Bar, choose App ➣ Category. This will bring up the Category screen, as in Figure 9.11.

FIGURE 9.11

All your applications, and their categories

3. Next to the name of each application, you'll see an arrow and a category name. Tap on the arrow to bring up a pick list of categories to which you can assign the application.

4. Tap on the category you want to use. The pick list box will close and you'll return to the Category screen.

5. Tap Done to close the Category screen and return to the Application Launcher. Your newly installed application will now be filed in its new Category.

Deleting Applications

The old rule of computing that says anything you install can be deleted applies to the Palm as well. So, if you find you're running out of memory on your Palm organizer or that application you installed isn't as useful as you thought it would be, just get rid of it.

While you need to HotSync your Palm to your desktop PC to install applications, you can delete them directly from your Palm organizer—no extra help required.

 TIP You cannot delete the four basic Palm applications. These are installed in the Palm's ROM (Read Only Memory). Applications you install yourself go into the organizer's RAM (Random Access Memory), so they can be deleted as you wish.

To delete an application you've installed:

1. Tap on the Application soft button to open the Application Launcher.

2. Tap on the Menu soft button to open the Menu Bar.

3. From the Menu Bar, choose App ➤ Delete. This will open the Delete screen, as in Figure 9.12.

FIGURE 9.12

Kiss your app goodbye.

4. Select the application or database you wish to delete and tap on the Delete command button. This will open the Delete confirmation dialog box, which you can see in Figure 9.13.

FIGURE 9.13

Are you sure?

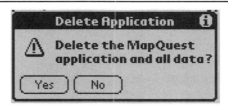

5. Tap Yes to complete the deletion. The confirmation dialog box will close, and you'll be returned to the Delete screen.

6. Tap Done and this screen will close and return you to the Application Launcher. The application you deleted will be gone.

Well, we've strayed from what you can do during a HotSync long enough. Let's explore some of the other things HotSync can do.

PART

II

The Applications

HotSyncing under Special Circumstances

In a perfect world, every Palm organizer would have one (and only one) desktop PC of its very own. And no two Palm devices would ever have to share that desktop PC. Oh, and we'd all be millionaires who never had to work again.

Ah, but reality is harsh. And there may come a time when you and your beloved have to share a single desktop PC, though you each have your very own Palm organizer. And, regrettably, you may need to HotSync that precious Palm with your desktop PC at home and the one in your office. Fortunately, none of these things is hard to do. We'll walk you through the process of HotSyncing two Palms to one desktop PC (be it a Windows system or a Macintosh), and also syncing one Palm to two different desktop PCs.

Two Palms, One Desktop PC

The family with multiple Palm organizers is most lucky. Rather than leaving each other notes on the refrigerator, you can just beam To Dos to each other. Fortunately, you don't need to have two desktop PCs for two Palms to happily co-exist. Nor do you need to install the Palm Desktop software twice—one installation per desktop PC is all you need. What you absolutely must have, however, is a unique username for each Palm organizer (and user) HotSyncing to the desktop PC. The first person who HotSyncs has it easy. Their username will be set up automatically with the very first HotSync. This will also take care of setting up all the necessary Palm Desktop folders, too.

To set up another user on the same desktop PC, launch the Palm Desktop software, and then:

1. Choose Tools ➤ Users from the menus along the top of the screen. This will open the Users dialog box, as in Figure 9.14. You'll see only one name in the list at this point.

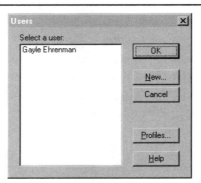

2. Click New to open the New User dialog box, which you can see here.

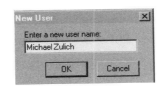

3. Enter the name for the second Palm user here, then click OK to close this box and return to the Users dialog, where you'll see the new user listed, as in Figure 9.15.

FIGURE 9.15

Now there are two.

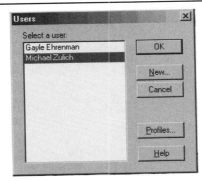

4. Click OK to accept this new user and close the dialog box. All the necessary Palm Desktop folders will automatically be created.

Each Palm user syncing with a desktop PC gets their very own set of folders in the Palm Desktop software. This lets each user maintain his or her own DateBook, Address Book, Memo Pad, and To Do List records. See Chapter 10 for more on using the Palm Desktop software.

TIP Macintosh users need to add new users through the HotSync Manager. Choose Users ➤ Show Palm User List. This will open the Palm Users dialog box. From this box, click the New User icon, enter a second username in the New Palm User dialog box, then click OK. This will return you to the Palm Users box. Close this box and you're ready to HotSync.

Now that you've added a new user, it's time to get that user HotSynced to the desktop. To do this:

1. Place the second user's Palm in the Cradle and press the HotSync button.

2. After a second or two, the Users dialog box will open, with both usernames listed (as in Figure 9.16).

*Pick the user
you prefer.*

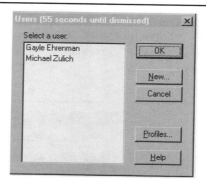

3. Click the second user's name, and click OK. The dialog box will close, and the HotSync will complete.

You only need to add the second user's name once, but you will have to pick the proper user each time you HotSync—no matter who you are. This is necessary so the HotSync manager knows which Palm its communicating with, and can synchronize with the proper folders on the Palm Desktop software.

 TIP Synchronizing multiple Palms on a single Macintosh works the same way it does on a Windows PC.

One Palm, Two Desktop PCs

These days, most of us are fortunate (or unfortunate, depending on your point of view) enough to have a computer at home and another at work. It's easy to HotSync your Palm to both desktop PCs, even if one machine is running Microsoft Windows and the other is a Macintosh.

Essentially, all you have to do is set up each of the desktop machines for HotSync as if it were your very first HotSync. Go through all the steps we outlined earlier in this chapter to complete your very first HotSync or a subsequent HotSync as the situation dictates on your first desktop PC (we'll call it Computer 1).

Then, install the Palm Desktop software (either the Windows or Macintosh version) on your second desktop PC (we'll call it Computer 2) and perform a routine HotSync. HotSync Manager will automatically create the username (you assigned this to your Palm when HotSyncing with Computer 1). It will also set up the necessary Palm Desktop folders, so you're ready for business.

Using a single Palm with multiple desktop PCs can get a bit confusing. When we first tried this, we were never sure where we entered information, and which system (Computer 1, Computer 2, or our Palm) had the most recent data. To alleviate this confusion, we adopted a simple rule: Enter data into the Palm Desktop software of Computer 1 or directly in our Palm organizer only. The Palm Desktop on Computer 2 was used as a read-only application.

And, when we HotSync, we choose to synchronize the files on the Palm with Computer 1, but use the Handheld Overwrites Desktop option when HotSyncing with Computer 2. This way, we're never overwriting current data with out-of-date information. We'll explain more about what this HotSync option does and how to set it in the next section.

Customizing Your HotSync

In the previous section, we explained some special HotSync situations and hinted at ways you can use HotSync options to better control them. Now, let's look at how you can customize HotSync operations, and when you'd want to use these options.

You have four choices for what action HotSync can take with each application installed on your Palm organizer. Your choices are:

- Synchronize The Files
- Desktop Overwrites Handheld
- Handheld Overwrites Desktop
- Do Nothing

Each of the main applications on your Palm (and some of the secondary applications) has a conduit. This conduit specifies how a HotSync should update data for that application. These options determine that "how." You can learn more about conduits in Chapter 22.

PART

II

The Applications

By default, a HotSync synchronizes all files between your organizer and the Palm Desktop software. This ensures that both your Palm and your desktop PC have the latest data. In general, you should keep the Synchronize Files option set unless something has gone wrong with either your Palm or your Palm Desktop software, or you are syncing one Palm and two computers.

The Desktop Overwrites Handheld option copies data for the application from your desktop PC to your Palm, replacing any data already on your organizer. This option is useful if your Palm has crashed and lost data.

The Handheld Overwrites Desktop option replaces the data on your desktop PC with the data from your Palm organizer. Choose this option if you rarely HotSync and do all your data entry on your Palm.

The Do Nothing option changes nothing in the application. Neither the data on your Palm nor on your desktop PC is touched during the HotSync. Choose this option for applications to keep from synchronizing applications you don't use, such as Mail or Expense.

You specify options on an application-by-application basis, so it's possible to get just the results you want from a HotSync.

To customize HotSync application settings:

1. Click the HotSync icon in the Windows system tray (the bottom-right corner of the taskbar). This will open the HotSync Manager menu.

2. Click Custom. This will open the Custom dialog box, as in Figure 9.17.

 TIP If you have the Palm Desktop software open, choose HotSync ➤ Custom from the menus at the top of the screen.

FIGURE 9.17

Customize all you want.

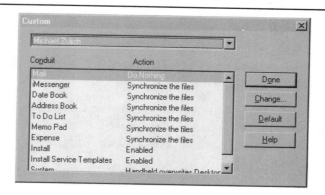

3. Select your username from the list at the top of the Custom dialog box.

4. From the part of the box that lists Conduit and Action, click the application you want to customize. It will be highlighted.

5. Click Change. This will open the Change HotSync Action dialog box, as in Figure 9.18.

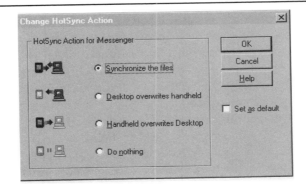

FIGURE 9.18

What do you want to change?

6. Click the option you want to invoke for this application.

7. Click OK to accept this setting.

8. Repeat steps 4–7 to change the HotSync action for other applications.

9. Click Done to accept your settings and make them active.

 TIP The custom HotSync settings you just configured will be in effect for your next Hot-Sync only. After that, the action will go back to the default. If you want to use the option you specified on a continuing basis, click the Set As Default check box in the Change Hot-Sync Action dialog box. This will make your selection the default HotSync action for that application.

 TIP Macintosh users: To customize your HotSync settings, open the HotSync Manager application, then choose HotSync ➢ Conduit Settings from the Menu Bar (or press ⌘+H). Double-click the application you want to customize. This will open the Settings dialog box. Click the action you want to invoke for this application; if you want to make this action the default, click Make Default. Then click OK. Repeat to configure other applications. Close the Conduit Settings dialog box when you're done.

PART

II

The Applications

Restoring Palm Data

Sometimes, in spite of your best efforts, misfortune may befall your Palm organizer. Maybe you didn't change the batteries quickly enough, or maybe you installed some nasty software that caused your Palm to crash. It doesn't matter. If your Palm should lose all its data, there's no reason to panic. You can restore it all from your desktop PC—if you HotSynced.

If your Palm has crashed, you'll need to reset it before you can proceed. Turn to Appendix B for tips on rendering your Palm operational again. If you're dealing with dead batteries (or a Palm V that's lost its charge), add new batteries or recharge it.

After your Palm has been restored to a healthy state, just pop it in the cradle and get ready to HotSync. Follow the directions in the previous chapter to customize your HotSync. Set all the conduit actions to Desktop Overwrites Handheld. Then push the HotSync button on the cradle, and all your data will be restored. It's just like magic!

Now do you see why we kept pestering you to HotSync your Palm?

Of course, once you have all that data on your desktop, you'll want to act on it. That's where the Palm Desktop software comes into play. Turn to the next chapter for a walk-through of that application.

CHAPTER **10**

Using the Palm Desktop

L et's get one important detail out of the way: You don't ever have to use the Palm Desktop software if you don't want to. The only reason you must install it is to add the HotSync Manager and Install utilities to your computer.

The Palm Desktop software is what's known as a PIM or personal information manager. You may be familiar with PIMs like Microsoft Outlook or Lotus Organizer. The Palm Desktop works much like these applications. In fact, if you already use one of these PIMs, or any of the others that support syncing to the Palm, you don't need to make a change; you can HotSync your Palm with one of those applications by using special software or conduits. We discuss conduits in Chapter 22.

But, if you're looking for a quick and easy way to view your Palm data from your desktop or to enter information in a hurry, the Palm Desktop is a useful tool. In fact, we know people who enter all their appointments, addresses, and To Dos using the Palm Desktop, and then just HotSync it over to their Palm device so they can always have that information handy.

The Palm Desktop software comes in a version for Microsoft Windows–equipped PCs (called Palm Desktop Software 3.0.1) and for Macintosh machines (called Palm Desktop 2.1). Both versions offer the same applications: the Date Book, the Address Book, the To Do List, and the Memo Pad. The Macintosh Desktop doesn't refer to the applications by their Palm-given names, though. Instead, it calls the Date Book the Calendar, the Address Book the Contact List, the Memo Pad the Note List, and the To Do List the Task List. Whatever they may be called, they're the same applications as on the Palm organizer itself, which is why HotSyncing data from the Desktop to the Palm is seamless. If you're not sure how to HotSync, turn back to Chapter 9.

There are a few other differences between the Windows and Macintosh versions of the Palm Desktop. For example, the interfaces of the two applications are different. In addition, the Windows version offers an Expense button, which opens a Microsoft Excel spreadsheet filled with your Palm Expense data; the Macintosh version doesn't offer this capability. That version does offer a couple of tricks the Windows version doesn't. The Mac version of the Palm Desktop lets you create banner events (events that span multiple days) and lets you choose a designer look for the application (it calls them Decors). The Mac version also offers something called the Instant Palm Desktop, which lets you create appointments, tasks, events, and more, as well as search for contacts without opening the Desktop software. We'll explain more about using these features later.

Let's start by exploring the interface of both the Windows and Macintosh versions of the Palm Desktop.

Learning Your Way Around

The Palm Desktop software looks appreciably different depending on the type of computer you're running it on. On a Windows system, it looks like a standard Windows application, with a series of drop-down menus along the top of the screen, a toolbar just underneath that, and then a series of buttons along the left edge. On a Macintosh, the Palm Desktop looks like a standard Macintosh application. You get a Menu Bar (which has different items on it than the Windows Menu Bar) and a toolbar just underneath the Menu Bar. Of course, both versions of the Palm Desktop display a main window, which is where you enter and view information; this will change depending on which application you're using and what view you're in.

Let's take a tour of each of the interfaces.

The Windows Interface

Like most Windows programs, the Palm Desktop has just a few basic elements, which you can see in Figure 10.1.

FIGURE 10.1

The Palm Desktop for Windows

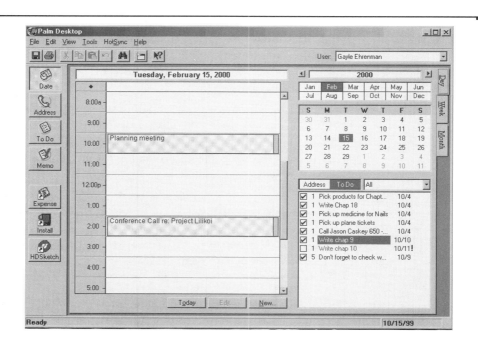

PART

II

The Applications

The Palm Desktop for Windows displays:

- A Title Bar, which is the colored bar along the top of the screen displays the name of the application that is in use. This bar doesn't get used for any program activity.

- A Menu Bar, which is the bar just under the Title Bar lists the drop-down menus. These work just like the menus on your Palm organizer; click one to see the options within it.

- A Toolbar, which is the row of icons just under the Menu Bar; click one of these icons to perform a particular task.

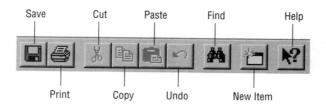

- A Launch Bar, which is the row of icons along the left side of the screen corresponds to the four main Palm organizer applications. Below these, you'll see two buttons: one for Expense, which opens the Microsoft Excel spreadsheet linked to the Palm Expense application, and one for Install, which launches the Palm Install tool for installing applications on your organizer. Turn back to Chapter 9 for tips on using Install.

- A Main Window, which is the largest part of the screen, situated between all the other stuff. What you see here will vary depending on which application you have open, but it will always be divided into two panes. The pane on the left side of the screen shows general information for the application, while the pane at the right shows more detail.

 NOTE By default, when you first launch the Palm Desktop, you'll see the Date Book (in Day View) open in the left pane of the screen, and a monthly calendar and the To Do List displayed in the right pane of the screen.

The various interface elements function here just as they would in any other Windows application, such as Microsoft Word or Adobe Photoshop. Click the Menu Bar to see the drop-down list of menu options (or use the standard Windows keyboard commands of Alt+ the underlined menu letter); then click the menu option to use it. The Toolbar and Launch Bar work the same way—just click the icon for the action you want to perform.

The Palm Desktop for Windows doesn't offer many options for configuring its overall operation. The few it does offer are all accessible by clicking Tools ➤ Options. This will open the Options dialog box, as in Figure 10.2.

FIGURE 10.2

Configure the display.

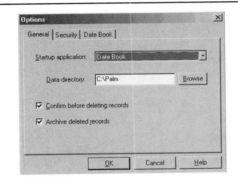

The General tab lets you choose which application displays when the Palm Desktop opens, what directory data is stored in, and how deleted files are handled. The Security tab lets you specify whether password identification is required when launching the Desktop. The Date Book tab lets you choose what time and day of the week to use as the starting point for the Date Book. Just click the tabs at the top of the Options dialog box to move from one to another; click the check boxes to select an option; or click the arrows to open pick lists of options. They're all standard Windows application operations.

 TIP If any of the terms or concepts we've referred to here are unfamiliar to you, you'll need to start with a book on using Microsoft Windows. Try the Sybex book, *Mastering Windows 98 Premium Edition* by Robert Cowart.

We'll get into the various actions you can perform with the Palm Desktop after we give a brief tour of the Macintosh interface.

The Macintosh Interface

Like the Palm Desktop for Windows, the Macintosh version has a rather simple surface, as you can see in Figure 10.3.

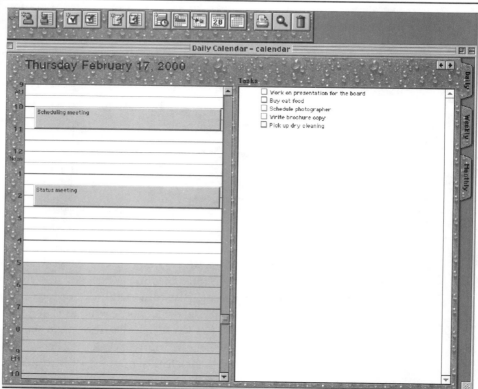

FIGURE 10.3

The Palm Desktop for the Mac

The Palm Desktop for the Mac displays:

- A Menu Bar, which is located at the top of the screen, this element lists all the drop-down menus and works just like the Menu Bar on your Palm organizer.
- A Toolbar, which is the row of icons just below the Menu Bar. Click one of these icons to carry out a particular action.

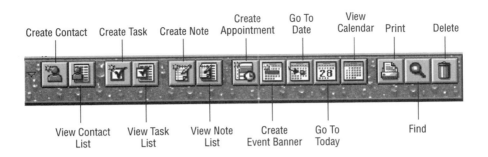

Create Contact   Create Task   Create Note   Create Appointment   Go To Date   View Calendar   Print   Delete

View Contact List   View Task List   View Note List   Create Event Banner   Go To Today   Find

- A Main Window, which is the large area under the Toolbar; what you see here will differ depending on what application you have open.

 TIP Referring to the bulk of the Macintosh Desktop screen as *the* Main Window is a bit misleading. The Macintosh Desktop allows you to have every one of its applications open at the same time, so you can display multiple windows of information. Whichever window is currently active will be displayed on top.

You have a couple of options for how the Palm Desktop for Macintosh diplays. For example, you can have the Toolbar docked or floating. By default, it is docked or fixed at the top of the screen. To change it to floating, so you can position it anywhere on the screen:

1. Click Edit ➤ Preferences. This will open the Preferences dialog box, as in Figure 10.4.

FIGURE 10.4

Set your Preferences.

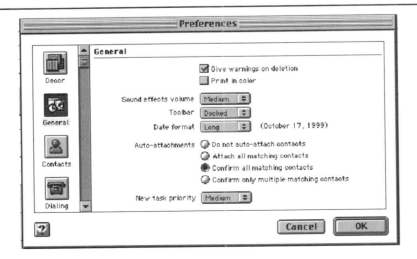

2. Click the General icon in the left pane of the dialog box.

3. In the middle of the screen, you'll see the word Toolbar with a gray box next to it. Click the arrows in this box to open its pop-up menu.

4. From the pop-up menu, click Floating to make the Toolbar movable. You could also click None to eliminate the Toolbar from the screen.

5. Click OK to accept the change and close the dialog box.

6. Click the Toolbar and drag it wherever you'd like on the screen.

You also can choose what the Desktop looks likes by changing its Decor. To do this:

1. Click Edit ➤ Preferences. This will open the Preferences dialog box, as in Figure 10.4.

2. Click the icon for Decor in the left pane of the dialog box. The right pane will change to show you a list of choices and a preview of what they look like, as in Figure 10.5.

FIGURE 10.5

Time for redecorating.

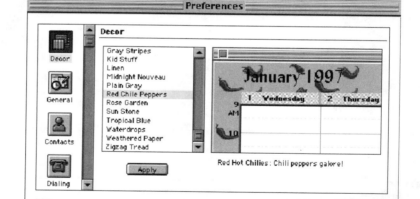

3. Click the various choices in the list to see them previewed. When you've found one you like, click Apply to select this Decor and see it on your Desktop.

4. Click OK when you're happy with your selection. This will close the Preferences dialog box.

You can change other aspects of the Palm Desktop program through the Preferences dialog box, as well. Clicking the Contacts icon gives you a range of choices for how your contacts are displayed, including the default labels, number of custom fields, and format for phone numbers. The Calendars dialog box lets you pick the start and end time used in Day View, as well as the first day of the week and time interval to use for appointments. The Dialing dialog box lets you configure the Palm Desktop to work for auto-dialing. Fonts lets you select the font to use for the Contact, Task, Note Lists, Note Body, Daily, Weekly, and Monthly Calendars.

You can make even more choices through the General Preferences dialog, which we used to configure the Toolbar. Here, you can also set the sound effects volume, the date format, and the priority assigned to new Tasks. You can also configure Auto-Attachment options—which are unique to the Macintosh version of the Palm Desktop.

The Auto-Attachment feature automatically attaches a contact to new notes, tasks, and appointments, much the same way you can attach a note to an event. So, if you type in "Lunch with Mike," Auto-Attachment will look for a contact named Mike. If it finds one, it will attach the contact to your appointment in the Date Book.

Using Auto-Attachment, you can choose to attach all matching contacts (adds every Mike in the book); confirm all matching contacts (opens a dialog box listing all Mikes and asks you to pick the right one); or confirm only multiple matching contacts (if it finds just one Mike, it attaches it; otherwise it asks for confirmation). You can also choose the Do Not Auto-attach Contacts, which keeps Auto-Attachment disabled.

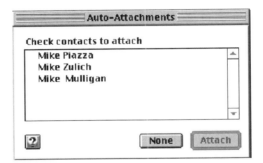

We've just scratched the surface of the Palm Desktop for Macintosh interface and its capabilities; explore for yourself to get to know everything the Palm Desktop can do.

TIP If any of the terms or concepts we've explained here are unfamiliar to you, refer to a book about using the Macintosh.

Now let's jump in to the Palm Desktop applications.

Using the Applications

The Palm Desktop applications work very similarly to their organizer counterparts and generally give you all the same options and functions. We'll explain how to carry out the most important tasks within an application, but cannot address all the functions of the Palm Desktop software.

 TIP The step-by-step instructions for completing a task should apply to both the Windows and Macintosh versions of the Palm Desktop. Where there's a difference, we'll explain the Mac method in a tip like this one.

The Date Book

Like the Date Book on your Palm organizer, the Palm Desktop provides three different views: Day, Week and Month. Day View is the default view, and the one that's most useful for adding appointments. To change to either of the other views, just click the tab for it on the right side of the screen.

Week View shows an entire week's worth of appointments, as you can see in Figure 10.6. Unlike the Palm organizer's Week View, the Palm Desktop's version displays the name of your appointments, rather than just representing them as bars. It also has a special region at the top of each day (represented by a diamond), where it places untimed events. You can add and edit appointments from this view.

Month View shows all the appointments you have scheduled in a month. You'll see more detail about your appointments here than in the Month View on your Palm organizer, but less than you get with either Day or Week View. Untimed events are indicated by an asterisk, as in Figure 10.7. And, you can't actually add or edit events from within this view. Trying to do so will kick you back into Day View.

FIGURE 10.6

A week's worth of fun

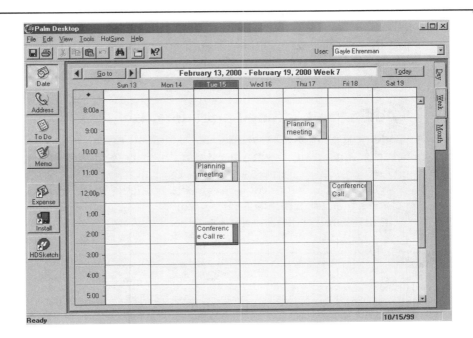

FIGURE 10.7

A mad, mad month

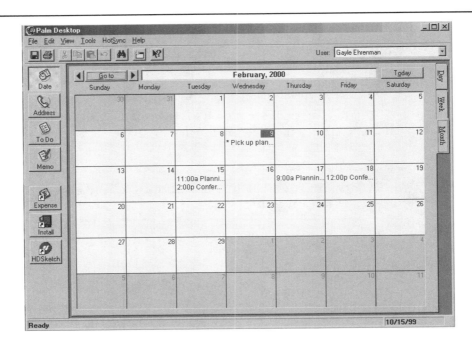

PART

II

The Applications

TIP Mac users: You can't create untimed events in the Macintosh version of the Palm Desktop. Instead, you have to create an Event Banner that lasts one day. We'll let you figure out how to do this on your own.

Adding and Editing Appointments

Adding appointments to the Palm Desktop Date Book is just as easy as adding them to the Palm organizer—maybe easier if you're more comfortable typing than using Graffiti.

To add an appointment, you can either click the New button at the bottom of the screen, then fill in the details in the Edit Event dialog box (see Figure 10.8), or enter the appointment directly in the Date Book.

To enter an appointment directly into the Date Book:

1. If the Date Book is not open to Day View, switch to it by clicking the Day tab at the right of the screen, or by entering Alt+D.

 TIP Mac users: Either click the Daily tab at the right of the screen, or click the View Calendar icon on the Toolbar.

2. Click the date you want for this appointment from the monthly calendar in the top part of the right pane. The Date Book will turn to the day you selected.

 TIP Mac users: Click the Go To Date icon on the Toolbar.

3. Click anywhere on the line next to your appointment's start time. A box will open on that line, with a blinking insertion point (see Figure 10.9).

FIGURE 10.9

An appointment in progress

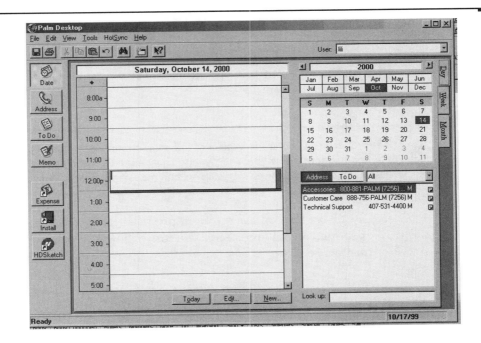

 TIP Mac users: You will see the Appointment dialog box, shown in Figure 10.10.

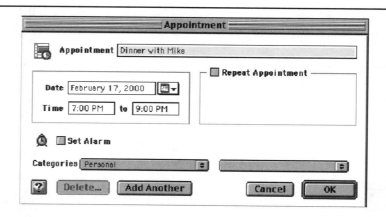

4. Type the subject of your appointment. The subject will appear on the appropriate line in the Date Book.

 TIP Mac users: Enter the subject of the appointment in the New Appointment box of the Appointment dialog box. You can also change the date and time of the appointment, assign up to two categories, set an alarm, and make it a repeating appointment.

5. Click anywhere on the screen or press the Tab key to accept this entry. The appointment you just entered will turn yellow to show that it's been added to the Date Book.

 TIP Mac users: Click OK in the Appointment dialog box when you're satisfied with your choices. The dialog box will close, and you'll return to the Date Book screen where the appointment will be displayed.

The appointment you added will automatically be assigned a length of one hour (or for Mac users, whatever time interval you specified in Preferences). To change the length of the appointment:

1. If the Date Book is not open to Day view, switch to it by clicking the Day tab at the right of the screen, or by entering Alt+D.

TIP Mac users: Either click the Daily tab at the right of the screen, or click the View Calendar icon on the Toolbar.

2. Click the appointment you wish to select. A dark gray bar will appear at its right edge, and a dark green bar will appear along the bottom.

 TIP Mac users: Your appointment will change color from gray to white, and you'll see arrows at its top and bottom edge, as well as a grabber bar on its left edge.

3. Click and hold on the bottom line of the appointment; your cursor will turn into a two-headed arrow. Drag down your cursor to make the appointment longer. To make it shorter, drag your cursor up. The appointment time will increase or decrease in half-hour intervals.

4. Let go of the mouse button when you're satisfied with the duration of the appointment.

To change the time of an appointment, just click and hold on the gray bar (the grabber bar, for you Mac users). Your cursor will turn into a four-headed arrow on the PC or a hand on the Mac. Drag the appointment to its new time, and let go when you get there.

 NOTE You can always change the date, time, and duration of an appointment through the Edit Event dialog box. On the PC, with the event selected, click the Edit button at the bottom of the screen to access this dialog box. Or, you can select the event, then double-click on the dark gray bar at its right edge. On the Mac, double-click the event.

Creating a Repeating Appointment

The prevailing attitude in most companies seems to be that any meeting worth wasting time on once is worth wasting time on an ongoing basis. So, if you're like us, and you have standing meetings that happen the same day and time every week, you'll want to set them up as repeating appointments.

PART

II

The Applications

To create a repeating appointment:

1. If the Date Book is not open to Day View, switch to it by clicking the Day tab at the right of the screen or by entering Alt+D.

 TIP Mac users: Either click the Daily tab at the right of the screen or click the View Calendar icon on the Toolbar.

2. Create an appointment, following the instructions in the previous section.

3. Click the appointment to select it, then click the Edit button at the bottom of the screen (or choose Edit ➤ Edit Event). This will open the Edit Event dialog box.

4. Click the None button next to the word Repeat. This will open the Change Repeat dialog box, which you can see in Figure 10.11.

FIGURE 10.11

How often must we endure this meeting?

 TIP Mac users: From the Appointment dialog box, click the Repeat Appointment check box. Select the frequency for the meeting from the interval pop-up menu. Specify the last date when the meeting should occur in the Until box, or choose a date from the pop-up calendar. Leave the Until date blank if this meeting will repeat indefinitely.

5. Click the repeat pattern you want (Daily, Weekly, Monthly, Yearly) to select it, then specify the time frame (every two weeks, for example). Specify an end date by entering it in the text box or picking it from the pop-up calendar. Leave End On set to No End Date if this meeting will continue for all eternity.

6. Click OK to accept your selections. The Change Repeat dialog box will close, and you'll return to the Edit Event dialog.

7. Click OK to close the Edit Event dialog box. An open circle with an arrow in it will appear next to your appointment to show its repeating status.

 TIP Mac users: You will not see an indication that an event repeats in the calendar. It will just appear on the appropriate Date Book pages.

There's one thing you should remember about repeating events: Every time you change one, you'll be asked if you want to change only this specific appointment or every one in the series. You always have the choice to change one or all. However, changing the text of the event, even if you chose to only Change Current, will change the text for all the events.

Attaching a Note to an Appointment

As with the Palm organizer, you can attach a note to any appointment. Macintosh users can not only attach a note, but a contact as well. Page back to the section on The Macintosh Interface for information on the Auto-Attachment feature.

For, now let's focus on attaching a note using the Palm Desktop for Windows. (Instructions for doing this on the Mac Desktop follow.) To do this:

1. If the Date Book is not open to Day View, switch to it by clicking the Day tab at the right of the screen or by entering Alt+D.

2. Create an appointment, following the instructions in the previous section.

3. Right-click the appointment you want to attach a note to. This will open a pop-up menu.

4. Click Note from this pop-up menu. This will open the Note Editor screen (see Figure 10.12).

 TIP If the event you want to add a note to is selected, the pop-up menu won't contain Note. Instead, you'll see an Edit option. Click Edit, then choose the note icon from the Edit dialog box that opens.

PART

II

The Applications

FIGURE 10.12

Start typing that note.

5. Enter the text of your note in the Note Editor screen.

6. Click OK when you're satisfied with your note. The Note Editor will close and you'll return to the Date Book where you'll see a note icon next to the name of your appointment.

Mac Desktop users have two different techniques for attaching a note to an appointment. Which one to use will depend on whether you're attaching a new note to an existing appointment (or vice versa), or if you're attaching an existing note to an existing appointment. It sounds more complex than it really is. We'll explain how to attach a new note to the appointment we just created. Check the Mac Desktop's Help files for guidance on attaching one new item to another.

To attach a new note to an existing appointment:

1. Either click the Daily tab at the right of the screen, or click the View Calendar icon on the Toolbar to open the Date Book to Daily view.

2. Click the appointment to which you want to attach a note.

3. From the Menu Bar, choose Create ➤ Attach to ➤ New Note. This will open the Note dialog box, which you can see in Figure 10.13.

4. Based on the appointment information, the title, date, and time will automatically be assigned to the note, but you can type in new ones.

5. Type in the text of your note.

6. Click the close button in the top-left corner of the dialog box to accept the Note and attach it to your appointment. The dialog box will close, and you'll return to the Date Book. There you'll see a file folder with a paperclip icon to indicate an attachment. The techniques we've outlined here for attaching a note to an appointment using either the Windows or Macintosh Palm Desktop work for all the Palm Desktop applications. Follow the same steps to attach a note to a Contact or a To Do.

FIGURE 10.13

Your Note goes here.

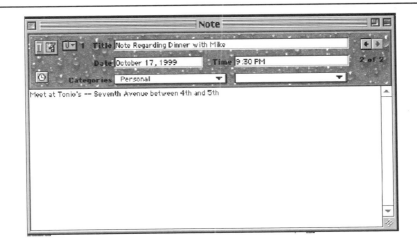

Deleting an Appointment

Decided that lunch with the in-laws isn't such a good idea after all? Well, just wipe that appointment right off your calendar. To delete an appointment from the Date Book:

1. If the Date Book is not open to Day view, switch to it by clicking the Day tab at the right of the screen, or by entering Alt+D.

 TIP Mac users: Either click the Daily tab at the right of the screen, or click the View Calendar icon on the Toolbar.

2. Click the appointment you want to delete. The yellow box around the appointment will be shaded to show that it's selected.

3. Press the Delete key on your keyboard, or right-click the appointment to bring up a pop-up menu of choices and click Delete from this menu (or, choose Edit ≻ Delete from the Menu Bar). This will bring up the Delete Datebook Event dialog box, as in Figure 10.14.

 TIP Mac users: Press the delete key, click the Delete icon on the Toolbar, or choose Edit ≻ Delete from the Menu Bar. You'll see the Delete warning box, as in Figure 10.15.

PART

II

The Applications

FIGURE 10.14

*Adios appointment–
PC style*

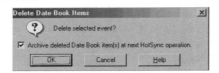

FIGURE 10.15

*Au revoir appoint-
ment–Mac style*

4. Leave the archive box checked if you want the appointment moved to an archive file (we'll explain how to do that later in this chapter); deselect it if you want the appointment deleted forever. Click OK to get rid of that pesky appointment and close the dialog box.

 TIP Mac users: You won't see an archive check box because the Mac Desktop automatically archives all deleted records. You can't disable this option.

If you delete a recurring event, you'll be asked if you want to delete just this instance or all of them in the sequence. The choice is yours.

There are other things you can do with appointments, including marking them private or adding alarms to them. Or, in daily calendar view, you can drag-and-drop an item from the Address or To Do pane to the calendar. We'll let you discover these options and features on your own.

The Address Book

The Palm Desktop Address Book, just like its tiny little Palm organizer-based companion, offers you two different views of your contact information: List View and Detail View. This is true whether you're working with the Windows Desktop or the Macintosh version. What you see in the List View will differ, depending on your Desktop version, however.

In List View, the Windows version of the Palm Desktop shows a limited selection of contact data—just names and work phone numbers. But, next to the List View, you'll see the Detail View for a selected Contact, as you can see in Figure 10.16. The advantage to this approach is that you don't have to change views from List to Detail—just select a contact, and all its information is displayed on screen.

FIGURE 10.16

One screen, two views

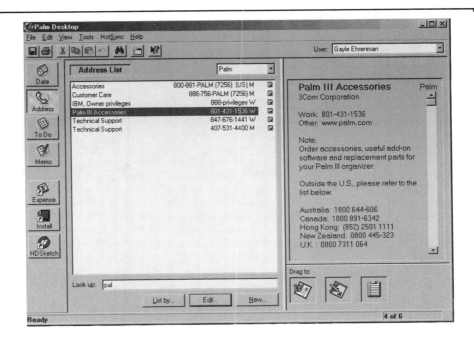

The Macintosh Desktop handles these matters differently. For starters, it opens the Contact List (remember, this is what it calls the Address Book) independently of the individual contact view. However, you can display this List full-screen, so you can see virtually every piece of information you've entered for every contact in your list (see Figure 10.17). If there's something that isn't readily visible, just scroll across until the column you want is displayed. This isn't a pretty approach, but it is efficient. We know folks who never look at individual records, preferring instead to just keep the Contact List displayed at all times.

FIGURE 10.17

The biggest of lists

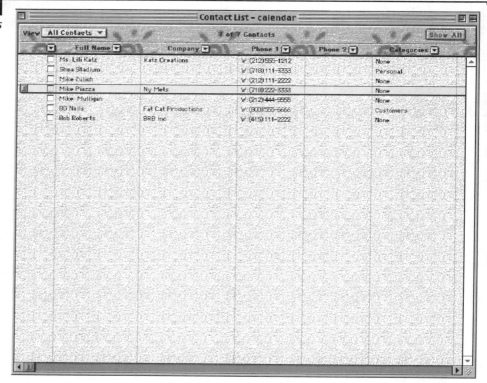

You open a contact in Detail View (which is much more attractive, in our estimation—and we believe looks *do* count) by double-clicking it from the list. You can see an individual contact displayed in Figure 10.18.

NOTE Windows Desktop users: You may have noticed Drag To buttons in the bottom-right corner of the Address Book screen (they also appear on the To Do List and Memo Pad screens). These represent non-Palm applications you can drag an item to. Clicking an item and dragging it onto one of these icons will launch that application (Microsoft Word, for example) and add the item you just dragged over to a new document. This is particularly useful if you want to add a name or memo to a report you're writing in Word.

Enough about the look of the Lists. Let's start entering information.

FIGURE 10.18

A contact close up

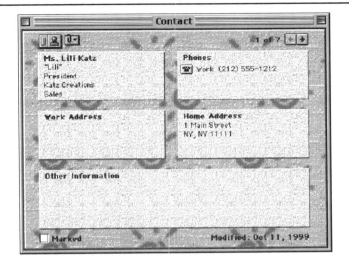

Adding and Editing an Address Book (or Contact List) Entry

To bring up the Address Book, just click the Address Book button at the left side of the Desktop screen. Or, you can choose View ➤ Address Book from the Menu Bar. Or, press F3. The main window will switch over to display the Address Book.

 TIP   Mac users: Click the Contact List icon on the Toolbar or choose View ➤ Contact List from the Menu Bar.

To add a new entry:

1. With the Address Book open, click the New button at the bottom of the screen, or choose Edit ➤ New Address from the Menu Bar, or press Alt+N. This will open the Edit Address form, which you can see in Figure 10.19.

FIGURE 10.19

Adding a new name

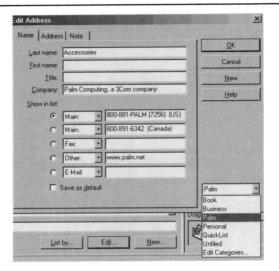

 TIP Mac users: Click the Create Contact icon on the Toolbar or choose Create ➢ Contact from the Menu Bar. Or, you can enter Apple+Option+C. Any of these will open an individual contact record and a form for entering information into that record (see Figure 10.20). By default, the Name Entry form will open. Fill in whatever information you'd like in this screen. When you're ready to add phone numbers, click in the Phones text box of the individual record. A form for adding phone numbers will open. To choose which phone number should display in the Contact List, click its check box. Follow this format to fill in all the information you'd like to add to this Contact.

2. Type the information you want to record in the appropriate text boxes of the form. You can add as much or as little information as you like.

3. Choose which phone number or e-mail address will display in the List View by clicking its radio button. You'll see a circle to show that it's selected.

4. Click the Address tab to add a street address for your contact.

5. Click the Note tab if you want to add a Note to this contact. Use this tab if you want to add a Note after you've added this contact to your Address Book.

6. Click OK when you're done entering information. The Edit Address form will close and the entry will be added to your Address Book.

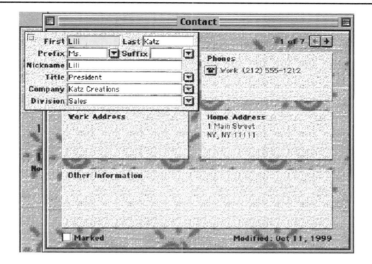

FIGURE 10.20

The Contact form

TIP   Mac users: Click the close box in the upper-left corner of the contact record when you're finished entering information.

To edit an Address Book (or Contact List) entry:

1. With the Address Book open, double-click the name of the person whose record you want to change. Alternatively, you can click it once to select it, then click the Edit button at the bottom of the screen. Or, you can select the entry with a single click then right-click to display the pop-up menu. Select Edit from this menu. The Edit Address form will open.

TIP   Mac users: Double-clicking the entry from the Contact List will open the individual contact record. Click in the Names, Phones, Address, or Other Information box to open the editing form. Make all your changes and repeat in the other boxes of the record.

PART

II

The Applications

2. Select any information you want to change by clicking and dragging, then type the new information. Whatever you enter will replace the old information.

3. Click OK when you're finished editing. The Edit Address form will close and you'll be back in the Address List.

 TIP Mac users: Click the close box in the upper-left corner of the contact record when you're finished editing. The contact record will close, and you'll be back in the Contact List.

Looking Up A Name

If your Address Book list is very long, scrolling probably isn't an efficient way to find just who you're looking for. Instead, let the Palm Desktop find the name for you.

To look up a name:

1. With the Address Book open, start typing the name you want to find in the Look up text box at the bottom of the screen. After you type just a couple of letters, the Palm Desktop will highlight the first name in your Address Book List that matches what you've just typed.

2. If the highlighted name isn't the one you're looking for, keep adding letters until you get an exact match. You can open the record you want by double-clicking it, or, if the record is highlighted, by pressing the Enter key on your keyboard.

 TIP Mac users: You don't even need to have the Contact List open to locate a contact. Just click the Find icon on the Toolbar (it's the magnifying glass). This will open the Find dialog box, which you can see in Figure 10.21. Click the Contacts icon in this box, then start typing the name in the Starts With text box. A list of possible matches will appear in the dialog box. Either scroll through the list to find the name you want, or keep typing until you get an exact match. Double-click the name to open the contact record. (Or, click the name once, then click the Display button). This style of Find works on the Windows desktop, too.

FIGURE 10.21

FIGURE 10.21

The Finder of lost
Contacts

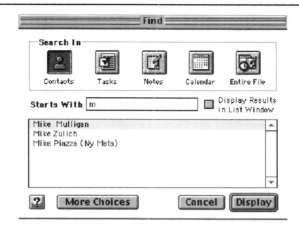

Categorizing Your Contacts

There's one big difference between how the Windows Desktop and its Macintosh counterpart handle categories. The Windows Desktop lets you assign just one category per contact (the same holds true for Memos and To Do List items). The Macintosh Desktop lets you assign up to two categories per item—and you can even categorize appointments.

To categorize a contact:

1. With the Address Book List open, double-click the name you want to assign to a category, or click the name once and click the Edit button. This will open the Edit Address form.

 TIP Mac users: You can double-click to open the record, then click in the Other Information box to access the proper form. Pick the category or categories you want to assign to this contact from the two drop-down menus at the bottom of the form (see Figure 10.22). Or simply click the contact once in the Contact List, then choose Edit ≻ Categories from the Menu Bar. Pick the category you want to assign from the list. Repeat this process to assign a second category.

PART

II

The Applications

FIGURE 10.22

Pick a category from the list.

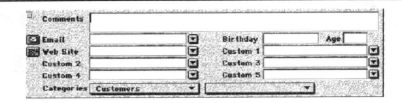

2. If it's not already selected, click the Name tab at the top of the form.

3. Click the arrow next to the Category box in the bottom-right corner of the form. This will drop down a list of category choices.

4. Pick the category you want from the list.

5. Click OK when you're done to close the Edit Address form and return to the Address Book List.

 TIP Mac users: Click the Close button in the top-left corner of the contact record to close the record and return to the Contact List.

Of course, you can create your own categories or edit the existing ones. Just choose Edit Categories from the Category drop-down list, and proceed as if you were editing categories on your Palm organizer.

If you add a category to the Palm Desktop that doesn't exist on your Palm organizer, it will be created for you upon your next HotSync—but only if you have HotSync set to either Synchronize the Files or Desktop Overwrites Handheld.

 TIP Mac users: You, too, can edit categories by choosing Edit Category from the drop-down list within a contact record form. Or, choose Edit ➢ Categories ➢ Edit Categories from the Menu Bar. Continue as if you were working on your Palm organizer.

You can do a number of other things with the Address Book (aka Contact List), including renaming custom fields, attaching notes, and deleting entries. You'll have to figure that stuff out on your own. We've given you a good grounding in the basics and introduced the menus and dialog boxes you'll need.

If you're not sure how to start, try the techniques we laid out for you in the Date Book section—chances are excellent that they'll work.

The To Do List

As we've mentioned before, the To Do List in the Windows Desktop is known as the Task List in the Macintosh version. But this is not the only difference between the two.

In the Windows version, the To Do List displays a list of items on the left and details of the To Do you've selected on the right. You can see this in Figure 10.23.

FIGURE 10.23

The Windows To Do List

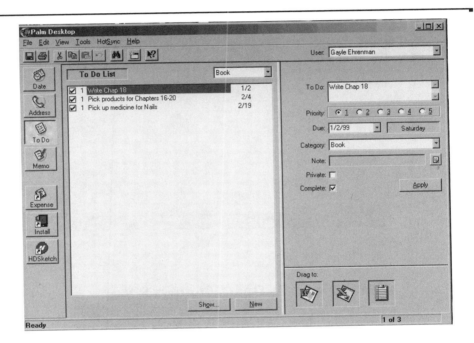

In the Macintosh version of the Desktop the Task List looks a lot like the Contact List—everything in columns spread across the screen. The name of the task appears in the left column, followed by columns for the Priority, Due Date, Category, and Completed Date. Double-clicking a task from the list will open its individual record, which displays the same information as the Task List. You can see both the list and an individual task record in Figure 10.24.

Working with To Dos: Windows Style

Much as it may seem like your To Do List adds items by itself, you are actually the one in control. We list everything you can do with a To Do in the following series of steps. You don't have to set all these options at once. You can return to a particular To Do to change options any time by simply clicking it in the To Do List.

To add a To Do to your list:

1. With the To Do List open, click the New button at the bottom of the screen (or choose Edit ➤ New To Do from the Menu Bar, or press Alt+N). A rectangle appears after the currently selected To Do List item, and the insertion point appears in the To Do text box on the right side of the screen.

2. Type the text of your To Do in the text box on the right side of the screen.

3. Assign a Priority to your To Do by clicking one of the radio buttons next to Priority on the right side of the screen. A black dot will appear to show you which priority is selected.

4. Assign a Due Date for your To Do by clicking the down arrow next to Due. This will drop down a menu of choices. Click either Today, Tomorrow, One Week Later, No Date, or Choose Date. If you click Choose Date, the Select Date dialog box will open. Click the date you want to assign to your To Do, then click OK to close this box.

5. Assign a Category to your To Do by clicking the Category box. A drop-down menu of choices will appear. Click the category you want to assign to this To Do, or click Edit Categories to add, rename, or delete a category. This will open the Edit Categories dialog box. Click New to create a new category, then proceed the same way you would to create a new category on your Palm organizer. Or, click the name of a category and then Rename or Delete to carry out one of those actions.

6. Click the Note icon to add a note to this To Do. The Note Editor will open. Type in the text of your note, then click OK to close the Note Editor and return to the To Do screen.

7. Click the check box next to Private to mark the note private.

8. Click Complete if you want to mark this To Do complete.

PART

II

The Applications

9. Click Apply when you're finished setting options. All the choices you made will be reflected in the To Do List. To cancel To Do input, click anywhere else in the application. This discards your changes.

Once you've categorized your To Do List items, you'll want to view them by category. To do this, just click in the Category box in the upper-right corner of the left pane of the To Do List. This will drop down a menu of To Do List categories. Click the one you want to display, and the To Do List will change to show only those items assigned to the category.

You can also determine what gets displayed in the list side of the screen. Click the Show button at the bottom of the screen (or press Alt+O) to open the Show Options dialog box.

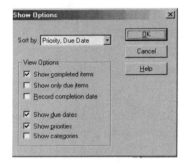

Here you can choose how to sort To Do List items; whether or not to display completed items; whether to record the date an item was completed; and whether or not to display the due date, priority, and category of To Do List items. You pick the Sort By option from a drop-down menu (click in the Sort By box, then pick an item from the list). The other options are all simple check box choices: Click in the check box to select it; click again to deselect the option. Click OK when you've finished setting options; the Show Options dialog box will close and you'll return to the To Do List, which will have changed to reflect your selections.

Working with Tasks: The Macintosh Way

Don't be confused: A Task is merely a To Do that lives on your Mac. It still needs to be created, categorized, and completed.

To create a Task:

1. Click the Create Task icon on the Toolbar (or choose Create ➤ Task from the Menu Bar). The Task dialog box will open, as in Figure 10.25.

FIGURE 10.25

A tisket, a task-et.

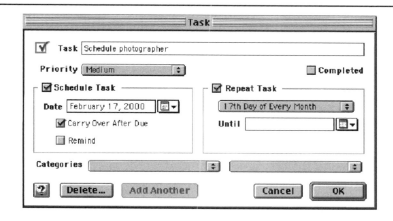

2. Type the text of your To Do in the text box next to the word Task.

3. Tap in the box next to Priority to see a drop-down list of priorities you can choose from. Click one to assign that priority to your task.

4. Click in the Schedule Task check box to assign a Due Date to this task.

5. Enter a due date in the Date box, or click the calendar button next to that box to pick a due date from the pop-up calendar.

6. If you want the task to stay on your Task List after its due date is passed, click the Carry Over After Due check box.

7. Click the Remind check box if you want to be reminded that this task still needs to be completed. Type in the number of days prior to the due date that you should be reminded in the Days Before box.

8. Click in the box next to Categories to access the drop-down list of categories. Click one in the list to assign the task to that category. Repeat the process in the next Category box if you want to assign a second category to the task.

9. If you've completed the task, click the Completed check box.

10. If this task will be a regular occurrence, click the Repeat Task check box.

11. Click the Repeat box to see a drop-down menu of Repeat options. Click one of these choices to select it.

12. Specify an end date for the recurring task by typing in a date in the Until box or by clicking the Calendar icon, then pick a date from the pop-up calendar.

13. If you want to create another task, click the Add Another button, and start over. Otherwise, click OK to close the Task dialog box and return to the Task List.

PART

II

The Applications

Of course, you don't have to set all these options at once. Just double-click a task from the Task List to open the Task dialog box. From there, you can set any of the options we just specified.

You have a few options for how items are displayed in the Task List. Click the View box in the upper-left corner of the Task List to decide whether to see All Tasks, This Week Uncompleted, or Today–Uncompleted. You'll also see options for Memorize View and Delete View. Choosing Memorize View will bring up the Memorize View dialog box; this box lets you specify a name for the view, and whether or not to memorize the Current Sort, Column Arrangement, and Window Positions. With the exception of naming the view, all these choices are made through check boxes.

The Current Sort refers to how you currently have your Task List columns sorted. You sort columns by clicking the down arrow next to the Column name, then choosing Sort from the pop-up menu. This will sort the Task List using that column as the primary criteria. For example, clicking Priority will sort the Task List so that the items you've assigned the Highest Priority are at the top of the list, followed by those of High priority on down.

Alternatively, you can set the sort order by choosing View ➤ Sort from the Menu Bar. This will open the Sort dialog box, as in Figure 10.26.

FIGURE 10.26

Click and sort.

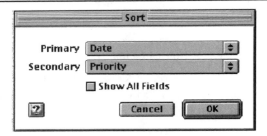

By clicking the Primary and Secondary boxes, you can choose two criteria for sorting the Task List. We generally find using Date as the Primary sort criteria and Task as the Secondary to be the best arrangement. This orders the Task List by Date (with oldest Tasks at the top of the list), and alphabetically (with multiple Tasks assigned to the same Due Date arranged from A to Z).

Sorting the Task List via the Menu command will override any manual sorting you've done by clicking the column sort options.

Now that you've got the To Do List down, let's move on to the Memo Pad.

The Memo Pad (or The Note List)

It's been awhile, so we'll remind you that the Macintosh version of the Palm Desktop calls the Memo Pad the Note List. But what's in a name anyway?

We've shown you how to attach a note to various items, but now we'll show you how to create a free and independent note. It's quick, it's painless, and you'll love it—just wait and see.

In some ways, creating a memo or note with the Desktop software is easier than creating one on the Palm organizer. If you're like most people, it's easier and quicker for you to type out a block of text than it is to enter it using Graffiti or the Palm's on-screen keyboard.

Both the Windows and Macintosh versions of the Palm Desktop present a List View of all your memos (or notes, on the Mac side). Creating memos is a very different process on the two different Desktops.

Working with Memos: The Windows Way

Let's start by switching over to the Memo Pad screen. To do this, either click the Memo Pad button on the Launch Bar, choose View ➤ Memo Pad from the Menu Bar, or press the F5 key on your keyboard.

The Memo Pad screen looks a lot like those of the Address Book and the To Do List. You'll see a list of all your memos in the left pane of the screen, and the text of the memo you've selected on the right side. If you can't see all the text, just click the scroll arrows along the right edge of the right-hand pane to scroll through the memo. Alternatively, you can click in that text box, then hit the Page Down or Page Up keys on your keyboard (or use the directional arrow keys) to navigate through a long memo.

To create a memo:

1. With the Memo Pad open, either click the New button at the bottom of the screen, choose Edit ➤ New Memo from the Menu Bar, or press Alt+N. A rectangle will appear at the bottom of your Memo List, and the insertion point will appear in the text box on the right side of the screen, as in Figure 10.27.

2. Type in the text of your memo in the text box.

3. Click the Apply button at the bottom of the memo text side of the screen. The title of your memo (its first line) will appear as the last item in the Memo List.

 TIP You can copy and paste text into a memo from a word processing document, another memo, or even from a Web page. Select the text you want to copy, then press Ctrl+C. This places the information on the Windows clipboard. Switch to the Palm Desktop Memo Pad, click the memo you want to paste the text in (or start a new memo), then press Ctrl+V. The copied text will now be in your memo.

PART

II

The Applications

FIGURE 10.27

The Memo Pad screen, ready for text

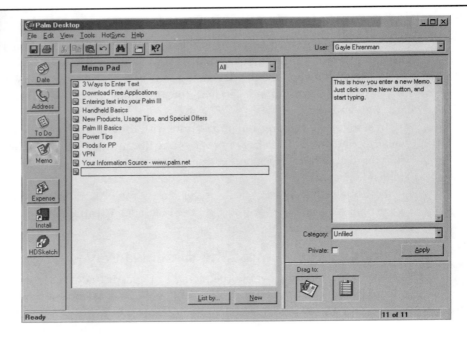

4. Click in the Category box to see the drop-down list of Categories. Click one from the list to assign it to this memo.

5. If you want to mark this memo private, click the Private check box. A check-mark will appear in the box. A key will appear next to the name of any memos you marked private next to their names in the Memo List.

 TIP Choose View ➤ Hide Private Records from the Menu Bar to eliminate those items from the Memo List. Choose View ➤ Show to add them back to the display.

6. Click Apply when you're satisfied with your choices.

Once you've categorized your memos, you'll want to view them by category. To do this, just click in the Category box in the upper-right corner of the left pane of the Memo List. This will drop down a menu of memo categories. Click the category you want to display, and the Memo List will change to show only those items assigned to that category.

Making Memos: Macintosh Style

OK, so they're really Notes. We just couldn't resist the alliteration. Whatever you call those text-based things that aren't Contacts, Appointments, or Tasks, they still serve the same purpose: They give you a convenient way to save text.

You don't have to open the Note List to create a new note, but you do need to have it open to see them all. To open the Note List, click the Notes List button on the Toolbar, or choose View ➤ Note List from the Menu Bar.

The Note List screen looks a lot like the Contact List and Task List. It displays a series of columns in a single window, as in Figure 10.28.

FIGURE 10.28

The Note List

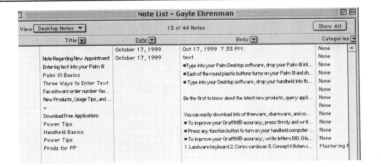

The title of the note appears in the left column, followed by column's Date, Body, and Categories. You can adjust the width of a column by clicking an edge and dragging out to make it wider or narrower.

In the top-left corner of the Note List is the View box. This lets you access a unique feature of the Mac Desktop: the ability to see just the freestanding notes you've created or to see every note you've created, including the ones attached to a Contact or To Do. Click in the box next to View to see your choices. Choose Desktop Notes to display only the freestanding notes or All to see every note you've created. When All Notes are displayed, the ones that are attachments will have a file folder icon next to their title.

Double-clicking a note from the list will open its individual record, which displays the same information as the Note List in a more readable form.

To create a note:

1. Click the Create Note button on the Toolbar. This will open the Note screen, as in Figure 10.29.

FIGURE 10.29

A nifty new note

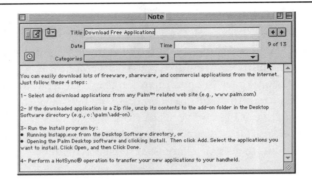

2. Type a name for your note in the Title box.

3. Enter a date for your note in the Date box. By default, the date will be set to the current date.

4. Enter a time for your note in the Time box. By default, the time will be set to the current time.

5. Click the Category box to see a drop-down list of categories. Click one to assign it to this note. Repeat this step using the second Category box if you want to assign two categories to this note.

6. Click the alarm clock icon if you want to add the current date and time to the text of your note.

7. Click in the white text box and start entering the text for your note.

8. If you want to attach this note to a Contact or Task or Appointment, click the file folder icon in the upper-left corner of the Note box. This will pop up a list of choices. Click one of these Attach To choices to attach the note to a new or existing item.

9. Click the close button in the upper-left corner of the box to close the note.

That covers most of the note-able features of Macintosh notes. Now let's move on to archiving.

Archiving Old Records

By now, your Palm organizer is probably starting to fill up with records and applications. It may even be running out of memory. No biggie. You can clear stuff out from your Palm and save it on your desktop PC, just in case. That's why your Palm organizer has a Purge option for items that are older than a specified time period in the Date Book and completed items in the To Do List. The Purge feature gives you an option to save an archive copy of purged items on your desktop PC.

 TIP For more on how to purge items, turn back to Chapters 5 and 6.

You can also choose to save an archive copy of all deleted items. The only way to view and manage archived items is through the Palm Desktop software.

To view an archived item on the Windows Desktop:

1. Open the application you want to view the archive for. If you want to view archived memos, click the Memo Pad button on the Launch bar.

2. Choose File ➤ Open Archive from the Menu Bar. This will open the Open Archive dialog box.

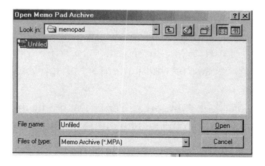

3. Click the name of the archive file you want to open. You will see a file for each category of records you deleted. For example, if you deleted and archived records from the Business and Personal categories, you'll see archive files for each of those. Since Datebook events can't be categorized, you'll just see one archive file for all deleted and archived Datebook items.

4. Click OK to open the archive you selected.

In the lower-left corner of the Palm Desktop status bar you will see the word Archive. The Palm Desktop title bar will read CategoryofDeletedItem.MPA (Archive). This indicates you are working with an archive file. Don't worry if you don't see all the items currently in your organizer—they're still safely tucked away in your current file.

Everything that was in that memo will appear as a new list of items in the Palm Desktop application you were working in. Archived items that were assigned categories will maintain those categories.

To return to your current data set, simply Select File ➢ Open Current. Now, we're guessing that if you opened an archive, it's probably because you accidentally deleted an item you'd like to get back (either that or you're hopelessly nostalgic). To recover an archived item:

1. Follow the steps above to open the archive. This archive can be a Memo, To Do, Address, or Date archive.

2. Find and then click the item(s) you want to restore to your Palm organizer. A bar will appear over the item to show that it's selected. You can select multiple items by pressing Shift+click (to select consecutive items) or Control+click to select non-consecutive items.

3. Press Ctrl+C to copy the item, or choose Edit ➢ Copy from the Menu Bar. The item will be copied to the Windows Clipboard, but you won't get any indication that this has happened.

4. Choose File ➢ Open Current from the Menu Bar. Your current set of application data will appear, opened to the application you were working in.

5. Press Ctrl+V or choose Edit ➢ Paste from the Menu Bar. The archived item will be pasted in to your current set of application data, and will appear selected in the List.

6. Place your Palm organizer in the cradle and perform a HotSync to restore the previously archived item onto your organizer.

On the Macintosh Desktop, the process is almost the same. But the way the Mac handles archives is very different. Where the Windows desktop creates a separate archive file for each application, category, and user (so you wind up with an Address Book archive, a Date Book archive, a To Do List archive and a Memo Pad archive), the Mac creates just a single archive file per user. It calls this file User Data Archive. To find it, go to the folder for Palm ➢ Users ➢ your username.

To open a Mac archive:

1. Choose File ➢ Open from the Menu Bar. This will open the File Open dialog box, as in Figure 10.30.

FIGURE 10.30

Pick a Mac archive.

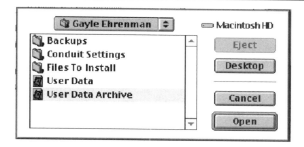

2. Click the name of the archive file you want to open.

3. Click OK to open this archive. You'll see all its information within the various application lists.

Follow the instructions from the Windows desktop list to restore archived items to your Palm organizer.

Don't go restoring everything from an archive to your Palm organizer, or you'll soon be out of space again. Just think of archiving as a safety net for when you absolutely must get an item or two back from oblivion.

If your Palm organizer should ever lose all its data, you'll want to restore it from the backup file created when you HotSync. Turn back to Chapter 9 for help on restoring.

PART III

Your Palm and the Outside World

LEARN TO:

- *Configure and use the Palm modem*

- *Perform a modem HotSync*

- *Use e-mail*

- *Access the Web and e-mail with the Palm VII*

- *Browse the Web*

- *Send faxes*

CHAPTER **11**

Getting Ready to Communicate

The Palm's size and weight makes it easy to carry everywhere you go—that's exactly what Palm Computing would like you to do. And why not? You use it to store your address book, make memos, carry around handy little programs to make your personal and business life a little easier. What else can you do? Well, how about surf the Web, download your e-mail, or send faxes. All you need is a Palm modem, a phone line, and about five minutes to configure the appropriate software. Doesn't get much easier than that.

 NOTE Turn to Chapter 20 for information on the modems available for your Palm device—there are several varieties available. In Chapter 12, we'll look at using the Palm and the modem to access e-mail. Turn to Chapter 14 to learn about browsing the Web through your Palm. Lastly, everything you need to know about faxing through your Palm is covered in Chapter 15. Palm VII users should turn to Chapter13.

And if all of the above wasn't reason enough to get a modem for your Palm device, how about HotSync via modem? Yes, that's right, HotSync via modem. That means that you don't need to be anywhere near your Palm cradle to update the contents of your Palm Desktop software. So, let's get started.

Setting Up Your Modem

Some communications devices are complex and some are simple—if you find a simple one, let us know! Generally, setting up a modem is anything but simple, especially if you've tried setting up that modem on your PC. What with interrupts, IRQs, and memory addresses, you could spend hours getting everything to work properly. Well, that's definitely not the case with the Palm modem. Nothing could be simpler, really.

The Palm modem is one of the easiest hardware accessories to install since it basically just clips onto the Palm. Here's what you need to do:

1. Remove the modem from its box and install the two AAA alkaline batteries. Be mindful of the batteries' orientation (its positive and negative ends). The battery compartment in the modem illustrates the correct position. Remember, the positive end of the battery has the pimple.

2. Connect the modem to the Palm device. The 10-pin connector at the bottom of the Palm device must mate smoothly with the 10-pin connector on the modem. This process is exactly like placing the Palm into its cradle.

3. Be sure that the Palm snaps into place. There is a mechanical latch on the back of the Palm V modem and one on the sides for the modem that fits the Palm III series and Palm VII. Be sure that this latch is engaged.

4. Connect an analog telephone line to the modem using the standard RJ11 connector. A 6-foot extension cable with RJ11 connectors is included with the modem. Analog telephone lines are the standard phone lines used in just about every American home. The RJ11 connector is that square, clear plastic connector on the end of all telephone lines.

 WARNING   Do not connect your modem to a digital telephone line, like those available in most offices and hotels. These lines will not work with your modem and can cause permanent damage. If you should connect your modem to a digital line by accident, the modem will emit five beeps as a warning. Disconnect the line and look for another. If you are in a hotel, be sure to use the line marked data port, fax line, or modem line.

Under normal operating conditions, you should be able to eke out about two hours of modem use or 150 HotSyncs per set of AAA batteries for a Palm V modem or four hours of continuous use with a Palm III series or Palm VII modem. When you've run down the battery life to about 20 percent, the modem will emit three short beeps as a reminder that you'll soon need new batteries. A Palm V modem will repeat the beeping in 5-minute intervals until the batteries are dead or you insert fresh batteries. A Palm III series or Palm VII modem will beep when you have four minutes of battery life left, and then beep at you every minute until either it totally dies or you get fed up and change the batteries.

Setting Up Your Palm Device to Work with the Modem

Chances are that your Palm will work just fine with the Palm modem; as we stated earlier, it is one of the simplest add-on devices. But just in case you feel the need to tweak the settings (or understand what they are), we'll take a look at each.

All of the modem settings are made through the Palm's Preferences screen. Turn on your Palm and tap the Applications soft button, then the Prefs icon to open the Preferences screen. From here you can make various choices (by default, the Palm OS sets each of the following preferences for you).

PART

III

Your Palm and the
Outside World

1. In the upper-right corner of the Preferences screen, tap the Category pick list and select Modem. This will open the Modem Preferences screen, which you can see in Figure 11.1.

The Modem Preferences screen

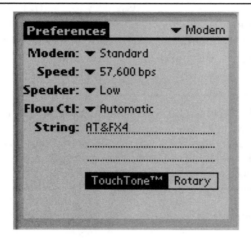

2. Tap on the arrow next to Modem to see a drop-down list of all of the available modem alternatives. Select your modem from the list. Remember, you must select the exact model from this list for the modem to work properly.

3. Tap the arrow next to Speed to see a drop-down list of modem speed options. Tap on the speed you want to select. You should select the maximum speed that your modem will allow.

4. Tap the arrow next to Speaker to see a drop-down list of speaker volume options. Select the speaker volume setting that meets your needs. By default, the Palm OS selects Low, but you can choose Medium or High, or even turn off the speaker if you like.

5. Tap the arrow next to Flow Control to see a drop-down list of options for modifying the modem's transmission buffer. The modem uses this buffer to hold data as it is received and sent, ensuring that it never experiences an overflow or underflow condition. It's best to leave this setting at automatic and let the Palm OS handle the details.

6. Depending on your Palm device you may or may not have a Country pick list. If you do, select the country you are in.

7. The String field should be left untouched. This field uses standard AT commands (ATtention commands used by all modems) to fine-tune its operation. Unless you are familiar with AT commands, you should accept the default.

8. The TouchTone/Rotary setting allows you to select the type of phone line you are using. The default is TouchTone, which is the standard in just about every part of the U.S. However, there are still many communities that use the old rotary style telephone service. Select the service supported in your area.

Setting Up Your Palm to Connect to the Internet

Through the Preferences screen, you can also set up the Palm to connect to the Internet. Once on the Internet, you can browse the Web, download e-mail, or send faxes. As we mentioned earlier, the Palm OS will generally handle all of the Preference settings for you. But if you must tinker, here's what you need to do and know. Turn on your Palm and tap the Applications soft button, then the Prefs icon to open the Preferences screen.

1. In the upper-right corner of the screen, tap the Category pick list and select Network to view all of the available Internet service alternatives. This will open the Network Preferences screen, which you can see in Figure 11.2.

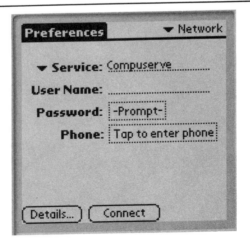

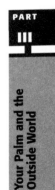

PART

III

Your Palm and the Outside World

2. From the Service pick list, select your Internet Service Provider (ISP), such as CompuServe.

TIP If your ISP is not listed, tap the Menu soft button to access the Menu Bar, then choose Service ➤ New. This creates a new connection service. Enter the name of the service on the Service line, then tap the Details command button. This will open the Details screen where you can specify settings unique to your ISP, such as Connection Type, Idle Timeout, and IP Address. If you're not sure what these settings are, accept the defaults.

3. On the User Name line, enter your username for the ISP you selected above. This field displays only two lines of text though it will accept multiple lines. Remember to add any periods in your username, but leave off the @ and service name, as this is addressed in the previous field. This field should look like this: bill.gates.

4. Tap the Password field and enter your password for the selected ISP. Once you've entered the password, tap OK, and the Palm displays the word Assigned in the password field. You may choose to leave this field blank and enter your password during login. If you do, this field displays the word Prompt.

5. Tap the Phone field to open the Phone Setup screen, which you can see in Figure 11.3. On this screen, you can enter a telephone number and other settings. Enter the phone number for your ISP.

FIGURE 11.3

The Phone Setup screen

6. Tap the Dial prefix check box to enter any dialing prefixes, like a 9 to dial out of a phone switch.

7. Tap the Disable Call Waiting check box and add the appropriate numeric code to disable this feature. If you have call waiting and do not disable this feature while logging into your ISP, any incoming call will terminate your Internet session.

8. If needed, tap the Use Calling Card check box to charge the cost of this call to your phone company calling card. Enter the calling card number in the field. To ensure that your calling card number gets properly transmitted to the local phone company, you should add several commas before the calling card number. Each comma represents a two-second delay after dialing the ISP's phone number. The Palm OS default includes four commas for an eight-second delay. You may need more depending on your local carrier.

9. When you have included all of the appropriate information, tap OK to save the settings and return to the Network Preferences screen.

10. Tap Connect from the Network Preferences screen to call your ISP. While you are connected, a small blinking cursor will appear in the upper-right corner to the right of the Category listing.

 NOTE Before you can connect to your ISP, you'll need an Internet application, such as a Web browser or e-mail client, to take advantage of the ISP connection. See Chapters 12 and 14 for more information.

11. When you're finished accessing the Internet, return to the Network Preferences screen and tap Disconnect to close the connection.

 WARNING The Phone Setup dialog box settings described above are accurate for AT&T and Sprint long-distance services. For MCI long-distance, reverse the phone number and calling card information. That is, put the calling card information into the phone number field, and the phone number into the calling card field. As of this writing, we don't know how the MCI/Sprint merger will affect these fields.

Performing a Modem HotSync

Perhaps one of the most interesting aspects of the Palm and Palm modem combination is a modem HotSync. This means that you don't need to be anywhere near your desktop computer or the Palm's cradle to update information on the desktop or Palm.

PART

III

Your Palm and the
Outside World

> **NOTE** Before you can use your Palm's modem to HotSync remotely, you must perform at least one local (in the cradle) HotSync. You need to do this to set up the HotSync manager and Palm log files. Also, don't leave Modem set as your default HotSync method or you won't be able to use your desktop PC's modem for dialing out to the Internet.

Configuring the Palm Desktop Software

To perform remote HotSyncs, you first need to set up the HotSync manager on your desktop computer. Then set up your Palm's preferences to allow remote synchronization. To set up your desktop computer, perform the following:

1. Turn off all background communications programs, such as PC Anywhere, on your desktop computer.
2. Click the HotSync manager in the system tray, make sure that Modem is checked, and select Setup. This will open the Setup dialog box.
3. From the Setup Dialog box, select the Modem tab, which you can see in Figure 11.4.

FIGURE 11.4

The Setup dialog box

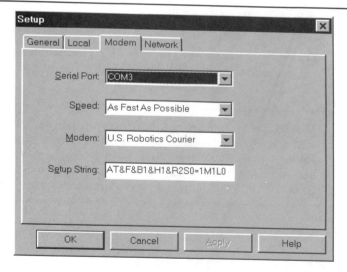

4. Ensure that all of the listed options accurately describe your desktop modem. If not, correct the discrepancies.
5. Click OK.

Configuring the Palm Device

Now you need to configure the Palm device for a remote HotSync. Follow these steps:

1. Tap on the Application soft button to open the Application Launcher. From the Application Launcher screen, tap on the HotSync icon. This will open the HotSync screen, as in Figure 11.5.

2. Below the Modem Sync icon, tap the Enter phone # field. This will open the Phone Setup screen, as in Figure 11.6.

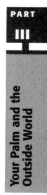

PART

III

Your Palm and the Outside World

3. On the Phone # line, enter the phone number that connects to your desktop computer's modem. For most of us that is our home or office phone number. Don't forget the 1 to access out-of-area code phone numbers.

4. Tap the Dial prefix check box to enter any dialing prefixes, like a 9 to dial out of a phone switch.

5. Tap the Disable Call Waiting check box and add the appropriate numeric code to disable this feature. If you have call waiting and do not disable this feature while logging into your ISP, any incoming call will terminate your HotSync session.

6. If needed, tap the Use Calling Card box to charge to cost of this call to your phone company calling card. Enter the calling card number in the field. To ensure that your calling card number gets properly transmitted to the local phone company, you should add several commas before the calling card number. Each comma represents a two-second delay after dialing the phone number. The Palm OS default includes four commas for an eight-second delay. You may need more depending on your local carrier.

7. When you have included all of the appropriate information, tap OK to save the settings and return to the HotSync screen.

8. Tap the Menu soft button to open the Menu Bar and then choose Options ➤ Modem Setup.

9. Setup your Palm modem as described above in the "Setting Up Your Palm Device to Work with the Modem" section.

Selecting Conduits for the HotSync

Now that you've configured the Palm Desktop software and the Palm device to accept a modem HotSync, you must select the applications you want to synchronize. You select these applications through the Palm device's Conduit Setup. Just follow these instructions:

1. Tap on the Application soft button to open the Application Launcher. Tap the HotSync icon to open the HotSync screen.

2. Tap the Menu soft button to open the Menu Bar, then choose Options ➤ Conduit Setup (see Figure 11.7). This will open the Conduit Setup screen.

FIGURE 11.7

Choosing Conduit
Setup

3. Tap the check boxes to select or deselect an application for the remote HotSync. The default is to synchronize all applications.

4. Tap OK to save your settings. The Conduit Setup screen will close and you'll return to the HotSync screen.

Completing the Modem HotSync

Once you have configured the Palm Desktop software, Palm modem, and Palm device, you are ready to perform a modem HotSync. To follow through on the modem Hot-Sync, do the following:

1. Connect the Palm modem to the Palm device, and connect the phone line to the modem.

2. From the Palm device, tap on the HotSync icon from the Application Launcher and tap the Modem Sync icon. Or, simply press the HotSync button on the modem.

3. Wait for the HotSync operation to complete before disconnecting the modem or phone line, or before powering down the Palm device. Turn to the next chapter to find out how to use your modem to access Internet e-mail.

PART

III

Your Palm and the
Outside World

CHAPTER 12

Using Your Palm as an E-mail Device

Surprising as it may seem, your Palm device maintains its well-earned likeness to a Swiss Army Knife by managing e-mail in addition to everything else that it does. You can download and read your e-mail, and create and send e-mail all through the built-in Mail application. Of course, unless you own a Palm VII, you'll need a modem to connect to your ISP/mail server. In this chapter, we'll look at the Palm's e-mail capabilities and features in more detail.

 TIP The Macintosh does not support the Palm Mail application. Mac users should turn to the section on third-party e-mail applications for information on tools that will work with that operaing system.

Using the Mail Application

The Palm's built-in e-mail application, which is simply called Mail, works like most any other e-mail client by providing all the e-mail management capabilities you need while you're away from your desk. The one thing that it can't do is connect directly to your e-mail service provider—for that you need to use your desktop computer's modem and whatever e-mail client you normally use on your desktop PC. Basically, the e-mail flows to your desktop computer, and a HotSync puts a copy on your Palm. This lets you collect all your e-mail, copy it onto your Palm device, and take the whole mess on the road. You can read all of your messages, delete the spam, reply to important messages, and be ready to upload the changes to your desktop computer once you're back in the office. Through the HotSync, any changes made on the Palm will reflect on the desktop and vice versa. So your e-mail inbox will always be the same on both devices. As you'll see, Mail is efficient and useful.

To configure e-mail synchronization between your desktop and your Palm:

1. From Windows Start, select Programs ➤ Palm Desktop, and then select Mail Setup. This starts the mail setup program. The first dialog box allows you to select a user. See Figure 12.1.

2. Select a user and Click OK.

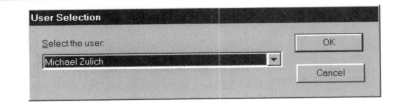

FIGURE 12.1

Select a user.

3. From the Mail Setup screen (see Figure 12.2), select your desktop e-mail application from the Synchronize With drop-down list and click Next. Mail Setup will configure the conduit, and then you simply click Finish on the final screen to complete the e-mail setup.

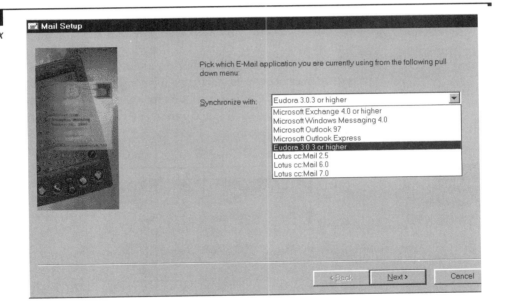

FIGURE 12.2

Mail Setup dialog box

PART

III

Your Palm and the Outside World

Next, you need to configure the HotSync Manager to handle your e-mail messages. You have several options to choose from, each offering a different set of features. To configure HotSync:

1. Click the HotSync icon in the system tray and choose Custom.

2. From the Custom dialog box (which you can see in Figure 12.3), highlight Mail and click the Change button.

FIGURE 12.3

HotSync's Custom dialog box

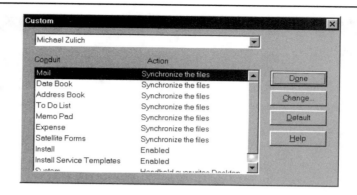

3. In the resulting Change HotSync Action dialog box (which you can see in Figure 12.4), you have three main options to choose from. Select the option that meets your needs and click OK. The Synchronize the Files option synchronizes all mail files between the Palm device and the desktop computer. The Desktop Overwrites Handheld option assumes that the desktop computer is always the master copy and is therefore always correct. Using this option, you will delete all of the e-mail on your Palm each time you HotSync. The last option, Do Nothing, does exactly that—essentially, this option turns off the e-mail synchronization.

FIGURE 12.4

Change HotSync Action dialog box

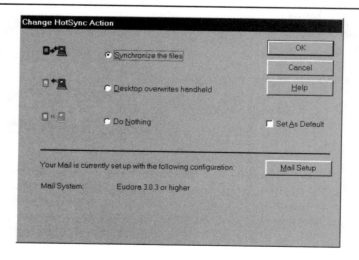

4. Once you have made your choice, you can click the Set As Default check box to set the above choice as the default option. Doing this means that the selected choice will be in effect until you actively make a change. If you do not choose this option, the custom settings will apply for the next HotSync only.

E-mail is now set up to run between your desktop computer and the Palm device. Download your e-mail through your desktop computer as you would normally do, and then HotSync. On your next HotSync, all your desktop e-mail will be synced to your Palm. It's that simple.

TIP If you want to keep your mail HotSyncing to a minimum, keep your e-mail client's inbox clean. We prefer to filter all mail from mailing lists to a separate folder, so those hundreds of messages don't get passed to the Palm Mail application. To do this, use the filtering features of your desktop e-mail client.

You can view and read e-mail on your Palm by tapping the Mail icon in the Application Launcher. This opens the mail Message List (see Figure 12.5), which lists your downloaded e-mail in two columns: the left-hand column displays the sender's address while the right-hand side displays the subject line. This information is truncated due to the Palm's diminutive screen, but you get enough of this data to make sense of the message. Additionally, at the very top of the screen, the Palm OS lists the number of messages currently in your Palm inbox and the number of unread messages that you have. Urgent messages are in bold, and messages previously opened, say on the desktop, are preceded by a small checkmark.

FIGURE 12.5

The Message List

You can sort the Message List e-mail just like you can on any full-featured desktop application. The Palm OS and the Mail application allow you to alphabetize your mail based upon the sender's e-mail address, the message subject, or the date sent. The date that you received the message is stored along with the sender's e-mail address and subject, but by default the date is not displayed. To show the date or to sort your e-mail messages by date, tap the Show button at the bottom of the screen. This returns the Show Options dialog box. From the drop-down list, select the sort column. Tap the Show Date check box to add the date field to the e-mail Message window.

To open any message, just tap anywhere on the sender's address or the subject area of the message. Once you've opened a mail message (as in Figure 12.6), you'll have fullview of the message, not truncated bits, though you won't have fullview of the header information. To save display space, the Mail Application only displays the To:, From:, Subj:, and Date: fields along with the message itself. If you desire more header information, like a CC: list, then tap the Complete Header Mode icon in the upper right-hand corner of the screen. The Abbreviated Header Mode icon, also in the upper right-hand corner of the screen and to the left of the Complete Header Mode icon, will return the message to its abbreviated form.

FIGURE 12.6

The Mail Message screen

You can create e-mail messages on your Palm device and then HotSync them to your desktop for transmission to your e-mail service. This useful feature lets you use your Palm to compose messages while on the road. To create a message, follow these steps:

1. From the Mail application on your Palm device, tap the New button in the lower left-hand corner. This opens the New Message window with To:, CC:, Subj:, and Body: fields. You can see this screen in Figure 12.7.

FIGURE 12.7

The New Message screen

2. Tap the To: field and enter the complete e-mail address of your recipient using Graffiti or the Palm's built-in keyboard.

 TIP You can find a recipient's mail information quickly by using the Look Up feature. Choose Options ➢ Look Up from the Menu Bar, then enter the first few letters of the name you want to find on the text line of the Look Up screen. The list of names will scroll to the name that matches your entry. Tap on the name to add it to the To: line of your message.

3. Tap the CC: field to enter the e-mail address of any copy recipients. Use a comma followed by a blank space to separate multiple CC: recipients.

4. Tap the Subj: field to enter the message's subject.

5. Tap the Body: field to enter the message's text.

6. Tap the Send button in the lower left-hand corner to queue the message for transfer at the next HotSync.

Replying to a previously received e-mail message is even easier than creating an e-mail message from scratch. To reply to an e-mail:

1. From the Message list, tap anywhere on the message to open the message.

2. Tap the Reply button at the bottom of the screen. This will return the Reply Options dialog box.

PART

III

Your Palm and the
Outside World

3. Tap the options that meet your needs. The Include Original Text check box will attach the original message to your reply. The Comment Original Text option places a ">" before each line of the original message.

4. Tap OK to proceed to the reply screen.

5. The reply screen is the message screen. Add another e-mail address or cc someone, and compose your message.

6. Tap the Send button in the lower left-hand corner to queue the message for transfer at the next HotSync.

 NOTE HotSyncing transfers new mail to your desktop system's outbox or message queue. You will need to send mail from there to deliver your newly tapped messages.

We talked about the Send button at the bottom of both the New message and Reply message screens. The Cancel button is self explanatory, but we haven't described the Details... button. The Details... button is available wherever you are able to forward mail to your ISP. Pressing this button returns the Message Details dialog box with the following delivery choices:

• The mail Priority drop-down list allows you to apply a Low, Normal, or High priority to your message.

- The BCC check box allows you to forward a copy of this e-mail to someone without including their name(s) in the address header.

- The Signature check box attaches signature text to the message.

- The Confirm Read check box enables confirmation that the recipient has opened the e-mail. This, of course, does not confirm that they have read the message, just that they have opened it. All confirm read options work this way.

- The Confirm Delivery check box sends a confirmation back to you that the recipient's e-mail system has received the message for delivery to the addressee.

All of this message handling leads to one thing, and one thing only: you must HotSync your Palm device to your desktop computer in order for the e-mail to go anywhere. Once you've run a HotSync, the messages will move from the Palm to your desktop e-mail application and wait there until you connect to your ISP. The next time you connect to your ISP and send your desktop e-mail, your Palm edited/created messages will be on their way. When sending mail, the desktop e-mail application usually picks up new e-mail messages, too. Then, depending upon the HotSync options that you selected, HotSync will or won't copy those new e-mails to the Palm device.

If you choose to sync all e-mail to your Palm, then you may be interested in filtering the mail to further refine the download. Through a Palm filter, you can more precisely determine the type of messages to download. To create a Palm e-mail filter, perform the following:

1. Tap the Mail icon in the Application Launcher.

2. Press the Menu soft button.

3. From the Menu Bar, choose Option ➤ HotSync Options.

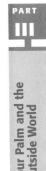

4. Select the Local HotSync setting from the Settings for drop-down list.

5. Beneath that selection are the four main filter options available to you. Select the option that you desire.

- The All option synchronizes all of your e-mail (both incoming and outgoing) between your desktop computer and the Palm device.

- The Send Only option forwards all the outgoing e-mail from your Palm device to your desktop but does not pick up any incoming e-mail.

- The Filter selection allows you to set parameters for what mail gets downloaded. Through the Filter settings, you can build rules that accept only messages from a specific individual (or excludes all messages from that person) or only messages with a selected string of words. You build these rules through a combination of drop-down lists and text.

- The Unread option synchronizes only messages that you have not opened (read) on your desktop computer.

- The Truncate button allows you to adjust the maximum size of incoming messages. You can select a message size from as small as 250 characters in length to a maximum of 8000 characters. Be mindful that the longer the maximum size, the longer it will take to HotSync all of the information to your Palm. Also, allowing longer messages will more quickly eat up your Palm's available memory. On the flip side, choosing a message length that is too short will truncate the tail end of your messages.

6. Tap OK when you have selected your HotSync configuration.

 TIP We've only scratched the surface with the Palm's Mail application and suggest that you turn to the Palm Organizer Handbook for more details.

Third-Party E-mail Applications

If you find that the Palm's built-in Mail application just doesn't meet your needs, or if you desire a few more features (or bells and whistles), then take a look at these three e-mail applications. Before you do, however, here are a few industry-standard e-mail terms that are used throughout these applications.

IMAP4   The Internet Message Access Protocol 4 is designed for hand-held devices like the Palm. It allows you to download message headers and bodies separately so that you can reduce the amount of data transmitted, and subsequently reduce the amount of data stored on your Palm.

NNTP   The Network News Transfer Protocol is a sending and receiving protocol for news groups.

POP3   The Post Office Protocol version 3 is probably the most widely used e-mail protocol. Most ISPs support POP3.

SMTP   The Simple Mail Transfer Protocol, is *the* standard mail protocol.

MultiMail Professional

Though not unique, MultiMail Professional is unusual in that it supports e-mail retrieval directly to your modem-equipped Palm device. That means you don't need to be tethered to your desktop while you HotSync and obtain your e-mail, which can be a real bonus while on the road.

MultiMail Professional installs easily—just one PRC file. Once installed, MultiMail works in parallel to the standard Palm Mail application: that is, both applications remain on the Palm device so you can choose either e-mail application. Configuring MultiMail to interface to your ISP and to your e-mail account is pretty simple—just follow the included instructions. And reference Chapter 11 for information about configuring your Palm modem. You can see what MultiMail Professional looks like in Figure 12.8.

FIGURE 12.8

MultiMail Professional

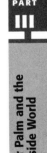

PART

III

Your Palm and the Outside World

As part of the install, MultiMail offers four e-mail protocols to chose from: IMAP, NNTP, POP3, and STMP4. Which option you choose depends upon your ISP's mail service.

MultiMail Professional lets you receive your mail and attachments, send mail, respond to incoming messages, and file incoming messages in a series of folders. This last feature is similar to that supported by any desktop computer's e-mail system. The caveat is that MultiMail Professional takes about 200KB of the Palm's precious memory and stored messages gobble up even more memory. So, be wise with the messages that you save.

MultiMail Professional is just a quick download away at www.actualsoft.com and costs $39.95.

Palmeta Mail

So you don't need or want to access your e-mail while on the road—at least not through your Palm device. But you'd love to read your e-mail and sort through the morass of office politics. Palmeta Mail may address your needs, and do so with a little more flair than the Palm OS Mail application.

Palmeta Mail requires a desktop computer with a modem to access your ISP, so it's more akin to the Palm Mail application than it is to MultiMail Professional. Nevertheless, Palmeta takes your e-mail (the e-mail from your desktop computer) and imports it to your Palm as MemoPad items whenever you HotSync. Palmeta also sets up Inbox, Outbox, and Sent categories on your MemoPad, so managing your e-mail becomes easy. You can read your messages and respond to those that you wish. These messages are held in the Outbox until the next HotSync, when they are sent to your desktop computer's e-mail application and forwarded to your ISP.

Like the Palm Mail application, Palmeta also copies the e-mail from your desktop computer so you will always have a copy there. Its real strength, however, is in its ability to handle complete e-mail messages, breaking the message into multiple parts.

You can configure Palmeta to interface to a multitude of e-mail programs, such as Netscape Communicator and Navigator, Microsoft Exchange, Windows Messaging, Outlook 97, Internet Explorer with Outlook Express 4, Eudora Pro and Lite, Microsoft Mail and Fax, Lotus Notes, and Novell Groupwise—applications not supported by Palm's standard Mail application.

You can download an evaluation copy of Palmeta Mail V1.73 from www.Palmgear.com. For $35.00 you'll receive a registration number that turns the time limited evaluation copy into a full-fledged, working copy.

HandMAIL 2.0

Similar in concept to MultiMail Professional, HandMAIL does not require a desktop computer to download e-mail. Using your Palm device and Palm modem, HandMAIL will interface directly to your ISP, and both download and upload e-mail. You can see it in Figure 12.9.

FIGURE 12.9

HandMAIL

HandMail is just as easy to use as its rival, MultiMail Professional, and provides a similar list of features and tools. In addition, HandMAIL supports AOL. HandMAIL requires a Palm modem to connect to your ISP, allowing you to access e-mail through virtually any telephone jack. No HotSync is required. HandMAIL also lets you create up to five different mailboxes on the Palm, so not only can your Palm handle your business mail, it can also handle your personal mail—and that leaves three more mailboxes.

HandMAIL is available from www.smartcodesoft.com for $49.95. This download includes everything that you'll need, from documentation to the PRC files.

PART

III

Your Palm and the
Outside World

CHAPTER 13

The Wireless Wonder: Accessing E-Mail and the Web with Your Palm VII

Y ou can set up any Palm organizer to send and receive e-mail and make an Internet connection, but it takes some doing. You need to get a modem, configure your Palm device to work with it, set up an account with an ISP, configure your Palm to work with the account, get e-mail and Internet software, and install that on your organizer. Then you're finally ready to link up with the outside world. Phew!

That approach is really your only alternative if you have any Palm organizer other than the VII. Fresh from the factory, your Palm VII has everything you need to send and receive e-mail and access the Internet.

The Palm VII communicates through the Palm.Net service, which functions as an ISP devoted to the Palm VII. All you have to do is activate your Palm.Net service and you're ready to go. If you haven't yet taken the Palm.Net plunge, turn back to Chapter 7 for instructions on getting started.

Managing Your Wireless Account

Way back in Chapter 7, we discussed all the things you can do through the Palm.Net application that comes installed on your Palm VII. But there are some Palm.Net account functions you can't control from your organizer. For those, you'll need to turn to the Palm.Net Web site (www.palm.net). Palm VII users should check in to this site regularly to find out what's new with their wireless service. We make it a regular stop on our surfing safaris.

The Palm.Net Web Site

If you haven't figured it out by now, the Palm.Net name covers multiple related applications. Palm.Net is the name of the network that provides wireless Internet service for the Palm VII; it's the name of the Query Application that lets you track your service usage from your Palm VII; and it's a Web site where you can manage your account, find new PQAs to download, and basically do anything you can do from the Palm.Net query application—plus a whole lot more.

You can find coverage maps on the Palm.Net Web site, which make it easy to figure out if wireless service is available in your area (see Figure 13.1). You can also check the status of your account from the site and even change your service plan and billing information. To perform these account management tasks, you'll need to log in with the username and password you created when activating your Palm.Net service. After that, making changes is easy.

There are also a couple of things you can do from the Palm.Net Web site that you can't do any other way—such as designating an address to receive copies of all your outgoing messages, and deleting blocks of messages. You carry out both of these actions through the My Account area of the Web site. You can see this area in Figure 13.2.

FIGURE 13.1

Does your area have coverage?

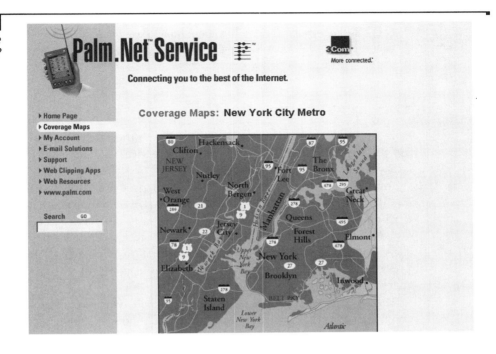

FIGURE 13.2

Specify a forwarding address

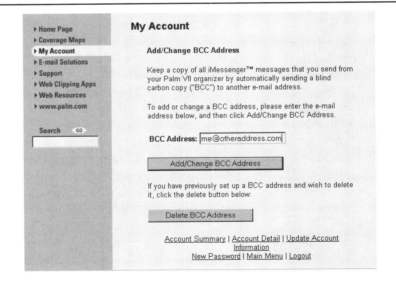

PART

III

Your Palm and the Outside World

NOTE We explain about more about how to use the Blind Carbon Copy feature and why you need it later in this chapter.

Which Service Plan Is Best?

Palm.Net service is either incredibly expensive or the bargain of the century, depending on how you use it. We'll help you pick a service plan and make the most of your kilobytes.

Initially, there were two Palm.Net service plans: the Basic Plan, which cost $9.99 for 50KB or approximately 150 Palm VII screens of data transmission; and the Expanded Plan, which costs $24.99 for 150KB or roughly 450 Palm VII screens of data transmission. Each kilobyte of data you send or receive in excess of your monthly allotment costs $.30. So, five screens of information (at about 1KB per screen) costs $1.50. That's about the average number of screens you're likely to traverse just to check baseball scores.

These plans work just fine for light-to-moderate wireless communication use, but you'll spend big money with these plans if you send lots of e-mail, check the sports news daily, or execute more than a couple of stock trades a month.

If you plan to use your Palm VII as your primary communications tool, you'll want to look in to the newly added Volume Plan. This one costs $39.99 per month for 300KB of usage, which works out to around 900 screens of information; you'll still pay $.30 per KB for every bit beyond the monthly allotment.

Most users would do well to start with the minimal level of service and see how much of their monthly transmission allotment they use. You'll need to do this for about two months before you'll get a clear picture of your wireless usage—it's the new toy factor at work. We blew almost a full month's worth of transmissions the first week we had our Palm VII, just because it was so much fun. After that, we tapered off to a more reasonable level.

Whichever plan you choose, you'll want to keep a couple of fundamental Palm.Net principles in mind. Remember that messages you send and receive count against your kilobyte allotments, as do Web clipping requests and the information that returns from those requests. Opening a PQA doesn't usually incur you any charges, because those applications are stored locally. (See "Web Clipping with Your Palm VII" later in this chapter for more on how PQAs operate.)

So, you probably should be selective in who you give your Palm.Net address to and limit its usage for checking your mail from other e-mail addresses. If you do need to interact with your standard, non-Palm.Net e-mail account, be sure to use the filtering tools built-in to both your desktop software and third-party Palm-based mail tools to keep from downloading anything but the most important messages. If you're like us and receive about 50 messages per day at just one e-mail address (and we have several addresses), you can easily exhaust a full month's service allotment in just one day if you're not careful. We've taken to filtering out the advertisements, newsletters and mailing list messages before downloading mail to our Palm VII. Sometimes, we'll filter out everything except mail originating from a particular user, such as our editor.

Beyond filtering your mail, you might want to consider using your Palm.Net account for sending messages, but redirect replies to an alternate, desktop PC–based mail address. We explain how to set this up in "The Inbox" later in this chapter.

Sending and Receiving Mail with iMessenger

If you've ever used an e-mail application, whether on your desktop PC or even the Mail application on the Palm, you'll have no trouble using the iMessenger wireless e-mail application on the Palm VII. iMessenger follows the basic organizing principles of every e-mail application on the planet.

The biggest difference between sending and receiving e-mail on the Palm VII and on your desktop PC is that on the Palm VII, you have to raise the antenna to make a connection. Other than that, the differences are minimal.

iMessenger Basics

Like most desktop-based e-mail applications, iMessenger is organized into a series of folders. There's an Inbox, where your newly received messages go; an Outbox, where messages wait to be sent; a Deleted folder, where the messages you deleted from the other folders linger; a Filed folder, where the messages you save are stored; and a Draft folder, where messages in progress are held. Each of these folders appears as a list, like the list view of the Mail application.

Be default, iMessenger opens to the Inbox. You access the other folders the same way you change categories in other Palm applications:

1. Tap the pull-down menu in the upper-right corner of the screen. You'll see a list of folders, as in Figure 13.3.

2 Tap the folder you want to open from the list.

PART
III

Your Palm and the Outside World

FIGURE 13.3

They're folders, not categories.

The biggest difference between the folders in iMessenger and the categories used by other applications is that the iMessenger folders are uneditable. You can't rename them, delete them, or add new ones. And, you can't arbitrarily move messages from one folder to another—with the exception of moving messages from Inbox to Filed or from Outbox to Draft.

Like other Palm applications, iMessenger has a Menu Bar and some options you can set. The two menus available from the Inbox are Message and Options. Under the Message menu, which you can see in Figure 13.4, you have one choice—Purge Deleted.

FIGURE 13.4

The Message menu

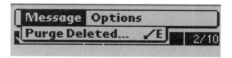

The Purge Deleted option comes in handy because deleting a message in iMessenger doesn't really make it go away. It just moves into the Deleted folder. If you want to rid yourself of messages from the Deleted folder, you have to use Purge Deleted. Just choose it from the Message menu, and those useless messages will be gone for good.

TIP The Deleted folder has a 50K maximum capacity. When Deleted reaches capacity, it automatically removes the oldest files in the folder from your system. This is the only time you don't have to purge files to get rid of them.

The Option menu offers more choices. Here, you can choose a font for displaying message lists (it works the same as in other Palm applications, so we won't explain it here), set Preferences, choose to Show Log, or find out About iMessenger. You can see the Option menu in Figure 13.5.

FIGURE 13.5

The Option menu

Preferences lets you decide how messages are displayed in the various message lists; any choices you make here will apply in all the iMessenger folders. You can see the Preferences dialog box in Figure 13.6.

FIGURE 13.6

iMessenger Preferences

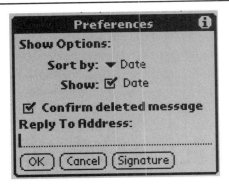

PART

III

Your Palm and the
Outside World

Preferences gives you the option to sort messages by:

- Date, which sorts messages by date in descending order, showing the most recent message at the top of the screen.

- Sender, which sorts messages by the sender's e-mail name, displaying messages in ascending alphabetical order based on the first word of the From field of a message.

- Subject, which sorts messages by subject in ascending alphabetical order.

By default, the message list includes a date column in its display (as in Figure 13.7). You can turn off this feature or reactivate it by tapping the Show Date check box in the Preferences dialog box.

FIGURE 13.7

Showing the Date

Show Date displays the date for messages downloaded on a different day than the one they were sent, or the time for messages downloaded on the same day they were sent. You may want to turn off this option to leave more room for displaying the From and Subject fields.

From the Preferences dialog box, you can also choose to confirm all deletions. Tapping the Confirm Deleted Message box activates this option. You'll see a confirmation dialog box when you choose to delete a message, as in Figure 13.8.

FIGURE 13.8

Are you sure you want to delete that message?

You'll also notice a Reply To Address line in the Preferences dialog box. This option lets you reroute replies to your messages to any e-mail address that you specify. Any messages you send from iMessenger will list your Palm.Net address in the From field. People who choose to reply to your message will automatically be sending messages back to this address, unless you redirect your mail using the Reply To Address option. To specify another address for replies, from the iMessenger Preferences dialog box:

1. Tap the edit line under the words Reply To Address.

2. Use Graffiti or the on-screen keyboard to enter the address where you want to receive replies to your messages. For example, you would enter me@another-address.com (see Figure 13.9).

3. Tap OK in the Preferences dialog box to accept this address and return to the message list.

There's one last option you can configure through the Preferences dialog box, though it's a bit hidden. Next to the OK and Cancel command buttons at the bottom of the screen, there's a third button labeled Signature. This button lets you specify a signature that you can add to messages you create. This signature can be different from the one you set in the Mail application. Also, your signature isn't automatically added to every message you create; you must choose to include it on a message-by-message basis. We explain how to add a signature to a message in the section on creating messages later in this chapter.

To create a Signature, with the iMessenger Preferences dialog box open:

1. Tap the Signature button at the bottom of the screen. This will open up the Signature screen.

2. Enter the text of your signature using Graffiti or the on-screen keyboard. Your text can be as long or short as you like. You can see an example of a signature in Figure 13.10.

PART

III

Your Palm and the Outside World

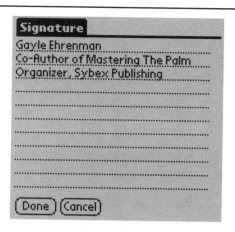

3. When you're satisfied with the text of your signature, tap Done to save the text. This will bring up the Signature dialog box, which explains how to add the signature you just created to your messages.

4. Tap OK to close this dialog box and return to the Preferences dialog.

That covers everything you can do through the Preferences dialog box, but there are two other choices on the Options Menu. These are Show Log, which displays a record of your most recent wireless transaction (see Figure 13.11) and About iMessenger, which displays the version number of the iMessenger application installed on your Palm VII.

The Inbox

By default, iMessenger opens to the Inbox message list screen. This screen displays a list of all the messages you've downloaded (except for those you've filed). It shows the e-mail address of the message sender, the subject of the message, and optionally, the date or time the message was sent. As you can see in Figure 13.12, messages you haven't read yet have a dash in the far-left column. Messages you have read are marked with a check. There is a third symbol you won't see in the Inbox—a diamond. This is used to indicate a message you created, so you'll only see it in the Outbox, Filed, Draft, and Deleted folders.

FIGURE 13.12

The Inbox
message list

From this screen, you can create new messages, open a message to read it, check for new messages, and set preferences for iMessenger (which we just finished explaining).

TIP Tap on the checkmark or dash next to the sender column to see a pop-up menu of commands you can carry out on this message from within the Inbox message list. Your choices (which you can see in Figure 13.13) include File and Delete Message. Tapping on File will move the message from your Inbox to the Filed folder; tapping on Delete Message will move the message to the Deleted folder; tapping on Read will open the message.

PART

III

Your Palm and the
Outside World

FIGURE 13.13

File that message the easy way.

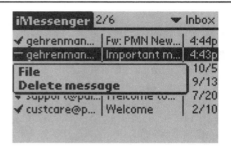

Creating and Sending Messages

Creating and sending messages with iMessenger couldn't be easier. You don't need to raise the Palm VII's antenna to access iMessenger or to create a new message. But, you must raise the antenna when you're ready to send your messages.

To create a new message, with the iMessenger application open to the Inbox message list:

1. Tap on the New command button at the bottom left of the screen. This will open the New Message screen. The To field will be highlighted.

2. You need to designate a recipient for your message. You can either enter their e-mail address using Graffiti or the on-screen keyboard, or you can look up a name from your Address Book.

3. To use the Look Up feature, tap on the Menu soft button to open the Menu Bar, then choose Options ➤ Look Up. This will take you to the Look Up screen, which you can see in Figure 13.14. Look Up will only display those entries from your Address Book that include an e-mail address.

FIGURE 13.14

Look up an address.

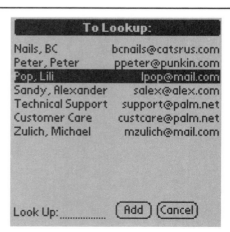

4. Scroll though the Look Up list using the scroll button or the on-screen scroll arrows until you reach the name you want. Tap the name to select it (you'll see a black bar over it to show that it's selected).

5. Tap the Add button to add this e-mail address to your message. This will return you to the New Message screen, where the name you selected will appear on the To line.

 TIP To add multiple recipients, follow step 2 or steps 3 and 4. If you enter names manually, make sure to separate them with a comma. If you add names via Look Up, the commas will be added automatically.

6. Tap the line next to Subj to add a subject for your message, using Graffiti or the on-screen keyboard.

7. Tap the line next to Body to compose the body of your message. Again, you can use Graffiti or the on-screen keyboard to complete this task. You can edit your message using the standard cut, copy, and paste functions accessible from the Edit menu.

8. When you're finished writing your message, either tap the Check & Send button at the bottom left of the screen or tap the Outbox button (next to Check & Send) to move the message to your Outbox. From there, the message will be sent the next time you log on to Palm.Net. If you choose Check & Send, the Palm VII will log on to Palm.Net, check for new messages, and send the message you just created. If you choose Outbox, you'll see the Send Later dialog box, as in Figure 13.15.

FIGURE 13.15

This message can wait.

PART

III

Your Palm and the Outside World

9. If you'd rather forget about this message for a while, tap the Cancel command button. You'll see the Save Draft dialog, as in Figure 13.16. If you tap Yes in this dialog box, your message will be moved to the Draft folder. If you tap No, the message will be deleted. Tapping Cancel will take you right back to the New Message screen, so you can work on your message some more.

FIGURE 13.16

Save it or trash it?

 TIP If you've moved a message to the Outbox, but changed your mind about it, don't panic. You can choose to delete the message, edit it some more, or move it into the Draft folder for future consideration. Go to the Outbox message list by tapping the drop-down folder list in the upper-right corner of the screen, then tap the diamond shape at the left of the recipient's name for the message you want to alter. (The diamond shape is used to indicate a message you composed.) This will bring up a pop-up menu of choices. From that menu, tap Move to Draft, Edit, or Delete message, depending on what you want to do. If you choose Edit, the message will open in a New Message screen.

But wait, before you send off that message, don't forget to add your signature—the one you created through the Preferences dialog box. To add your signature, with the message you just created open:

1. Tap the screen at the point in the body of the message where you want your signature to appear. In general, this will be at the very end of the message.

2. Tap the Menu soft button to open the Menu Bar.

3. From the Menu Bar, choose Options ➤ Add Signature (see Figure 13.17). The signature text you specified will appear in the body of the message.

FIGURE 13.17

*Paste in your
signature.*

TIP   You can also add a signature by entering the Graffiti command stroke, followed by a Graffiti Z.

Checking for New Messages

The best part about e-mail is getting messages. With iMessenger, the process of downloading new messages is simple—it's hard to get it wrong, as long as you remember to raise the antenna of your Palm VII before you try to retrieve your mail.

The process works virtually the same way it does in any standard desktop e-mail package. But, there are a few things you should know.

What You Can't Do With iMessenger

From an organizational perspective, iMessenger may look just like a desktop e-mail application, but it has some functional limitations those applications do not. These limitations are not oversights on the part of the Palm developers; rather, they've been put into place specifically to minimize the strain on iMessenger and the Palm VII's wireless communication capabilities. Here's a rundown on the limitations:

Message Length   iMessenger was designed to work with short messages. It can completely download messages with 500 or fewer readable characters. For messages with 500–50,000 characters, it downloads the first 500 characters and tells you how many characters are left to download. You can choose to download as much of the rest or the message as you like, or just ignore it. Messages with more than 50,000 characters are returned to sender as undeliverable—you will not receive any notification.

PART

III

Your Palm and the
Outside World

Download Capacity   iMessenger can only download a maximum of 60,000 characters in a single wireless transaction. If you have too many messages (or one that's too long) to download at once, you'll have to log back on to Palm.Net to retrieve the rest. You have 30 days from when you start downloading a long message to retrieve the remainder. After that, it's deleted from the Palm.Net network.

Distribution Lists   iMessenger offers only a To field; it does not support CC or BCC for messages you create or receive. If messages you receive use the unsupported fields, iMessenger tacks the names from those fields on to the end of the To list. Your address will always appear first in any distribution list. Sometimes, though, a distribution list may be truncated. This is because iMessenger allots a maximum of 300 of the first 500 characters to the distribution list. (A maximum of 100 characters of the first 500 goes toward the Subject field, and the remaining 100 characters are given over to the body of the message.) Any characters beyond the 300 allotted to the distribution list will be cut off; this is indicated by an ellipsis at the end of the distribution list.

Attachments   iMessenger doesn't do attachments. If someone sends you a message with a plain old ASCII text file attachment, iMessenger will append that text at the end of the body of the message. Other types of attachments just don't download; you'll get a warning that the message has a non-downloadable attachment when you open the message it belonged with.

Now that we've gotten all the technical stuff out of the way, let's start downloading mail.

To check for new messages, from the Inbox message list, just tap the Check & Send button at the bottom of the screen. This will download any messages waiting for you on the Palm.Net network, and send any messages you have queued up in the Outbox.

You'll see a Transaction Progress dialog box (as in Figure 13.18), which will let you know if your Palm VII succeeded in making a connection and if it completed the Check & Send operation.

FIGURE 13.18

*Progress in the
making*

Since iMessenger downloads no more than 10 messages at a time, the Transaction Progress dialog box will let you know if there are more messages waiting for you on the network.

You can tap the Cancel button at any time during a wireless transaction to end it. Keep in mind, though, that any messages downloaded before you cancel the connection will count against your monthly kilobyte allotment. So think before you check!

 NOTE You'll also see the Check & Send button in the list screen for all the other iMessenger folders. It works the same way all the time.

Reading Messages

When iMessenger finishes downloading messages, they go directly into your Inbox. All these messages are downloaded in compressed format to help them get to you a little bit quicker; the messages are automatically converted to an uncompressed format when you open them for reading.

To read a message, tap the message you want to read from the Inbox list screen. A full message screen will open. At the top of the message, you'll notice the header. By default, all you'll see is an abbreviated header displaying just the From and Subj lines.

Notice the two icons in the top-right corner of the screen—we're referring to the icons with the different number of lines on them (see Figure 13.19). These are the header icons.

FIGURE 13.19

The long and short of it

The icon with fewer lines on it, which will be highlighted when you first open a message, is the Abbreviated Header icon. The one with more lines is the Complete Header icon. Tap this icon now to see the full header for the message you have open.

With the Complete Header option active, you'll see not just the From and Subj lines, but also the To line and the Date, as in Figure 13.20.

FIGURE 13.20

*All the header info
you could ask for*

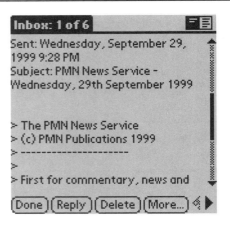

The Complete Header takes up a lot of screen real estate, but allows you to see everyone the message was sent to. In most cases, the Abbreviated Header will provide all the information you really need, and allow more of your message's body text to be displayed and read at a glance.

If your message is too long to fit on a single screen, you can scroll to see the rest by tapping the scroll bar along the right side of the screen or by using the Scroll button.

You can move to the previous message in the Inbox list by tapping on the left-most of the two arrows in the bottom-right corner of the screen. Tapping the arrow to the right takes you to the next message in the list.

 TIP You can open and navigate through messages in the other folders using these same techniques.

When you read a message that's longer than 500 characters, you'll see a button labeled More at the bottom of the screen, next to the Previous and Next navigation arrows. You can see what we mean in Figure 13.20 above.

Tap the More button and you'll see the Retrieve More dialog box. What you see in this box will depend on how many more characters remain to be downloaded. For messages with fewer than 500 character remaining, the Retrieve More dialog box will detail just how many more characters remain, and provide two buttons: Get Rest and Cancel. Tapping Get Rest will download the remainder of the message; tapping Cancel will leave the rest undownloaded and return you to the message screen.

If your message has more than 500 characters left to download, the Retrieve More dialog box will look more like the one in Figure 13.21.

FIGURE 13.21

*The text just keeps
coming.*

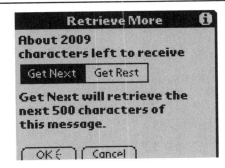

You'll still see how many characters are left to download, but you'll have the choice to Get Next, which retrieves the next 500 characters, or Get Rest, which downloads the remainder of the message. And, of course, you can choose to Cancel and forget the whole thing.

 TIP Unless you're absolutely certain that you need the full text of that long message, don't download it all. You're paying for every KB you download, one way or another.

No matter how long the message is that you're reading, you'll see Done, Reply, and Delete buttons at the bottom of every message screen.

Tap Done when you're finished reading the message. This will return you to the Inbox message list screen (or the list screen for whatever folder you're working in).

If you want to get rid of the message, tap Delete. Unless you turned off the Confirm Deleted Message option in the Preferences dialog box, you'll see a Delete Message confirmation box. From this box, tap Yes to move the message into the Deleted folder or No to leave the message where it is.

If you want to file the message, tap the Menu soft button to open the Menu Bar, then choose Message ➤ File. Alternately, you can enter the Graffiti command stroke followed by a Graffiti L. Either way, the message will move to the Filed folder.

Of course, you can also reply to that message. We'll tell you how next.

PART

III

Your Palm and the
Outside World

Replying to Messages

Replying to a message is as simple as tapping the Reply button that appears at the bottom of every message screen. That's oversimplifying things a bit, but it's a good place to start.

Here's what you do:

1. From the Inbox list, tap the message you want to reply to. This will open the message.

2. Tap the Reply button at the bottom of the screen. This will open the Reply Options dialog box, as in Figure 13.22.

FIGURE 13.22

Reply requested

3. To reply to the message, choose Sender next to Reply To, which will place the address of the person who originally sent you the message on the To line.

4. Tap in the Include Original Text box to paste the text of the original message into the body of your reply.

5. Tap in the Comment Original Text box if you want to have the original text marked in your reply. This option will place a > at the beginning of each line of the original text, as in Figure 13.23.

6. Tap OK when you're satisfied with your choices. The dialog box will close and the New Message screen will open, with the To line filled in.

7. Compose the body of your message using Graffiti or the on-screen keyboard, and edit the original text (if you chose to include it).

8. Tap Outbox to place the message in your Outbox folder from where you can send it the next time you log on to Palm.Net, or tap Check & Send to log on and send the message immediately.

If you'd rather forward the original message to a different party, follow steps 1 and 2. Then, choose Forward from the Reply Options dialog box. This will take you to the new message screen, where the text of the original message will appear as the body and the To line will be blank, as in Figure 13.23. You can add an address the same way you would if you were creating a new message. Then, pick up from steps 7 and 8 above.

FIGURE 13.23

Fill in a forwarding address.

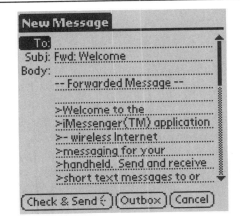

Alternate E-Mail Solutions

One of the early criticisms of the Palm VII was that it only provided access to the Palm.Net e-mail service. This meant that users needed to maintain yet another e-mail account, besides the one they already use at home and work.

Now that the Palm VII has gone national, that criticism is moot. There are a handful of third-party applications that let you download messages from Internet-based services, such as MindSpring and Worldnet, to your Palm VII. There are even applications that let you download Web-based e-mail, such as mail from Hotmail or Yahoo accounts.

The one catch is that the e-mail system you're trying to hook up with must be either POP3 or IMAP compatible. This shouldn't pose too much of a problem, since virtually every e-mail service supports at least one of these Internet mail standards.

PART

III

Your Palm and the
Outside World

NOTE POP3 (Post Office Protocol 3) and IMAP (Internet Message Access Protocol) are both protocols used for retrieving e-mail from a mail server. Most mail servers use the older POP3, but some that are based on the newer IMAP standard are starting to appear.

How E-Mail Works

Explaining how the whole e-mail process works is beyond the scope of this book, but we'll try to give you a quick understanding of how you can get your Internet mail onto your Palm VII.

When you sign up for Internet service with an ISP, you are paying for an Internet connection for a monthly fee. Typically, this fee includes an e-mail account. Your ISP maintains a mail server (think of it as the post office) that you dial in to using client software, such as Eudora Pro, Microsoft Outlook, or Netscape Messenger. This client software resides on your desktop PC. It communicates to the mail server at your ISP through a series of communications protocols, including POP3 and IMAP. Because most mail servers understand these protocols, you can use any client that supports them to download and read your mail.

These same principles apply when accessing Internet e-mail on your Palm VII. You install a client application on your Palm VII, dial out to the Internet, and the client application communicates with the mail server at your ISP to locate and download your e-mail.

 TIP Not sure what protocols your mail system supports? Check out the E-Mail Solutions Help page on the Palm.Net Web site (www.palm.net/email_solutions/help/) for tips on finding out the answer.

Web-based e-mail, those free mail accounts that let you read your mail only in a Web browser, may not support either POP3 or IMAP. So, you'll need a different client to access these mailboxes. You can find clients for Yahoo! mail and Hotmail on the Palm.Net Web site.

The Tools for Getting Internet E-Mail onto Your Palm VII

There are two ways to get e-mail on your Palm VII organizer. You can access your mailbox directly using any third-party e-mail application (such as the ones we mention in Chapter 12) on your Palm VII, or you can forward your messages to your Palm.Net iMessenger account. For accessing corporate e-mail systems such as Lotus

Notes or Microsoft Exchange Server, you'll have to forward messages to your Palm. You'll need your network administrator's help and permission to get this set up.

There are two third-party applications you can use to access your POP3 and IMAP accounts: ThinAirMail and iPopper. Both of these applications are actually Palm Query Applications, and can be downloaded for free from the Palm.Net Web site (www.palm.net). Both applications leave the mail you download to your Palm VII on your mail server, so you can also download it on your desktop PC.

 TIP You will need to have an active Palm.Net account as well as an ISP account to use Internet e-mail tools. Mail you download with these applications will be billed against your monthly transmission allotment.

ThinAirMail (ThinAirApps.com, www.thinairapps.com) offers access to both POP3 and IMAP mailboxes. You must download it, install it on your Palm VII, and then configure it for use with your Internet e-mail account. Rather than downloading entire messages, ThinAirMail retrieves the sender's name and subject of the e-mail, so you can preview your messages before downloading them. For long e-mail messages, ThinAirMail retrieves the first kilobyte and gives you the option to download the rest of the message. You can also filter your e-mail to retrieve only messages from a particular person, with a certain subject, or sent on a specific date.

The other Internet mail application, iPopper (Corsoft, www.corsoft.net), works only with POP3 compatible mailboxes. Like ThinAirMail, you need to download, install, and configure this e-mail client on your Palm VII. After that, it's easy and intuitive to use, and provides complete e-mail functionality. Like ThinAirMail, iPopper downloads just the sender's name, the e-mail subject, and the date. You then decide which messages to download. You can also perform all the standard filtering to limit which messages get downloaded to your Palm VII.

If you would rather not install a mail application on your Palm VII, you'll want to look at Visto Assistant (Visto Corp., http://corp.visto.com/palm.html), which can forward your messages to your iMessenger Inbox. Visto Assistant (which is also free) runs on your Windows PC. It works with POP3 mail, as well as proprietary e-mail systems such as Lotus Notes and Microsoft Exchange Server.

Visto Assistant checks your e-mail periodically, and forwards any new messages that match your optional filtering criteria to your Palm VII. The big catch is that for this application to work, you must leave your PC turned on and connected to your e-mail account. If your ISP charges you by the hour, you're looking at a heck of a bill—not to mention what you'll rack up in telephone charges. For these reasons, this solution is better suited to accessing corporate e-mail than your personal account.

PART

III

Your Palm and the Outside World

Web Clipping with Your Palm VII

A Palm VII does not live by e-mail alone. Chances are, your Internet needs don't end there, either. This is precisely why the Palm VII provides Web access via Palm Query Applications (PQAs) and a technology it calls Web clipping. Web clipping isn't exactly like Web surfing, but it's the best approach we've seen for corralling the Internet and making it work in a small, limited environment like the Palm operating system and the Palm VII.

The Difference between Clipping and Browsing

Think about the typical Web page—it's big, loaded with colors, and slow to download. And that's on a desktop PC with a reasonably fast dial-up connection. Now think about your Palm VII—it's tiny, runs on batteries, offers a slower connection speed than the average modem, and gets billed for every kilobyte it downloads. When you look at it that way, the Internet doesn't seem like such a great thing. If you're surfing, that is.

Fortunately, Palm Computing came up with a way to access the Internet that makes sense for the Palm VII. It's called Web clipping, and it eliminates the need for lots of fast bandwidth and a big screen with color support. If you think of the Internet as a newspaper, and Web clipping as clipping an article out of the newspaper, you'll get the basic idea. With Web clipping, you only get the information you're interested in, and don't have to deal with all the extraneous stuff.

Here's how Web clipping works. Your interaction with the Internet is based on queries and responses, rather than a series of hyperlinks as in Web browsing. Essentially, you ask for a piece of information, and it's returned to your Palm VII. This interaction is controlled through a PQA, which is stored locally on your Palm VII. PQAs are request forms; there's a place where you enter data, such as a stock symbol to look up or a news topic. Since the PQA itself is stored on your Palm VII like any other application, only your data request gets sent out over the Internet. This keeps response time quick and the actual amount of data being transmitted to a minimum. In a typical application, the query you send out averages about 50 bytes; less than 500 bytes (compressed) are returned to your Palm VII. The process is so efficient that in most cases, the information you requested will be returned to your organizer in less than 10 seconds.

How to Use a PQA

Your Palm VII comes with a handful of PQAs installed and includes a bunch more on the Palm Software CD. We can't begin to describe how to use each and every PQA;

that would be like trying to tell you how to navigate every site on the Internet. Instead, we'll walk you through using two of the pre-installed PQAs that use all the usual PQA functions.

For the purposes of this discussion, we'll primarily use the ESPN.com PQA because its design and operation are representative of what you'll encounter in most PQAs, and we're really big sports fans. (As we write this, basketball season has just gotten under way, and we have high hopes for the NY Knicks, but then, we are eternally optimistic about the hometown teams.) So now we have the perfect excuse to keep checking the box scores. We'll also briefly use the Weather Channel PQA to show one feature that's not included in ESPN.com.

Before we go any further, let's explain a few of the principles of a PQA application.

- You tap to select an item or perform an action, the same way you would with any other Palm application.
- You enter text, when necessary, using Graffiti or the on-screen keyboard.
- Interface conventions, like scroll bars, pick lists, check boxes, command buttons and menus, work the same way in a PQA as they do in any other Palm application.
- You access the Menu Bar in a PQA the same way you do in other Palm applications.
- You can cut, copy, and paste information to an edit line just as you usually do.

Now, let's look at some of the interface conventions that are unique to a PQA. Start by opening the ESPN.com PQA. You do this the same way you open any application: Tap the Applications soft button, then tap the icon for ESPN.com from within the Application Launcher screen. The ESPN.com PQA will open immediately, whether or not you've initiated a Palm.Net connection. You'll see the home page for this PQA, which is installed on your Palm VII. You can see it in Figure 13.24.

PART

III

Your Palm and the Outside World

FIGURE 13.24

What sport interests you?

First, notice that the different sports categories are underlined, just as a hot link would be in a standard Web application. The underlining indicates a link; tapping it will send out a request for information, and return a new page. This is the query part of a PQA. Take a good look at the line for Baseball. That little curved icon next to it is the over-the-air icon.

This indicates that tapping on this option will initiate a wireless transaction. The minute you start a wireless transaction, you're incurring cost—either in the form of a deduction from your monthly kilobyte allotment or actual money, if you've run through that allotment.

At this point, you should raise the antenna on your Palm VII to connect to the Palm.Net service. Anything you tap from this home page will send a request out to the Internet; the information you requested will quickly be returned to your Palm VII. For the purposes of this demonstration, tap Baseball from the ESPN.com home page. Now tap Scores. You've just sent your first query to the Internet. As the information you requested is being located and downloaded to your organizer, the words Connected (or Sending) will appear at the top of the screen, followed by an icon like this one:

This circular icon is the Stop icon. You can tap it to Stop the transaction you just initiated. For now, though, just let the request go through.

What you see on the screen now is the response to your query, otherwise known as a Web clipping. You'll notice an arrow at the top of the screen, about halfway across (see Figure 13.25). This is the Back arrow. It works just like the back arrow in your Web browser. Tapping it will take you to the last page displayed in the Query application. Tapping it repeatedly will take you all the way back to the Application Launcher.

FIGURE 13.25

Take one step back.

Let's send another query. Tap the line that says News. This will open the first news screen. In the top-right corner of the screen, where the category pull-down would appear in a regular Palm application, you'll notice the word History. Tapping this will drop-down the History list, as in Figure 13.26.

FIGURE 13.26

Review your clippings.

This list works just like the History list in a Web browser. It displays all the clippings you've received for the PQA you're working in. It will show the name of the clipping and the time it was downloaded. You can tap any clipping in this list to return to that screen.

There's one last thing we'd like to point out on the Baseball News clipping screen. See the ESPN.com logo at the top-left of the screen? This is the title area of the screen. You can tap it to find out how big the clipping you just received was, as in Figure 13.27.

PART

III

Your Palm and the
Outside World

FIGURE 13.27

Tapping on the title area of a PQA will show you how many bytes a clipping contains.

Sometimes, sending a query will involve more than just tapping a screen. For some interactions, you'll need to enter text or use a pick list to get more specific information. The ESPN.com PQA doesn't use these techniques, so we'll move over to the Weather Channel for this example.

Tap the Weather icon in the Application Launcher to open the Weather Channel PQA, and then tap Find A City. As you can see in Figure 13.28, the Weather Channel PQA requires you to either pick a state from the Pick List, or enter a city name or zip code on the text line to get weather information for that region.

You work with these options the same way you would with any Palm application. Scroll through the pick list using the scroll arrow on the side of the box (or enter the first few letters of the state you want to automatically advance the list). When you get to the state you want, tap it to highlight it, then tap the Go State command button.

FIGURE 13.28

Either pick or write.

TIP You can also paste information from a standard Palm record into the text line of a Palm PQA. You do this the same way you copy and paste in any Palm application.

If you'd rather enter a city or zip code, just tap the text line to activate it, then use Graffiti or the on-screen keyboard to enter the city or zip code for which you want information. Tap Go to launch the query.

Pick lists and text lines are common elements in PQAs that let you search for specific information, such as a name, a movie listing, or a stock symbol. News and general interest PQAs will generally just offer options that you tap to access.

One option every PQA will offer is the ability to copy information from the application to paste into a memo, Address Book record, or any other basic Palm application. You can't select part of a PQA page or just some of the text from a clipping. You have to take the whole clipping.

To copy a clipping:

1. Make sure the clipping or page you want to copy is displayed on the screen.

2. Tap the Menu button to open the Menu Bar.

3. From the Menu Bar, choose Edit ➢ Copy Page (see Figure 13.29).

FIGURE 13.29

Copy a clipping.

4. Open the application you want to paste the clipping into.

5. Create a new record.

6. Tap the Menu button to open the Menu Bar.

7. From the Menu Bar, choose Edit ➢ Paste. The clipping will appear in this new record.

PART

III

Your Palm and the Outside World

TIP Copying a clipping always starts at the top of the current page, no matter what is displayed on the screen. Copy Page copies only tables and texts; it doesn't pick up icons or other graphics.

That about sums up the basic functionality of PQAs. It's time to start exploring on your own.

Five Must-Have PQAs

The PQAs installed on the Palm VII and included on the Palm Software CD are great to start with, but there are thousands of other PQAs ripe for the downloading. You can find good ones on the standard software download sites we discuss in Appendix A. The Palm.Net Web site is also a great resource for new PQAs. Once you've downloaded these PQAs to your desktop PC, you install them the same way you would any other Palm application. Here are five PQAs we consider must-haves, all of which can be downloaded from www.palm.net/apps.

Internet Movie Database   This listing of 6,500 movies is the perfect tool to have for those trips to the video store. You can search by title, actor, director, etc., and get detailed information.

Starbucks Coffee Store Locator   Keep yourself appropriately caffeinated with the Store Locator. It lists every Starbucks in the continental U.S., so you'll never have to go latte-less.

Amazon.com Anywhere   Shop from your Palm VII with this PQA that provides access to Amazon auctions and products. It even delivers Amazon.com reviews, product ratings, and prices, so you can make informed purchases.

PDA Dash Palm News   Keep up to date on the latest Palm news, rumors, and reports with this daily newsletter.

Vicinity BrandFinder   Looking for the nearest gas station, fast food restaurant, or hotel? BrandFinder can help you find the closest name-brand provider. Perfect for when a Big Mac attack strikes you in an unfamiliar city.

If you're looking for full Web surfing capabilities or you're not lucky enough to have a Palm VII, turn to the next chapter to find out about applications that let you surf the Web.

CHAPTER <u>14</u>

Browsing the Web

Contrary to popular belief, there were tools for surfing the Web with your Palm organizer long before there was a Palm VII. Of course, as you discovered in the previous chapter, what the Palm VII does isn't really Web surfing; it's Web clipping. So even you Palm VII users might want to keep reading and see what they're missing. You're not precluded from using any of the stuff we talk about here; you'll just need to forget about the wireless connectivity for a while and plug in like the rest of the world. Before we jump into the requirements and software options you have for browsing the Web, let's consider the basic premise of Web browsing a la Palm.

On your desktop PC, chances are excellent that you use either Microsoft Internet or Netscape Navigator to wend your way through the World Wide Web. Hate to break it to you, but you won't find either of those tools for the Palm platform—they're too big in size, require too much screen real estate to work properly, and are too slow to run properly on the Palm.

But there are a couple of things that those big browsers share with their petite Palm brethren: caching and offline browsing. Caching is simply a fancy term for saving stuff in memory to speed up page load times. In the case of a Web browser, the first time you visit a Web page, your browser saves its graphics on the hard drive of your desktop PC. By saving the graphics, your browser can spit them right back out when you enter the appropriate URL, rather than waiting for them to download. This way, the next time you visit the page, it will load more quickly—whether that next visit happens ten minutes after the first visit or ten days later.

Palm browsers take caching a step further. They cache entire pages rather than just graphics. This serves two purposes. It enables you to surf the Web without having an active dial-up connection. That's called offline browsing, which your desktop PC browser can do, though you may have never tried out that feature. Of course, caching entire pages means faster load times, as well.

With that out of the way, let's look at what you need to start browsing and what your software options are.

What You Need

First things first: You must have a modem. It can be a snap-on Palm modem or a desktop modem specially rigged to hook up with your Palm organizer (we discuss this more in Chapter 11). But if you don't have a modem, you don't get to surf. Or do you? Hmmm… Read the section on channel managers to find out about accessing Internet content without a modem. For this discussion, you'll need a desktop PC with a modem.

Next, you need an Internet account with an Internet Service Provider, such as AT&T Worldnet, Earthlink...you know the drill.

Then, you need to get the modem and your ISP communicating. It's easier to configure your Palm for Web access than it is for e-mail. All you need to know is the name of your ISP, your username, password, and the number you dial for connection with your ISP. You set all this up through the Network Preferences screen. If you're not sure how it's done, or your ISP isn't listed in the Service list, flip back to Chapter 11 for some step-by-step assistance.

 TIP If you use a channel manager, you don't need a modem for your Palm and you don't need to do any configuring on the device. You will need a desktop PC with a modem and an active ISP account. And you'll need to HotSync.

With all the setup out of the way, it's time to pick an Internet application. You have a few choices here—you can go with a Web browser that's just a browser; choose one that provides channel management capabilities for better offline browsing; pick one that also lets you access news groups; or choose a separate news reader.

We'll give you a brief rundown of each of the leading applications in these categories next.

Browsers and Channel Managers

There's one basic difference between a browser and a channel manager. A browser works directly with Web content and requires a modem to operate, at least initially.

A content manager, on the other hand, can put Web content on your Palm, even if it doesn't have a modem. Instead, it uses the modem and Internet account on your desktop PC to access specially formatted, hosted Web content and pushes that content out to your Palm when you HotSync.

We'll explain how a channel manager works a little later in this chapter. First, let's take a look at two of the most adept Palm browsers.

Browsers

A Palm Web browser works very much like a standard desktop Web browser. It dials up, makes a connection through your ISP, and provides access to pages located somewhere out there on the Web.

Of course, Palm Web browsers are operating under a bit of a disadvantage compared to most desktop Web browsers. They're dealing with slower connection rates in most cases, a smaller display area in every case, a slower processor, and less memory. But, Palm browsers have a couple of tricks up their sleeves to make you forget their limitations.

HandWeb ($49.95, SmartCode Software, `www.smartcodesoft.com`) speeds up Palm browsing by giving you the option to view Web sites as text only. Of course, if you're feeling adventurous or really patient, you can choose to view images or cache them for viewing later. And HandWeb works with any Internet service, except AOL. A demo version of HandWeb, which lets you visit only the URLs hard-coded into the application, can be downloaded from the SmartCode Web site or from a number of other Palm shareware sites.

HandWeb makes it easy to create and save bookmarks for sites you visit often. In fact, as you can see in Figure 14.1, the HandWeb's opening screen is its bookmark list.

FIGURE 14.1

Tap on a site to open it.

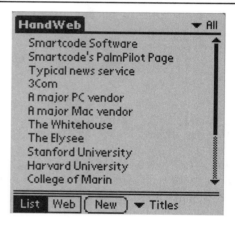

To go to one of these pages, you simply tap on its name. This will open a pop-up menu of choices, which include Open, Edit, Move to, Duplicate, and Delete. With these options, you can open a bookmark, edit it, move it to a different category, duplicate it (perhaps to file it in multiple categories), or delete it. HandWeb offers the usual Web navigation features, including a cache and history list for quickly returning to pages you just visited. It also gives you forward and back buttons and the ability to reload pages.

HandWeb lets you store Web pages for offline browsing, download files, and interact with Web-based forms. It supports cookies, password authentication, proxies and redirection. It does not support frames, so some Web sites may not display properly. It also doesn't support SSL (Secure Socket Layer) encryption, which is the standard form of protection when submitting sensitive information (like your credit card number) over the Web. In spite of these limitations, HandWeb will work fine for basic Web browsing. We'd advise leaving images turned off—they're slow to download and don't look all that good anyway.

ProxiWeb (free, ProxiNet, `www.proxinet.com`) gives you the full Web experience, graphics and all, yet still manages to load pages up in a hurry. This tiny 120K Web client offers everything HandWeb does, and then some. To use ProxiWeb, you have to sign up for a ProxiNet account, but that's free; you still use your regular ISP for Internet access.

 TIP You'll need to sign up for a ProxiNet account from your desktop Web browser before you can even download the ProxiWeb client.

The ProxiNet account gives you access to the ProxiWare servers, which let ProxiWeb do its magic. These servers function as custom proxy servers, intercepting your page requests and processing the Web page's data by filtering out extraneous HTML code and converting color graphics into the four shades of gray that can be displayed on the Palm organizer. The result is a streamlined Web page optimized for the Palm organizer.

ProxiWeb is exceptionally fast and easy to use. It has the look and feel of a desktop Web browser and supports many of the same features. For example, it supports HTML tables, frames, forms, and cookies, as well as Triple DES and SSL 3.0 encryption for secure transactions. It supports both GIF and JPEG images, and lets you view images as thumbnails or full-size. You can see a full-size image in Figure 14.2.

PART

III

Your Palm and the
Outside World

FIGURE 14.2

*A Palm-perfect
Web page*

ProxiWeb even lets you download compressed archives (like Zip and StuffIt files) and install applications. Like HandWeb, it lets you track your browsing history and save bookmarks, as well as save pages for offline browsing.

 TIP   Palm VII users can connect to ProxiWeb wirelessly—no modem required.

For online modem or mode-free browsing, it's hard to beat ProxiWeb. It's fast, easy to use, and free—what more could you ask for?

These are not the only online Web browsers available, but they are two of the best. Check the Palm shareware sites for other options. We list some of the best sites for Palm software in Appendix A.

Channel Managers

The title of this section really should be Channel Manager—because there's only one entrant in this category worth mentioning. Our pick for best Palm Channel Manager is (drum roll please)... AvantGo (free, AvantGo, www.avantgo.com). Like ProxiWeb, AvantGo requires you to sign up for a free service account (called AvantGo.com) and uses your standard ISP for Internet access. And again like ProxiWeb, this service provides access to a custom caching server that strips out extraneous material from Web sites, converts and compresses graphics files, and delivers an optimized Web page to your Palm organizer.

The biggest difference between AvantGo and ProxiWeb is that AvantGo is really optimized for offline browsing. It uses a channel metaphor; for example, you don't visit the Yahoo Web site, you visit the Yahoo channel. When you first sign up for AvantGo.com service, you'll be asked what subjects interest you. AvantGo will download a handful of channels based upon your responses. These are fully-prepped and downloaded Web sites that you can view without making a modem connection; AvantGo downloads them to your desktop PC, then transfers them to your Palm when you HotSync.

TIP You'll need to initially configure AvantGo from a desktop PC equipped with a modem and a Palm cradle. Be prepared to HotSync multiple times to complete the process. To speed the process along, set up a custom HotSync with all the conduits, except for Install, set to Do Nothing.

That's what makes AvantGo primarily a channel manager rather than a true Web browser (though it has some Web browsing capabilities just recently added to the program). You can see a list of our starting channels in Figure 14.3.

FIGURE 14.3

Our AvantGo channels

You really don't need a modem to use AvantGo. You simply perform a HotSync while you connect to the Web. The channel content is stored directly on your Palm for viewing whenever you like. If you have a Palm modem, you can modify your AvantGo.com profile and do some real-time Web browsing online. AvantGo can access any Web page and reformat it for delivery to the Palm organizer. However, it offers such an extensive list of channels and such good offline viewing capabilities, you may never feel the need to surf at all.

Whether you surf or confine yourself to offline channel use, you'll be happy to know that AvantGo supports all the standard Web formats, as well as HTML tables and SSL encryption. It does not support frames, however, and cannot use the Palm VII's wireless connectivity for online surfing. Still, if you don't have a modem or are primarily interested in browsing offline (which is much, much quicker than real-time surfing on the Palm), AvantGo is an excellent choice. AvantGo also supports updating channel content via modem, but no PC is required after installation.

News Readers

There's more to the Web than just surfing. If you're hooked on newsgroups, there's no reason to leave them behind just because you're away from your desk. A handful of Palm news readers are available that let you read news postings online or offline.

Our favorite online news reader is NewsPad (`http://members.tripod.com/~hokamoto`). This free utility lets you read NNTP messages posted on Internet newsgroups. All you need is the name of your Internet Service Provider's news server and a Palm modem. It takes a long time to download postings, and reading messages is a bit of a chore. NewsPad does not support attachments or let you post messages back to the newsgroup. But it does work reliably and keeps you up to date on the latest news threads.

For offline news reading, we prefer PalmReader. This shareware application ($10.00, `www.mindspring.com/~lior/PalmReader.html`; a free 20-day trial version is available) lets you download newsgroups to your Palm for later viewing. You manage Palm-Reader through a simple desktop application (Windows-only, unfortunately) and can limit both the number and size of messages to download. You can see the Windows desktop in Figure 14.4.

Because it works through your desktop PC and a HotSync, you don't need a modem to use it.

FIGURE 14.4

A list of the news-groups you want to monitor

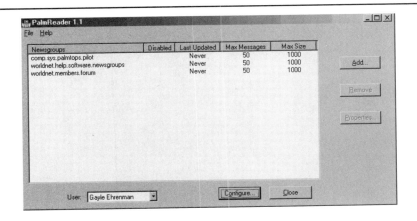

TIP Only download the newsgroups that you really can't live without. Each message averages 1K of Palm RAM, so just one active newsgroup can eat up all of your organizer's available memory.

NewsPad and PalmReader are just a drop in the bucket as far as Web tools for the Palm go. Search the usual Palm shareware sites and you'll turn up IRC, ICQ, and Chat applications, as well as terminal applications, Web servers, FTP tools, and other assorted Web goodies.

So what are you waiting for? Get yourself a modem and start surfing. Since you're investing in a modem anyway, turn to the next chapter to learn about using it for faxing.

PART

III

Your Palm and the Outside World

CHAPTER 15

Faxing and Printing Palm Style

Sometimes, the Palm organizer manages to amaze us. Turns out this little computing dynamo, which replaced our hulking Filofax, can easily take the place of another business tool—the fax machine. With a little help from a modem and some third-party software (or for the Palm VII a free PQA and fax-for-fee service), the Palm organizer can send and receive faxes. Tack on some more third-party software, and the Palm becomes print-enabled. Is there no limit to what this thing can do?

Getting Started

Your Palm will require different tools depending on whether you're faxing or printing. Both tasks will require you to buy and install third-party applications since no single application can do both.

Faxing Requirements

To turn your Palm organizer into the world's smallest and most portable fax machine, you'll need a couple of extras. For starters, you'll need a modem and a third-party fax application, if you're using any Palm model other than the Palm VII. Palm VII devices can use their wireless capabilities to send a fax, but they'll require different software than other Palm devices.

You can use the little Palm snap-on modem appropriate for your Palm. Or, you can use a standard desktop PC modem connected to your Palm organizer via a special cable. Either approach will work just fine, though the Palm-specific modem is much more portable, runs on batteries and, more importantly, is much easier to configure properly than a desktop PC modem. Conversely, desktop PC modems were never intended to be portable, so they tend to be a bit on the hefty side. And, most come with a big brick of a power source, so you need not just an electric outlet, but one that can accommodate that big brick. Still, you may not need to go out and buy a desktop PC modem. They've become so ubiquitous, you probably have one lying around that you're not using. To make an external desktop PC modem work with your organizer, you'll need to purchase a special modem cable, which has a 25-pin connector on one end and a HotSync connector on the other. The last time we checked, Palm Computing no longer offered this cable on their Web site; try some of the online Palm stores. Adventurous types can try building their own cable. Directions are available on the Palm Web site (www.palm.com/devzone/hdk/images/cablemod.gif).

TIP Make sure that any desktop/PC modem you're hooking up to your Palm for faxing is a Class 2 Fax modem. The documentation that came with the modem will have this information.

Unless you're lucky enough to be using a wireless modem, you'll need a phone jack to plug your modem into. Just as your standard paper-based fax machine requires a phone line to reach out and touch someone, so does your Palm organizer. It's a wonder-device, but it isn't a miracle worker. Faxing is just another form of communication, like e-mail or the Internet—it demands a connection, too.

 TIP If you need help configuring your modem or Internet account, turn back to Chapter 11, where we explain the basics of using your Palm organizer to communicate with the outside world.

Finally, you'll need a third-party fax application. If you're working with any Palm model other than the Palm VII, you basically have two choices: HandFax, ($49.95, SmartCode Software, www.smartcodesoft.com) or Mobile WinFax, ($49.95, Symantec, www.symantec.com). Both of these applications are commercial software, with limited demo versions available for download from their respective Web sites and other leading Palm shareware sites. We'll give you a rundown of the capabilities of these products later in this chapter.

TIP If you're feeling thrifty and adventurous, troll the sites for an older, somewhat buggy, and no longer supported fax application called DBFax .2b3. The last time we checked, the $13.95 shareware product was still posted at PalmGear (www.palmgear .com). DBFax was one of the first fax applications for the Palm, but it's no longer being advanced or triaged, so don't expect all the bells and whistles of the more expensive applications or any tech support if you encounter bugs.

Printing Requirements

Printing is probably the least advanced communications medium for the Palm organizer. Out of the box, the Palm can't print directly to a printer. It requires third-party software, and even then it won't work with every printer. The printer must have either a serial port or an IR port and it must "speak" PCL, Epson emulation, or PostScript (three common printer definition languages). Some IR-equipped printers include the Canon BJC-80 and BJC-50; the Hewlett-Packard DeskJet 340CBi, LaserJet 6P and 6MP, as well as the LaserJet 2100 series; and the Citizen PN60I. There are point-of-sale IR printers too, like the Citizen PD-04 and Seiko DPU-3445.

You're more likely to find a serial port on an older printer than a newer model. One currently available printer that has a serial port is the Epson LX-300 Dot Matrix printer. To take this route, you need to plug your HotSync cradle or HotSync cable into the serial port on the printer. You may also need an adapter to make the connection between the 25-pin serial port on your printer and the 9-pin serial port on your HotSync cradle. One of these adapters comes with your Palm organizer, so if you're not already using it to connect your cradle to your desktop PC, you're in luck.

 TIP Mac users: Your MacPac cable (the 9-pin to Mac serial adapter) may be all you need. The AppleTalk connector on some printers may also function as a straight serial port. It has been reported that both the HP 855C and HP DeskWriter 310 work using this cable.

If your printer doesn't have a serial port, you're going to need to take an extra step—adding a more expensive serial-to-parallel converter. You can find these at your local electronics store, or order one directly from the printing software vendor.

If you have a printer with an IR port, you're in luck. No cables are required. Just make sure that your Palm organizer is no further than about 20 inches from your printer and that it has a clear line-of-sight to the printer's IR port.

In terms of printing software, you basically have only one choice of application: PalmPrint, ($39.95, Stevens Creek Software, www.stevenscreek.com). A demo version of the program is available for download from the Web site. We'll discuss this application later in the chapter.

TIP Printing directly from your Palm organizer can be a bit complicated. You can avoid the whole thing by printing your data from the Palm Desktop software, or if you're away from your desk, just sending a fax to a nearby stand-alone fax machine. This works great when you're on the road. Every hotel in the free world has a fax machine where you can receive faxes for a minimal charge.

Faxing

As we mentioned earlier, which software you use will be determined by whether you're using a modem to make your fax connection or you're using the built-in wireless capabilities of the Palm VII. First, we'll give you an overview of the two modem-dependent fax applications for the Palm, then we'll explain the unique setup you use to fax wirelessly with the Palm VII. You'll have to learn how to use these programs on your own. They're all fairly full-featured applications that we couldn't do justice in this space. Fortunately, since they are commercial programs, they come with detailed directions and offer tech support, in case of emergency.

Applications That Use the Modem

There are two third-party applications that fall into this category: HandFax from SmartCode Software and Mobile WinFax from Symantec. There are lots of subtle differences between the two programs (which we'll get into in a bit), but there's one big, overriding difference that may make your buying decision for you. Both programs can send faxes, but only Mobile WinFax can receive faxes as well. It's also the only application that offers a desktop component for managing your faxes. That said, let's take a quick look at each of these modem-dependent fax tools.

NOTE The demo version of HandFax is extremely limited. It lets you send partial memos and write brief faxes, but always puts SmartCode's name and company logo on the cover sheet. And, the logo creation portion of the program does not function in the demo. The Mobile WinFax demo, on the other hand, gives you access to the full range of features, but expires after 30 days.

HandFax is the older of the two applications, and for a time, was the most full-featured fax application available for the Palm platform. While it's lost that honor to Mobile WinFax, don't count HandFax out yet. SmartCode's parent company, Smart-Code Technologie, was acquired by Palm Computing a short while back, but so far no plans have been announced for the future of this application.

As it stands, HandFax is easy to configure and use, and has one little feature not found in Mobile WinFax. It includes HandPaint, a bitmap editor that lets you create and add your own logo to your faxes. You can even use it to add your "signature" to a fax. This tool is very basic; you're better off creating a logo in another graphics application and then importing it here. Just make sure the logo doesn't exceed 160 by 48 pixels, and that it's in black and white.

HandFax's core functionality is equally simple. It lets you send Memo Pad memos as faxes or write a fax using Graffiti or the on-screen keyboard. Really, the program is best suited to send an existing memo; HandFax's opening screen shows you a list of all the memos on your Palm to help get you started (see Figure 15.1).

FIGURE 15.1

Pick a Memo to Fax.

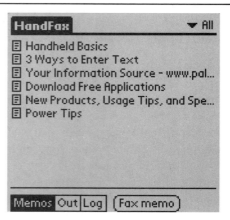

HandFax can look up names and phone numbers from the Address Book, and automatically adds relevant cover sheet, subject, and sender information to your faxes (cover sheets are optional). It provides an Outbox, so you can compose faxes and save them for sending later, and it keeps a complete log of all your fax transactions. This makes it easy to see what faxes you've sent and even re-edit them for sending again.

Composing and sending a fax couldn't be simpler than it is with HandFax. If you really only need basic capabilities, and don't want to fuss with a lot of options, Hand-Fax can do you proud. Its faxes are small, quick, and professional looking.

At the other end of the spectrum lies Mobile WinFax, which may just be the most full-featured Palm application on the planet. Don't be surprised if the name of this application sounds familiar—it's the Palm computing version of the leading desktop PC fax application, WinFax Pro (also from Symantec). If fact, if you already use that application, you'll gain an extra level of productivity from Mobile WinFax.

When it comes to faxing, there isn't much you can't do with Mobile WinFax. Like HandFax, Mobile WinFax lets you send a Memo as a fax or create a fax from scratch. It also lets you draw maps, annotate text, sign documents, and write short notes using your stylus. All of this is done freehand, rather than pixel by pixel with drawing tools, as in HandFax. Of course, Mobile WinFax can also look up names and fax numbers from the Address Book and it maintains a full log of all incoming and outgoing faxes.

But there are a number of things Mobile WinFax can do that HandFax can't. For starters, it can forward received faxes. And did we mention that it can receive faxes either directly or via HotSync? Which brings us to another important difference: Mobile WinFax includes a desktop component that can be used as a fax manager. You can see the Mobile WinFax Desktop in Figure 15.2.

FIGURE 15.2

You can view and manage faxes in the Mobile WinFax Desktop.

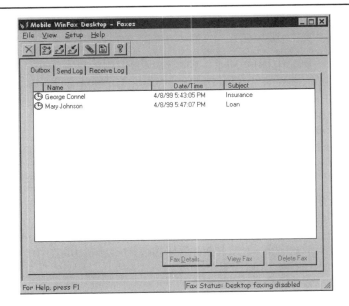

Besides simple fax management, the WinFax Desktop also lets you receive faxes on your desktop PC, and then HotSync them over to your Palm for reading, annotating, and forwarding. It also has a special HotSync trick: You can create a fax on your Palm, specify a file to be attached (it can be any file residing on your desktop PC), and then HotSync to send the fax, complete with the file attachment, from your desktop PC. You can also use the Mobile WinFax Desktop to convert PC documents to images that can be uploaded to your Palm for faxing via modem. Trust us, it's much simpler than it sounds.

We've really only scratched the surface of Mobile WinFax. This application really does give you all the functionality of a desktop PC fax program in a Palm size package. If you're serious about faxing from your Palm, this is the tool to choose.

Wireless Faxing with the Palm VII

You don't need a modem or one of the programs we discussed above to fax from your Palm VII. There are two options available that let you use the Palm VII's built-in wireless capability to send all the faxes you want.

 TIP If you want to be able to receive faxes on your Palm VII, you're going to have to invest in a modem and Mobile WinFax. As we write this book, both of the Palm VII fax applications are send-only.

The two Palm VII fax solutions both come from Rovenet.Com (www.rovenet.com). Both options require you to download a free PQA and then pay a service fee.

If you only need to send an occasional fax, choose P7-Fax. This service will cost you $.75 per fax you send; faxes can be any length. The first time you start P7-Fax, you'll see an account setup form for specifying credit card information; your card will be hit with a $5 deposit fee. The charge for any faxes you send will be deducted from this deposit.

P7-Fax provides a generic cover sheet, lets you send faxes only to the U.S. and Canada, and limits you to 6 faxes per month.

If you're going to need to send more faxes, you'd do well to sign up for Rovenet.com's Send-A-Fax service. This is a more high-end, customized solution that uses the JFAX.COM Internet faxing service to send faxes anywhere worldwide. In order to use this system, you must pay a one-time $35.00 Send-A-Fax Software Preparation fee; a one-time $14.00 JFAX activation fee; a $12.50 JFAX monthly charge; and then roughly $.05 per fax page for US faxing.

For this money, you get customized cover sheets, unlimited worldwide faxing, customer support, and what Rovenet calls "powerful utilities." We couldn't tell you what these are because the whole thing was just a little too rich for our taste.

The advantage to this approach is that you don't need a modem or a telephone connection and you don't have to pay phone charges. If you have a Palm VII, it's true faxing freedom. In our opinion, it's only worthwhile if you need to send a lot of faxes from remote locales. For more mundane faxing chores, you're better off investing in a Palm modem and a standard fax application.

Printing from Your Palm

Of course, you know that if you want to create a paper version of your Date Book or Address Book, the best approach is to do it from the Palm Desktop software (just choose File ➤ Print). However, if you absolutely must print directly from your Palm organizer and have access to a printer but not the PC you HotSync to, there is a tool that makes this possible.

Your sole option here is PalmPrint, from Stevens Creek Software. You can download a demo version of the application from the company's Web site, `www.stevenscreek.com`.

PalmPrint includes two basic components: PalmPrint and SnailMailer. The Palm-Print engine, which you can see in Figure 15.3, lets you print memos, portions of your To Do List, or anything you've placed on the Palm Clipboard (the invisible portion of the Palm OS that holds any text you've selected and either cut or copied, but haven't yet pasted back in to an application).

FIGURE 15.3

What do you want to print today?

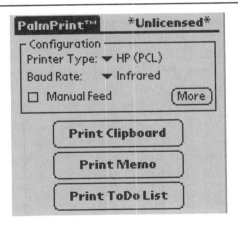

PART

III

Your Palm and the Outside World

SnailMailer, which requires the PalmPrint engine, lets you print envelopes and mailing labels from the names in your Address Book or information from any individual Address Book record. You can see SnailMailer in Figure 15.4.

FIGURE 15.4

From Palm to paper with SnailMailer.

The basic SnailMailer functionality comes free with PalmPrint. For an extra $19.95, you get a version of the program that lets you create and save up to eight sets of mailing lists, which can be different from the categories in your Address Book. For example, you can create a customer list for sending a mass mailing or a Christmas card list for spreading holiday cheer. You also get mail merge capability so you can create memos with a spot for address information, then fill it in with information pulled from the Address Book.

Stevens Creek also offers another free package, called Mail/P, that replaces the standard Palm Mail application and adds the ability to print e-mail messages.

Bet you never realized your Palm could do all this stuff? Amazing what you can accomplish with a little ingenuity, some third-party software, and a few cables.

Now that your Palm has made a connection to the outside world, it's time to explore some of the other things it can do. Turn the page to read about alternate uses for your Palm organizer.

PART IV

Alternate Uses for Your Palm

LEARN TO:

- *Use databases for better productivity*

- *View and create images*

- *Play games*

- *Organize your free time*

CHAPTER **16**

Tools for Better Business and Productivity

I f you thought your Palm organizer was a powerful business and productivity tool right out of the box, wait until you add a few software extras to the mix. Virtually every type of business application you use on your desktop PC has a Palm counterpart. Unlike Windows CE handheld devices, Palm organizers don't offer miniature versions of your desktop applications. So you won't find a compact version of Microsoft Excel for your Palm, but you will find a powerful spreadsheet application designed to take advantage of what the Palm operating system offers and also link up with your desktop spreadsheet application. You can also find powerful Palm database and personal finance tools.

We'll tell you about some of the top tools in these categories. In addition, we'll tell you about some applications that can help you organize your thoughts, make sure your memos are correct, transfer your desktop documents into Palm formats, and generally make you more productive.

The majority of the software we highlight in this chapter is commercial software—which means you have to pay for it. But Palm software developers agree with us on one important point: You should be sure an application does what you need it to do before you shell out your hard-earned cash for it. So, almost all of the commercial applications we've included here offer limited-time demo versions, which you can download from the Web. Most of these demo versions offer all the functionality of the registered, bought-and-paid-for versions; the big difference is that the demo version will only operate for a fixed period of time, usually 15–30 days. After that, either you pay up or you find yourself some new software.

This seems quite fair to us. After 15 days, you should know whether or not you really need a piece of software. If you decide to buy after the demo period is up, you'll be rewarded with more than just the right to keep using your new favorite application. Commercial applications, such as those included in this chapter, generally offer better documentation than shareware, as well as free technical support. In many cases, the software you pay for offers a more sophisticated user interface than shareware, too. And, of course, you're getting a piece of software that will help you execute an important business function; that's got to be worth something.

Databases

When you think of a database, what comes to mind? A giant, hulking application that's hard to work with, slow, and scary? Think again. Databases have been shrunken down to Palm sized, and they're easy enough for mere mortals to master.

There are three Palm database applications that share the market equally. You can author your own databases easily with any of these tools, or use any of the hundreds of existing databases available for download from the Web. In Chapter 19, we discuss some lifestyle applications that are really nothing more than database files that run on one of these database engines.

The three leaders here are JFile Pro, HanDBase, and MobileDB.

 NOTE Each of the three leading Palm database programs has its own file format, so don't automatically assume that a database you create in one can be read by the others.

JFile Pro   ($19.95, Land-J Technologies, www.land-j.com) offers pop-up lists, in-place editing of certain field types, check boxes, and the ability to easily duplicate records in a database, all of which make it easier to create your own databases. It also lets you password-protect individual databases and export records to the Memo Pad. JFile Pro includes a Windows PC–based application that can convert Comma Separated Value (CSV) files, which you can generate from a spreadsheet application, to and from JFile Pro PDB format databases. Macintosh users will need a third-party application, like Palm Buddy or JFile Converter, which are available separately. Be warned: JFile Pro has a new file format, so it can't read plain old JFile databases. You'll need to download a conversion utility from the Land-J Web site in order to use your old database files with this version.

HanDBase   ($19.95, DDH Software, www.ddhsoftware.com, free 30-day trial available) offers all the easy-to-use features of JFile Pro and then some. We find it a bit easier to use than JFile Pro, and more powerful. Like JFile Pro, HanDBase offers a full selection of pop-up menus for setting up your fields (see Figure 16.1). And it makes it as easy as possible to create, view, and modify databases on your Palm organizer.

FIGURE 16.1

Use the pop-up menus to set up your database with HanDBase.

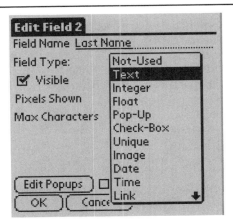

HanDBase lets you add notes and images to your database files, and even link multiple relational databases to each other. It even offers pop-up menus, which make it easier to add fields from another database. There's no limit on the number of pop-up values or multiple pop-up fields that can be grouped together and filled in automatically. There are a variety of utilities available (third-party and from DDH) for importing spreadsheet data into a HanDBase database, as well as a desktop application (free for registered users) for working with your HanDBase files on any computer running Microsoft Windows. There's even a third-party program that can link your HanDBase databases to Microsoft Access.

For those who'd rather just use existing databases, DDH Software provides a whole library of free downloads on their Web site. For really robust database capabilities, HanDBase is hard to beat.

MobileDB   ($14.95, Mobile Generation Software, www.mobilegeneration.com, no time limit, but until you register, you can only create and install up to two databases) is the most modest of the database offerings. It doesn't have all the features of its more powerful competitors, but it has the same core functionality as those applications. MobileDB comes in two versions: MobileDB, which lets you author and view databases, and MobileDB Lite, which only lets you view databases. MobileDB Lite is entirely free. In addition, there's a Windows 95/98/NT version of the software that is free. This application lets you easily create and edit MobileDB databases for use on your Palm organizer. It has an Excel-like interface that lets you import and export data in comma- or tab-delimited formats.

Like HandDBase, MobileDB offers a slew of databases you can download for free. If all you need is simple database capability, this is the tool to choose.

 TIP   Some of the leading enterprise-class databases have come out with stripped down versions for the Palm organizer, which let you peer into the mammoth databases back at the office. IBM has released a version of its DB2 database, DB2 Everywhere for Palm organizers; Oracle has a version of its database, Oracle Lite, that runs on the Palm, as well. Check with your IT department to see if your corporate data store is Palm-enabled.

Spreadsheets

Where would the world of business be without the spreadsheet? There's no more useful tool for charting and tracking lots of numerical data. While you can't view hundreds of cells at a glance on a Palm organizer, the Quicksheet and TinySheet spreadsheet applications serve up all the most important spreadsheet functions in its compact form.

Quicksheet ($49.95, Cutting Edge Software, www.cesinc.com, 15-day trial version available) is the most full-featured spreadsheet application available for the Palm organizer. It can automatically synchronize entire spreadsheets to or from Microsoft Excel via HotSync. Quicksheet includes 45 built-in functions with support for many scientific, financial, date/time, and statistical calculations, as well as numerous cell formatting and editing functions. It supports up to 15 named sheets per workbook and lets you link sheets. If you're looking for desktop-style functionality, Quicksheet is the spreadsheet for you. You can see Quicksheet in action in Figure 16.2.

FIGURE 16.2

The spreadsheet goes vertical with Quicksheet.

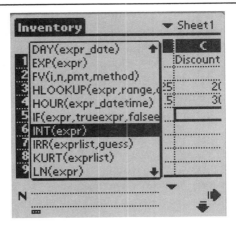

TinySheet ($19.95, Iambic Software, www.iambic.com, 30-day trial version available) is not quite as powerful as Quicksheet, but can handle all the basic spreadsheet calculations. TinySheet is ideal for "what if" calculations and it offers many familiar spreadsheet features, including 31 built-in functions for scientific and financial work, easy entry of series data, complex formulas, cut and paste, and adjustable column widths. It doesn't offer the direct Microsoft Excel links offered by Quicksheet, but it does let you import and export data from desktop spreadsheet applications. For modest requirements, TinySheet is up to the task.

Personal Finance

Whether your interest lies in managing your own money or keeping track of the myriad computations of the business world, there's an application out there for you. The following is just a small sampling of the many finance-related applications available for your Palm organizer, but it gives you a taste of the two primary types of finance software available: expense trackers and calculators.

Pocket Quicken   ($39.99, LandWare, www.landware.com, 15-day trial version available) turns your Palm organizer into a portable money manager. This companion to the desktop version of Quicken 99 lets you record checking, credit card, and cash transactions while on the road, then easily upload the information to Quicken on your desktop PC via a HotSync. You can track any type of transaction for multiple accounts, including checks, credit cards, cash, deposits, withdrawals, splits, and transfers. You can also use your desktop categories and classes for organizing and grouping expenses. Data entry is fast and simple. We know of no better tool for keeping your Quicken records up to date and accurate.

Financial Consultant   ($29.95, LandWare, www.landware.com, 15-day trial version available) calculates expenditures rather than just tracking them. This powerful calculator was designed specifically for real estate, retailing, and business professionals who need to use their Palm organizers for making financial decisions. You can solve problems using Algebraic, RPN, and Forms-based environments. There are tools for calculating savings, loan, and mortgage problems; generating amortization schedules; figuring out loan balances, retail markups, ratios, discounts; and much more. Financial Consultant even includes statistical and scientific functions, all presented within a flexible, easy-to-grasp interface (see Figure 16.3).

FIGURE 16.3

*Calculate almost any-
thing with Financial
Consultant.*

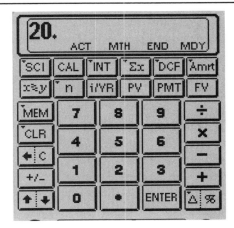

Organization

You wouldn't think that a powerful organizer like the Palm would need any more
help in the organization department. But, we found a couple of tools that can help
you better organize your To Dos, appointments, and memos, as well as your thoughts.

Actioneer   ($19.95, Actioneer Software, www.actioneer.com, 30-day trial ver-
sion available) takes care of all the hard work for you. Actioneer can distribute
individual items to multiple programs easily. You set up keywords that tell
Actioneer which Palm application should receive your event. For example, you
can have it store a message with the word Call in it in both your To Do List and
Date Book (see Figure 16.4). You enter events in Actioneer, and it passes them
to the appropriate applications. It's easy to use and efficient.

FIGURE 16.4

*List your call in
multiple applications
with Actioneer.*

BrainForest Mobile Edition ($30, Aportis Technologies, www.aportis.com, 30-day trial version available) makes it easy to get your thoughts in order. This versatile outlining tool organizes ideas into trees that have branches and leaves you can sort, move, and organize as you see fit. BrainForest is great for organizing action items, tracking ideas, and planning projects. It lets you import and export text to and from the Memo Pad and To Do List, and is intuitive to use. BrainForest is also available in a Professional Edition ($39.95 or $9.00 upgrade for registered Mobile Edition users) that includes a stand-alone desktop application for Windows and Macintosh users, expanded export and import capabilities, and a mini-project planning chart. For those who need some help keeping their projects on track, it's a great tool.

Productivity

As much as we hate to make sweeping generalizations, that's exactly what we're doing in this category. Productivity tools are those that make it a little easier to get your work done, or that make it possible for you to accomplish tasks you couldn't tackle any other way. The products we've included here have very little in common, other than meeting one of those two definitions. Any way you slice it, these applications will make your life a little easier.

Thesaurus and Spell Checker ($15, DDH Software, www.ddhsoftware.com, 30-day trial version available) offers more than 50,000 cross-referenced and indexed entries. It operates in two modes: Thesaurus and SpellCheck. In Thesaurus/Dictionary mode, you simply write word on the text entry line and tap on the Find Word command button. A list of synonyms appears in a box on screen. SpellCheck mode works the same way, except here you'll either get a message that confirms the word is spelled correctly, or you'll get a list of similarly spelled words to choose from. You can also look up words from within Memo Pad; you just copy the word in question, run the thesaurus, and see the results. It's a straightforward, fast, and effective way to better your use of the language.

Backup Buddy NG ($29.95, Backup Buddy Software, www.backupbuddy.com, 30-day trial version available) runs entirely on your Windows PC, and backs up everything installed on your Palm organizer when you HotSync—including all the Hacks, third-party applications, and databases you've installed. If you install even half the programs we recommend, you're going to need this helpful tool.

A regular HotSync backs up the standard Palm applications and all the associated data, but doesn't touch all the extras you've installed. Backup Buddy offers a streamlined interface and automated backups, but it does give you lots of room for customization (see Figure 16.5).

FIGURE 16.5

Choose which applications to back up.

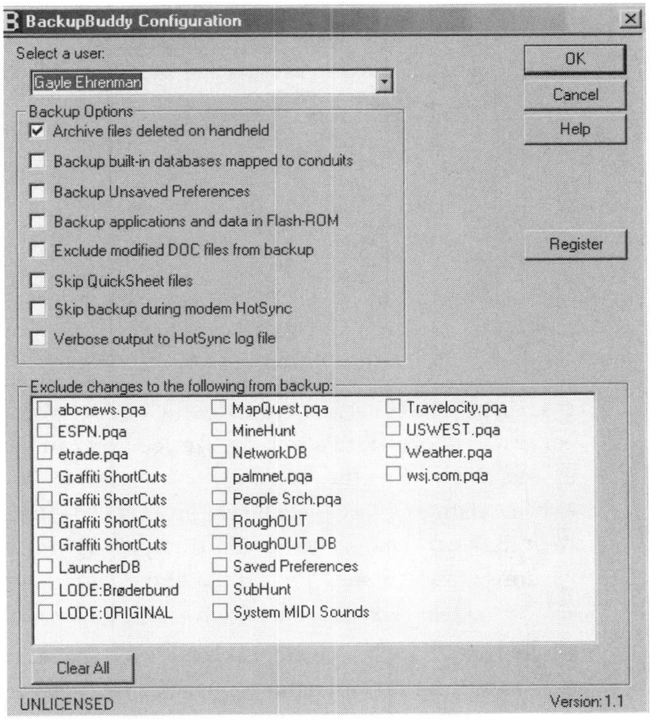

Once it's installed, Backup Buddy runs transparently; you just press the HotSync button on your Palm cradle, and Backup Buddy does its thing. Your HotSyncs may take a bit longer than usual, but if your device should crash, you'll appreciate having a backup version of all your applications and data.

Documents To Go   ($39.95, DataViz, www.dataviz.com, 15-day trial version available) lets you view word processing and spreadsheet files, like Word and Excel, right on your Palm Organizer. Documents To Go includes software that runs on your Windows PC (see Figure 16.6), which handles converting desktop files into Palm-suitable versions.

FIGURE 16.6

Convert desktop documents to Palm format with Documents To Go.

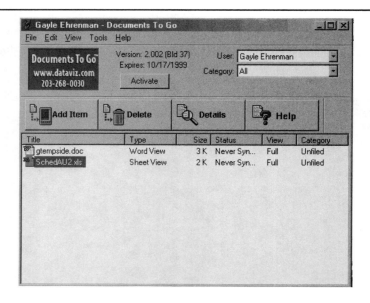

Documents To Go also includes two viewers (Word View and Sheet View) that get installed on your Palm organizer, so you can view those converted documents. Converting files is a one-click operation, and viewing them is just as easy. Documents To Go even synchronizes the documents on your Palm with their desktop versions when you HotSync, so you always have the most recent versions close at hand. You can't edit converted documents with Documents To Go, but at least you can take them with you.

BeamBox ($5 shareware, Inkverse, www.inkverse.com) makes it possible to beam any application, database, Hack...whatever to other Palm users. The only things it won't let you beam are copy-protected databases (which you shouldn't be beaming anyway) and BeamBox itself. The interface is quite simple: You choose which items you want to send, then tap the Beam command button. The person you're beaming to also needs to have BeamBox installed. But for $5, why wouldn't they? As an added plus, BeamBox has a mechanism that translates registered software to unregistered (demo) software during beaming. This lets you share your favorite software with your friends without worrying about violating licensing agreements or stealing.

Desktop To Go ($49.95, DataViz, www.dataviz.com, 15-day trial version available) lets you synchronize your Palm organizer's Address Book, Date Book, To Do List and Memo Pad to the corresponding functions in Microsoft Outlook and Schedule+. Desktop To Go works with the Palm's HotSync capability, and lets you work with custom Outlook fields, limited date ranges, and more. It's the ideal solution for making your Palm talk to Outlook.

Intellisync   ($69.95, Puma Technology, www.pumatech.com, no trial version available) merits mention even though it is the only commercial product we've come across that doesn't offer a free trial version. Still, we had to include it here for one simple reason: It is without a doubt the most powerful tool for syncing up your Palm organizer with whatever desktop personal information manager you use. Intellisync intelligently transfers your Palm data to Lotus Notes, Lotus Organizer, Microsoft Outlook, Novell GroupWise, Goldmine, Symantec ACT!, DayTimer Organizer, and many more applications. It is fully customizable, and offers powerful filtering and full conflict resolution, so you can be certain that your data goes exactly where you want it. After you've set up the initial mappings, this conduit application works as a simple HotSync. Simplicity and power make it hard to top Intellisync.

CHAPTER <u>17</u>

Using Your Palm as a Graphics Tool

Forget about Photoshop-like image retouching, and forget about having millions of colors, huge canvases, and high resolution at your disposal. Basically, abandon all thoughts of true digital artistry when you endeavor to use your Palm organizer as a graphics tool.

Sure, there are plenty of graphics applications out there just aching for you to download them. But let's be realistic here. Your Palm organizer is not as well-endowed as the average desktop PC of even three years ago, let alone what passes for a graphics workstation today. Where those systems have ultra-speedy processors of up to 500 MHz, your Palm has a more modest speed of around 17MHz. And where standard desktop PCs have hundreds of megabytes of RAM, your Palm organizer has a maximum of 4MB for a Palm IIIx (2MB for the Palm III, V, and VII). Same goes for storage—your Palm is definitely at a disadvantage here as well since it uses its memory for processing and storing files, while your desktop PC has a dedicated hard disk that deals with the storage issues.

All of these differences are important when working with graphics, which tend to be great big resource hogs that will suck up every CPU cycle and every chunk of memory they can wring out of your computer.

We haven't even mentioned the biggest drawback to working with graphics on your Palm organizer—it's the Palm's total lack of color. Palm devices from the IIIx on up can deliver a whopping 16 shades of gray. Earlier Palm organizers were capable of only 4 shades of gray, which amounts to white, light gray, and black (you try to distinguish between dark gray and black on the Palm's tiny screen; we sure can't). Even 16 shades of gray can hardly compare to the 32 million colors most desktop PCs are capable of displaying. But, for the Palm world, it's a big step in the right direction.

We're not trying to discourage your from even attempting artistry on your Palm organizer. We're merely trying to manage your expectations so you don't expect too much.

With the help of the right applications, your Palm is surprisingly adept at graphics handling. These applications work within the constraints of the Palm's physical dimensions and computing capabilities so the Palm can really shine. They've simplified the features sets of the standard desktop-based graphics applications, so only the operations that the Palm's processor can handle within a reasonable amount of time remain. This means you won't find sophisticated image editing filters like blur or polarize—those monsters require a computer to move hundreds of thousands of pixels in a matter of seconds. But you will find basic paint brushes, erasers, and a good selection of fill patterns. And while you won't find the range of drawing tools we've become accustomed to in desktop illustration software (even the best Palm programs don't have a polygon tool, for example), you will find the standard shape, line, and text tools, as well as basic object-oriented operations. Think of your Palm as an image viewer and a place to create simple graphics and you'll do just fine.

TIP Don't worry if you don't know the difference between drawing and painting. There's a graphics primer coming up later in this chapter.

Viewing Images

This may seem like a strange place to start. After all, if we haven't created any images on the Palm, what do we have to view? Ah, so many things! Chances are good that you have a treasure trove of digital images lurking somewhere—either things you've shot with a digital camera, scanned in from a standard photo, downloaded from the Internet or created using a drawing or painting program on your desktop PC. With the right tools and a tiny bit of work, these images can be converted into Palm-viewable images.

 TIP So why would you want to view images on your Palm anyway? Maybe just to keep a picture of your loved ones nearby. Or maybe to keep an important map, drawing, or diagram close at hand—particularly important for when you're at a remote location, yet still need to be informed.

For starters, you'll need a Palm image viewing utility and an image converter. The best viewer we've found is ImageViewer III, from Art Dahm (http://palm.dahm.com). This shareware image viewer has been around since 1997, and is the de facto standard for Palm imaging. Virtually every graphics program for the Palm platform supports the ImageViewer file format. ImageViewer III is a shareware program that displays a 10-second countdown before you can use it in its unregistered state; it costs just $12.95 to register and eliminate the irritating countdown. You can use ImageViewer to display scrollable grayscale (4-level or 16-level, depending on your device) pictures, maps, drawings, or diagrams in its own image format.

To get images into the ImageViewer format, you'll need the Image Converter utility, which is also from Art Dahm. This Windows 95/98/NT application converts standard desktop graphic files, like BMP, GIF, and JPG files, into a format that ImageViewer III can read.

> **TIP** Attention Macintosh users: You can download and install ImageViewer III, but you'll need a different image converter utility. Try the Macintosh Image Converter from Lemke Software. You can download this shareware application from www.lemkesoft.de. It offers more image editing tools than the standard Image Converter, but it's easy enough to convert files from Mac formats to ImageViewer format. Be prepared for a big download—the file weighs in at 3.07MB.

Converting Images

First, let's take a look at how you convert images from standard formats to ImageViewer format. We'll be using the Windows Image Converter utility.

Image Converter can work with files on your hard drive, as long as they're in GIF, BMP, DIB, JPG, RLE, TGA, or PCX format. Files you download from the Web will likely be in either GIF or JPG format. Windows Paint creates files in BMP format. The other formats are more specialized, but still fairly standard. Alternately, Image Converter can grab whatever image is in your Windows clipboard (something you've copied from a document, perhaps) or grab a portion of your screen display.

Choose what you'd like Image Converter to convert (see Figure 17.1), then choose a name for the converted file. Next, choose the username for the Palm organizer you want this image to go to on the next HotSync.

FIGURE 17.1

Pick a file, any file.

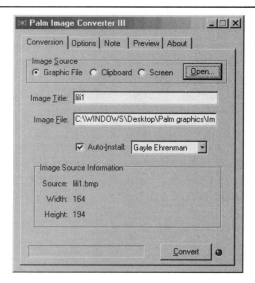

That's really all you have to do to convert a file, but there are some more things you can do to get the best possible conversion. We recommend taking a look at the Preview, so you can see what all those colors in your image will translate to when you convert them to 16 shades of gray (see Figure 17.2). You can toggle between the original Windows version of your image and its Palm version.

If you don't like what you see, click the Options tab to configure the conversion to your liking. If your Palm is capable of displaying 16 shades of gray, and you're not pressed for memory, go with that option; it will yield the greatest subtlety in your image. Likewise, choose Error Diffusion dithering; it produces the smoothest, least blocky shading. Finally, choose what you want the application to do if your image is too large to be successfully converted.

 TIP For the best possible conversion, make some adjustments in your favorite image editing package. If the resolution of your image is above 166 dpi, reduce it; if the image is large in size, crop it. Try fiddling with the brightness and contrast, too. You can also reduce the number of colors before you convert the image. The color reduction algorithms used by most image editing packages are more sophisticated than those used by Image Converter. This will ultimately produce a more attractive grayscale image.

When you next HotSync your Palm to the desktop, this new image will be installed on your organizer.

Looking at the Results

Now that you have a picture on your Palm that's ready for the ImageViewer, let's fire up the application and take a look. Remember, you'll have to install ImageViewer on your Palm organizer first. See Chapter 9 if you can't remember how this is done.

Tap on the ViewerIII icon in the Application Launcher to open ImageViewer. If you haven't registered the application, you'll get a 10-second delay before you can do anything. OK, once that's over with, you'll see a list of all the compatible images installed on your organizer, as in Figure 17.3.

FIGURE 17.3

*The ImageViewer
images*

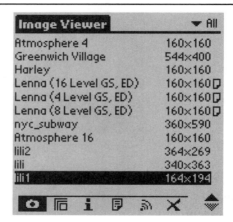

Just tap on one of the names in this list to open the image. You can see the results in Figure 17.4.

You'll notice a row of icons along the bottom of the ImageViewer's list screen (see Figure 17.3). From left to right, these icons are View Image, Preview Image, Image Details, Image Notes, Beam Image, and Delete Image. To execute the action, tap on one of these buttons, then on the name of an image on the list. You can also access these icons while viewing an image by tapping on the Menu soft button.

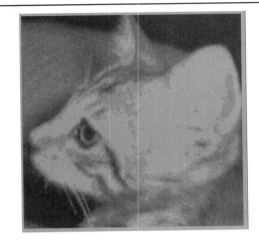

FIGURE 17.4
The final masterpiece

Drawing on Your Palm

No, we're not suggesting you get out the permanent markers and start scribbling
across the screen. Instead, load up a drawing program and use your stylus to create a
digital illustration of that widget you're brainstorming, or a map to the buried treasure. We'll let you decide what to draw.

A Crash Course in Graphics

Digital graphics come in two varieties: vector and bitmap. Drawings or illustrations that
you create with desktop programs like Adobe Illustrator or CorelDraw are vector graphics. Photos and paintings that you create with Adobe Photoshop or Metacreations'
Fractal Painter are bitmap graphics. Screen captures are essentially photos of what's on
your computer screen, so those too are bitmap graphics.

So what's the difference? Here's where we start getting technical, so pay close attention.

Vector graphics are made up of objects—lines, shapes, and text. (Technically, these
graphics are made up of mathematical descriptions of elements that specify the dimension, fill, line width, color, etc. of the object.) Because everything you create in a vector
graphic or drawing program is an object, it remains fully editable. So you can create a

Continued

CONTINUED

whole panorama and come back to just change the color of the roof on the house, for example. You can also overlap objects (overlay the roof on the house), change their order (put the roof behind the house), and even change their size and color.

Bitmap graphics, on the other hand, are made up of hundreds of thousands of individual pixels (those tiny little dots that make up everything you see on screen). Each pixel is defined individually as to its location and status (black, white, or one of the displayable shades of gray). So, the picture you create using a screen capture utility or a painting program is actually a map of all the many pixels you have laid down. Bitmap graphics are both less and more flexible than vector graphics—you can go in and erase a single pixel, but you can't draw a circle and then move it somewhere else on the screen without altering the underlying drawing (as you can with vector graphics). If you create a farm scene with a house set against the sky and grass, it's all one picture; you can't move the house or change its size after you've painted it.

This is really a vast oversimplification, but it will at least help you understand the difference between drawing and painting on your Palm.

When it comes to drawing programs for the Palm, the choices are rather limited. Despite an intensive search, we were only able to come up with two: PalmDraw and QDraw. Each has some unique features, but we still wish they did more.

PalmDraw

This shareware program from Brad Goodman (www.oai.com/bkg/Pilot/PalmDraw/) will cost you $10.95 to register, but it's money well spent. You get the usual shape tools, such as rectangle, circle, freehand drawing, and line, plus you get a Bezier curve tool—a sophisticated curve tool that lets you determine the arc of the curve by tugging on handles. Unfortunately, you don't get any fill patterns nor do you get line weights—so your drawings are going to be strictly black and white (with the emphasis on the white; see Figure 17.5 to see what we mean). Icons for the various drawing tools are displayed at the bottom of the screen. Just tap an icon to use that tool. Object actions are stashed in the menus.

FIGURE 17.5

*Notice the lack of
fills in this PalmDraw
illustration.*

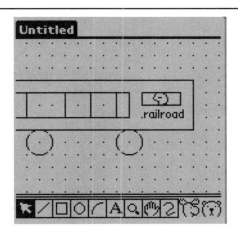

Don't despair the lack of detail in your drawing. PalmDraw does offer PalmDraw
Conversion Tools for converting your illustrations to Windows WMF files. You'll have
to download that utility separately, but it does work nicely. Regrettably, they do not
offer similar tools for the Macintosh platform. Those users can try choosing File ➢
Export to PostScript, which will export the drawing to a PostScript file. When you
HotSync, the file should appear in your Backup folder.

PalmDraw has one other interesting trick up its sleeve—the ability to print directly
to a PostScript printer with a standard serial port. You just plug your HotSync cradle
into the printer's serial port and use PalmDraw's Print To Serial command (located on
the File menu).

QDraw

This freeware program from Quantum World is quite robust (if you're using it to
develop your own Palm application, you're expected to pay a nominal fee; download
it from one of the major shareware sites). It lets you do everything you can do with
object-oriented graphics: move, resize, change their order, modify text, and more. It
has all the standard drawing tools, including a rounded rectangle (you can even
change the degree of roundness on the corners), various line weights, a good selection
of pattern fills (missing from PalmDraw), and a snap-to-grid option (ideal for precise
placement of objects). You can view thumbnails of all your images (much nicer than a
list of names) and create drawings of 160 by 160 or 320 by 320 pixels.

You access the drawing tools by tapping the arrow icon at the lower left of the
screen. This brings up the tool palette, which you can see in Figure 17.6.

FIGURE 17.6

The tools of QDraw

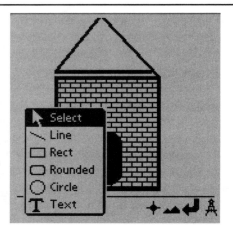

Similarly, tapping the circle button brings up the fill pattern palette, while tapping the line button lets you choose a line weight. The other icons along the bottom of the screen let you snap to grid, zoom in or out, return to the thumbnail screen or launch QPaint (a companion painting program). Object actions, such as group or ungroup, are accessible from the four menus. Just tap on the Menu soft button to see your choices.

Painting on Your Palm

Now that you're an expert at drawing on the Palm, we'll just jump right in to your choices for painting on your Palm. And no, they do not include latex, enamel, or oil-based paints. Despite these omissions, your choice of painting programs is much broader than for drawing tools—or any other type of graphics tools, for that matter. Search on any of the leading shareware Web sites (you can find their URLs in Appendix B), and you'll find upwards of a dozen applications that fit the bill. Rather than bore you with a discussion of each (really, they differ little), we'll just cover the most basic and the most advanced: DinkyPad and TealPaint.

TIP Any program that has sketch, paint, or doodle in its name is probably a bitmap graphic tool.

DinkyPad

This shareware application from Daggerware (www.daggerware.com) offers just bare bones painting capabilities, but it's indispensable. Though it is in fact a bitmap graphic tool, DinkyPad works more like a graphical notepad that lets you take free-hand notes or make quick sketches over a virtual canvas that's larger than your Palm's screen. DinkyPad supports a drawing space with a height of up to 2040 pixels (you use the Palm's scroll buttons to get to it all). And, since it compresses all its stored images, each one weighs in at just a couple of K.

The painting tools are extremely basic—you get just pen, circle, line, rectangle, and eraser tools, in a choice of five weights. You can see all the paintings on your Palm in the thumbnail viewer, and add a text note to each image (see Figure 17.7). You can use a text note either as a file name or as a way to quickly jot down a phone number that you'll later add to the Address Book. If you want to download your DinkyPad paintings to your desktop PC, look for DinkyView; you should be able to find it at the major shareware sites.

FIGURE 17.7

A modest DinkyPad painting

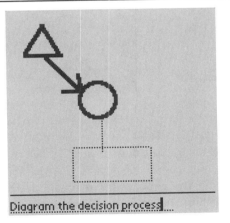

Diagram the decision process

TealPaint

At the opposite end of the power spectrum from DinkyPad lies TealPaint. This $17.95 shareware program from TealPoint Software (www.tealpoint.com) is as full-featured and professionally designed as any shrink-wrapped application.

TealPaint's interface is intuitive and strongly resembles what you get with a desktop PC paint program. It consists of two main screens: the drawing page (where you create your masterpiece) and the index page (where you can see all the pictures you've created). You can see thumbnails for up to four images at a time; the scroll buttons can help you navigate to the rest.

The painting tools lie at the bottom of the drawing page. Tap the Tool button, and a palette pops up to offer you the following tools: line, freeform, shape and text tools, a selector tool, a magnifying glass, and a paint can (for filling selections). You can see the tool palette in Figure 17.8.

FIGURE 17.8

The TealPaint tool palette

Next comes the Pattern Selector button, which pops up a palette of patterns to choose from. There's also a brush selector button, which lets you choose the pen tip shape for the selected painting tool. The last two buttons are Undo and Done. Undo reverts the last action you've taken (we wish it had multiple levels of Undo, but we're being greedy); Done saves your image and returns you to the index page.

These are just the basics. TealPaint also offers a complete set of operations, accessible via the menus. Besides the usual cut, copy, and paste, you'll find a Screen Grab tool that allows you to captures what's on your screen to a file, as well as a basic animation tool that lets you create the individual pages of a flipbook animation.

You can get your screen captures and other TealPaint images onto your desktop PC by HotSyncing. At that point, a new file (called pictures, by default) will be placed into the Backup folder inside your username folder within the Palm Desktop folder. To make those pictures viewable, you'll need Paintmgr—a Windows 95–only utility for converting your TealPaint pictures to Windows BMP files. Macintosh users should look for the TealPaint Mac Utility Pack for import, export, and viewing tools.

We've barely scratched the surface here. Try TealPaint for yourself, and see what it can do.

Exploring Other Graphics Options

There's more to the wonderful world of graphics than just drawing, painting, and viewing images. However, those are the categories that are best represented on the Palm platform, and they're the ones the majority of people use on a regular basis.

Here we'll give you a quick rundown of some other Palm graphics applications that may meet your particular need.

Charting Magic Chart 1.1 is virtually the only game in town. This shareware application from Patrice Nolin (`www.geocities.com/SiliconValley/Lakes/6481/`) costs $20.00 to register. It takes data from Memo Pad memos to create line, pie, and histogram charts.

Fonts If you want to create your own Palm fonts, you should use Handy Pilot Font Editor (shareware, $25.95, Alexander Ovcharenko, `http://www.sochi.com/~sandy/fe/`). This bitmap font editor lets you use Palm OS fonts as a template for creating your own. You can store your new fonts in RAM (if you've registered the software) and transfer them to the desktop by HotSyncing.

Animation The animation capabilities of the Palm are limited, but Flip (shareware, $19.00, Andermation, `http://www.flippad.com`) makes it easy for even the most artistically challenged to create cute little flipbook animations.

Sketching on Your Desktop RoughOut (commercial $39.95, 20-day free trial, Informal Software, `http://www.informal.com`) lets you sketch on your desktop PC (sorry, no Mac support) using your Palm as a real-time drawing device. Since you can import graphics to both the desktop component and the Palm, it's a great tool for annotating diagrams and maps, or for adding a signature to a PC document. The one drawback is that your Palm organizer must be in the cradle (which needs to be connected to your PC) for RoughOut to work. Still, it's a unique and useful concept.

Backgrounds   If you can't live without a background image on your Mac or Windows PC, you'll be pleased to hear that BackDrop EZ (freeware, Twilight Edge Software, http://www.twilightedge.com) lets you turn any ImageViewer picture into a background screen for your Palm IIIx, V, or VII.

Capturing Screens   If TealPaint is more than you need, but you'd still like to capture screens for use on your desktop (or in your own Palm book), Snapshot (Freeware, Joseph Strout, www.strout.net./pilotsoft/) is for you. This tiny 3K application can capture grayscale, black, and white Palm screens and save them to ImageViewer format. You can then view the captures on your Palm organizer or HotSync them over to your desktop. It's simple and effective.

CHAPTER **18**

Fun and Games for Your Palm

We firmly believe that all work and no play makes the Palm a dull device. Fortunately, there are thousands of application developers out there who seem to agree with us, judging by the sheer number of shareware and freeware games available for the Palm platform. Heck, in our search, we uncovered no less than five different variations on Tetris; if you're interested in old standards like Solitaire or Blackjack, you have even more choices. It's probably safe to say that if there's a game you enjoy playing on your desktop PC or even (gasp) in the analog world, there's a variation of it available for the Palm.

Though you can find Palm versions of first-person shooters along the lines of the PC giant Doom, the gaming experience will hardly be comparable. Forget about 3D, high-resolution graphics, high-speed movement, and cinematic sound effects. By now, you should know that's not what the Palm is all about.

Games for the Palm are much more subdued than their big-budget desktop PC counterparts. Palm games are more like the second generation of digital games—not quite as graphically challenged as Pong, but not as lush as Myst. Think of PacMan, and you're headed in the right direction.

Palm games may be more modest in their graphics, sound, and speed than their desktop counterparts, but they're also considerably more modest in their cost. While the $50 PC game is far from unusual, you'd be hard pressed to find a Palm game that costs more than $15.

So what do you need to play games on your Palm? Absolutely nothing but time and a fresh set of batteries (or a fresh charge if you're a Palm V user). All the games we found run right on top of the Palm operating system—no helper applications required. Though Palm games may be largely based on desktop PC games, they're written from scratch for the Palm platform. So, even though the premise behind TetrisV for the Palm and its PC-based counterpart may be the same, that's where the similarity ends. Under the covers, the code for the games is entirely different, as is the look and playing experience. With Palm games, you're getting an experience created to take advantage of what the Palm platform offers, rather than a dumbed-down version of a PC game that just makes you ache for what you're missing.

 TIP If you're planning to play lots of games on your Palm, stock up on batteries. The constant screen redraws and processing required by games will drain a battery faster than a month of regular application use.

Without much trouble at all, we came up with a baker's dozen of games and other amusements that make the most of the Palm platform. There are so many good games out there, it was hard to contain ourselves. But, our editor wouldn't let us do a whole book on Palm games, so we'll just let you expand your gaming repertoire from here.

 NOTE All the games mentioned here were downloaded from the PilotZone (www.pilotzone.com). You can probably find them at the other major Palm software sites listed in Appendix B, as well. All can be loaded from Windows or Macintosh machines.

Card Games

It seems like there are as many variations of solitaire as there are Palm organizers at Silicon Valley cocktail parties. But for our money, one version of Klondike (the traditional solitaire game available on every Windows machine in captivity) plays pretty much the same as the next. We're partial to unusual variants of the single-player card game, and if we can get them in the same package as some other card games, we're even happier.

We found just the thing in SeaHorse Game Pack 1. This $15 shareware program includes three games: Euchre (a bridge-like game that is more complicated to describe than it is to play), Crazy 8s (the classic card matching game we all played with our Nanas growing up), and Four Corners (a solitaire variant that calls for you to move cards to the corners of the layout). All of the games come with thorough playing instructions, are well-designed, and are fun to play. We'd forgotten how much fun Crazy 8s could be! The unregistered version of the Game Pack is exactly the same as the registered version, except it doesn't maintain game state (so if you leave the game and come back, it starts all over again) and doesn't save any game stats.

The other must-have card game for the Palm is Blackjack. Hey, if it's good enough for Las Vegas, it's good enough for us. Some folks may want to download one of the many blackjack games that let you bet, but we're so lousy at the whole gambling thing, that we could manage to go bust with even virtual money. So, we'll stick with the Gizmo Suite. This $5 shareware bargain includes Backjack (blackjack—which you can see in Figure 18.1) and PokeMe (5 card draw).

 TIP In Backjack, the dealer only has to hit on anything under 17. You can't double down or split a hand.

Both games come with a twist: Your opponent is Gizmo, a sarcastic dog who really hates to lose. So kick his canine keister and avoid the taunts, but don't miss this game.

Gizmo is a sore loser.

Board Games

Board games seem to translate really well to the Palm platform, so prepare to lose hours of productivity to these old favorites.

Triv, a $15 shareware version of Trivial Pursuit is our new favorite productivity killer. In case you've been living in a cave since the 80s, we'll explain the concept: You answer short trivia questions to earn pieces of pie. When you have a piece of pie for each of six categories, you win the game. Triv also offers some variations on the theme, including a Quick Quiz, which awards points for correct answers (you can see it in Figure 18.2); you can play against the Palm or against up to four human opponents.

The questions are challenging, but not brain busting; the only quibble we have is that the game layout is a bit busy. But, with 510 questions in the unregistered version and 8,000 available to registered users, we're not likely to grow tired of this one any time soon.

TIP Attention Macintosh users: Triv also offers a Module Creator for the Mac (sorry, no Windows) that lets you create your own question sets.

FIGURE 18.2

*We are the masters
of trivia.*

No game collection would be complete without a fun word game, so we always keep Wordlet handy. This $15 shareware version of Boggle has everything the analog version does, except the sound of the letters banging against the plastic dome when you shake them up. Like the real-world version of the game, the point of Wordlet is to create as many words as possible out of adjacent letter cubes laid out in a 4x4 grid. You earn points based on how many words out of all the possible combinations you come up with. You'll need to register this game before the 15-day trial period runs out, or you'll be out of luck when the Wordlet craving hits.

Our final selection in the board game category is an oldie but goodie with a Palm-only twist. IR Battleship combines all the fun of the fleet-sinking original, along with multi-player support via IR. So, you can either try to locate and sink the Palm's fleet of ships, or you can put that IR port to good use and try to sink your boss' fleet. Now isn't that a dream come true! The graphics are simple but appealing, and the game play is true to the original. The game expires in 30 days, unless you pay $15 to register it. We think it's worth the money for some head-to-head naval maneuvering.

TIP If you're into two-person gaming, check the shareware sites for IR-enabled versions of Chess, Checkers, Othello, Gin, and more. PilotZone even has a whole section devoted to IR games.

Action and Adventure Games

The Palm games available in this category are certainly more modest than their desktop PC counterparts, but they still offer some good exploring and shooting opportunities.

Those of you old enough to remember the 80s will no doubt have fond memories Lode Runner, one of the best of the early side-scrolling adventure games. The Palm version, dubbed Load Runner, uses the same concept as the original (collect all the jewels on the screen while avoiding the guards who protect them). The animated graphics are simple but interesting, and the game play is fairly speedy. The unregistered version gives you five levels of play; registering for $10 gets you extra levels and the ability to create your own levels.

Those of you prefer your gaming with a touch of violence can get your kicks from Ray Gin, a first-person shooter in the style of Doom and Quake. The goal here is the same as in every other game in this genre: Explore the maze-like environment, picking up everything that doesn't move and blowing away everything that does.

TIP Ignore Ray Gin's instructions for how to play—they're wrong. To shoot, press the Memo Pad button. Pressing the Date Book button turns you to the left and the Address Book button turns you to the right. The scroll button controls forward and backward motion (up for forward, down for backward).

The graphics here are incredibly simple—take a look at Figure 18.3 if you don't believe us. Your foes are represented by moving triangles, and the movement is far from smooth scrolling. But, if you really need a portable way to vent your frustrations, Ray Gin is just about the only game in town. And it's free!

FIGURE 18.3

*That triangle can
kill you.*

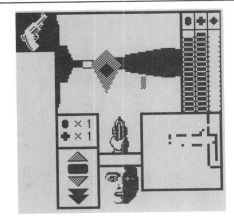

Classic Arcade Games

The three games in this section are really a blast from the past. In many ways, they bring digital gaming full-circle.

Way back in 1982, Donkey Kong made its debut on one of the original handheld gaming devices, Nintendo's "Game & Watch" series (it turned up later in arcades). The version for the Palm platform, called Donkie Kung Jr. is every bit as much fun as that early game. The premise is the same, too: Your dad (Donkie Kung) has been caged by the evil Maryo; you, as Junior, must free the old man, while avoiding evil birds and other assorted baddies. The animation is surprisingly detailed and speedy.

Overall, it's good old-fashioned fun. Registering for $5, earns you the right to have your high score listed on the developer's Web site (www.pilotfan.com), so brush up on your jumping and climbing.

We're happy to say that hopping a frog across a Palm screen is a bit tougher than it was in the days of Atari (oh, how we long for a Palm-supported joystick instead of navigating with the hard buttons), but it's every bit as much fun thanks to Froggy. This version of arcade favorite Frogger calls for you to safely navigate five frogs across a busy highway, a crocodile-infested river, and other hazards.

TIP The funny blob on the first row of logs is a lady frog. Escort her home to earn 200 bonus points.

The game play is smooth, though the graphics are a bit small to see clearly at times (take a look at Figure 18.4). The unregistered version delivers two levels of amphibian fun; the $10 registration fee buys you more adversaries, levels, and two secret features.

FIGURE 18.4

Don't turn into amphibian roadkill.

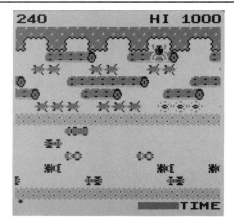

Those who prefer a more abstract challenge won't want to miss TetrisV. This block-arranging game is a perfect duplicate of the PC favorite of the 80s. Arrange the falling blocks into complete rows to wipe them off the board and earn points. Let the playing board fill up with incomplete rows and you lose. Keep at it long enough, and you'll be seeing falling blocks in your sleep. This $8 shareware game is every bit as addictive as the original.

Random Amusements

The three titles we're calling amusements are hard to categorize. They're not exactly games, but they certainly aren't productivity applications. Two of them are downright silly, while believers would consider the third quite serious. Whatever you call them, all three deliver entertainment in a compact arrangement.

There's no other way to describe Psychic Rabbit than to say it's a one-trick bunny, but that trick is a fun one. The bunny deals out some cards, you pick one in your mind, and then the bunny tells you what card you picked. We have no idea how this one works, but that wily (and free) rabbit is right most of the time.

Voodoo Doll is another one-trick—or more accurately, one-stick—piece of free entertainment. This one lets you name your victim, then stick pins into the doll (just tap your stylus where you want the pins to go). As you can see in Figure 18.5, this doll is not shy about expressing its discomfort with your actions. It's a harmless way to exact a measure of revenge on those who've done you wrong.

FIGURE 18.5

Take that, you fiend!

TAP (Tarot Assistant for Pilot) is much more benign, though it too dwells in the realm of the mystical. This $5 shareware program lets you lay out the tarot cards and interprets them for you. It's entirely text-based, so you don't get to see the lovely graphics of a tarot deck. But it offers a handful of different layouts to choose from, and its readings of the cards are traditional. Ignore its message at your own risk!

CHAPTER 19

Better Living through Palm Software

Bet when you first bought your Palm organizer you thought it was just a nifty little device that would help you get better organized. And now… Well, if you made it this far into the book, you're not sure how you ever managed before the Palm organizer. We're about to make that Palm even more indispensable for you, by describing some tools that help you pursue the things that are really important to you—health, happiness, and exotic locales—all using your Palm.

We tend to refer to the shareware and freeware applications in this chapter as lifestyle software. These little applications won't make you work more efficiently but they're not just for fun either. They're not as serious and the business and productivity tools we discussed in Chapter 16, but they're not as flat-out frivolous as the games we discussed in the previous chapter, either. Instead, they're applications that make it easier to pursue the interests that make your particular life more interesting. Whether you're interested in exercise, making music, reading, fine dining, cars, exotic drinks, or exotic locales, there's bound to be something here that piques your curiosity.

 TIP Many of the applications we've included here, and in fact many of the lifestyle applications available for downloading, are customized database files loaded with information on a particular topic. We'll tell you what database the application requires and where you can get it. For full descriptions of the database applications themselves, see Chapter 16.

The twelve applications we've included here barely scratch the surface of the thousands of freeware and shareware lifestyle offerings just waiting for you out there on the Web. Search one of the shareware sites we've highlighted in Appendix A, and you're sure to find something that caters to your needs.

 TIP All of the applications we've included here can be downloaded from PalmGear (www.palmgear.com). You can probably find them at the other major Palm software sites listed in Appendix A, as well. All can be loaded from Windows or Macintosh machines.

Travel

Whether your travels take you around the world or around the corner, there's a Palm application that can make your journey a bit more enjoyable.

Time Traveler is the Palm equivalent of a software suite. It includes three separate applications, Time Book, Time Place, and Time Travel, which cover a lot of ground within the travel arena. The three shareware applications cost $29.95 to register; the downloadable demo versions expire after 30 days. Time Book works as an international version of the standard Palm Date Book that's really at its best when you have to schedule a rendezvous in another time zone. You specify the time and time zone you live in, a description for your event, and where (geographically) that event is being held. Time Book will automatically calculate the time difference and fill in the time at your event locale. This is great if you need to make a three-way cross-country (or continent) phone call. You can have your mother in New York call in at 5:30 PM (local time) and your sister in Hawaii call in at 12:30 PM her time—without having to calculate all the time zone changes yourself. You can specify the time for the call in either local time or event time (the time for the location where the event is being held), and Time Book will calculate the other time for you and log the event. It's a nifty tool for the peripatetic Palm user.

Time Place is a very, very simple application that just calculates time differences (kind of like Time Book without the Date Book functionality). You just specify where home is (in our case, it's New York City), and Time Place figures out what time it is in various cities and countries around the world. In case you were wondering, when it's 9:00 AM in NYC, it's 12:30 AM + one day in Adelaide.

The third piece of the Time Traveler bundle is Time Travel—easily the most disposable application of the bunch. Time Travel keeps track of where you're going and how you're getting there. It offers a place to list your flight (or cruise) number, departure and arrival locations, and length of stay. Time Travel uses this information to reset your Palm's clock to local time. We wish it also let you keep track of where you're staying once you get to your destination and that it let you beam listings to other Palm users. Still, combined with the other Time Traveler applications, it's a useful tool for frequent fliers.

After that long flight, you're bound to be hungry, so don't miss TealMeal. This handy little $13.95 shareware application lets you find a restaurant that meets your dining requirements—whether they're based on price, cuisine, atmosphere, or some combination thereof. As you can see in Figure 19.1, it's an easy program to use and lets you choose from more cuisines than you can shake a Kebob at.

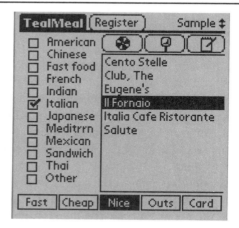

Say you're in San Francisco and desperately want cheap Italian food. Just select Italian and Cheap, and TealMeal will see what it can come up with. Of course, you'll need to make sure you have the San Francisco database loaded. But not to worry, there are a bunch of free city databases available for download from the TealPoint Software site (www.tealpoint.com). And TealMeal can manage multiple databases, so if your travels take you to San Jose as well, you're in luck—but only for 30 days, when the trial runs out. Register to ensure your dining needs will be met.

If you're travels take you further afoot, make sure you know what you're eating with Translator7. This free PQA (which means it's only for the Palm VII users out there), is a surprisingly quick translation tool. You just enter the word you want translated and pick the language you want it translated to. Translator7 then dials out over Palm.Net and returns the translation to you. The company that published this PQA, Snakefeet.com, runs a Proxy server that hooks you up to the language resources of www.travlang.com. Don't worry; you don't have to know any of this since it's all seamless and fast. Translator7 translates English to and from German, Dutch, French, Spanish, Portuguese, Italian, Danish, Swedish, Norwegian, Finnish, Frisian, Afrikaans, Latin, Czech, Hungarian, and Esperanto, and from those languages back to English. It also translates from most of those languages to most others. This is indispensable if you want to know what Scungilli is, and if it's something you really want to put into your mouth.

Health

First, let's clear up a common misconception: Owning a Palm organizer will not make you thinner or more physically fit. Nor will it force you to put down the brownie and drop into push-up position. It's not a drill sergeant, after all. But, if you're trying to clean up your act and lead a healthier lifestyle, there are plenty of Palm-based tools to help you along.

For those of you out there who actually do follow an exercise regimen, WorkOut Tracker is the next best thing to a personal trainer. This application makes it easy to record all the information from your workout right on your Palm organizer. You can record information for each exercise, customize exercises to suit your needs, and group exercises into routines. Workout Tracker provides a long and customizable list of all your exercises, organized by date. Each exercise has customizable fields, so you can record the information that you need. You can chart your progress over days or weeks via graphs (see Figure 19.2).

FIGURE 19.2

*Slow but steady
progress.*

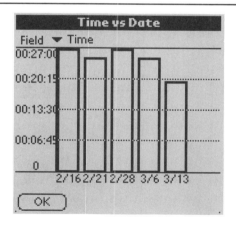

The downloadable version of WorkOut Tracker is a 30-day demo; it costs $19.95 to register the program. Pay the money! This is a great tool for monitoring your progress along the road to physical fitness—or your slide into slothdom, as the case may be.

Exercise alone won't help you hit your goal weight. You need to cut back on the junk food, too. DietLog Weight Watchers ($59.00, 15-day trial version available for download) can help you track everything you eat in the course of the day. This version of DietLog (an excellent Palm program in its own right) is customized to follow the Weight Watchers 1-2-3 Success plan, which counts points instead of calories. Diet-Log Weight Watchers (which is not endorsed by the Weight Watchers organization) has a full database of foods and point values. The program can help you calculate your point range (which is based on factors such as your height, starting weight, age, sex, and goal weight) and tally up the points you consume throughout the day. You can add any foods or recipes that are missing from the list and even see reports on your consumption for a day or week (did I really use up 20 percent of my points on snacks?). Those who are merely counting calories or trying to watch their fat intake should download standard DietLog—it has everything the Weight Watchers version does, except the point values. This one isn't shareware, but it's worth every penny.

Music

Bet you didn't know you could make music on your Palm. Well, we're pleased to tell you that this too is possible. The music you make won't sound like a symphony, after all the Palm has but a handful of tones in its repertoire. But just because you're away from your piano (or guitar, or drum kit) doesn't have to mean you're out of tune.

Put a drummer in your Palm with Pocket Beat. This tiny dynamo provides an animated drum kit that plays along with whatever beat you set (see Figure 19.3).

FIGURE 19.3

A drumming dynamo

It offers synthesized snare, kick, and hi-hats, and support for a variety of tempos. It also provides a count-off, continuous playback, as well as a bunch of stuff that music pros will appreciate, but fall on our tone-deaf ears.

We just like playing. But we're told that acoustic guitarists who can't always find band mates should love this one. Pocket Beat is shareware with a $12.00 registration fee. It requires PocketC to run, but that's included in the download file.

 TIP If Pocket Beat playback is sporadic, you may have too many Hacks installed that are sucking up all your resources. Uninstall some and try Pocket Beat again.

If you'd rather try your hand at composing rather than just playing along, check out miniGrid. This demo version of a larger application called miniMusic lets you draw a melody graphically on your Palm organizer. miniMusic lets you work with music in any of three views and save a categorized library of your compositions. You can find it at www.5thwall.com/minimusic/.

To use miniGrid, you just tap your stylus on the display (not the Graffiti writing area) to add a note and drag to stretch the note or change its pitch. When your notes are where you want them, tap on the play button to hear your creation. There's even an eraser so you can go back and fix your mistakes.

You'll need to know something about music to create a song that sounds any good, but it's fun just to noodle around, too. And did we mention that miniGrid is free? So what's stopping you from becoming the Palm's answer to Puccini?

Reading

You're probably thinking this is a very strange category to include here. After all, every Palm application requires you to read, now doesn't it? But, there's an entire category of software for the Palm called e-books (or e-text), which are full-length works of fiction, poetry, philosophy, medical references…you name it, and it's been converted into a document that can be read on your Palm organizer.

There are literally thousands of texts out there ready for downloading. And they're all free. If you can't find a book that appeals to you, you can easily create your own e-text. Perhaps one day, even *Mastering Palm Organizers* will be available as an e-book. Until that day rolls around, you'll have to content yourself with the likes of Shakespeare, Thoreau, Aristotle, and the King James Bible.

We're not about to debate the merits of Shakespeare over Aristotle. We'll leave the decision about what to download to your personal preference. Instead, we'll explain what you need to read e-books on your Palm and where to find a treasure trove of texts. The rest is up to you.

For starters, the majority of e-texts are in a format known as Palm Doc. Though it may sound like the file format used by Microsoft Word, it's really something entirely different. Palm Doc is a compressed format that requires a Doc reader, which is an application that displays the e-text and in most cases lets you search for particular words, add bookmarks (so you can find a favorite passage easily), and copy chunks of text for use in other applications.

There are at least a dozen different Doc readers available on the Internet. While they all serve the same basic purpose, they do it differently; and they can't all read each other's files. Every Doc reader should be able to read every Doc file you download, but some of the readers also offer proprietary file formats that can't be read by every other reader. Some Doc readers offer more sophisticated search capabilities, more font choices, and more robust bookmarking. Others are commendable for their small size and unique features. Try out the demo versions to decide what really matters to you. If all you want to do is scroll through a complete book, any of the readers will work just fine.

 TIP To get you started on your own Palm library, here are two great sources of e-books. Try PalmCentral (www.palmcentral.com), which organizes e-books by genre, and the Palm Etext Ring (head to www.webring.org and search on Palm), which links you to sites all related to e-books. You can even find some original works of fiction out there.

Two of our favorite Doc readers are AportisDoc Mobile Edition and TealDoc. Both are shareware applications that offer everything you could ask for in a Doc reader—and some things you never thought of, too.

AportisDoc Mobile Edition (it also comes in a free Reader version, which doesn't support bookmarks, and a $39.95 Pro version, which lets you convert Microsoft Word and HTML documents into DOC format) pretty much defined the standard for what a Doc reader should be. It offers a variety of ways to navigate through a document, including line-by-line, screen-by-screen, a customizable auto-scroll, powerful searching and bookmarking features (see Figure 19.4), and four display fonts. One of our favorite features is the automatic bookmarking option, which lets you specify text and a certain number of characters for AportisDoc to look for. So, for example, you can specify the word Chapter to have AportisDoc find and bookmark all the chapter headings in a document.

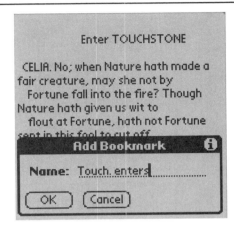

FIGURE 19.4

*Mark the really
important parts with
AportisDoc.*

AportisDoc Mobile Edition even lets you use a virtual screen that's wider than the Palm's 160 by 160 pixel screen. This is very useful if you are working with database reports. Searching for a particular passage is easy thanks to the command buttons at the bottom of the screen; if you prefer more reading room, you can switch to full-screen mode and eliminate the buttons.

AportisDoc Mobile Edition does not expire or have functional limitations, but you are expected to send in the $30.00 registration fee after 60 days of use.

 TIP If you really want to convert existing documents into Doc file, you can find utilities on most of the shareware sites that make this possible.

TealDoc is our other favorite Doc reader. This shareware application offers an almost identical feature set as AportisDoc Mobile Edition, with one major addition: it's the only Doc reader for the Palm that lets you display embedded graphic images, as well as inter- and intra-document links (which work like Web hyperlinks). Combined, these features let you read illustrated books and jump to different locations within a work. There aren't that many e-books that have taken advantage of these features yet, but they have great potential. You can see a Doc file with an embedded graphic in Figure 19.5.

FIGURE 19.5

An illustrated Doc

You can download documents that take advantage of TealDoc's unique capabilities from the TealPoint Software Web site (www.tealpoint.com). There, you'll also find utilities for the PC and Mac that let you convert existing Word, HTML, and Adobe PDF documents into TealDoc files.

Hobbies

We're not sure how you define a hobby, but we characterize it as anything you're passionate about that doesn't result in cash income (at least not on a regular basis). We surfed far and wide to see what Palm developers consider hobbies, and found a wealth of choices—wholesome and not so wholesome, well-designed and not so well-designed. We really do believe that there is a Palm application out there for every type of collector. For the most part, the hobby applications either deliver content or a way to organize content from your particular area of interest.

AutoBase is one of the organizing types of hobby applications. On the surface, it's vaguely reminiscent of the Palm Expense application—like that tool, AutoBase provides a form for holding a particular type of information. In this case, that information pertains to the maintenance records for your car (or cars; AutoBase can track multiple vehicles). So, if you're like a certain member of this writing team, you'll use AutoBase to log fuel purchases (complete with location, price, number of gallons, and odometer reading), oil changes, tire rotations, scheduled service, and sundry other auto things.

Since AutoBase isn't a database, it doesn't offer a way to filter or sort the entries by type, which means you can't easily find out how many miles per gallon your car averages over a period of time. Still, AutoBase offers built-in mileage-based reminders for tire rotations, periodic service and oil changes, and it's free—which makes it hard to beat.

For those who'd rather play bartender than auto mechanic, the application of choice is Palm Bar. This free database requires MobileDB to run. MobileDB is one of the leading Palm database programs, which can also be downloaded from PalmCentral. We discuss it in greater detail in Chapter 16.

 TIP You should install MobileDB before installing Palm Bar. You won't see an icon in the Application Launcher for Palm Bar. Just tap the MobileDB icon to open that application and you'll see Palm Bar in the list of installed databases. Tap Palm Bar from that list, and you're on your way.

Next time you're hosting a major shindig, and someone asks for a drink you never heard of, power up Palm Bar and start mixing. This handy little database has the lowdown on 219 different drinks, ranging from old standards like the Martini to oddballs like the Americana. Since it's a MobileDB database, you can filter the records based on any column—perhaps to find all the bourbon drinks (see Figure 19.6).

FIGURE 19.6

Name your poison.

There's nothing fancy about Palm Bar itself (all the cool functionality is provided by MobileDB), but if you're dying for a Cuba Libre, Palm Bar's for you. If you invent a drink, you can even add it to the list.

If you'd rather create new recipes for food than drinks, go with the appropriately named Recipes. Like Palm Bar, this is a free database-driven application. However, Recipes requires HanDBase to run. We'll tell you more about HanDBase in Chapter 16.

Recipes doesn't come populated with other folks' instructions for creating a meal, rather it provides a well thought-out, portable place for you to build your own recipe database. To make things a little easier, Recipes provides a pop-up list of frequently used terms (such as Preheat Oven) that you just tap on to add to your instructions. This list is fully customizable, so if your concoctions call for a less common action, such as scalding, you can add it yourself. The database is fully sortable (we only want to see desserts made with chocolate), customizable, and even lets you beam your recipes to loved ones (let's see you do that with index cards). Just don't drop your Palm into the food processor!

CHAPTER **20**

Accessorizing Your Palm

Don't know about you, but we seem to surround ourselves with things that want other things. For example, we bought new cameras, and they wanted lenses, filters, and different kinds of film. It just goes on and on.

Our Palm organizers are no different. We outfitted them with all kinds of software, but they want more. Fortunately, plenty of accessories are available to choose from. Some of the accessories even have their own accessories.

Of course, they're all very practical and go a long way toward enhancing the Palm computing experience. We'll bet you can't stop with just one.

Cases

Every Palm deserves a safe, secure home. The bottom of your purse, backpack, or briefcase just won't cut it. At best, your Palm will pick up bits of tissue lint rattling around there and can accidentally turn on and drain the batteries. At worst, your Palm's screen can get scratched and the buttons jammed. Now we know you want better than that for your new favorite organizer. So, be a sport and buy your Palm its very own case. There are choices in virtually every price range and style, ranging from the sporty to the avant-garde to the chicest of the chic. Search on any of the sites offering Palm merchandise for sale, and you'll find a large selection. We'll highlight a few of our favorites here.

If you're an accident waiting to happen, the Bumper ($39.99, Concept Kitchen, www.conceptkitchen.com) is the case for you. This one is made of impact-resistant plastic, so it can survive some pretty hard bumps and bruises (see it in Figure 20.1). We've seen it dropped from about four feet, and its precious Palm cargo emerged unscathed. It's also water resistant, so there's no reason to cry over spilled latte. Just don't take your Palm for a swim—that's more than the Bumper can handle.

The Bumper has a hideaway lid, two stylus holders, an IR window, and loops for attaching wrist or shoulder straps. It even comes in a choice of colors: sports yellow or asphalt gray. Unfortunately, the Bumper doesn't fit the Palm VII, though it can accommodate every other Palm model.

If you're looking for something just as rugged but a bit more fashion-forward, take a look at RhinoSkin's Titanium Slider Hardcase ($99.95, RhinoSkin, www.rhinoskin.com). These cases aren't cheap, but they are durable and practical. The hard lid slides under the base when your Palm is in use to make a compact bundle. The case is lined with neoprene to provide extra cushioning for your organizer. You can even access the IR port while your organizer is in the case.

FIGURE 20.1

*A Bumper for
your Palm.*

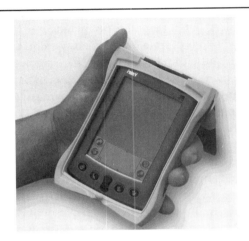

While the titanium cases aren't sized to accommodate a Palm VII (they work fine for Palm III series and Palm V organizers), RhinoSkin does offer a cordura nylon case that fits the Palm VII (and other models) just right. Made out of the same rugged fabric as backpacks, the Rhinopak 1000 Sport case costs just $26.95, but offers water resistant design, extra pockets for storing business cards, and a plastic insert that protects your Palm's screen. It's a sporty-looking black case that won't take up a lot of room in your briefcase.

If fine leather and refined styling is more to your liking, check out the offerings from Dooney & Bourke (www.dooney.com). Their $49.95 Palm V case is as sleek and stylish as the Palm V itself. It uses the Palm V's attachment rail to hold the device in place, and offers one card slot on the inside of its cover. The $49.95 Palm III case has a tongue and loop closure and uses Velcro to hold the Palm in place. Both cases are made of soft but resilient all-weather leather that gets better with use. Alas, they don't offer any Palm VII cases and have no plans to add them to the line (even though we begged!).

Other fine leather cases are available from Coach (www.coach.com) and Palm Computing (www.palm.com). At the time we wrote this, Palm Computing was the only company offering a leather case for the Palm VII. Their top-of-the-line offering is the Premiere Slim Case, made out of napa leather and selling for $39.95.

Replacement Styli

There is nothing inherently wrong with the stylus that comes with the Palm organizer. It works just fine and has the advantage of fitting nicely in the provided slot in the organizer. But, many users (us included) find it a bit too thin and small for using over long periods of time. Fortunately, we don't have to cramp our hands holding on to that tiny little thing any longer. There are hundreds of different replacement styli on the market. These range from the bargain basement to the think-twice-about-it pricy. Many come from traditional pen companies, who know a thing or two about writing comfort.

The Pilot Pen company is one of the leaders in the replacement styli market. They have a number of different models, some of which offer and pen and stylus in one. The newest model, the Chameleon by Pentopia ($18.95, www.pentopia.com), not only offers a pen and stylus rolled in one, it even fits in the stylus slot on your Palm organizer. It looks very much like a Palm III series stylus, but the cap unscrews to reveal a refillable ballpoint pen. There's even a reset pin hidden in the pen body.

Pilot Pen also offers a full line of stylus-only models that range in price from $1.50 for one that looks like a disposable stick pen to $9.95 for a Dr. Grip version with an ergonomic cushioned contour grip and a retractable tip. Their top-of-the-line model, the $29.95 T2300, combines a stylus, ballpoint pen, and a mechanical pencil in one sleek silver package. It's very convenient and oh so stylish.

If you'd rather not have to carry a stylus with you, consider the PenCap Stylus ($9.99 for a pack of four, Concept Kitchen, www.conceptkitchen.com). This little plastic device slips over the end of any stick-style disposable pen, turning it into a stylus. It can even double as a pen cap when you need to use the pen for non-Palm writing. You can see it in Figure 20.2.

The PenCap Stylus writes well on the Palm screen, is comfortable to use, and cheap enough not to worry about if you lose.

Cross' DigitalWriter Duo ($35.00, Cross Pen Computing Group, www.cross-pcg.com) lies at the opposite end of the luxury spectrum. This stylus/ballpoint pen combination has all the sleek, understated styling of a Cross pen. And it's just as comfortable in your hand thanks to its wide barrel and flexible stylus tip, which comes closest to providing a pen-on-paper feel of any stylus we've tried. It comes in a variety of colors, so you can match your stylus to your case. Now that's accessorizing!

FIGURE 20.2

The PenCap Stylus

Care and Maintenance

A clean Palm is a happy Palm. You already know enough not to bathe your Palm in a tub full of bubbles, or to spray window cleaner on its delicate screen. But that doesn't mean you should neglect the screen completely. There are special tools for protecting it from scratches and nicks, and gentle cleaning products that can keep it pristine for the life of the device.

Keep your Palm screen free of scratches by applying a WriteRight screen overlay ($27.99 for a pack of 12, ConceptKitchen, www.conceptkitchen.com). These clear vinyl overlays fit directly over the screen of your Palm organizer. They're slightly textured, so besides protecting your screen from scratches, they also improve Graffiti recognition and cut glare. They adhere to the screen through static cling rather than glue—so you'll never have a sticky mess to clean up. Each overlay lasts about a month. We wouldn't think about taking our Palm out without one.

TIP   Some folks find the overlay a bit hard to see through on the screen, but like the improved Graffiti recognition. If you fall into this category, trim the overlay so it covers just the Graffiti writing section of the screen and get the best of both worlds.

No matter how careful you are, your Palm screen will pick up some dust and nicks through routine use. And if you're going to use a WriteRight overlay, you should clean the screen thoroughly before sticking it on. We know of no better product than Screen Clean kit ($19.99, Concept Kitchen, www.conceptkitchen.com), which is an all-in-one screen cleaning kit (see Figure 20.3).

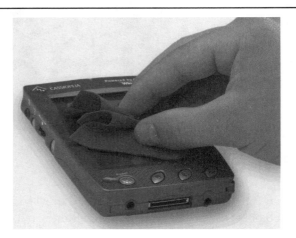

The kit contains 12 Brain Wash packets (a wet and dry solution that restores your screen to its original condition) and a Karma Cloth (a soft leather chamois for gently dusting and polishing the screen). You can use the Karma Cloth for daily fingerprint removal and the Brain Wash for once a month heavy cleaning. Together they'll keep your Palm screen shiny and bright for years to come.

Productivity Enhancers

Dress it up though we may, we haven't forgotten that the Palm is still a first-rate business and productivity tool. So, we've rounded up a bunch of accessories that help you communicate with the outside world, input information better and faster, and use your organizer for other purposes besides organizing. All of the accessories in this category are hardware devices; most require you to install some software on your organizer in order to use them. All are worth the little bit of extra trouble.

If you write lots of memos on your organizer or just can't get up to speed with Graffiti, you really need the GoType keyboard (LandWare, www.landware.com). This hardware keyboard comes in two models: The $79.95 GoType, which works with all Palm models except the Palm V, and the $89.95 GoType Pro, which works with the Palm V only.

Both models offer the same basic functionality. You just plug the keyboard into your Palm's HotSync connector, load the GoType software from your desktop PC (you only need to do this once), then start typing. Both devices draw a small amount of power from your Palm organizer. The 11-oz. keyboard is light enough to carry around (you can even buy a case for it), but sturdy enough for everyday use. The keys have a good tactile response that should appeal to even the fussiest touch typists.

Both GoType models work with all Palm operating systems and all Palm applications. Both also offer customizable function keys and let you access menu commands and ShortCuts. The GoType Pro also includes an additional serial port, so you can HotSync without removing the Palm from the keyboard, and it has an integrated power input so you can charge your Palm V while it's connected. Whichever model you choose, you'll find it's an indispensable tool for fast text input.

Ever come home from a trade show with a pocket full of business cards, and no ambition to input them into your Palm? (Who hasn't?) Then the CardScan Executive ($299.00, Corex Technologies Corp., www.cardscan.com) is the perfect device for you. CardScan Executive includes a business card scanner, OCR and database software, and a Palm conduit. Still, it's a Palm accessory in only the loosest sense: You hook up the card scanner to your desktop PC, the OCR software turns the scanned pixels into editable text, then places the information—name, phone number, e-mail address—into the proper fields in its desktop database. You HotSync your Palm to get the information into your Address Book. The scanner is surprisingly quick and its optical character recognition is acceptably accurate. Though this device requires a desktop PC to operate, it still offers the best way we've found to get business card information into the Palm (short of beaming, that is).

If you'd rather input information through voice dictation than text, Jet Talker ($149.00, DynaFirm, www.dynafirm.com) is the product for you. This device snaps on to the HotSync connector on any Palm organizer but the V, and lets you record up to 34 minutes of voice memos. The Jet Talker has its own memory for storing messages, weighs just under 3 ounces and runs on two AAA batteries. You can organize your memos into 15 categories, each of which can have 15 subcategories. A simple software interface lets you fast forward, rewind, pause, and delete messages and create personalized voice alarms. The sound quality isn't exceptional, but it's definitely decipherable. Doctors, lawyers, and others who need to take lots of notes in a hurry will love this one.

If you'd rather pull information in from the Web than input it yourself, a modem is a must. Palm Computing (www.palm.com) offers models for the Palm III series, the Palm V, and the Palm VII. All plug in to the HotSync connector of your organizer, run on two AAA batteries (an AC adapter is optional), and provide about 5–6 hours or operation or 150 remote HotSyncs on one set of batteries. The Palm III and VII models sell for $129.00; the Palm V version is $169.00. All of the modems have a maximum data transfer rate of 33.6Kbps, and work with any standard ISP account you may have. And, you'll need to plug in to a phone line to make a connection.

 NOTE   You'll need special software on your organizer to browse the Web or read your e-mail; we explain all about this in Chapters 12 and 15.

For those who'd prefer an entirely wireless connection (and don't mind paying for it), Novatel Wireless offers the Minstrel III modem ($369.00, www.novatelwireless .com). This pocket-size wireless modem looks like a cradle for the Palm III and, not surprisingly, plugs in to the Palm's HotSync connector. It works with any Palm III series or Palm VII organizer; rumor has it a version for the Palm V is coming soon.

The Minstrel III is capable of transmission speeds of up to 19.2Kbps (slower than the connected modem), but since it's wireless can send and receive Internet data or perform a remote HotSync without being plugged in to a phone jack. It uses a rechargable battery that should provide about 6–8 hours of use. The biggest drawback to this one is that you have to set up an account with a wireless service provider, rather than use your standard ISP account. In addition, the Minstrel uses a wireless technology called CDPD, which isn't available everywhere. Check with your local cell phone service provider about availability; most service providers also offer wireless data service for $20.00–$50.00 per month.

Take your Palm on the road with the Earthmate Road Warrior Edition ($219.95 for Palm III and VII or Palm V version, Delorme, www.delorme.com). Earthmate delivers a complete GPS navigation solution for the Palm organizer. It includes everything you need to use maps, rout directions, and a GPS on your organizer. The kit includes an Earthmate GPS Receiver, Street Atlas USA and Solus Pro software, and an adapter cable for connecting the GPS to your Palm.

The Street Atlas software runs on your desktop PC. You upload maps and route directions from this application to your Palm and view them there using Solus Pro. The GPS Receiver uses satellite-positioning data to tell you where you are at any given time. If you're the sort that gets lost easily, this system is a great addition to your Palm toolkit.

Attention Palm V users: You can leave home without your cradle. The Emergency Charger (Tech Center Labs, http://members.aol.com/talestuff) can charge your Palm V in a pinch. This handy device comes in two versions: the $29.95 PalmV Emergency 9V Charger and the $34.95 PalmV Emergency CarCharger. Both devices serve the same purpose: they provide a way to charge your Palm V when your cradle is nowhere in sight. Both devices plug in to the HotSync/charge connector on your Palm V and hook up to a power source. The 9V Charger uses a standard or NiCad 9-volt battery as its source, while the CarCharger plugs in to the cigarette lighter in your car. Both devices use a limited constant current (same as the Palm V cradle) and both offer an LED indicator that lets you know how the charge is progressing. We've found the devices to be effective in limited use, but neither has been endorsed by Palm Computing.

We found another nifty, reasonably priced device just for Palm V users. As you've probably surmised by now, the accessories you bought for your previous Palm device are useless to your Palm V. Accessories created for the Palm Professional or Palm III can be plugged into any Palm III series organizer and even the Palm VII, but not into the Palm V, which has a different HotSync connector. However, you can now invest $14.99 in the Bridge for Palm V (Midwest PCB; www.midwestpcbdesigns.com). This little piece of plastic with a built-in circuit board does but one thing: it lets you plug Palm III accessories into your Palm V organizer. Just snap the Bridge into your Palm V's Hot-Sync connector, then plug your accessory into the Bridge. It's a great tool for salvaging your existing accessories—and saving money you would have spent on new ones.

PART V

Advanced Techniques

LEARN TO:

- **Improve the Performance of your Palm Organizer**

- **HotSync Beyond the Palm Desktop**

- **Write Your Own Palm Applications**

- **Debug Your Applications**

CHAPTER **21**

Using HackMaster to Improve the Performance of Your Palm Organizer

We all like our Palms for their small size and quick response. Turn on a Palm and you're immediately ready to go: enter a new contact name and phone number to the Address Book or confirm an appointment in the Date Book. Then turn it off. This entire operation probably takes 10–12 seconds, or less than half the time that an average desktop or laptop computer takes just to boot up. Because the Palm is designed for this purpose, it is a speedy performer, which is more they you can say for your great big general purpose computer. What we gain in speed and simplicity, however, we trade off in the ability to modify or customize our Palm organizers. They are simply what the factory made them—or are they? Don't judge a Palm's flexibility by its seemingly singular purpose.

Tweaking for Better Performance

Unlike a desktop or laptop computer, Palm organizers offer little in the way of quick and simple performance tweaks. However, that doesn't mean that you lack options and must accept your Palm just the way it is.

There are many ways to optimize these gems; heck, you can even write your own application programs. All it takes is a little planning and a few of the techniques that we will talk about here.

There are many books and magazines devoted to exploring the plethora of optimization tips for our computers. Be it DOS, Windows, or Mac OS 8.X, there is at least one publication loaded with tricks and tips to make that computer run more quickly or more efficiently.

Many, if not most, of these tips require you to modify your computer's operating system in some way to make the computer run faster. These modifications may be as simple to enact as selecting a radio button from a application's menu, or they may require that you become one with your computer and "monkey around under the hood."

Fortunately, Palm organizers are incredibly fast straight out of the box, and there is little anyone can do to make them faster. But you can personalize them by removing all possible roadblocks, which translates to faster use.

Even if you're satisfied with the Palm's operating speed, you still may want to monkey around under the hood. We'll explain how you can personalize your Palm in three ways: by using Palm OS modifications called Hacks (discussed in this chapter); by adding a link or a conduit to a new desktop application (see Chapter 22 for more information on conduits); and by writing your own complete Palm application (covered in Chapters 23–27).

TIP For information on Web sites that offer Palm OS hacks, conduits, and complete applications for free (or inexpensive download fees), see Appendix A.

HackMaster

Developed and distributed through an outfit called DaggerWare, HackMaster is the product of Edward Keyes, a programmer and graduate student at MIT. DaggerWare/Keyes introduced HackMaster as a shareware product back in 1996 with the hopes of making it the standard development tool for the Palm OS. Over the past few years, HackMaster has garnered a following and a fair share of attention—and it's still a shareware product. DaggerWare determined that you could write a Palm OS extension and attach it to any one of several system routine traps. A trap is similar in concept to an interrupt on a PC; both are basically event handlers. Whenever that system routine is called, so will the newly written OS extension. Simple in concept, but quite complex in practice.

Among its many virtues, HackMaster manages Hack files by providing a common interface to us, the users. Installing and un-installing Hacks are a snap, and HackMaster even manages each Hack file's status so multiple Hacks won't clobber each other.

A *Hack* is a standard Palm resource file, created in some flavor of the C programming language. These resource files possess a .PRC file extension and look just like a "normal" Palm application except that, once installed, they may not look or react like a "normal" Palm application. Though each Hack program is installed and managed through HackMaster, the Hack program itself may never display on the Applications Launcher. That's because some Hacks modify the behavior of the Palm device and are always running in background. For example, Fitaly Keyboard for Palm OS, a keyboard extension from Two Solutions, installs and looks like a standard Palm application. You'll even have an icon in the Applications Launcher and you'll also need HackMaster to run the Fitaly Hack. On the other hand, LeftHack, a tool that makes the Palm more lefty friendly, blends into the background once installed. No icons, no indication that this program is running except, of course, that your screen now looks quite different. We'll look more closely at these and eleven other Hacks later in this chapter.

 NOTE Creating a Hack is something that should only be undertaken by an experienced programmer. DaggerWare assumes "a fairly high level of Pilot programming knowledge."

PART
V

Advanced Techniques

You can download HackMaster directly from DaggerWare (`www.daggerware.com`) or from several other Palm Web sites (such as `www.palmgear.com`). Version 0.91 is the most recent version (as of August 1999) though all versions are backward compatible. Additionally, HackMaster takes just 10KB of your Palm's memory once it is installed. As a shareware application, HackMaster is distributed free of charge.

Installing HackMaster

HackMaster and Hacks are really very easy to install and use. We'll just need to install HackMaster prior to installing any Hack applications. We also need to be mindful of the order in which we install Hacks—sometimes they react poorly and will not peacefully co-exist.

To Install HackMaster:

1. Copy HackMaster to the add-on folder in your Palm Desktop directory.

2. Access the Palm Desktop software on your PC or Mac, then click the Install button to activate the Install tool, as shown in Figure 21.1.

FIGURE 21.1

The Install Tool

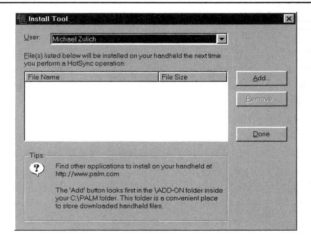

3. Click the Add button.

4. From the Open dialog box, choose Hackmstr.prc (see Figure 21.2).

FIGURE 21.2

The Open window
with HackMaster
highlighted

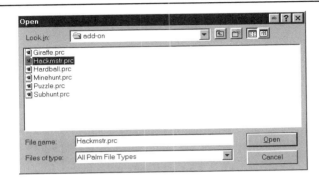

5. Click Open. Click Done and then OK in the resulting dialog box, which informs you that your program will be installed the next time you HotSync your Palm organizer.

6. Perform a HotSync to install HackMaster.

Once you have installed HackMaster onto your Palm device, you'll find its icon nestled between your Graffiti and HotSync icons, as shown in Figure 21.3. Hack-Master is running and ready to do its magic.

FIGURE 21.3

HackMaster on the
Applications menu

Once you have HackMaster installed, you can load each individual Hack application onto your Palm device. Follow the above procedure substituting the Hack file name for the HackMaster file name in Step 3. Hacks don't generally appear as icons on the Application menu, so don't become alarmed if you see nothing different after loading a new Hack. You'll need to install and configure each Hack application through HackMaster.

Tap the HackMaster icon to see a list of the Hacks that you have downloaded to your Palm device. Tap the check box to the left of the Hack filename to install the Hack, as shown in Figure 21.4.

 TIP It's best to install Hacks one at a time and not in large groups. Hacks work at a very low level inside your Palm, using memory and CPU resources in some very odd, though creative, ways. HackMaster tries hard to prevent Hacks from interfering with each other, but it does not concern itself with how the Hack interfaces with the other applications on your Palm. So, it is possible that a Hack will cause your Palm to lock up and require a soft- or hard-reset. With that in mind, it is prudent to load one Hack at a time. If your Palm locks up, you'll know which Hack is the offender.

FIGURE 21.4

The HackMaster
Install screen

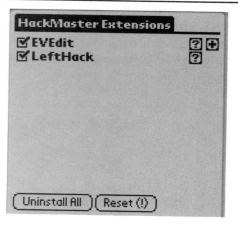

Tap the (?) help icon to the right of the Hack filename for information and instructions for using the Hack. Some of these are pretty thin, so don't expect too much. Additionally, some Hacks may have a Plus (+) icon to the right of the (?) help icon. Generally, these are used to access the user preferences or install a customization menu. Just tap this icon to access the menu.

 WARNING If you have loaded several Hacks and are having problems with them, try uninstalling each and reinstalling them in a different order. Hacks are sometimes sensitive to the order in which they were loaded.

Now that you've installed HackMaster, you're ready to enter the world of Hacks.

The Lucky 13: Hacks You Can't Live Without

Hacks come in all flavors and varieties, but the one thing that seems common to them all is their ingenuity: these tiny programs can solve many problems and cure a plethora of shortcomings. Here are our top 13 most useful Hacks, and a couple tips that address Palm IIIx and Palm V owners only. These Hacks are available for downloading from the Web.

Managing and Launching Your Applications

These four Hacks will let you customize your Palm device.

Hack 1: Launcher III

This freeware Hack, shown in Figure 21.5, replaces your Palm's built-in applications launcher with a series of menu tabs. All of your applications are automatically organized into the APPS, UTILS, and GAMES tabs. Don't like how Launcher III arranged your applications? Just drag-and-drop the application to the preferred tab. Don't like that application anymore? Drag it to the trash can. Tap the lower-left corner of the Palm's LCD screen and change the date, time, and day of the week views. You can also view the battery and memory status in either percent of total or actual level.

PART

V

Advanced Techniques

FIGURE 21.5

Launcher III

Launcher III uses 30KB when installed on a Palm device. You can download it from www.benc.hr.

Hack 2: PopUp Favorites

If Launcher III seems like too much of a change from the standard Palm Application Launcher, or if you don't want to change the look of your Palm's application menu, then you might want to try PopUp Favorites, shown in Figure 21.6. With this Hack you can define a pen stroke, or attach a single or double tap of the stylus to each application. These actions reduce your need to scroll or tap through multiple screens. You're essentially making shortcuts.

*PopUp Favorites
Setup screen*

PopUp Favorites takes 25KB when installed and, as shareware, is available for $5 from www.benc.hr.

Hack 3: AppHack

Ever wish that you could *really* customize your Palm—like change what the buttons do? Well, this tiny Hack lets you do exactly that. But it not only lets you redefine your Palm's hardware buttons, it goes several steps beyond what the Palm OS allows. AppHack (shown in Figure 21.7) inserts a menu between the hard button and the application. Press a hard button, and a menu pops up with a list of applications. Using this approach, you can assign up to six applications per button (with the aid of the up and down buttons).

AppHack is extremely memory-frugal and needs only 9KB when installed. You can download this freeware gem from several Web sites, including www.palmgear.com and www.tucows.com.

FIGURE 21.7

*AppHack
Configuration screen*

Hack 4: SilkHack

So, you really enjoy re-configuring your Palm's hard buttons? How about re-configuring the soft buttons? SilkHack divides each soft button into four quadrants and lets you assign an application to each quadrant. Pick an application from the list on the left and tap a quadrant. That function is now associated with that corner of the soft button. By default, the upper left quadrant of the Apps, Menu, and Find buttons are not reconfigurable, so you can't inadvertently lock yourself out of these functions. But, that leaves thirteen re-configurable quadrants that are completely programmable to your individual needs. SilkHack is shown in Figure 21.8.

FIGURE 21.8

*SilkHack configuration
screen*

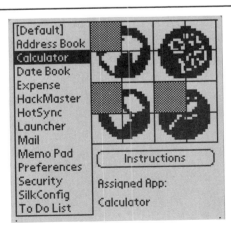

Buying SilkHack might be the best investment you could make for your Palm. This shareware product costs just $10, and needs only 7KB of memory. You can find it at www.palmgear.com.

 TIP If you own a Palm IIIx, you may have noticed the horizontal and vertical streak and shadow lines across the screen. Streak Hack (a $5 shareware Hack downloadable from www.interlog.com/~nbridges) eliminates these streaks, which are particularly noticeable in the Calendar and Date Book applications. The developer also claims an 8% performance increase when using this Hack—but we haven't been able to verify that claim.

Editing

If the Palm has one weak link in its chain, it is data entry while on the road. Graffiti is nice and the Palm keyboard works well, but wouldn't you like something less cumbersome—and inexpensive?

Hack 5: Fitaly Keyboard for Palm OS

The standard computer, or QWERTY, keyboard was designed in the days of manual typewriters, and was laid-out in that unusual format (QWERTY, that is) in an effort to reduce typing speed. In those old manual days, the typewriter's keys could collide with each other if the typist was faster than the typewriter's mechanical linkage. The keyboard was arranged to slow down a typist. Not exactly what we need today. So, along comes the Fitaly keyboard (named for the second row of keys), designed to make typing faster and easier for someone using a stylus.

You can download a demo version of Fitaly (shown in Figure 21.9) from www.twosolutions.com, and buy a license for $25. Be forewarned though: the Fitaly design works nicely, but it does take some time to break the QWERTY habit. Fitaly is a large application and will take 78KB of memory.

FIGURE 21.9

Fitaly Keyboard

Hack 6: TealScript

Palm's Graffiti is handy, but a little difficult for most people to master. Well, what if you could customize Graffiti to your own handwriting? That's what TealScript does for you: It lets you "train" Graffiti to understand your hand. You can't change Graffiti, but you can make minor changes to it by configuring TealScript to recognize your handwriting. So if you find Graffiti's K a little difficult to write (a problem for some lefties), fear not—just train TealScript to recognize your version. TealScript in shown in Figure 21.10.

FIGURE 21.10

TealScript Graffiti Profile

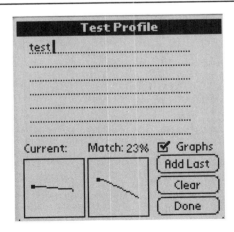

PART

V

Advanced Techniques

TealScript is shareware and costs $16.95. You can download TealScript from www.tealpoint.com. You might also need a memory upgrade if you have a lot of information in your Palm or if you have an older Palm device; TealScript takes 102KB when installed.

Hack 7: EVEdit

Well, now that we have several handy ways for entering text into our Palm devices, how do we manipulate that text? Enter EVEdit. This clever Hack, shown in Figure 21.11, gives us complete word processor-like editing control over our text, and includes a series of drop-down menus for easy navigation through its many features. Each menu is custom-configurable and provides access to all of EVEdit's functions through soft pen strokes. Select a word, a paragraph, or an entire entry with a double-, triple-, or quadruple-tap of your stylus. You can cut, paste, undo, find and replace, and use any or all of the ten clipboards EVEdit provides.

FIGURE 21.11

EVEdit drop-down
menu

You can download this $16 shareware product from www.tucows.com. EVEdit takes 43KB when installed.

Utilities

Every computing device and operating system has, and needs, utility programs—those little tools that help us fix the messes we create by not paying attention, or supplement what the device/OS manufacturer thought that we would want or need. These are perfect venues for Hacks.

Hack 8: GadgetHack

GadgetHack, shown in Figure 21.12, lets you easily toggle between utility applications and invert the screen to white-on-black. It provides a "soft" off button, Graffiti help, and one-touch time, date, and voltage read-outs. Each of these features, called gadgets, uses an icon. The icons for these selected features replace the application title bar and give you instant access to GadgetHack's utilities.

At $4.95, GadgetHack is a fairly inexpensive shareware application. When installed, it requires just 12KB of memory. You can download GadgetHack from `http://ourworld.compuserve.com/homepages/mcdan`.

FIGURE 21.12

GadgetHack configuration screen

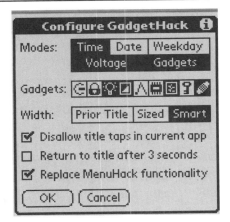

PART

V

Advanced Techniques

Hack 9: GlobalFind

If you sometimes remember someone's name, or a note that you wrote, not by the first characters, but by some in the middle (does that new contact spell his name Geoffrey or Jeffery?), the Palm's Find function won't be much help. But GlobalFind will find any set of characters anywhere in any word. Fill in the "ff" string and tap Search. You will find every instance of a double f on your Palm. Search for "pp" and find all your "support" entries. (See Figure 21.13.)

FIGURE 21.13

*GlobalFind's
Find menu*

GlobalFind is a $5 shareware Hack and is available at http://klyatskin.da.ru/. Your $5 gives you the password necessary to unzip the GlobalFind compressed file. Once installed, it takes a miniscule 1KB of memory.

Hack 10: MultiClipHack

If you've found the Palm's clipboard to be too limiting, then this little Hack may expand your viewpoint. MultiClipHack increases the size of the Palm's clipboard to 32KB and provides a total of 16 clipboards. A simple, configurable pen stroke activates the clipboards (see Figure 21.14).

FIGURE 21.14

*MultiClipHack
Preference screen*

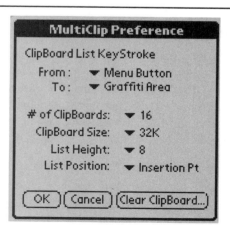

Yet another $5 shareware product. You can download MultiClipHack from www.tucows.com. Once installed, this hack takes just 11KB.

Miscellaneous Hacks

Here are a few Hacks that don't really fit into any of the other categories, but are just as useful. Whether it changes the tone of your alarms, automatically adjusts the clock with seasonal changes, or makes the Palm easier to use for lefties, one of these Hacks will make you and your Palm more efficient.

Hack 11: 3AlarmHack

So, you record an appointment and set the alarm, but you find that the Palm's alarm is just too short. You really need an extended alarm tone—and that is where 3AlarmHack can help. This Hack lets you set the length of the original alarm tone, as well as set a repeat interval, much like a snooze alarm. There are also seven alarm tones to choose from. You can even turn on the Palm's backlight or make it flash to really get your attention. (See Figure 21.15.)

FIGURE 21.15

3AlarmHack set-up screen

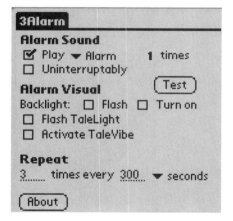

3AlarmHack is freeware, takes only 15KB when installed, and is downloadable from http://home.att.net/~foursquaredev.

TIP For Palm V users: The cover of the Palm V rests against the up and down buttons and, with just a little pressure, can prevent an alarm from sounding. PalmVHack (a $5 shareware Hack available from www.rgps.com) will disable the up and down buttons and ensure that your alarms will sound. PalmVHack takes just 4KB once installed.

Hack 12: Daylight Savings Hack

Forgetfulness seems to be a hallmark of most Palm users—that's why we have our Palms in the first place. So, do we remember to adjust the Palm's clock for daylight savings time? Probably not, and that's where this little Hack can really help. Load Daylight Savings Hack (shown in Figure 21.16) and never worry about Spring back and Fall ahead again. Or is that Spring forward and Fall back? Just select the month, day, and time daylight savings time begins and ends, and Daylight Savings Hack will automatically reset the Palm's clock.

Daylight Savings Hack is freeware and downloadable from www.tucows.com. For only 4KB of memory, this Hack will make sure that all of your alarms sound at the correct time.

FIGURE 21.16

Daylight Savings Hack setup screen

Hack 13: LeftHack

Though we right-handed people may not notice, the screen on our Palm devices is designed for righties; scroll bars, scroll arrows, and command buttons are all located on the right side of the screen, making it easy for us righties to reach. Well, what if you're left-handed? All of these navigation "aids" then become difficult to use. Left-Hack shifts all icons to the right and moves scroll bars and scroll arrows to the left side of the screen. No longer will a lefty worry about accidentally activating an application while reaching for the scroll bar. (See Figure 21.17.)

FIGURE 21.17

LeftHack and scroll bar on left

LeftHack is a $5 shareware Hack available from www.tucows.com. Once installed, it takes a tiny 3KB of memory.

PART

V

Advanced Techniques

CHAPTER **22**

HotSyncing beyond the Palm Desktop

The convenience of a Palm device is in its size and rapid response. Just reach into your pocket, hit one of the five buttons and retrieve the necessary information. Getting that information into the Palm is another thing. And what about installing applications? The Palm Desktop addresses all of that for us, and we never give it a second thought. Well, now it's time for second thoughts. Just how does the Palm Desktop move data between your computer and your Palm? It's done through marvelous pieces of software called conduits, the traffic cops between the Palm device and the HotSync application.

An Overview of Conduits

A conduit is basically the software interface between your Palm device and the Palm Desktop, and is required for just about every interaction between the two. For example, when you invoke a HotSync, you access one of the Palm's standard built-in conduits. The HotSync Manager application moves data, and relies on a conduit to manage the transfer. The conduit properly synchronizes data from the Desktop to the Palm device, and vice versa.

Conduits work in many different ways and provide several services, including the following:

- They synchronize the data stored on the Palm device to the desktop computer.
- They back up data from the Palm device to the desktop computer.
- They install new applications on the Palm device.

Each of these services is provided by a different conduit, which allows you to share data between the desktop computer and the Palm device.

As stated earlier, the HotSync Manager application uses conduits to manage the movement of data from the Palm device to the desktop computer and back. The Hot-Sync Manager oversees the entire process and calls each of the required conduits, built-in or third party, to perform their synchronization. Depending upon the application in use, HotSync may call only one or several conduits. HotSync then loads the conduits into memory, moves the data, and removes the conduits from memory. During this process, the conduit inspects each record to determine its status (whether it should be backed up, copied, or ignored).

When you press the HotSync button, the HotSync Manager determines if the Palm device is a valid user by reading the user ID. The user ID is a random number produced by the HotSync Manager after the Palm device's initial synchronization or after its first synchronization following a hard reset. Each Palm device has a unique user ID. Hot-Sync stores the user ID on both the Palm device and in the Palm Desktop software on the desktop computer, so they can identify each other. HotSync then locates the proper database in the Palm Desktop software for that user ID and notifies the desktop to prepare for synchronization.

Next, HotSync locates the creator ID and finds the conduit associated with that ID. The creator ID is a unique identifier assigned to each database and application on the Palm device. HotSync uses the creator ID to identify the databases stored on the Palm device and their associated conduits. It then adds these conduits to the list of applications and program modules that HotSync will run. If HotSync cannot find a creator ID, it will look for the backup bit. The backup bit is a flag or identifier that is set to a specific value determined by the conduit. If this flag is set, HotSync will call the Backup conduit for that specific database.

At this point, the Palm device and the desktop computer are synchronizing. HotSync has called the Install conduit and installs any new applications from the desktop to the Palm device. Any application sitting in your "add-on" folder will be automatically loaded by the Install conduit. HotSync will then call all other conduits registered to the creator ID and allow each to perform its intended function. If you are running HotSync version 3.01, it will call the Install conduit again to perform any installs that may have been generated by the registered conduits. No other version of HotSync performs this step. At this point, the Backup conduit is invoked to copy any data marked for backup.

 TIP To verify your HotSync version, click the HotSync Icon in the System tray. Then select About from the menu. There you will see what version of HotSync is running. If HotSync is not currently running on a Windows PC, click Start ➢ Programs ➢ Palm DeskTop ➢ HotSync Manager to proceed.

HotSync now updates the synchronization information (the date of the HotSync, and the number of records updated) on both the Palm device and the desktop computer, and then notifies the desktop that the synchronization process is complete.

Programming Conduits

The HotSync Manager accesses conduits through an entry point. An entry point is a function call or code handle used to call the conduit. A conduit may have several entry points, but all conduits must have the following three:

- `GetConduitVersion`, which returns the conduit version
- `GetConduitName`, which returns the name of the conduit
- `OpenConduit`, which starts the conduit

PART

V

Advanced Techniques

The Install Conduit

The Install conduit is provided by Palm Computing and is one of the standard, built-in conduits on the Palm device. It installs new applications or databases on to the Palm device. The Install module calls the Install conduit when you click the Install button or double-click the executable file. You can also run the Install conduit by double-clicking the INSTAPP.EXE from within the Palm directory on your desktop computer. However you start the install process, the Install module copies all files with PRC and PRB extensions to the install directory, and lines up the appropriate conduit to perform the actual installation. A flag is set to indicate each conduit needed to complete the install process.

At HotSync time, the HotSync Manager looks for these conduit flags and starts each respective conduit using the OpenConduit command. This begins the synchronization process.

If you are using HotSync Manager version 3.01 or newer, the Install conduit is called twice—once as described above and again after the synchronization process is complete. The second call of the Install conduit installs any applications queued for installation as a result of the synchronization process.

Once all conduits have completed their tasks, HotSync Manager completes the installation process by notifying each desktop application that the synchronization process is complete. The Palm OS also apprises each application on the Palm device of the installation status of each related database applications that were installed. HotSync Manager then sends a message to the user and makes an entry to the HotSync log.

The Backup Conduit

The Backup conduit, like the Install conduit, is provided by Palm Computing as a built-in conduit. And just like the Install conduit, you start the Backup conduit by invoking the OpenConduit command. The Backup conduit runs after all other conduits have completed their tasks. Files and databases destined for backup must have their backup flag bit set by another conduit. The Backup conduit then looks for files or databases with the flag bit set and copies those files or databases from the Palm device to the desktop computer.

The Backup conduit is probably the most heavily used of all the conduits. It's a prime candidate for those Palm application used only on the Palm device and accessed only on the Palm device. For example, any information you enter on the Palm but want stored on the desktop for safekeeping probably uses the Backup conduit.

Once all conduits have completed their tasks, HotSync Manager completes the backup process by notifying each desktop application that the backup process is complete. The Palm OS also apprises each application in the Palm device of the status of each related database or additional application that was backed up. HotSync Manager then sends a message to the user and makes an entry to the HotSync log.

Synchronization Types

To make synchronizations efficient and fast, HotSync must move the smallest amount of data possible. HotSync Manager achieves this through two types of record-level synchronization: FastSync and SlowSync.

FastSync, the faster and preferred method, forwards data between the Palm device and the desktop only if the data has changed since the last synchronization. An unmodified record is left in place. This is the synchronization method.

Every database and record has a modification flag that indicates whether that database or record has been modified since the most recent synchronization.

HotSync Manager determines if a FastSync is possible by interrogating the Palm device for the user ID and the PC ID of the most recent synchronization. HotSync then compares this information to the data stored on the desktop computer. If the values match, HotSync Manager assumes that the modification flag on each record is accurate and dependable and allow the conduits to perform a FastSync. If not, Hot-Sync looks to perform a SlowSync.

SlowSync, the slower method, is the fallback for those occasions when FastSync cannot be used. Typically, SlowSync is employed when the record status flags are not reliable and a discrepancy exists between the Palm device and the desktop computer. In this case, SlowSync will compare each record in the Palm device to each record on the desktop computer. It will then determine the best method to synchronize the data and will communicate that information to the appropriate conduit.

On some occasions all records must be copied irrespective of their condition or status flag. If a database has been deleted from the Palm device or the desktop computer, or if a new application is installed, then the synchronization will result in all records being copied from the Palm device to the desktop computer or vice versa. That usually results in a SlowSync, copying each and every record and guaranteeing a complete and accurate database.

Interfacing Conduits to the HotSync Manager Application

Conduits and the HotSync Manager application work closely together to ensure that all of your data is accurately and safely handled. Whatever you enter onto your Palm device is captured by the desktop computer for safekeeping and record storage. Likewise, the information that you enter into the Desktop Manager is forwarded to your Palm device to guarantee that you have the most up-to-date data.

Conduits and the HotSync Manager work together in three ways:

- During a synchronization process, the Hotsync Manager uses one of the three conduit entry points to gain access to the conduit required for data transfer.

- A conduit can call the log function of the HotSync Manager and add an entry detailing the last transaction.

- During a HotSync, some conduits interface directly with a desktop application. To prevent data from being overwritten, HotSync, or the conduit itself, must provide a notifier DLL (dynamically linked library) to the desktop application.

A notifier DLL is used to inform an application that both the desktop computer and the conduit can modify data, and ensures that only one changes data at any given time. HotSync generally calls the notifier DLL, which in turn notifies the desktop application. Notifier DLLs are usually created by the conduit developer, since they know exactly how their program interfaces with both the HotSync Manager and the desktop application.

The HotSync Manager application can use one of three categories of conduit entry points: required entry points that are part of the conduit, an optional entry point provided by the conduit developers for special or dedicated purposes, and a file-linking entry point that links a file to the conduit. We will look at these categories individually in the following sections.

Required Entry Points

There are three required entry points (mentioned above) that every conduit must support. These entry points, or call points, allow the HotSync Manager, or an application, uniform access to any conduit. With that, a conduit developer only needs to contend with standardized entry points and be completely comfortable that their conduit will interface properly to the HotSync Manager.

GetConduitVersion

The GetConduitVersion function returns both the major and minor version numbers of the desktop computer's conduit to the HotSync Manager.

GetConduitName

The GetConduitName function returns the display name of the conduit and a status flag that indicates whether the call was successful.

OpenConduit

While the other two required functions return information about the conduit, the OpenConduit function performs an action. To start up the conduit, HotSync Manager calls the OpenConduit function. This call begins the synchronization process.

GetConduitInfo

The GetConduitInfo function is a superset of the GetConduitVersion and GetConduit-Name functions and is used to retrieve complete conduit information such as the conduit name, MFC version used to develop the conduit, and the conduit's default action. This one command lets you retrieve the information otherwise obtainable through two commands. We'll look more closely at conduit details in the section on developing conduits.

Optional Entry Points

There are two optional conduit entry points that you can use to customize a conduit's operation, depending upon the version of HotSync Manager you are running. Version 3.0*x* uses CfgConduit, while versions prior to 2.*x* use ConfigureConduit. In either case, the basic functionality is the same.

CfgConduit/ConfigureConduit

The CfgConduit function is invoked by HotSync Manager version 3.0 when you attempt to customize a conduit through the Custom command of the HotSync Manager application.

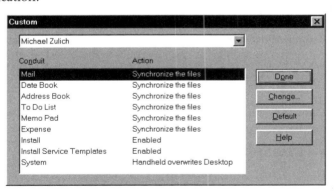

This can also occur through the Change command of the HotSync Manager application's Custom dialog box.

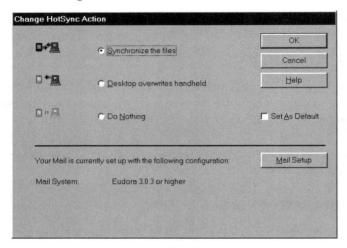

The `ConfigureConduit` function provides the same result for HotSync Manager versions prior to 3.0. Calling either function will return the same screens.

When trying to customize a conduit through one of the above methods, HotSync Manager calls the `CfgConduit` or `ConfigureConduit` function, depending upon the HotSync version, and displays one of the above screens. Through these screens you can specify the conduit's actions.

File Linking Entry Points

File linking allows you to automatically update your Palm device to an external data source, such as data that does not reside on your desktop such as a network database. In this case, the conduit must create a link to the server data file through one of the four file linking entry points. Older versions of HotSync Manager were called file linking subscribing. Palm Computing has maintained this nomenclature, so some of these conduit entry points use the term subscriptions.

ConfigureSubscription

The `ConfigureSubscription` function retrieves file link details from the active conduit. For example, `ConfigureSubcription` delivers information about the files on the network server that are linked to the conduit.

ImportData

When called by the HotSync Manager, the ImportData function loads data from a linked file. The ImportData function then displays a dialog box from which we can choose field details for the imported data.

SubscriptionSupported

The SubscriptionSupported function tells HotSync Manager if the conduit supports file linking. If the conduit does support file linking, then it returns a flag value of 0.

UpdateTables

Once HotSync Manager determines that the conduit does support file linking, and once data field details have been made, the UpdateTables function will update the databases on both the Palm device and the desktop computer.

Notifications

Because some desktop applications and their conduits can modify data, HotSync Manager uses notifications to prevent a free-for-all of updates and overwrites. These notifications ensure that only the desktop application or the conduit are changing data at any one time.

Through the notifier DLL, HotSync Manager forwards a notification to the desktop application in a format that the desktop application can understand. This notification then acts to control the data changes and prevents an unintentional overwrite.

Palm Computing provides a notifier DLL, pdn20.dll, that can notify all of the Palm Desktop organizer applications. All other applications should provide one notifier DLL of their own if their application requires notification. If a conduit accesses data from a desktop application but does not interface to that application, then it does not require a notifier DLL.

Developing Conduits

As mentioned above, a conduit is a DLL on a Windows-based system. Like any other DLL, you can create a conduit using any one of several tools, including:

- Palm's Conduit Development Kit version 3.0 and Visual C++ version 5.0 or greater for Windows-based systems
- Palm's Conduit Development Kit version 3.0 with Metrowerks CodeWarrior Release 5 for Mac OS systems

- Palm's Conduit Development Kit version 3.0 (Java Edition) with Visual J++ or Symantec's Visual Café for Java for Windows 95/98 and NT
- Satellite Forms from Puma Technologies, though without the aid of the Conduit Development Kit
- Pendragon Forms from Pendragon Software Corp., also without the aid of the Conduit Development Kit

Conduit Types

The conduit you create must perform several tasks, the most crucial being synchronizing data between the Palm device and the desktop computer for a specific application. With that in mind, the conduit must be able to open and close the Palm device's databases; add, delete and modify records on both the Palm device and the desktop computer; and support FastSync wherever possible.

Additionally, the conduit must conform to one of the following three conduit types:

- A conduit type that synchronizes a custom database on the Palm device to a custom database on the desktop computer. An example of this conduit type is a custom-designed inventory tracking database that resides on both the Palm device and the desktop computer.

- A conduit type that synchronizes a built-in database on the Palm device to a custom designed database on the desktop computer. For example, this conduit might bridge the Palm's Address Book to a custom designed contact manager used in lieu of the standard Palm Desktop software application. Microsoft's Outlook 98 and Symantec's ACT! each have conduits of this type, which link the Palm device to their desktop applications.

- A conduit type that synchronizes a built-in database on the Palm device to the standard Palm Desktop software application. In this case, your conduit replaces a conduit provided by Palm Computing and performs the same function. Though Palm supports this application of the conduit, it is difficult to see why anyone would attempt to use it when the Palm provided conduits work just fine. It is, not surprisingly, the least used of the conduit types.

Each of the above synchronizations falls into one of the four synchronization classes:

Mirror Image This conduit modifies data on both the Palm device and desktop computer, making identical copies of the data on each. The conduit must resolve data conflicts without the user's intervention. An example of a mirror image synchronization is the Palm Date Book or the Address Book applications.

Uni-directional This conduit type modifies data in one direction only by copying data from one platform to the other. This synchronization class is the fastest and should be used as often as possible. An example of a uni-directional synchronization is an informational download of read-only data (perhaps a product pricing database) from the desktop to the Palm device.

Transaction-Based A conduit from this class handles data on a case-by-case basis, allowing the desktop computer to perform additional processing to the data between synchronizations. This is probably the slowest of the synchronization classes since the conduit must examine each record separately. An e-mail program is a good example of the transaction based conduit, since processing must occur separately at both the Palm device and desktop computer level.

Backup The backup conduit copies all data from the Palm device to the desktop computer without any exceptions. This is the default conduit for most applications and the simplest to implement.

Design Goals

There are several design goals that you must keep in mind while developing a conduit. With these goals, you will minimize user intervention, guarantee data integrity, and make the HotSync process quick and reliable. If you miss on any one of these points, you reduce the application's reliability and usefulness.

You should try to reduce the amount of times the user has to place the Palm device in the cradle and press the HotSync button. The process should be automatic, and the user can simply watch the synchronization occur.

The conduit should include sufficient intelligence to handle conflicts and prevent data loss under all circumstances. This includes handling duplicate data during a mirror image synchronization and a connection loss while HotSyncing. In either case, the conduit should gracefully administer to the error, note the situation in the log, and notify the user to the existence of the error. Though this may seem to fly in the face of reducing user intervention, it is a necessary step in preventing data loss and represents a very small number of occurrences.

If you follow the above guidelines, you will likely design a conduit that is reliable and fast. Speed is, of course, the overall design requirement, and if you reduce the amount of data that is transferred, you can guarantee a speedy HotSync.

The Sync Manager API

The Sync Manager API is the interface to the HotSync Manager and allows communications between the desktop computer application and the Palm device. It also provides access to the databases and allows you to modify and move records. Using Sync Manager, you can control communications between the Palm device and the desktop computer during the synchronization process. Sync Manager uses the HotSync transport to accomplish this, and since HotSync addresses the connection type (direct cable/cradle, modem, or network), the conduit just needs to concern itself with the data.

Before using a conduit with Sync Manager, you must register the conduit with the SyncRegisterConduit function. Once this is accomplished, you can use the conduit freely throughout the application. To un-register the conduit, a process you should undertake when you no longer need the conduit, you must call the SyncUnRegister-Conduit function.

To create a new database on the Palm device, invoke the SyncCreateDB function. This command not only creates the database, but opens it for further processing. Likewise, you can call SyncOpenDB to open an existing database on the Palm device.

Below is a code example that employs both the SyncCreateDB and the SyncOpenDB functions taken from the ObtainRemoteTables function of Palm Computing's Expense conduit.

```
rval =
SyncOpenDB(m_rSyncProperties.m_RemoteName[m_CurrRemoteDB],0,m_remHandle);
// create the remote databse if it's not there
if (rval == SYNCERR_FILE_NOT_FOUND &&
  m_rSyncProperties.m_SyncType !+ eHHtoPC)
{
CdbCreateDB dbInfo;
memset(&dbInfo, 0, sizeof(dcInfo));
dbInfo.m_Creator = m_rSyncProperties.m_Creator;
dbInfo.m_Flags  = eRecord;
dbInfo.m_CardNo  = (BYTE)m_rSyncProperties.m_CardNo;
dbInfo.m_Type    = 'DATA';
strcpy(dbInfo.m_Name, m_rSyncProperties.m_RemoteName[m_CurrRemote]);
if (!(retval = SyncCreateDB(dbInfo)))
{
  m_RemHandle = dbInfo.m_FileHandle;
  }
}
```

Special Considerations for Databases

Since nearly all Palm applications are databases, and each database is merely a collection of records, you need to become familiar with handling data records. Every record has a unique identifier within a database, and each record belongs to a data category. Every database uses an application information block to identify the names of data categories used in that database. Flags on each record identify whether that record is marked as archived, busy, deleted, modified, or private. Lastly, a sort information block stores record ordering information for the database.

You can read data records from the Palm device through one of six different Sync-Read functions. Each automatically retrieves the next record until you have traversed through the entire database. The SyncRead functions allow you to read data records by record category, record ID, the next modified record, and combinations of the above.

Once you have read data records and completed your processing, you can write the resulting information back to the Palm device through a SyncWriteRec function. Additionally, you can write a resource record back to the Palm Device by using a SyncWriteResourceRec function.

To clean up a database and remove data records flagged for deletion, you can use the SyncPurgeDeletedRecs function, which deletes all records with their delete or archive flag set. The SyncResetSyncFlags function resets the modify flag on all records on the Palm device and also resets the backup date for the database.

Upon completion of all record processing, you must close the database. The Sync Manager application allows you to open only one database at a time, and failure to close an open database before exiting the conduit will prevent other conduits from functioning. To close a database, use the SyncCloseDB function.

Synchronizing to Third-Party Applications

Short of writing your conduit, there is really no way to connect your Palm device to anything but the Palm Desktop application. And as you have seen from the previous discussion, writing your own conduit is not a trivial task and best left to experienced programmers.

A few third-party applications offer Palm conduits, allowing you to connect your Palm device to their desktop application. These applications are similar in concept to the Palm Desktop in that they track contact names and addresses, and offer "to do" lists and calendar features. If you're satisfied with the Palm Desktop application, there is little reason to change. However, if you currently use one of these third-party applications, this can be a real bonus.

Symantec offers a conduit for their ACT! contact manager application. You can download this conduit, called a PalmPilot Link from the Symantec Web site at `http://www.symantec.com/act/palmpilot/index.html`. This 1.4MB download file requires ACT! 3.05 or later and Windows 95/98/NT.

Microsoft also offers a conduit for Outlook 98, Microsoft's contact manager/organizer. Outlook 98 also offers an e-mail manager in addition to contact management. Palm Computing includes the Outlook 98 conduit on the Palm Desktop Organizer CD-ROM that accompanies all Palm devices. To invoke the Outlook 98 conduit, select Synchronize With Microsoft Outlook when you install the Palm software on your desktop computer.

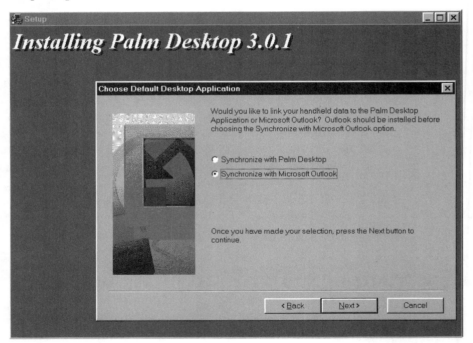

With the Microsoft conduit installed, your Palm device will synchronize with Outlook 98 instead of the Palm Desktop software.

 NOTE If you'd like more information on programming for the Palm platform, download the free developer's manual from Palm at `http://www.palm.com/devzone/docs.html`.

CHAPTER 23

Writing Your Own Applications

Writing an application for the Palm device is similar to writing an application for a desktop computer. Before you start, you must have a clear set of goals: what you intend to accomplish with this application, and how it will function. You should also know the application's resource requirements. The only real differences between a Palm device application and a desktop application are resources—the Palm has precious few. Keep that in mind as you proceed and you shouldn't have any problems.

 NOTE Any software development project is a serious task, and we assumed in the writing of this chapter that you have some programming experience. If you've never written a program before, we'd suggest that you search your local library or bookstore for any one of the many introduction to programming books.

Programming the Palm Device

The Palm platform imposes several limitations on you, the programmer. These limitations actually result from the Palm's strengths: its small screen, fast operation, and small size. But this is a mixed bag of strengths and weaknesses that we'll uncover in the next several sections.

Screen Size

The Palm screen measures a tiny 2⅜ by 2⅜ inches square, though Palm Computing claims that the screen is 2½ by 2½ inches. This small piece of real estate translates to a 160 by 160 pixel square. That's not much when compared to a standard desktop computer's 800 by 600 pixels. Because of this small size, you need to carefully design each screen that you use. Be sure not to crowd out important information or make the screen so busy that it is difficult to use.

Quick Turnaround

Unlike a desktop computer, which you might power-up and leave running all day, the Palm device is designed to be used frequently and for short periods of time. That means that the power-up process and access time to any application should be quick.

NOTE Palm OS does not have a wait cursor (such as the hourglass from Windows). The average Palm user accesses their Palm 15–20 times per day according to Palm Computing, making the quick turnaround design criteria quite strong.

You can also achieve quick turnaround by simplifying the user interface. You should aim to reduce the number of screens and dialog boxes that a user needs to navigate through. Keep the screen layout simple and consistent with other Palm applications. This will reduce the user learning curve and the associated frustration while improving user acceptance of the application.

Data Input

To speed up the time it takes to input data, you can try one of the keyboard add-ons like Fitaly Keyboard Hack discussed in Chapter 21 or the hardware keyboard from LandWare. However you do it, it's best to design your application with minimal data entry required. While any of the above products will meet the data entry needs, none are quick. Keeping speed and simplicity in mind, it's best to incorporate drop-down lists. This allows users to select information from a list instead of entering information free-form. You'll find that you can enter data quickly and without typos.

Memory

With the majority of Palm devices sporting anywhere from 512KB to 2MB of total dynamic memory and storage, your application must be memory frugal. Some Palm devices that support memory cards, like the Palm IIIx and others, may have more memory, but not much more since this memory is used both for dynamic and supplemental storage. Palm devices do not have much memory to spare since they do not support hard disks or PC Card devices. You must optimize your application to take advantage of the available memory while leaving behind sufficient memory for supplemental storage. This is a difficult balance to achieve and maintain.

Power

The Palm device runs on a set of alkaline batteries (unless you're using a Palm V, which uses a rechargeable Lithium-ion battery), which limits the device's overall processing power. The Palm devices are all built around a Motorola M68328 Dragonball chip.

PART

V

Advanced Techniques

Though powerful in its own right, it's no match for today's desktop or laptop processors. With that in mind, you must keep the computational aspect of your application to a minimum. Alternately, you can use the desktop computer to crunch through the calculations then HotSync the results to your Palm.

Backward Compatibility

Much like a desktop computer, applications written for the Palm device need to be backward compatible—at least to the oldest device still being sold by Palm Computing, which is the Palm III. With each product revision, Palm Computing has improved the Palm OS to include new features and functions. If you write your application to take advantage of a new function, the application will not work on a Palm device running an older OS version. For example, the Palm V uses Palm OS versions 3.1, and an application using features inherent to OS version 3.1 will likely prove problematic on a PalmPilot Professional, which runs Palm OS version 2.0. See Table 23.1 for Palm devices and their OS versions.

TABLE 23.1: PALM DEVICES AND OS VERSIONS

Device Name	OS Version
Pilot 1000	1.0
Pilot 5000	1.0
PalmPilot	2.0
PalmPilot Professional	2.0
IBM Workpad	2.0 and 3.0
Symbol SPT 1500	3.0
Qualcomm pdQ	3.0
Palm III	3.0
Palm IIIx	3.1
Palm IIIe	3.1
Palm V	3.1
Palm Vx	3.3
Palm VII	3.2

The Motorola MC68328 DragonBall Processor

The heart of the Palm device is the MC68328 chip, which powers every Palm device from the Palm III onward. Motorola designed the DragonBall chip for handheld and portable computers, like the Palm, to efficiently address all of our needs. The DragonBall runs at 16.67MHz while sipping battery power at 3.3 volts. It's fully compatible to the MC68000 chip family, sports two serial ports, supports PCMCIA version 1.0, and can address up to 4GB of memory. Motorola also includes built-in LCD control with 4-bit color. Clearly, the chip supports more features than Palm Computing has implemented, which may be a predictor of things to come.

Getting to Know the Palm OS

The Palm OS is radically different from current desktop computer OSs; it's actually more akin to desktop computer OSs of several years ago. The Palm OS is single threaded (it only handles one process at a time) and event-driven (it waits for the user to perform a function). Virtually all applications are implemented by calling Palm OS functions which, when called in groups, work together to implement a feature. Generally, these grouped functions use the same prefix for easy identification.

Functions are called using launch codes, a built-in capability of the Palm OS. Launch codes work by firing off an application and possibly several ancillary functions or applications as well. We'll learn more about features, functions, and launch codes in this section.

Using Launch Codes

Launch codes are the methods used to communicate between the Palm OS and one or several applications. You would use a launch code to start up an application and display its user interface. Likewise, you could use a launch code to start up a second application that is required for further processing by the current application. By using a launch code, you do not need to open the complete application but merely access the required functionality. Given the Palm's small screen and light processing power, this capability is a real bonus.

Launch codes may use a parameter block and/or a launch flag. A parameter block points to a piece of code that contains the parameter required to launch an application. A launch flag defines how the application should behave: whether or not the application should display its user interface, for example.

Every application should contain a `PilotMain` function, which is the entry point for all launch codes. The `PilotMain` will inspect a launch code to determine its relevance: whether or not the application is capable of processing the launch code. For example, through a launch code, you could simultaneously start the Calculator application on the Palm device and a search application that returns a text string. Since the Calculator application does not handle text data, `PilotMain` would make the determination that the search function is not relevant. If the action is not relevant, the two applications will co-exist without failure (albeit without any effect either). If the action is relevant, `PilotMain` will perform the action.

Normal Launch

A normal launch is, as the name implies, the common method for starting an application. A normal launch begins with a start-up routine, moves to the event loop, and then terminates with a stop routine. You can invoke a normal launch through the `sysAppLaunchCmdNormalLaunch` command. It begins by initializing the global variables needed by the application. Next, it finds the required database (or creates one) and locates the application-specific preferences and variables. Finally, it initializes all other variables as needed.

Programmatic Launch

You can launch an application from within another application or from the system itself. These are called programmatic launches and do not require a direct user interface. A programmatic launch is handled much like a subroutine; that is, the calling application must pass the required variable data to the subroutine.

The system function, `SysAppLaunch`, sends a launch code to a different application. The function supports several options, such as processing the passed variables and allocating new global variables.

Stopping

At some point after an application has been launched, you'll need to stop processing. For example, when you move from one application to another, the first application is halted and the second is commenced. You can stop an application using the `appStop-Event` command, which terminates all processing, cleans up outstanding activities, closes all open databases, and saves information.

Alarms

The Alarm is a commonly used feature of the Palm OS. The OS alarm manager supports real-time alarms and works closely with the time manager to do so. The alarm manager also sends launch codes to each application that has an alarm set. It first notifies the application that an alarm has been tripped, then allows the application to display a user interface screen. The alarm manager doesn't provide any dialog boxes or play an alarm tone, however. You must provide these capabilities as add-ons to your application.

Setting Alarms   You can set an alarm within virtually any application, but generally alarms are used to notify the Palm device user of some noteworthy event. The Palm's built-in Datebook application is a fine example of how to implement and use an alarm.

To set an alarm, use the AlmSetAlarm function and specify when the alarm should trigger and for which application. The following code listing shows the AlmSetAlarm function in use for the Palm Datebook application.

```
static void SetTimeOfNextAlarm (Ulong alarmTime, Dword ref)
{
   UInt cardNo;
   LocalID dbID;
   DmSearchStateType searchInfo;
DmGetNextDatabaseByTypeCreator (true, &searchInfo,
sysFileTApplication, sysFileCDatebook, true, &cardNo, &dbID):
AlmSetALarm (cardNo, dbID, ref, alarmTime, true):
}
```

Once you have set the alarm, you should set the PilotMain function to respond accordingly. PilotMain should then launch the sysAppLaunchCmdAlarmTriggered launch code, which notifies each application for which an alarm has been set. After each application has received this launch code, the alarm manager sends the sysAppLaunchCmdDisplayAlarm function to notify the applications to display the alarm.

 WARNING   Though you can set multiple alarms, an application can have only one alarm pending at a time. That means you cannot set multiple alarms to ring at the same time.

NOTE All alarms are set based upon the number of seconds that have transpired since January 1, 1904. To convert a date or time into the number of seconds, use the `TimDate-TimeToSeconds` function.

Procedure Alarms   If you are writing applications for the Palm VII (Palm OS version 3.2), you can take advantage of an additional set of alarm types called procedure alarms. A procedure alarm offers several features that differ from Palm's standard alarm. For example, a procedure alarm specifies a Palm OS function instead of an application. It also bypasses the need for launch codes and goes directly to the specific procedure. These functions are particularly useful if you want to perform a background task that is to be hidden from the user.

You can set a procedure alarm by calling `AlmSetProcAlarm`. This function is implemented as a macro that calls `AlmSetAlarm` and passes a function pointer. From here `AlmSetProcAlarm` functions similarly to `AlmSetAlarm` and will process only one pending alarm at a time.

Features

Features are a special set of variables used by the Palm OS to identify features/functions supported by the particular Palm device or an application. As defined by Palm Computing, "a feature is a 32-bit value that has special meaning to both the feature publisher and the users of that feature." This 32-bit value identifies the feature creator and the feature number or value, and should be registered with Palm computing.

Features are "published" by the system or by the application, which means that the feature is present and accessible through the Palm OS. Once a feature is published it will remain present until you un-register the feature or reset the Palm device. Even after you close an application, a feature registered by that application does not go away.

All Palm devices support the system version feature, which identifies the Palm OS version number. This information is stored in a feature table in system ROM. Starting with Palm OS version 3.1, this information is copied out to system RAM for easy access. A query to this feature will deliver the OS version number, allowing you to tailor your code accordingly.

Feature Manager   You can use the feature manager to interrogate the Palm device for its features. You can use `FtrGet` to obtain the feature creator and feature number. To obtain a complete list of features, call `FtrGetByIndex`. Each time you call this function you will receive the next feature in the list. If there are no features present, you'll receive an error code. To remove a feature, call `FtrUnregister`. Remember, features remain present until it is explicitly removed or the device is reset.

Feature Memory   Starting with Palm OS 3.1, Palm Computing added feature memory to Palm devices. Feature memory allows data to pass among applications, even if one of the applications is closed. Much like any other feature, feature memory remains active until explicitly removed or the device is reset.

 WARNING   Feature memory is a performance improvement and should be used sparingly.

Discovering Palm's Sound

Sound is not the Palm device's strongest feature. Nevertheless, it does support primitive sound that is good enough to handle alarms and provide aural feedback when coursing through the application menus. Oddly enough, the Motorola 68328 chip, in combination with Palm OS 3.0 or higher, creates and plays standard MIDI sound files. Of course, the sound hardware can play only one tone at a time through the on-board speaker, which basically confirms the original statement about Palm's sound.

But just because sound is not a Palm forte doesn't mean that users don't want or enjoy some form of aural stimuli. The Palm OS supports sound through several functions including the SndDoCmd, which plays single tones, and SndPlaySystemSound for the built-in system tones. System sounds include the Alarm, Click, Confirmation, Error, and Information sounds. Users can adjust the volume of these System sounds through the Preferences application.

Palm OS 3.0 supports the playback of standard MIDI files. These files are available to the user through the System MIDI Sounds database, and are played using the SndPlaySmf function. Each record in the Standard MIDI File database is, in itself, a standard MIDI file.

Asynchronous and Synchronous Sound

The Palm's ability to playback sound is handled in one of two methods: asynchronously or synchronously. In either case, the SndDoCmd function executes the operation.

- Asynchronously produced sounds are non-blocking, so that they can be interrupted by another sound command.
- Synchronously produced sounds are blocking and prevent other sounds from playing.

PART

V

Advanced Techniques

The SndPlaySMF function operates synchronously and blocks any other sound from playing except sound generated by any user event, such as the sound that is played when pressing a hardware button. In this case, the sound manager will suppress SndPlaySMF's synchronous playback and allow other sounds to play.

Playing Standard MIDI Files

As we learned earlier, standard MIDI files are stored as records in a MIDI database. This database is a type sysFileTMidi and contains the system alarm sounds as well as any other MIDI files you decide to create.

When playing back a MIDI file, you must identify the particular database and the record that holds the data. You should identify the database by name or database ID. Then you can use the SndCreateMidiList function to retrieve the specific record and obtain information about SMFs (Standard MIDI Files) from multiple MIDI databases. The returned info includes the record name, record ID, and database ID in tabular form.

Even if you know the name of a MIDI database, you must locate its database ID in order to open the database and retrieve Midi records. Use the DmFindDataBase function to obtain the database ID based upon the database name. Once you have found the database ID, you can use DmOpenDataBase to open the database and DmFindRecordByID to locate the individual SMF record. You can now either modify the record using the DmGetRecord function, or just playback the sound record with DmQueryRecord. The former function will mark the record as busy, preventing any other application from using it. Remember to close the database when you are through by using the DmClose-DataBase function.

Setting Sound Preferences

Since you can adjust or modify Palm's sound settings, a well-designed application must be aware of those settings and accommodate them into the application. Otherwise, the application could run in an independent fashion, ignoring the sound preferences and annoying the user.

The sound manager reads the stored sound preferences and caches their values for use when the Palm device is powered on. If you modify your sound preferences, both the stored value and the cached value are also modified. If you reset your Palm device, sound manager must read the default stored values and load them into cache before proceeding.

Be mindful that the Palm OS is backward compatible, so applications written for OS version 1.0 will function under OS version 3.2. However, the reverse is not necessarily true since an application written for version 3.2 may take advantage of a feature not supported in version 1.0. We'll look at the details below.

Palm OS 1.0   The earliest version of the Palm OS, version 1.0 captured only the alarm and system sound levels. These values were set using the `alarm-SoundLevel` and `sysSoundLevel` fields of the SystemPreferencesTypeV10 data structure (to obtain this data structure, use the `PrefGetPreferences` function). Each of the two data fields has a value of either on or off, represented by `slOn` or `slOff`. If the field is on, then the `sndMaxAmp` constant will determine the volume level.

Palm OS 2.0   With version 2.0 of the OS, Palm Computing introduced a new sound API for game sounds. Now you have three sound values: `prefAlarm-SoundLevel`, `prefGameSoundLevel` and `prefSysSoundLevel`. Using these fields, we can retrieve individual amplitude values for each. Just like OS version 1.0, these fields contain values of either `slOn` or `slOff`, and must map to `sndMaxAmp` to determine the volume level.

Palm OS 3.X   When Palm Computing introduced the Palm Pilot III, and Palm OS version 3.0, they also enhanced the sound preference settings that use discrete amplitude levels for alarms, games, and system sounds. Using the `PrefGetPreferences` function now delivers three newly defined sound fields: `prefAlarmSoundVolume`, `prefGameSoundVolume`, and `prefSysSoundVolume`. The values returned from each of these are the actual amplitude settings—you no longer need to map the `slOn` or `slOff` values to `sndMaxAmp`. This amounts to a great improvement in sound management, but the old functionality remains in OS version 3.X to maintain backward compatibility.

Resetting the System

Just like any other computer, the Palm device supports a hardware reset capability. When all else fails to rectify a problem, reset the device—just be sure to HotSync often to protect your data. A reset acts to clear cache memory and return system preferences to the default settings.

To reset a Palm device, you must use the reset button located on the back of the device. This button is situated within a small hole (to protect you from an accidental reset) in the back of the Palm's case. Insert the Palm's reset tip tool (this is located within the stylus) or a straightened paper clip into this hole.

Soft Reset

The standard, or soft, reset clears memory (the dynamic heap) and restarts the Palm OS, reloading drivers and variables. All applications receive a `sysAppLaunch-CmdSystemReset` launch code.

If you depress the up arrow key while performing a standard reset, you'll achieve all of the above with two exceptions:

- The Palm OS does not use the `sysAppLaunchCmdSystemReset` launch code. This option prevents all applications from launching and is useful if an application appears to cause a crash and prevent the system from booting. If you don't start this launch code, applications will not start.

- System patches are not loaded, so you can delete or replace them individually. If a patch is loaded, the file's status is open and prevents you from accessing the patch.

Hard Reset

A hard reset is a bit more drastic than a soft reset: it clears dynamic memory and restarts all applications, as well as clears all storage heaps. This means that programs, data, user information, etc., are lost, and the Palm device is brought back to its factory new condition. You can cause a hard reset by employing the standard soft reset while depressing the Power button. The Palm OS will ask for confirmation before completing this step, but once it is invoked, the Palm device is cleared of all that is not in the Palm system ROM.

Understanding the Power Modes

One of the design specifications of the Palm device was "instant on," which means no boot-up delay when you press the Power button. To accomplish this, the Palm device uses a constant trickle of power to maintain subsystems like the real-time clock and memory. That's a good thing since the only form of storage is RAM, and RAM requires electrical power to maintain its values. The Palm device uses a unique form of power management, and the on/off button merely brings the Palm device out of a low power mode. Effectively, all that is powered-off with the Power button is the LCD panel.

The Palm OS supports three different power modes: sleep, doze, and running. Transition between modes of operation is handled through the system manager.

- Sleep mode is the power-down mode, in which the LCD panel is blank and the Palm device appears to be powered off. The Palm OS puts as many peripherals as possible into low-power mode. The real-time clock and the interrupt generator are the only circuits left active, which saves power and extends battery life. Your

Palm device enters this mode whenever you depress the on/off button or when it shuts off automatically through the auto-off delay feature set in user preferences. Since the interrupt generator is still alive, any activity that generates an interrupt will bring the Palm back to life. For example, with your Palm device in power-down mode you can press any hardware button, or the on/off button, to place your Palm in an active mode.

- Doze mode occurs whenever the Palm device is in the power-on state but is not processing user input. Doze mode conserves energy without outwardly showing it. In this mode, the main clock is running, the LCD panel is powered on, and the processor is in halt mode, which means that it is running but not processing data. Your Palm device enters doze mode whenever it's powered on but has no input. Because everything is powered on, the Palm device will transition out of doze mode much faster than from sleep mode. In effect, that transition is instantaneous, taking only the time required to process an interrupt, such as a tap of the stylus.

- Running mode occurs whenever the processor is executing instructions, and the Palm device remains in this mode for however long it takes to process the user input. As soon as this processing is complete, the Palm device will enter doze mode again, slow down the processor, and conserve battery power. According to Palm Computing, a typical application enters running mode about 5 percent of the time.

Configuring the Real-Time Clock

No matter what power mode your Palm device is currently operating in, the real-time clock continues to run. This guarantees that your Palm will display the correct time and date whenever the device is raised to doze or running mode, and will generate an interrupt when an alarm is set.

The real-time clock and the programmable timer are part of the Motorola 68328 processor chip used on the Palm device. This clock generates one hundred system ticks per second, affording one hundred possible interrupts per second. The time manager allows you to access all of the timing resources of the built-in clock. The Palm OS utilizes a 1-second timer (one hundred system ticks) to track the real-time clock for date and time, and a 0.01-second timer (one for each system tick) for more refined timing tasks and system functions. The 0.01-second timer is not updated when the Palm device is in sleep mode and will reset to 0 whenever the device is reset.

Time in the Palm OS is measured using midnight on January 1, 1904 as the baseline. All time and timings are converted into seconds from that date, which creates a mighty large number. There are 86,400 seconds in one day and a little over 31.5 million seconds in a regular, non-leap year, which adds up to several billion seconds over the 95-year period.

To convert the current data and time to seconds, use the `TimDateTimeToSeconds` function. From here you can perform virtually any calculation, like measuring elapsed time between two variable days or the time from today to some day in the future. To convert seconds to a date, use the `TimSecondsToDateTime` function.

Floating Point Arithmetic

You can take advantage of floating point arithmetic through a floating point library provided in the Palm OS. Palm OS version 1.0 supported only 16-bit floating point arithmetic, but starting with Palm OS version 2.0 you have access to 32-bit and 64-bit floating point numbers.

With Palm OS version 1.0, you must explicitly link the floating point library, and this library adds about 8KB to the size of the resulting file. Fortunately, programs written for version 1.0 that use this library will run on newer versions of the Palm OS even though they do not require the library. This means that programs written for Palm OS version 1.0 are compatible to newer version of the Palm OS.

For Palm OS version 2.0 or later, it is not necessary to link the library since floating point functionality is built into the system ROM.

Application Design Guidelines

A Palm device serves multiple purposes, so it's very important that you design your application to co-exist with others. Since a user will likely come to rely upon these applications, you must be certain that your application does not clobber another application and that other applications don't clobber yours. Additionally, a user should be able to switch from one application to another easily and without fear of losing data. To that end, your application should do the following:

- Accept `sysAppLaunchCmdNormalLaunch` commands to launch other applications.
- Accept and use the system preferences including the formats for time, date, and first day of the week.
- Not obscure the Graffiti area or the silk-screened buttons. Remember the Palm display is 160 by 160 pixels in total.
- Accept alarm codes, low battery warnings, and system messages.

There are several other details that you should consider to ensure that your application interfaces properly to the rest of the Palm world, but these four are the most important.

Programming Conventions

To maintain uniformity across all Palm applications, Palm Computing uses a series of programming conventions. Just like any structured programming language, these conventions make it much easier to read the code and locate incompatibilities among applications. Here are a few examples of these conventions:

- Palm OS functions belong to families each with a two or three letter prefix such as SYS for system functions.
- All Functions and global variables start with a capital letter.
- Events, constants, and structures start with a lowercase letter.
- Generally, Macintosh `ResEdit` resource types start with a lowercase letter and follow with three capital letters.

Performance Tuning

There are probably as many ways to tune an application as there are programmers. Certainly, creating tight code is an imperative, but there are additional considerations when developing an application for the Palm device. As we have already learned, heap space and storage are at a premium, so your application must function in this limited space. Therefore, optimize your code for heap space, followed by operational speed, and then code size. You can accomplish this by carefully constructing your application not to use certain features or to operate in certain areas. For example, keeping an application size below 32K will improve performance since the application won't need to cross a memory boundary. If you must cross a memory boundary, arrange your subroutines so their use and location falls into the same 32K block. Additionally, you can limit the use of global variables and allocate memory chunks instead. Since a global variable is accessible anywhere in the program, you must allocate and maintain space for the variable, all of which use memory. You can also eliminate a potential dynamic memory bottleneck by keeping large structures off the stack.

Each of these techniques works to reduce the Palm's resources load and improve overall application performance.

PART
V

Advanced Techniques

Defining Creator IDs

A creator ID is a 4-byte value used to identify all databases associated with a particular application. The ID is unique to the application, and contrary to what its name implies, it does not identify the application's developer—just the database. Every database used on a Palm device employs a creator ID in the form of a value/type field. This field should be set to APPL (an application database). You should register your creator ID with Palm Computing using their Web page at http://www.pal.com/devzone/crid/cridsub.html.

The system launch window uses the creator ID to identify which database is associated with the application. The system also uses the creator ID to calculate the total memory that an application will use.

Managing Databases

Since nearly every application used on the Palm device is based upon a database, proper database management is crucial. For the sake of performance, records in a database are not compressed, but they must be tightly packed to save space. Additionally, each record should be a uniform size and format to reduce overhead processing. Be mindful when using the DmDeleteRecord function to delete unwanted records and not just remove them. A record marked for deletion on the Palm device will be deleted from the desktop software at the next HotSync, whereas a record marked for removal may not. At the next HotSync, the desktop software will still contain the removed record and may attempt to reload it to the Palm device.

 TIP These are only some of the issues involved in database Management. Consult the Palm OS Users Guide for the most up-to-date details. Visit www.palm.com/devzone, or purchase printed copies from www.fatbrain.com.

Making Applications That Run Fast

Speed is just about the most important aspect in programming for the Palm. Not only must the application run quickly, but the user must be able to access the application quickly, too. Basically, you need to change your outlook from the desktop computer world to the handheld world of the Palm device.

According to Palm Computing, a user should be able to access and use your application while using the telephone. That is, they should be able to carry on a conversation while creating appointments or selecting and using your application simultaneously and in real time.

Accessibility is also a concern for speedy operation. If an application is difficult to open or navigate, it will not be readily accepted. You can improve your application's accessibility by:

- Reducing the number of stylus taps required to add data and navigate through the application.

- Reducing the number of intermediate screens and the need to change screens.

- Using command buttons in place of dialog boxes.

- Using pick lists in place of data entry.

Making Applications Easy to Use

A successful Palm application must be easy to use, and require little to no training or instruction. Of course, that doesn't mean that the application should be so simple as to be useless, but rather that your application should be intuitive and relatively error-proof. You can start by keeping your application consistent to other Palm applications. This reduces the learning curve and increases a user's comfort level. Also, keep the application as straightforward as possible to reduce ambiguity and interpretation. And don't forget to keep the screen as free of clutter as possible. A cluttered screen is hard to read, and too many buttons and dialog boxes can be confusing.

Don't forget to add an application icon to the Palm Launcher. This makes the application easy for the user to start up and use, and adds visual proof that the application installed correctly. Keep the number of double-taps to a minimum since they can be cumbersome for some users. And remember to remove (instead of gray-out) menu items or other elements that have been made unavailable. This eliminates any ambiguity and frees up precious screen space.

Advanced Techniques

Getting to Know the Leading Application Development Tools

We've looked closely at the Palm OS and can clearly see that even though the operating system has many strengths, programming an application is not one of them. The

Palm OS is just what the name implies: an operating system. It was designed to run the Palm device, ensure that all of the Palm's features operate, allow users to address these features, and allow users to launch application software.

To create an application, you'll need to enlist the help of a different breed of software—software that simplifies the Palm programming process. This specialized software is commonly referred to as an application development tool.

There are many different types of application development tools, running the gamut from easy-to-use to complex, from limited functionality to full-featured, from free to frightfully expensive. Some tools can be purchased from third-party vendors, one is available directly from Palm Computing, but most are available directly off the net for free or for a very small price.

We don't know if these are truly the top ten of applications development tools, but we are sure that several of these are indispensable. Certainly no developer would attempt to create a new application (or ever debug an existing one) without POSE—the Palm OS Emulator. As for the rest, we choose these based upon their relative strengths, costs, flexibility, or some combination of these traits. With over three million Palm software developers, you can rest assured that these ten application development tools get quite a workout.

We'll take a close look at the constituents of our list, starting with the more popular and moving on to some interesting alternatives.

The Front Four

These four application development tools (or three application development tools and one utility) cover a broad range of complexity and functionality. POSE, the Palm OS Emulator, is not used to create a Palm application, but rather to test any application, created anywhere else, without the need to install the software onto a Palm device. As for creation tools, CodeWarrior receives the official sanction of Palm Computing and is a professional quality development tool: bullet-proof, extremely flexible, and complex. Chipmunk Tiny BASIC is easy to use and free to download. And Satellite Forms turns complex development projects into series of fairly simple forms manipulations.

 NOTE The version numbers we cite here were accurate at publication time. However, you should check with the software vendor to see if the software has been updated. Having the most recent version is vital to dealing with application development tools.

POSE Version 21d29

POSE is the Palm device hardware emulator program. This utility program, for lack of a better word, emulates the actions and processes of the Palm hardware as software on your desktop computer. With POSE you can test and debug your application without having to load the application onto a Palm device. This is a very handy tool because it's considerably easier to recover from an application crash on your desktop computer than the Palm device.

The hardware emulator looks and functions just like a Palm device. The hardware, soft buttons, and Graffiti work just as they do on the real Palm device. Your mouse pointer takes on the functionality of the stylus, and you even have a series of keyboard shortcuts to help with application program debugging.

POSE is a generic Motorola 68000 series hardware emulator, so you'll need some additional software files to make it work like your Palm VII or Palm IIIe. These files are ROM images and emulate the ROM of an individual Palm device, so there is an individual ROM image file for the Palm III, the Palm IIIe, the Palm IIIx, the Palm V, and the Palm VII. You can download the image file directly from your Palm device or apply to Palm Computing to receive these files. The Palm OS Emulator is shown in Figure 23.1.

PART

V

Advanced Techniques

FIGURE 23.1

Palm OS Emulator

POSE is extremely useful because it completely emulates each specific Palm device. POSE also allows you to test your application on any other Palm device. Now you'll know if your application will crash a PilotProfessional without the need to purchase one. Of course, when you have completed your POSE testing, it's always a good idea to test your application again on the physical device. Remember that old programming tenet: just because you haven't found a bug doesn't mean that one doesn't exist. Test, test, test.

POSE is a multi-threaded 32-bit program available for the MacOS 7.5 or higher and Windows 95, 98 and NT. You can download it for free from Palm Computing at www.palm.com/devzone/pose. See Chapter 27 for more detailed information about POSE and how to use it.

CodeWarrior Version 5.0

For the serious professional programmer, or anyone who wants to approach their application development from that angle, there is Metrowerks CodeWarrior. CodeWarrior is one powerful tool and is available in two distinct flavors: CodeWarrior for the Palm Computing platform version 5.0 and CodeWarrior Professional Edition version 5.0. Each is available for both the Mac OS and Windows environments. And CodeWarrior is fully sanctioned by Palm Computing.

CodeWarrior for the Palm Computing platform incorporates Metrowerks Integrated Development Environment (IDE), a C/C++ compiler, source and assembly level debuggers, as well as a linker. The tool also includes a GUI building tool called the Constructor that uses drag-and-drop elements to build and edit screens. You can download a trial version of the software directly from Metrowerks at www.metrowerks.com/pda/palm. However, this trial version is very limited because you cannot create new applications; you can only modify a series of pre-existing sample projects. A full-function version of CodeWarrior costs about $300 for either the Mac OS or Windows platform. CodeWarrior is shown in Figure 23.2.

CodeWarrior Professional Edition includes all of the features of CodeWarrior for the Palm Computing platform plus support for Java. Metrowerks includes a Java compiler with JDK 1.2.X Java Language Specification support and full SUN Java documentation, as well as Run & Debugging support for the latest JDK 1.1.X virtual machine and a Java linker. The Professional version is a little more costly, as you would expect, and runs around $360 for either the Mac OS or Windows platforms.

This is an all-purpose development tool, flexible enough for just about any variety of application you may need to create. Take a look at Chapter 26 for a detailed walk through CodeWarrior in action.

PART

V

Advanced Techniques

FIGURE 23.2

CodeWarrior

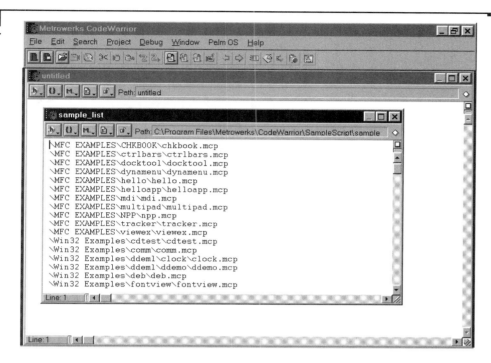

Chipmunk Tiny BASIC Version 0.96

Ah, venerable BASIC—the first programming language just about everyone learns. First developed at Dartmouth College in the early sixties as a language for teaching programming, BASIC has gone through many modifications and variations over the years. This version, called cbasPad, is a BASIC interpreter and text editor for the Palm device. It's a derivation of Tiny BASIC originally penned for early desktop computers with their extremely small amounts of memory. This makes Tiny BASIC/cbasPad ideal for the Palm device with its limited memory resources.

Like any other version of BASIC, cbasPad supports floating point numbers (IEEE single extended), string manipulations, Boolean logic, plus arrays and nearly 30 built-in functions. And because of its simplicity, cbasPad is extremely user friendly (see Figure 23.3). You should be able to sketch, write, and compile a single application in no time. But you must be prepared to do all of this on your Palm device since cbasPad has no IDE. You'll write your BASIC program in Memo Pad and load it into cbasPad for compiling.

FIGURE 23.3

cbasPad

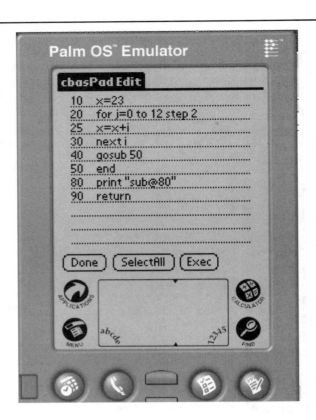

Unfortunately, cbasPad is not bug-free—something that you can probably guess from the from the software version number. Even the software's developer, Ronald H. Nicholson Jr., warns about bugs and buggy performance. But don't let that put you off. It's still a simple environment to work within, though we would probably not use cbasPad for a major or critical application.

You can download cbasPad for free from www.nicholson.com/rhn/palm.html, where you can also find cbasPad documentation and an FAQ. Remember, this is freeware, so don't expect tech support or documentation beyond what's on the Web site. You can, however, look for an older book on BASIC (circa 1980) for programming tips, tricks, and assistance. We'll work more deeply with cbasPad in Chapter 26.

Satellite Forms Version 3.0

Forms-based development tools are usually pretty easy to work with and can be quickly developed. Generally referred to as rapid application development tools, or RADs, forms-based technology removes language syntax and conventions from the development process since you work with a series of pre-defined forms and menus in a GUI. You define data fields and perform actions and calculations using menus, virtually guaranteeing that things will work from the outset.

Puma Technologies Satellite Forms version 3.0 is a forms-based RAD that perfectly fits the above description. Satellite Forms (shown in Figure 23.4) employs drag-and-drop simplicity with the power to create complex databases that you can link to Oracle, DB2, Lotus Notes, and MS Access databases, among others. It will even interface to Metrowerks CodeWarrior C code.

PART

V

Advanced Techniques

FIGURE 23.4

Satellite Forms

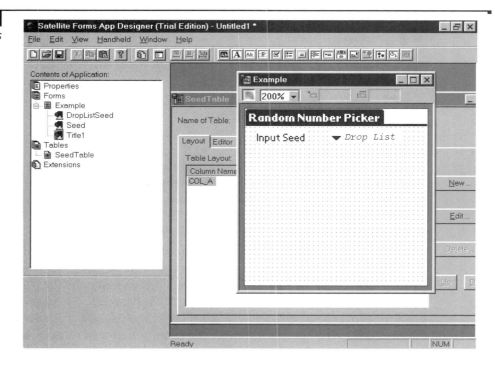

Satellite Forms core components include the application designer (the menu driven GUI), the forms conduit with ActiveX Control so you can transfer data to and from the Palm device, and the Satellite Re-Distribution Kit with its run-time engines allowing you to freely distribute your creation.

Satellite Forms comes in two editions: Standard and Enterprise. The Standard edition includes all of the tools that any developer needs to create a Palm application, including free run-time licenses. This version easily transfers data to MS Access and is best for entry-level development. It is available from Puma Technologies at `www.pumatech/com` as well as most software distributors for around $395.

Enterprise Edition includes all of the above plus all of the necessary network hooks such as the ability to connect your Palm to the network server and support for Oracle and Lotus Notes databases. Unless you're developing a network-based application, the Standard Edition is just fine (the Enterprise Edition costs $995). We'll use Satellite Forms to develop an application in Chapter 25.

The Backfield

This group of application development tools is comprised of some old standards and a few newcomers. Each is just as capable as the next, and all are comparable to the front four. The differences among these tools are purely in how they do what they do, not how well they do what they do.

CASL Version 2.6

CASL, or Compact Application Solution Language, is a BASIC-like proprietary, PDA programming language. CASL is object oriented and event driven; all actions undertaken by a CASL program occur in response to some event: a user tapping the screen, a timer executing, etc. Its proprietary nature comes from the fact that although CASL is BASIC-like, it is not BASIC, nor is it C++ or any other language.

The CASL compiler generates PDA independent p-code files. You must install a run-time interpreter (included with the software) onto your Palm device to interpret the p-code file into something that the Palm OS understands. The latest version of CASL, shown in Figure 23.5, also supports a p-code to PRC file function so you can convert your CASL application into a PRC file for easy download to a Palm device. Ostensibly, p-code programs can also be easily ported to Win CE devices using the appropriate PDA compiler.

FIGURE 23.5

CASL

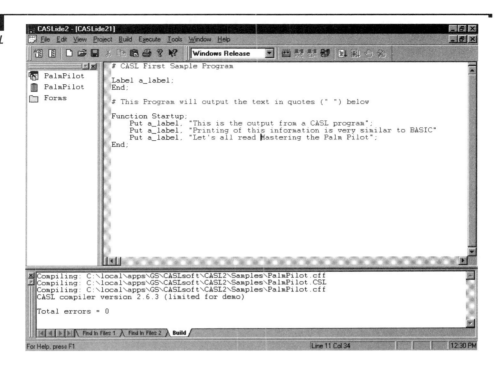

PART

V

Advanced Techniques

Written for Windows (95, 98, NT), CASL also includes an Integrated Development Environment, or IDE, that helps you to create, de-bug, and organize your CASL applications. You can write your CASL code in any ASCII text editor like Windows Wordpad, but the IDE offers some additional level of convenience.

CASL supports a range of programming feature/functions including over one hundred built-in functions, double word floating point variables, string manipulation, arrays and array manipulation, complete Boolean logic operators, and of course, objects and object modifiers.

Because CASL is highly reminiscent of BASIC, it is an easy language to learn and use. Its device-independent code may also appeal to developers looking to introduce an application for more than one PDA family.

You can download a limited-use (limited by your program size) demo copy of CASL for free from the Feras Information Technologies Web site at www.caslsoft.com. For $64.95, you can upgrade the free demo to a complete version of the software; Feras will e-mail a new compiler and a personal license key. That same $64.95 can buy you a complete version of the software without the need for the intermediate demo copy.

PalmFactory Version 1.0 Alpha 6

PalmFactory is a relatively new application development tool for the Palm device (hence the alpha 6 designation). PalmFactory is a menu driven database creation tool, modeled to some degree on MS Access. PalmFactory not only provides the tools for you to create a database application, but you can also create the application interface screen and its own icon. It's another menu driven RAD tool, so you don't need to worry about language syntax or nuance.

PalmFactory allows you to easily create a database and the GUI. You really don't need any programming knowledge or special skills, though an analytical mind helps. You use built-in tools to draw and implement radio buttons and check boxes, and to handle the differences between title fields and data entry fields. PalmFactory also allows you to create your own Palm Applications launch icon, or import one from Paint if you so desire. Palm Factory is shown in Figure 23.6.

FIGURE 23.6

PalmFactory

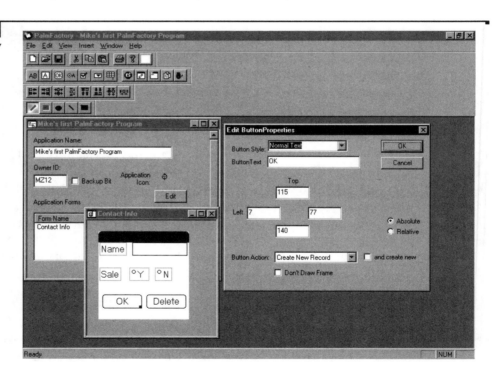

On the downside, PalmFactory is so new that there is little documentation on how to make the application work and not all features have been implemented. Nevertheless, the simplicity and flexibility make it a pleasure to work with.

Currently, PalmFactory is a free download from www.alcita.com/palmfactory. Palm-Factory is an evolving application so you should expect to see additions and modifications emerging shortly. It's ease of use should overrule all of its current shortcomings.

PocketC Version 3.03

PocketC is a Palm based C compiler that runs directly on your Palm device. Unlike most of the other tools mentioned here, there is no desktop computer development environment—all development is done on the Palm device. The PocketC compiler and other source code comes in PRC format, so you must HotSync them directly to your Palm device. You write a program as a Memopad record. Alternately, you can write your PocketC code on your desktop computer, copy the code to a memo using the Palm Desktop software, then HotSync the newly created Memo Pad record to the Palm device.

Once installed on your Palm device, the PocketC.prc file becomes an application, accessible through the Palm Applications launcher. You access PocketC like any other application, and then you can compile an application created on Memo Pad or select a previously compiled file (see Figure 23.7).

PART V

Advanced Techniques

FIGURE 23.7

PocketC

PocketC supports the standard built-in development functions you would expect from any C programming development tool. This includes event handling, string and math functions, graphics, sound, and basic system functions.

You can download a free 45-day trial version of PocketC from `www.orbworks.com`. For $18.50, you can obtain a complete, registered version of the software. Because there is no desktop computer interface, PocketC is not bound to any desktop OS—it's compatible with both the Mac OS and Windows. However, you must perform all of your compiling and debugging directly on the Palm device, which is not an ideal platform for this type of work.

Pendragon Forms Version 3.0

Pendragon Forms is another entry in the forms development arena that is easy to use. This RAD tool is visual and logical, and like the other forms based software, it doesn't require that you learn and understand code of any sort. And as you might expect, it's a quick learn.

Pendragon Forms, shown in Figure 23.8, is designed for database development, and accordingly the Forms Manager is the graphical design tool used to create data entry forms. Forms Manager is also an Access 97/2000 database application—a run-time version of Access is included with Pendragon Forms. Through Forms Manager, you can access Forms Designer with a mock-up of a life-size Palm LCD panel. Define a field using the Field Type drop-down list, keyboard, and pop-up options box. As you create these fields, they will populate the mock-up Palm LCD panel. Save the form and then "freeze" it so you can download the application to your Palm device.

Basically, that is all you need to create an application. The freezing process creates an Access database table automatically, so all of your data has a home. With every HotSync, data is moved from the Palm device to the Access database on the desktop. You can now manipulate this data in anyway you like on the desktop computer.

Pendragon Forms, like all forms based tools, is best used for database applications. Clearly you wouldn't want to attempt to develop a game with this tool—leave that to C/C++. But since Palm devices excel at database applications, Pendragon Forms is a very useful tool.

You can purchase Pendragon Forms from many software distributors or directly from Pendragon Software for about $150. You can also download a free 14-day evaluation version from Pendragon's Web site at `www.pendragon-software.com`.

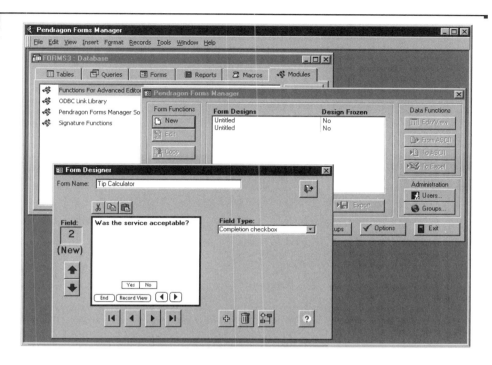

FIGURE 23.8

Pendragon Forms

Jump Version 1.0 Beta 4

With the exception of CodeWarrior, Jump from Greg Hewgill is probably the only other Java programming environment for the Palm device. Jump does not create Java applets nor does it have anything to do the Web. It simply allows you to use Java as a development language. You'll also need a Java VM, which is a Java compiler, as well as the Pilot Pila assembler and the Pilot Resource Compiler PilRC. More about these in the section on Assembler.

Jump reads the CLASS files produced by your Java compiler, and outputs Pilot assembler reads ASM files. You must then assemble these files with the Pilot Assembler from which comes the PRC file that you can HotSync to your Palm device. These resultant PRC files are fully functional Palm resource files and do not require Java to run. Jump does not support an IDE; it is basically a command line interpreter.

To get Jump to function properly, you'll need some additional software. You should have the latest Microsoft Java VM, which you can download as part of Microsoft's Java SDK. Most any Java compiler should work, though Hewgrill recommends Sun's JDK and Microsoft's Java SDK. You should also be able to use Symantec's

Café or Inprise's Jbuilder. Lastly, you need the Pilot Assembler (see the next section on Assembler language for more information).

For you Java zealots out there, Jump is a real bonus: with it, you can use their favorite language to develop applications for the Palm. But for those of you just starting out in application development, you might feel more comfortable with one of the IDE based development tools, like one of the RAD or C/C++ tools.

Jump is a free download from the Web at `http://hewgill.com/pilot/jump`.

Assembler

No matter how good the development tools become, you will always find a gear-head. You know that type: the kind of person who wants to do things the hard way, the old-fashioned way or both. This person shuns the more full-featured tools in favor of complete control (that person probably drives a car with a manual transmission and insists upon dicing onions with a chef knife instead of using the Cuisinart). Well, enough about us.

For the gear-head, purist, or the person looking to produce a compact application with absolute control, there's assembler code. And for the Palm environment there are several choices: the plain old Motorola 68000 class assembler, such as Pila, or one of the modified versions of assembler, such as EZAsm.

Seriously, assembler code is probably the most apt choice for the Palm environment. With assembler, you can create an extremely small application that, once compiled, runs very fast. The reduced size and fast operation works hand-in-glove with the Palm's reduced resources. Additionally, these same attributes keep power consumption down since assembler code application requires less memory space and less time to open, use, and close. Altogether, not a bad bunch of benefits!

 WARNING Assembler programming is not for everyone, not even every experienced programmer. Assembler code is very labor intensive to produce and, because it is a low-level development tool, you need to be extremely careful while writing your code. In assembler, you are working with bits and bytes (literally), and if you don't think in that fashion, you may want to look at other tools.

Pila Version 1.0 Beta 3   Yes, this is yet another beta development environment. Unfortunately, that seems to be the nature of quite a few Palm application development tools. Nevertheless, Pila is one of the Motorola 68000 series assembler environments. Short for Pilot assembler, the Windows-only Pila tool includes several elements that make assembler development a little easier. These include:

- PilRC, which is the Pilot Assembler resource compiler. You can use it to call/use user interface items such as icons and menus.

- PilDis, which is the Pilot disassembler. A disassembler will convert a compiled assembler language program to its assembler source code. This is very helpful as a learning tool, since you can really "see" how a specific application or routine is coded.

There is no IDE for Pila—you write your source code in any text editor, saving the resulting file with an ASM extension. You then assemble the program through a Pila command line option: `Pila program name.asm`. This creates a file with the same name as your source assembler code, only now that file has a PRC extension. Simple, straightforward, and extremely efficient. Of course, you really need to know Motorola 68000 assembler before starting. By the way, you can download Pila for free from `http://www.massena.com/darrin/pilot/tanda.htm`.

Though assembler code is always small and efficient, using it to program large applications is a very time-consuming and arduous task. Unless you're an accomplished programmer, think of a more user-friendly tool for that stock inventory database.

EZAsm Version 1.28   EZAsm is a modification of the standard assembler SDK (Software Development Kit). Originally developed for the Amiga, EZAsm is a hybrid development environment combining mostly Motorola 68000 assembler code and a little C. It sounds strange, but it makes for a much more user-friendly environment. For example, EZAsm supports an "`else`" clause just like C, obviating the need for branch condition codes.

In many ways, EZAsm is much like standard Pila: there is no IDE, and the EZAsm executable is applied to your assembler code that was created in an ASCII text editor. EZAsm is a WIN 32 console (read command line) application. Just like plain old Pila, you must write your code in something like Windows Notepad and save the resulting file with an ASM extension. The ASM file is applied to the EZAsm executable to create a compiled assembler program.

On the plus side, EZAsm does allow the "`else`" command and brackets, and it will automatically optimize your code for speed. This last item is a real benefit that frees you from the necessity of becoming an assembler expert.

The same caveats that apply to Pila, apply to EZAsm. Assembler code is very compact and quick to run, but it is also very difficult to create. You will likely find that larger applications for data manipulation might be easier to create using another tool. Assembler is not necessarily the wrong tool for a complex application, but using it to do so will be labor intensive. You can download EZAsm for free from `http://customers.doubled.com/~joes`.

CHAPTER 24

Creating an Application in Tiny Basic

I n this chapter we will discuss a usable application and how you can code it in one of the featured application development tools. If you've ever read any programming aids or textbooks, you'll recall that they typically start by walking you through a very simple program and then asking you to create it. Usually, these programs produce nothing more than a line or two of text that will print out on paper or to the screen. You know the type: the "My First Program" or "Hello World" programs that consist of little more than the title line. This approach is usually good because it shows you just how easy it is to create a simple program. Of course, the program's utility is suspect; after all, who needs a program that says "Hello World"? In addition, this example doesn't provide any clue as to just how difficult it is to create a real, usable program. So, with that in mind we will create a real, usable program in small steps so that you can follow along and learn.

Over the next three chapters we will use three different application development tools to create a program that just about any person, particularly business people would love to have handy. Our sample program is a tip calculator. Have you ever wondered just how much money is 15 percent of a $68.37 restaurant bill? We certainly have. And what about those three martini lunches, er... business lunches, where you don't want a 15% tip based upon the total bill, just the food portion? Well, that can be a real problem since most restaurants don't itemize the price of the olive! But you get the point.

We'd also like to define two terms that we've used interchangeably: program and application. There is little difference between these terms, but some people think of programs as any compilation of programming code that performs a task, while others usually think of an application as a compilation of programming code that performs an end-user task. Applications are always made of one or a series of programs. For example, a word processor like Microsoft Word is an application comprised of a series of programs that change fonts, create tables, etc. Even with this definition, many people still use the two terms interchangeably. So, let's take a close look at our program, er... application.

Creating a Tip Calculator

By design, our tip calculator will determine a tip based upon several factors: the total restaurant bill, the total drink portion of the bill, and, of course, the quality of the service. The old rule of thumb that says the tip for any restaurant bill should be based upon the total food bill including the cost of drinks does not take into account that a bottle of wine is not created by the restaurant and that it takes very little effort to serve it. Not to mention that the price of that bottle of wine can be considerably higher than anything else on your bill. So, with that in mind, our tip calculator will give you the opportunity to remove or include the drink portion of the total bill in the tip calculation.

Restaurant service varies with the quality of the establishment, the time of day or day of the week, and luck. Sometimes the service is exceptional, most times average, and sometimes poor. So, our calculator must provide a means to reflect the service quality in the tip. Our suggestion is to use a straight and clear percentage figure, such as "I think that the service was pretty good, and worth 18%." Our calculator will have the ability to figure a tip of whatever percentage you feel is appropriate—in this example 18%.

We now have the basis for our tip calculation. We will take the total restaurant bill, offer the choice to address the drink bill, then calculate the tip based upon a percentage of the adjusted total. If we turn that statement into a logical expression, it would look like this:

```
Total Bill less Drink Bill times Tip Percent equals the Tip.
```

Now, let's turn that logical expression into a mathematical one (don't worry, it's really quite simple):

```
(B-D)*S=T
```

where B is the Total Bill, D is the Drink Bill, S is the Tip Percent (or Service), and T is the calculated Tip. Alternatively, we can turn that one expression into two, to simplify the logic. We'll also turn the expression around, putting it into standard computer assignment form:

```
NB=B-D
T=NB*S
```

where NB is the Net Bill (the Total Bill less the Drink Bill) and T is the calculated tip, which is the product of the Net Bill times the Tip Percent. We can use either the first expression or the second two expressions to calculate the tip, but of course we can't mix and match!

 NOTE We will use these mathematical expressions throughout the next several chapters to create our tip calculator. So, keep them in mind!

Our first Palm device application development language is cbasPad Chipmunk Tiny BASIC, an easy to use derivative of Dartmouth BASIC. We will discuss more sophisticated tools (Puma Technology's Satellite Forms and Metrowerks CodeWarrior) in the next two chapters.

PART

V

Advanced Techniques

cbasPad Chipmunk Tiny BASIC

In this chapter, we will create our tip calculator using cbasPad Chipmunk Tiny BASIC. Like any other version of BASIC, cbasPad is easy to use and understand, which usually results in short development time (meaning, you can generally create an application quickly).

As described in Chapter 23, cbasPad is based on Tiny BASIC, which was originally written for early desktop computers that had miniscule storage capacity and even smaller amounts of RAM. Desktop computers of the day (late 1970s and early 1980s) were quite similar to the current crop of Palm devices: they had limited storage, limited RAM, and a relatively slow processor. Since the original Tiny BASIC was able to take advantage of these desktop computer limitations, it became an ideal candidate for Palm use. But cbasPad Tiny BASIC is under constant revision and is becoming increasingly more stable and user friendly. Fortunately, cbasPad Tiny BASIC is freeware, so obtaining a revised copy is as simple as directing your Web browser to www.nicholson.com/rhn/palm.html.

cbasPad Tiny BASIC Details

Freeware is always nice: there's no cost to you, so you can try out the software and not worry about buying something that just doesn't meet your needs. You can create just about any application you desire with cbasPad Tiny BASIC, though we'd shy away from database applications. Like any other version of BASIC, cbasPad just isn't the best tool to create a database (though there is probably someone out there who has done just that and will take umbrage with our last statement). Simplicity usually translates to reduced capability, and that defines cbasPad well. Unlike the other two development tools that we'll work with, cbasPad does not support an IDE (Integrated Development Environment), so there is no user interface. You must write your program or application directly in cbasPad, or alternatively import your code through the Memo Pad (more on that later). Either way, you don't have the benefit of any advanced tools or features for creating your masterpiece.

You may also find the dearth of documentation a little daunting; included with cbasPad is one short TXT file with a set of fundamental instructions. We suppose that we can't expect too much from freeware. The software's developer, Ronald H. Nicholson Jr., has said that he can devote his time to improving the software or writing documentation and has chosen to improve the software. We certainly can't fault him for that, but it does leave us without all of the information that we might need to complete an application. Given that cbasPad is based upon an old version of

BASIC, you might find some solace in an old BASIC manual, circa 1983, if you can find it. Try your local library, since it's unlikely that any bookstore will stock a nearly 20-year-old programming manual.

Additionally, though cbasPad is not bug-free it has gone through many minor revisions to correct errors and add new features. The latest version, 0.96, is quite stable and shouldn't present any major problems, particularly with our fairly simple application. So let's forge onward, install cbasPad, and create our tip calculator.

Installing cbasPad Tiny BASIC

Once you have downloaded cbaspad096.zip from Ron Nicholson's Web site at www.nicholson.com/rhn/palm.html and unzipped the files, you'll need to install the one PRC file to your Palm device. Using the Palm Desktop Install Tool (see Figure 24.1), load the cbaspad.prc file, and HotSync the Desktop to your Palm device. Figure 24.2 shows cbasPad loaded onto a Palm device.

Palm Desktop
Install tool

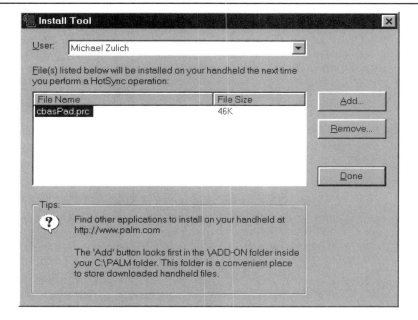

FIGURE 24.2

*Palm device
Applications Launcher*

 TIP When you load a new application to your Palm device while the Application Launcher is open, the Application Launcher will not immediately display the new application. The files will load, but you must exit the Application Launcher and return to it before you can see the new application listed.

At this point, you can access cbasPad just like any other Palm application through the Application Launcher. Tapping the cbasPad icon brings up the cbasPad memo editor shown in Figure 24.3 (all cbasPad programs are considered to be memos by the Palm OS) with the New, Edit, and Exec buttons at the bottom of the screen. In order to avoid any possible conflicts with the standard Palm application MemoPad, cbasPad uses its own memo database.

To start writing a new program, just tap the New button, which brings up the cbasPad Edit window (see Figure 24.4). You can use the Palm's built-in keyboard, Graffiti, or an add-on keyboard to write your code. Once your code is complete, just tap the Done button to save the newly created program. To test the new application, tap the SelectAll button to highlight the program and then the Exec button to run it.

FIGURE 24.3

Main cbasPad screen

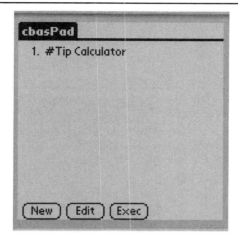

FIGURE 24.4

cbasPad Edit window

Once you have created an application, you can modify the code by highlighting the application in the cbasPad memo editor window and tapping the Edit button. This will bring you to the cbasPad Edit window and open the program for modifications.

You can also write your code through the Palm Memo Pad, rather than directly into cbasPad, and then "import" the Memo Pad file into cbasPad, shown in Figure 24.5. It may not seem to be any easier to create your program code through the Memo Pad, but using a regular keyboard and text editor can be a bonus.

FIGURE 24.5

cbasPad Import window

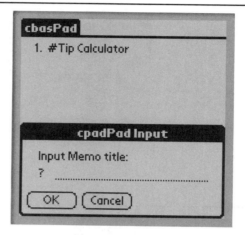

Using cbasPad Commands and Functions

Documentation for cbasPad is sketchy at best, and even with an old BASIC manual in hand you'll need to play with the language for a while before you'll feel comfortable. You can use if/then logic, the goto statement for flow control, and create subroutines and the gosub statement. cbasPad supports the standard set of BASIC commands and functions and has a few of its own.

We've listed the Palm-specific or modified commands below:

cbasPad Command	Description
dprint x	Prints the contents of x to a mini-dialog box
? x	Prints the contents of x to a mini-dialog box
dim	Defines the length of one dimensional arrays
Input "prompt", x	Displays Prompt in a dialog box and reads user input in variable x
print x	Appends x to the end of the cbasPad memo
fn 16	Returns the content of the seconds timer
fn 17	Returns the contents of the tick timer in 100HZ

cbasPad Command	Description
fn 18	Returns the memory address of the clipboard contents
fn 19	Returns the length of the clipboard contents
fn 20	Returns the scaled battery voltage
fn 22	Waits for two seconds and returns 0
fn 24	Returns decimal date
fn 25	Returns decimal time
fn 30	Displays a nine-line dialog box and returns the dialog button status
fn 33	Waits for a Graffiti character to be input and returns its ACSII value
fn 34	Returns the tick time of the last pen down
fn 38	Non-blocking form of fn 33
fn 39	Returns last input or dialog button status
fn 42	Clears the middle of the screen
fn 48	Returns the last pen tap x
fn 49	Returns the last pen tap y
grline x1, y1, x2, y2, 1	Draws a line starting at point x1/y1 and terminating at point x2/y2
grline x1, y1, x2, y2, 2	Draws a gray line at starting at point x1/y1 and terminating at point x2/y2
grline x1, y1, x2, y2, -1	Erases a line starting at point x1/y1 and terminating at point x2/y2
grline x1, y1, x2, y2, 4	Draws a rectangle with its upper-left corner at x1/Y1 and its lower-right corner at x2/y2
grline x1, y1, x2, y2, 5	Draws a gray rectangle with its upper-left corner at x1/Y1 and its lower-right corner at x2/y2
grline x1, y1, x2, y2, 7	Draws a filled rectangle with its upper-left corner at x1/y1 and its lower-right corner at x2/y2
grline x1, y1, x2, y2, -7	Erases the filled rectangle with its upper-left corner at x1/y1 and its lower-right corner at x2/y2
op "ds", a$, x, y	Places the content of string variable a$ at location x,/y

cbasPad Command	Description
op "ds", a$, n*1000+x,y	Places the contents of string variable a$ at location x/y in font n
op "sety", y	Replaces line y with the following print output
op "page", "new title"	Replaces the title of the output page with the string within quotes (new title)
op "page", "", n	Changes the output page to record n
op "page", "", -1	Creates a new output page and moves to it
op "dt", t$	Changes the fn 30 dialog box title to the value in the string variable t$
op "it", t$	Changes the input dialog box title to the value in the string variable t$
op "mfind", x$, n	Locates the MemoPad entry beginning with the contents of string variable x$, and returns the value of the memo index to n (n will be set to –1 if the test fails)
op "dbrd", "memo", n, m	Reads the MemoPad entry n into the built-in string array variable s$(0); m is the character offset, if m = –1 then read the next line
op "dbrd", "addr", n	Reads the AddressBook entry n into the built-in string array variable s$(0)
op "dbrd", "date", n	Reads the DateBook entry n into the built-in string array variable s$(0)
op "dbrd", "todo", n	Reads the Todo entry n into the built-in string array variable s$(0)
op "db", type, creat, i	Returns length of database record i
op "gnum", n	Returns the first number from line n of the current page
op "get$", n	Returns a string from line n of the current page
sound x, y, z	Plays a tone with a frequency of value x in Hz, for y mS and a volume of z (based on a scale of 0 to 64)
sersend addr, len, baud	Sends data at location addr of length len through the serial port at speed baud

cbasPad also supports the following five commands to write data to the Palm device, though if you are intent on doing this we'd recommend using one of the other two development tools discussed later in the book. cbasPad BASIC is just a little too difficult to work with in this environment.

op "dbwr!", "memo", n, 1	Appends the value in the built-in string array s$(0) to the end of the MemoPad memo number n with 1 line feed
op "dbwr!", "addr", n	Writes the contents of the built-in string array s$(0 … 18) to the AddressBook item n
op "dbwr!", "JBas:DBNAME", n	Writes the JFile database DBNAME record number n from the built-in string array s$()
op "dbwr!", "JBas:xyz", n, f	Writes record n, field f to JFile database "xyz"
op "dbwr!", DBOS:xyz", n, f	Writes record n, field f to DB database "xyz"

WARNING You can easily turn your Memo Pad, Address Book, and JFile databases into trash with the above five write commands. Use them with extreme caution.

In addition to these Palm specific commands, cbasPad supports the usual mathematical and programming functions. This short list includes a square root, exponential, log and trigonometric functions, as well as string processing and conversion functions.

A function is a built-in subroutine that performs some process on an external value and returns the processed value. We've listed some of these functions below:

cbasPad Function	Description
atn(x)	Returns the trigonometric value of the arc-tangent of x in radians
chr$(c)	Returns the ASCII value of string variable c
cos(x)	Returns the trigonometric cosine value of x in radians
eval(q$)	Evaluates string variable q as a numeric expression
exp(x)	Returns the product of e to the x power

cbasPad Function	Description
fre	Returns the free dynamic heap space
hex$(n)	Returns hex value of n
int(x)	Truncates the value of x to create an integer
len(a$)	Returns the length of string variable a
log(x)	Returns the natural log (base e) of x
mid$(a$, n, m)	Returns substring of a starting at location n with a length of m
mid$(a$, -n)	Returns the right string of (a$, n)
peek(a)	Returns 8-bit byte at address a
peek(a, 2)	Returns the 16-bit value at word aligned address a
peek(a, 4)	Returns the 32-bit value at word aligned address a
rnd(x)	Returns the pseudo-random integer in the range of 0 ... n-1
sin(x)	Returns the trigonometric sine value of x in radians
sqr(x)	Returns the square root of x
str$(x)	Returns the string representation of x
tan(x)	Returns the trigonometric tangent value of x in radians
val$(a$)	Returns the numeric value of string variable a$
varptr(y)	Returns the memory address of y

Understanding cbasPad Standards, Syntax, and Limitations

Like any programming language, cbasPad has a set of standards, syntax rules, and interpreter limitations. Most are similar to our old friend Dartmouth BASIC, but some are particular to this scaled-down Palm version. We'll look at the complete list and explain each item.

Standards

Every cbasPad program must start with the new command and end with the run command. These commands indicate the outer boundaries of the program code. You must precede all other lines of code with an ascending line number, such as 10, 20, 30, etc. To code in a comment or explanation, start the line with the # sign. All lines starting with the # sign are interpreted as non-executable code, so anything on that line is treated as a comment, even program code. The auto-numbering feature in cbasPad uses the # autonum comment feature. Place this comment/command at the start of your program (just after the new command), and cbasPad will automatically number all the lines of your code. By the way, the gosub and goto commands use line numbers and not line labels. Here's an example of commands, comments, and line numbering.

```
new
10 # this is a comment line
20 # and this is a sample of cbasPad syntax
30 a=b+c
run
```

There are a few more standards that we must live by to program in cbasPad Tiny BASIC. These are a few of the more pressing:

- Names of cbasPad variables cannot exceed 15 characters in length.
- All floating point numbers and variables use the IEEE single extended format.
- All string variable names must end with the $ character, and you are limited to a maximum of 30 string variables.
- The maximum length of a string variable is 31 characters.
- Complex string expressions don't work. The interpreter is buggy, but this may work in the next revision.
- All arrays must be defined or "dimensioned."
- cbasPad provides one built-in string array: s$(x). By definition, this array does not need to be defined. You may not create another.
- All keywords must be typed in lower case.
- Complex mathematical expressions generally require liberal use of parentheses.

Syntax

The cbasPad compiler includes a simple syntax inspector that will flag most syntax errors. Use a command improperly, and cbasPad will flag it and tell you which line in the code has a problem. It won't tell you the nature of the problem, just that you have a syntax error (see Figure 24.6).

FIGURE 24.6

cbasPad syntax error

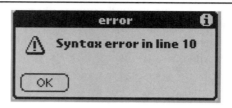

The syntax inspector doesn't catch every typing error or misplaced modifier. For example, the Motorola Dragonball functions, such as fn 16 that returns the seconds timer, requires a space between the fn and the function number 16. Leave out that space, and the function will return nothing, but cbasPad will not indicate the syntax error.

WARNING Carefully review all of your code, even after cbasPad gives it a clean bill of syntax help. The built-in syntax checker isn't perfect.

You have two print commands in cbasPad. The first, the standard print command, will append whatever follows the print command to the current cbasPad memo. For example, the cbasPad code line

```
10 print "this is the end of the program"
```

will literally copy the text in quotes to the end of the current program. The second print command is the dprint command (or its abbreviation, the ?). The dprint command will display whatever follows the command to the Palm LCD panel in a mini dialog box. So, the following line of cbasPad code

```
10 dprint "this is the end of the program"
```

will display the text in quotes on the Palm LCD panel. You could also use the ? abbreviation in place of the dprint command, so the line could look like

```
10 ? "this is the end of the program"
```

and this will produce the same results (the text in quotes would display to the Palm LCD panel).

As a twist on the straight dprint or information display, we have an additional command that will change the current output page. Using one of the graphical display commands, the op "page", −1 command, we can open a new output page and deposit the output there. This is similar, in effect, to the dprint command, though dprint will not change the output page.

Limitations

All cbasPad programs are limited to a length of 4000 characters. Remember, every letter, number, punctuation mark, etc. is a character. So, the command line

```
10 for k=10 to 100 step 3
```

contains 19 characters and six spaces, which are counted as characters given that a space has a numerical value and it too requires memory space. Fortunately, you can create a program in modules and connect the modules together with the `#include <$TITLE>` comment. cbasPad interprets this comment line as a far call to the file named TITLE. In plain English, cbasPas will link two or more programs through the `#include <$TITLE>` comment, inserting the program named TITLE in the exact location where the `#include` statement was used.

Here are a few more cbasPad limitations:

- Integer overflows will not always provide a warning.
- Forgetting the new command at the start of a program can result in the execution buffer not clearing.
- Peeks and pokes can lock up your Palm device.
- The `sersend` command will drain the Palm device's battery at an abnormally high rate.
- Floating point values occasionally calculate or print incorrectly.
- Not all syntax errors will provide line numbers.
- Nesting complex expressions can cause a stack overflow.
- Divide by 0, log(0) and overflows produce undefined results.

Creating the Application in cbasPad

Now that you have a rudimentary understanding of how cbasPad works, and how its command and functions operate, you can put that knowledge to work and develop your application. Remember, your application will calculate the tip for a restaurant bill based on the total bill less the total cost of drinks. This is a simple example with real-world merit.

So, let's re-examine our original equation introduced earlier in this chapter:

```
Total Bill less Drink Bill times Tip Percent equals the Tip
```

which we transformed into the following mathematical expression:

```
(B-D)*S=T
```

where B is the Total Bill, D is the Drink Bill, S is the Tip Percent (or Service), and T is the calculated Tip. We then transformed that one mathematical expression into two expressions, and reversed the order to arrive at standard computer assignment form:

```
NB=B-D
T=NB*S
```

where NB is the Net Bill (the Total Bill less the Drink Bill) and T is the calculated tip, which is the product of the Net Bill × S, the Tip Percent. We can now add the calculated Tip to the Total Bill amount to arrive at the Grand Total Bill (the total amount that you should pay). This equation looks like this:

```
GT=T+B
```

where GT is the Grand Total, T is the calculated Tip, and B is the Total Bill. Hopefully that's all really clear, and you're ready to begin programming.

Coding the Application in cbasPad

We will use a modular approach to code our application. That is, we will start by coding the calculation, then add our input/output commands, and lastly add any window dressing to make the application look a little prettier. We will also approach this exercise with simplicity in mind. Our code will get the job done in a very simple way—no complex code, no hidden programmer tricks, no special knowledge. The idea here is to display the strengths of cbasPad, and the ease and speed by which you can create an application. So, what we will do is get the program up and running quickly and logically, and leave the complicated stuff to you. With that in mind let's get going.

We'll assume that you have already installed cbasPad onto your Palm device; if not, see the section titled "Installing cbasPad Tiny BASIC" earlier in this chapter. From the Palm Application Launcher, tap the cbasPad icon to open the development tool, then tap the New button.

Remember that every cbasPad program must start with the New command and end with the Run command. Additionally, any line starting with the # is treated as a comment. You can place comment lines before the New command, and since the very first line of any program becomes the program's name, let's start off with a comment line entitled Tip Calculator. You can use Graffiti or the Palm's built-in keyboard to enter this info. Now let's code in our formulas:

NB = B – D   where NB is the calculated Net Bill (the difference of the Total Bill less the Drink Bill)

T = NB * S   where T is the calculated Tip (the product of the Net Bill times the Tip Percent)

GT = T + B   where GT is the calculated Grand Total (the sum of the Total Bill plus the Tip)

So our program should look like this, so far:

```
# Tip Calculator
new
100 nb=b-d
110 t=nb*s
120 gt=t+b
run
```

If we tap the SelectAll button to highlight the program code as shown in Figure 24.7, and then tap the Exec button, we can run our little beauty. But because we haven't defined any means for supplying input or output to our program, we have no real idea if it works or what it does.

FIGURE 24.7

Highlighted code sample

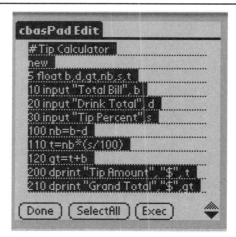

Let's include a data input command to accept the information that our program needs to calculate a tip. We can use cbasPad's input command to obtain this data. The input command takes on the following form:

```
10 input "Total Bill", b
```

When cbasPad encounters this command, it displays a dialog box to the Palm's LCD panel and forms the text in quotes into a question. In this case, we would receive a dialog box with the words Total Bill? inside it, as shown in Figure 24.8. The input command then provides a blank line for the requested data. That data becomes variable b.

We need to code two additional, similar lines for the Drink Total and the Tip Percent. The three complete lines would like this:

```
10 input "Total Bill", b
20 input "Drink Total", d
30 input "Tip Percent", s
```

FIGURE 24.8

Input screen

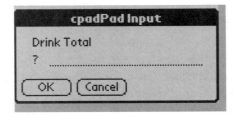

Our code should now look like the following listing:

```
# Tip Calculator
new
10 input "Total Bill", b
20 input "Drink Total", d
30 input "Tip Percent", s
100 nb=b-d
110 t=nb*s
120 gt=t+b
run
```

NOTE Though the line numbers in your cbasPad program must be sequential, cbasPad does not require that they follow any pattern. The numbering scheme used above is 100 percent legitimate.

We now need to add output commands—some way to display the results of our calculations. For that we will use cbasPad's dprint command. The dprint command uses a form similar to that of the input command, displaying a variable with a line of text. For our program, we will use two dprint commands: one for the calculated Tip and one for the Grand Total amount. These two commands look like this:

```
200 dprint "Tip Amount", "$", t
210 dprint "Grand Total", "$", gt
```

You'll notice that we added one additional parameter to each dprint command, the $. By placing the $ in quotes, we are able to display these along with the calculated data on the Palm's LCD panel.

So, now our almost complete program looks like the following:

```
# Tip Calculator
new
10 input "Total Bill", b
20 input "Drink Total", d
30 input "Tip Percent", s
100 nb=b-d
110 t=nb*s
120 gt=t+b
200 dprint "Tip Amount", "$", t
210 dprint "Grand Total", "$", gt
run
```

What makes this almost complete is the fact that we're missing a little piece of housekeeping code, the declaration statement. We use declarations to identify variables and their types to the program and the interpreter. The declaration statement should be the first line of program code, and should identify all of the variables that we intend to use. Since all of our data and calculated variables must be decimal numbers, we must declare our program variables as floating point numbers. We do this as follows:

```
5 float b, d, gt, nb, s, t
```

NOTE To download the following code, go to www.sybex.com and navigate to the *Mastering Palm Organizers* page.

The complete program now looks like this:

```
# Tip Calculator
new
5 float b, d, gt, nb, s, t
10 input "Total Bill", b
20 input "Drink Total", d
30 input "Tip Percent", s
100 nb=b-d
110 t=nb*s
120 gt=t+b
200 dprint "Tip Amount", "$", t
210 dprint "Grand Total", "$", gt
run
```

PART

V

Advanced Techniques

Tap the Done button to save the program. This action also returns you to the main cbasPad window, which should now list your new program as number 1.

TIP Since line numbers do not need to be consecutive, you can group portions of code within selected number ranges. This makes identifying the code segments a little easier.

TIP It's also good practice to leave large numerical gaps between line numbers. This lets you insert new lines of code without the need to renumber your entire program.

To run this new cbasPad program, highlight the program in the main cbasPad window and tap the Exec button. Then, cbasPad will respond by drawing a dialog box and asking for the Total Bill input data. The screen should look like Figure 24.9.

FIGURE 24.9

Total Bill input screen

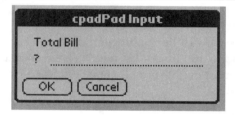

Enter a value and tap OK, and the program will draw the second dialog box and ask for the Drink Total. The program continues with the Tip Percent (see Figure 24.10), which may present a slight problem.

FIGURE 24.10

Tip Percent input screen

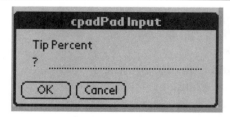

If you're like us, you might enter 15 percent as the number 15 and not the decimal number 0.15, which is the correct answer to the Tip Percent question. If you think in whole numbers, we can modify the program to accommodate that way of thinking. For the time being, enter the Tip Percent as a decimal percent, say 0.15, and tap OK.

Then, cbasPad displays a dialog box with the Tip Amount. Tap OK to get to the Grand Total dialog box (see Figure 24.11).

FIGURE 24.11

Tip Amount dialog box

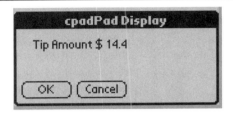

To adjust the Tip Percent calculation to accommodate whole numbers, such as 12 instead of 0.12, we need to modify line 110. All we need to do is divide S, the Tip Percent variable, by 100, which turns the whole number into a decimal percent number. From the cbasPad main menu, highlight the Tip Calculator program and tap the Edit button. This will open cbasPad program in Edit mode. Change line 110 to read as follows:

```
110 t=nb*(s/100)
```

By dividing the whole number Tip Percent variable by 100 we have created a decimal percent number. Now, if we re-run the program and enter a whole number, such 15, we will actually calculate a 15 percent tip. The complete and correct program now looks like the following:

```
# Tip Calculator
new
5 float b, d, gt, nb, s, t
10 input "Total Bill", b
20 input "Drink Total", d
30 input "Tip Percent", s
100 nb=b-d
110 t=nb*s
120 gt=t+b
200 dprint "Tip Amount", "$", t
210 dprint "Grand Total", "$", gt
run
```

With a little time, creativity, and a proper BASIC manual, you should be able to create a tight program with fewer input dialog boxes. What we've created is a simple, little program that solves a problem, and there is always room for improvement.

PART

V

Advanced Techniques

To make this application look better, try using the fn 30 function and the built-in string array, s$(x). The fn 30 function creates a separate dialog box that can be easily filled with the contents of the s$(x) array. The outcome is that you can use one dialog box for both input and output information.

We've learned a little about cbasPad Tiny BASIC, and how quick and easy it is to create a program. This is the real strength of cbasPad: we can create applications right on the Palm device; there's no need for a desktop computer. We'll see that with the other two applications development tools, creating an application is not quite so simple. Though, in their defense, these tools have quite a bit more power and capability. Read about each in the following chapters before you make any decisions regarding which applications development tool is best for you.

CHAPTER 25

Creating a Sample Application in Satellite Forms

Satellite Forms is a visual, forms-based application development tool that is very different from the other two tools (cbasPad Tiny BASIC and Code-Warrior) we spotlight in this book. Satellite Forms uses tables to collect, store, and process information, which makes it an ideal database management (DBMS) system. Satellite Forms stores data in standard dBase V format making the data tables relatively easy to transfer and access from other application development tools. Tables—think Excel spreadsheets or Access tables—are the preferred techniques for handling data in any DBMS. By design then, Satellite Forms is intended to be a database tool; use it to capture data records while on the road and then upload this information to your desktop computer when time permits. This model borrows its design from the original design model for the Palm device making for a perfect match.

Satellite Forms comes in two flavors: the Standard Edition and the Enterprise Edition. The Standard Edition is intended for the stand-alone user or developer—someone who will not perform their development over a LAN or the Web. With the Standard Edition you get free distribution rights to the Satellite Forms engine and all of the tools necessary to create applications and distribute them as you see fit. The Standard Edition retails for about $800—a very expensive tool, but a very capable one, too. The Enterprise Edition includes all of the features in the Standard Edition, plus network support for 10 simultaneous users, the ability to HotSync across a network connection, and Oracle Lite connectivity support. The Enterprise Edition is just a little bit more expensive with a suggested retail price of just a fin short of $1000. You might be able to find either of these application development tools for less through a VAR or other retailer.

Unlike the cbasPad Tiny BASIC project of Chapter 24, working with Satellite Forms allows us use of a full function IDE on the host or desktop computer. We will develop our application here, taking full advantage of the IDE features, not to mention the full-size keyboard. And just like in our cbasPad example, we will use the Palm OS Emulator (POSE) to test and debug the application.

Satellite Forms Version 3.1 Details

There are the four basic components of Satellite Forms:

The App Designer   The IDE used to develop forms and tables which are the basis for any application created through this development tool.

The Conduit   The data transfer mechanism used to move applications created within the IDE to your Palm device and vice versa.

The HotSync Extension Active X Control   The mechanism that simplifies integration with database applications (see the following explanation).

The Satellite Forms Engine   The mechanism that runs the Satellite Forms application on your Palm device. You'll need to download this Forms Engine to your Palm before you load any applications.

The App Designer is where you will spend most of your time. Not only is it where you create your application, it is the only "visible" component of the tool. The other three pieces (the conduit, HotSync Extension, and Forms Engine) are basically behind-the-scenes components that you can't live without. You must install all four components if you want Satellite Forms to run properly.

Forms, Tables, and Controls

Before you can undertake any development within Satellite Forms, you need to examine some of the fundamentals behind this application development tool. Satellite Forms is a relational database, meaning that all data is associated with some other piece of data. The relationship that you develop as you create the database will determine the association. Ideally, you would create a relationship that is either real or necessary for your database processing. For example, you could create a relationship between your name and address since your name is linked to your address. This relationship makes sense since you always relate your address to your name, and the relationship makes database processing a little easier. This relationship means that you don't need to handle an address when all you want is a name, or vice versa, and it allows you to use either piece of data or both, whichever is required.

Data, in our relational database, is stored in tables. Basically, these tables look very much like spreadsheets—columns for data types and rows for records or groups of data. Add a new record and you add a new row. The table grows as the database grows. When you're not viewing the data in spreadsheet form, you can view the data through a form. Forms let you organize data so that it is easy to read, grouping related data from several tables together. By presenting the data in a user friendly format (the form), you are able to ensure that it not only makes sense to the user but is easy to read. You can determine how the data in the form is seen and managed through controls, such as a pick list, that display allowable field info. We'll look more closely at tables, forms, and control in the next few sections.

Tables in Satellite Forms

Tables are the basic means for storing data in Satellite Forms. The App Designer creates tables for you, so you don't need to concern yourself with those details—just start the App Designer.

Each table must have a unique name as does each field in that table. These unique names are required to identify each piece of data. Ideally, these names (both table and field) should be descriptive of the data it represents, though it is not required. Additionally, you must assign a field type description that determines the nature of the data in that field to each field. Your choices include the following:

- Character field defines a field that accepts any printable character including the entire alphabet, numbers, punctuation marks, and symbols.

- Numeric field defines a field that accepts only numbers. This includes numbers that you may want to use for mathematical operations, such as cost figures, income, physical dimensions, and quantity. Numeric strings, such as a social security number or phone number, should be treated as character fields.

- True/False field accepts only a character response of "T" for true or "F" for false. Satellite Forms will accept no other input.

- Date field accepts only date information in the form of month/day/year using two digits to identify the month and day, and four digits to identify the year. For example, you would enter the date January 21, 2000 as 01/21/00. Fortunately, Satellite Forms does not force the Palm device to use this notation, but will bow to the Palm's setting determined through the Preference screen.

- Time field accepts data only in the time format of hours:minutes AM/PM, where both hours and minutes are represented by two digits. Satellite Forms uses a 12 hour clock, so 8:27 PM is represented as 08:27 PM and 11:06 AM is represented as 11:06 AM. Just like the data field, the time field defers to the Palm device's Preferences.

- Ink fields will accept input only from the ink control, and are used for signatures or drawings.

- Time Stamp fields establish compatibility with imported Oracle Lite tables and accepts an 8-bit integer.

Forms in Satellite Forms

Since forms are the means for viewing data—the window through which we organize and see the tables of our data—you must carefully craft how the form looks, works, and functions. The App Designer module of Satellite Forms is your form development tool, and how a form looks in this module is how it will look on the Palm device. Depending on the size of your table or the number of tables you choose to use, you may need multiple forms to obtain all of the necessary information. Just like windows in a house, you can have multiple windows (forms) to view your data. However, you can view only one table at a time. So you may need multiple forms per table, but can have only one table per form.

Forms that view tables of data are considered to be dynamic; that is, some portion of what you can and will see changes as the database changes. You can also have static forms: forms that display the same info regardless of the status of the database. A help screen, a title screen, and instructions are some examples of static forms.

Additionally, you can have (and likely will have) hybrid forms that contain a mix of dynamic and static elements. A form that displays database information is a dynamic form, but that form will contain both dynamic and static elements. The form's title is static, as are the field titles or any graphics. The displayed table information, on the other hand, is dynamic—this information will change with each record. How dynamic data is displayed on the form is determined by a control and is the topic of the next section.

Controls

Through App Designer features called controls, you determine how to display dynamic information. You can also design control buttons, like "Enter" or "Cancel," and determine the action that your form will perform.

The App Designer supports the following 15 controls:

- Title control displays a title across the top of the form.
- Text control displays static information such as a help field.
- Edit control lets you modify the contents of a selected field, which in turn modifies the data in the database.
- Paragraph control allows you to modify a multi-line field and works similarly to the Edit control.
- Check Box control creates a check box on the form. Check boxes are not mutually exclusive, so a user can check as many boxes as you create.
- Radio Button control works like the Check Box control except that the Radio Button controls are exclusive, so a user can select only one radio button.
- Button control defines how a button will behave. The Button control executes an action through a script or small program. For more information on scripts, see the next section.
- List Box control displays a table or portion of a table, and is the only way to view more than one record at a time. This control is useful for quickly comparing data across multiple records.
- Drop List control creates a drop-down list whose contents comes from a separate table.

- Lookup control displays the contents of a lookup table. Lookup tables are tables linked through one field of data. For example, your bank likely uses your bank account number to link personal information such as your name and address to financial information such as your bank account.

- Ink control lets you use freehand drawings or marks as a signature.

- Bitmap control displays bitmap images on the form.

- Auto Stamp control is not visible on the form, but records the current time and date, which is useful for time sensitive operations.

- Graffiti Shift Indicator control displays the Graffiti cap lock indicator, which is much like your keyboard cap lock indicator, on the Palm device's LCD panel.

- SFX Custom controls are special Satellite Forms controls such as the slider control that creates a slider bar.

Scripts

As the name might imply, Satellite Forms scripts are the means to perform standard program logic such as if/then operations, mathematical calculations, or data management. Scripting is event-driven and is based on an object model that includes forms, tables, controls, fields, and extensions, each having its own set of custom configurable properties.

The Satellite Forms scripting language is largely a subset of Microsoft Visual Basic, with nearly identical syntax. You have the use of local and global variables, full Boolean logic operators, and complete input/output control. Scripts add an additional level of processing to Satellite Forms that allows you to capture data and manipulate it all in the same application.

Show Script Icon

To access the Script Editor, open a project, go to the View menu in the App Designer and select the Misc Toolbar, if it's not already selected. Click the Show Script button in the toolbar or, alternatively, right-click on a form or control. Once you have accessed the Script Editor (see Figure 25.1), you can open the Forms and Event drop-down lists.

FIGURE 25.1

Script Editor

To start, use Select Form to identify the form that you will use as the basis for this script. From the drop-down list you can select every form created in your application along with Global Variables. Highlight a form, move on to the Events drop-down list, and select an event to associate with this script.

Your event choices are:

- AfterChange occurs after data in any control or form is modified.
- AfterLoad occurs after you load a form, but before an AfterChange event occurs.

- AfterOpen occurs after you open a form but before that form is loaded with data. This event will execute only when you open the form.

- AfterRecordCreate occurs after you create a new record but before you enter any other information. This event is useful in initiating records with preset information.

- BeforeClose occurs before you close a form but after you execute OnValidate event from the form.

- BeforeRecordDelete occurs before a record is permanently deleted but after a user makes the request.

- OnKey occurs when you press one of the hardware or soft buttons or enter a Graffiti character. Combined with the GetLastKey command, you can specify the exact button pressed or Graffiti character written.

- OnPenDown occurs when the stylus touches any portion of the screen.

- OnPenUp is the direct opposite of OnPenDown, and occurs when you lift the stylus from the screen. We're not quite sure when or why you would use this event, but Puma Technologies includes it anyway.

- OnTimer occurs once for each time period when the timer is set. Using the OnTimer frees the CPU from counting time periods for your script.

- OnValidate is a flag that is set when the entered data meets your validation criteria. OnValidate executes before the BeforeClose event occurs. This order can prevent a user from entering bad data and exiting the application.

All variables, whether local or global, are automatically declared as floating point, integer, or string depending on the value assigned. You can and should declare all your variables to ensure that they are all of the proper form before proceeding with your script. To declare a variable, use the dim keyword and one of the variable types: float for floating point numbers, int for integer numbers, or str for string variables. Unless you specifically select Global Variable, all variables are assumed to be local, accessible only within this one script, and exist only for the duration of this script.

Once you have completed a script you'll need to compile the code so that you can download it to the Palm device. To compile the script, click the Compile Changed button in the Misc Toolbar.

Compile
Changed Button

Extensions

You can add to the capabilities of Satellite Forms through extensions. Extensions, also called SFX plug-ins and SFX controls, are C programs that increase the utility of Satellite Forms scripts, add logic not included in the standard Satellite Forms package, and help to customize how Satellite Forms works. You can write your own or download an extension directly from Puma Technologies.

Since extensions are C programs, you can create virtually anything from a custom control to a mathematical function. For example, Puma Technologies includes a square root SFX plug-in and a SFX control called Slider, which is a graphical slider. But because we're talking about C programs, extensions are not for everyone. Try the download route before attempting to create your own. Try the Puma Technologies Web site for downloadable extensions.

Installing Satellite Forms

Installing Satellite Forms is a little different from installing any other applications development tool. You must install the IDE portion of the tool (the App Designer) on your desktop computer, then install the Satellite Forms Engine onto your Palm device. Satellite Forms requires both pieces for your application to function. Frankly, you can't develop your application without the App Designer on your desktop, so that's a no-brainer.

Version 3.1 of Satellite Forms typically arrives on a CD-ROM, so we'll explain the CD-ROM installation for the standard edition.

1. Load the CD-ROM into your CD-ROM drive.

2. If Autorun is enabled on your computer, the install process will begin on its own. If Autorun is not enabled, look for and execute the Setup.exe program found in the CD-ROM root directory.

3. Read the license agreement (see Figure 25.2), click Yes to agree to the terms, and continue. If you click No, the install will cancel and you will need to start over again.

4. Fill in your name, company name (Satellite Forms requires a company name and will not let you proceed without one—make up a name if you don't have a company name), and the product key code. You can find this code on the back of the CD-ROM jewel case. The code is case sensitive so be mindful of capital letters (see Figure 25.3).

FIGURE 25.2

*Satellite Forms SE
Version 3.1 Install
Screen*

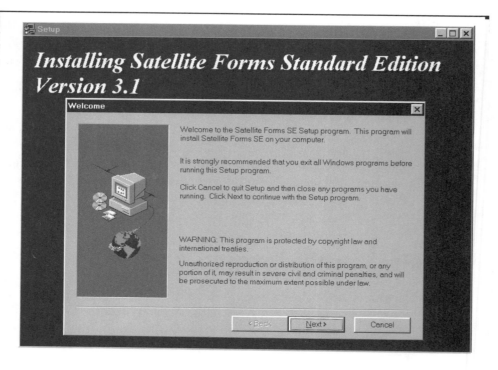

FIGURE 25.3

Enter Key Code Screen

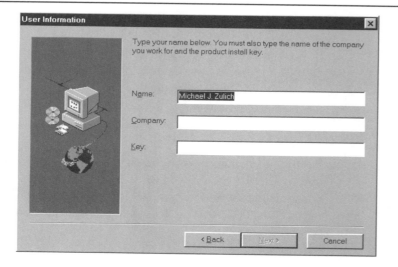

At this point, the install provides online instructions detailing the best method for handling an upgrade. If you are upgrading from an older version of Satellite Forms, carefully follow the instructions presented on this screen, shown in Figure 25.4. If you aren't upgrading, click OK and the install will complete.

FIGURE 25.4

*Satellite Forms
Warning Screen*

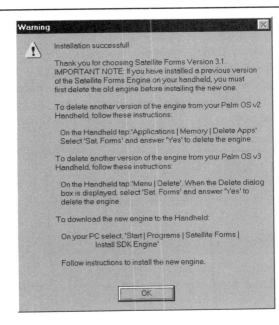

Contents of Installed Folders

The Install program creates a Satellite Forms SE folder with seven files and three sub-folders. The contents of the Satellite Forms SE folder includes:

- App Designer is the main Satellite Forms application that includes the IDE.
- Icon Maker is an application that creates Palm OS icons. Create an icon here to identify your Satellite Forms application and download it to your Palm device.
- Install SDK Engine is an install tool that moves files from the desktop computer to the Palm device. It's identical in nature to the Install tool in the Palm Desktop software.
- Install Work Order RDK Sample is a Satellite Forms sample application used to test the Satellite Forms installation.
- RDK Help is online help for the RDK command line options.

- Readme provides the latest information regarding Satellite Forms, the installation process, and program fixes.
- Uninstall is the uninstall program.
- Doc folder holds all of the on-line documentation for Satellite Forms version 3.1.
- Project folder is empty at installation but should be used to hold your applications.
- Samples folder holds sample files and applications.

The install program will also place a Satellite Forms SE version 3.1 menu pick list in your Programs menu.

Now that you have installed Satellite Forms on your desktop computer, you must install the Satellite Forms Engine on the Palm device. Satellite Forms applications will not function on the Palm device without the Satellite Forms Engine.

 WARNING You must delete any older versions of Satellite Forms from your Palm device before installing this new version.

Deleting an Older Version of Satellite Forms

To delete your current, older, version of Satellite Forms, perform the following:

1. From the Palm's Application Launcher screen, tap the Menu soft button.

2. From the Menu Bar, choose Delete.

3. Select Satellite Forms from the Delete list, and tap the Delete… button.

4. Tap Yes to confirm your selection.

5. Tap Done to return to the Application Launcher.

Installing the Satellite Forms Engine

To install the Satellite Forms Engine on to your Palm device, use the following procedure:

1. From your desktop computer, click the Install SDK Engine menu item from the Satellite Forms SE version 3.1 menu pick list in the Program menu.

2. Select a username and click OK. Figure 25.5 displays the Install Tool screen.

FIGURE 25.5

Installing the Satellite Forms SDK Engine onto a Palm device

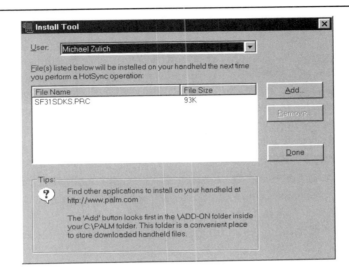

3. HotSync your desktop computer to the Palm device. This loads the Satellite Forms SDK Engine onto the Palm. You can see its icon in Figure 25.6.

FIGURE 25.6

Palm device with Satellite Forms Engine installed

You can also use the Palm Desktop Install tool software instead of the Install SDK Engine tool in step 1.

Download the Sample Application

To ensure that the installation on both the desktop computer and the Palm device worked, you should download the sample application and run through its features. There's little reason to believe that something has gone wrong with the installation, given that it's relatively simple and straightforward. Nevertheless, it's always good practice to test everything. Besides, running through this process is also good practice for loading your own application to the Palm device.

To download the sample application you'll need to start from the App Designer module of the Satellite Forms SE version 3.1 application on your desktop computer.

1. Open the App Designer and click File/Open. See Figure 25.7. From the Open submenu, navigate to the Samples folder and double-click the Projects subfolder.

2. Double-click the Restock subfolder, highlight restock.sfa, and click Open.

FIGURE 25.7

Open submenu

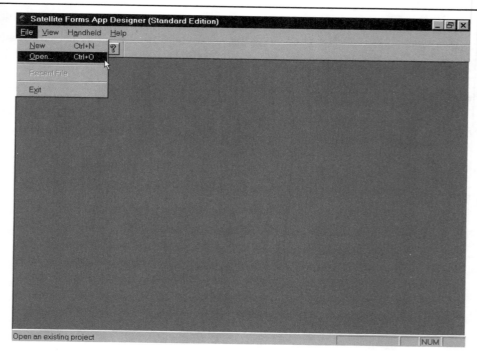

3. Select Download Application To Handheld from the Handheld menu. You'll see the confirmation dialog box shown in Figure 25.8. Now HotSync.

FIGURE 25.8

Download
confirmation

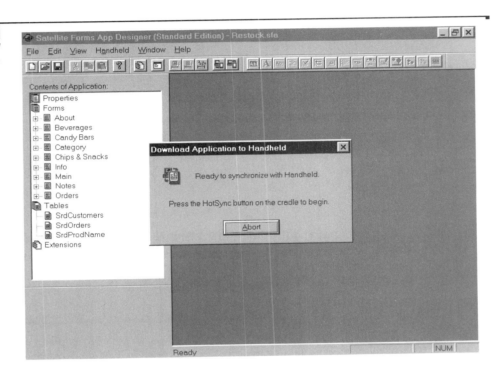

4. After the HotSync completes, tap the Satellite Forms icon in the Palm's Application Launcher and select the Store Restocking Demo. The LCD panel on your Palm device should look like Figure 25.9. Tap on the Store Restocking Demo to run that application.

5. Next, highlight Joe's Food Mart.

You'll notice that there are three buttons at the bottom of the screen. The Info button provides information about the client, the Orders button lets you input/record new orders, and the About button presents the "Powered by Satellite Forms" logo required to meet the license agreement.

FIGURE 25.9

*LCD panel on your
Palm device*

This example, and the others in the Samples folder, will give you a good idea of what Satellite Forms can do and how it can look. Try playing with a few other sample applications to familiarize yourself with the process of moving the application to the Palm device, and to give yourself some ideas of how to use the program's features.

 TIP You'll probably want to remove these samples from your Palm device when you have finished examining their features. This will free valuable memory on your Palm.

Removing the Satellite Forms Engine

If you've decided that you've had enough of Satellite Forms and want to remove it from your Palm device, you can easily delete the Satellite Forms Engine. From your Palm device, perform the following:

1. From the Application Launcher screen, tap the Menu soft button.

2. From the Menu Bar, choose Delete.

3. Select Satellite Forms from the Delete list, and tap the Delete... button.

4. Tap Yes to confirm your selection.

5. Tap Done to return to the Application Launcher.

The Satellite Forms IDE

Satellite Forms' IDE, the App Designer, has the familiar look and feel that we associate with virtually every other development tool or end user application. Basically, the App Designer (see Figure 25.10) looks like any software package from Microsoft or Adobe: a menu bar at the top, a toolbar just beneath that, and the bulk of the screen devoted to a design/work space.

FIGURE 25.10

The App Designer

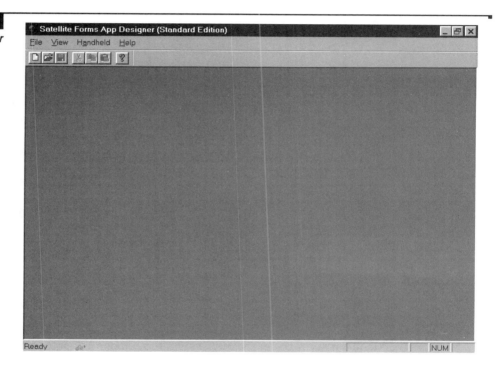

Let's open the App Designer and take a close look at its features. To do that, you should create a new project or application by clicking File/New on the Windows Menu Bar. This action changes the view and properties of the screen from the default view and should look like Figure 25.11. It adds several new buttons to the toolbar and vertically separates the workspace into two panes. The left pane, about 20 percent of the screen, is called the Contents window, which displays the contents of the current project in hierarchical form. This method of displaying the project uses a form similar

PART

V

Advanced Techniques

to Microsoft's directory tree structure. The remaining 80 percent of the screen is called the workspace and is just that: the place where you will create your application.

FIGURE 25.11

The new application window

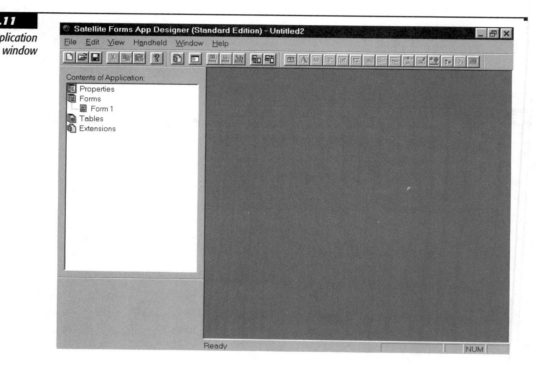

The Menu Bar

The Menu Bar at the top of the App Designer screen has six commands: File, Edit, View, Handheld, Window, and Help. These menu commands react and respond similarly to other graphical applications—each menu holds several submenus. Additionally, some Menu commands are context sensitive and depend upon what you're doing or where you are in the application. Most Menu commands also have keyboard shortcuts.

The File Menu

The File menu, illustrated in Figure 25.12, includes all of the file maintenance activities such as file open, save, and exit.

FIGURE 25.12

File menu

The File menu includes the following commands:

- New (CTRL+N) creates a new Satellite Forms application.
- Open (CTRL+O) opens an existing Satellite Forms application through the Open file dialog box, as shown in Figure 25.13.

FIGURE 25.13

Open file dialog box

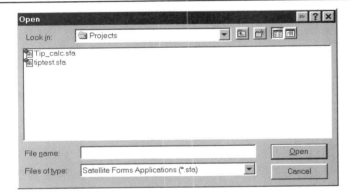

- Close closes the current application and will prompt you to save if you haven't already done so.
- Save (CTRL+S) saves the current application with the current file name. By default, Satellite Forms will open the Save As dialog box if you haven't previously saved the file. This allows you to avoid having to create files with those default files names like application1.
- Save As saves the current application but gives you the option to change the file name or location.
- Recent File List displays a list of the most recently accessed Satellite Forms applications. This list makes easy work of finding previously saved applications.
- Exit closes the current application and exits the App Designer. Fortunately, Satellite Forms will prompt you to save your file if you haven't already done so.

The Edit Menu

The Edit menu should look like Figure 25.14 and holds all of the application editing functions such as cut, paste, copy, and insert.

The Edit menu includes the following commands:

- Cut (CTRL+X) cuts the highlighted element, placing it on the clipboard for use elsewhere.
- Copy (CTRL+C) copies the highlighted element, placing it on the clipboard for use elsewhere.
- Paste (CTRL+V) pastes the contents of the clipboard at the cursor point within the application.
- Delete (DEL) deletes the highlighted element, removing it entirely from the application.
- Select All (CTRL+A) selects every object/element in the current window and highlights them for further editing operations.
- Insert Form inserts a new form into the application at the cursor's location.
- Insert Table inserts a new table into the application at the cursor's location.
- Import Table imports a table into the application at the cursor's location. You can import any ODBC compliant table.
- Bring Control to Front will bring the selected control to the front, giving it a higher priority over other controls.
- Send Control to Back is essentially the opposite of the Bring Control to Front. The Send Control to Back takes the current control, modifies its priority, and moves it to the end of the list.
- Object Properties opens the selected object's property box.

The View Menu

The View menu holds the commands for setting toolbars, scripts, and extensions. Figure 25.15 displays the View menu contents.

FIGURE 25.15

The View menu

- Scripts (CTRL+T) opens the Application Scripts window which looks like Figure 25.16.

FIGURE 25.16

The Applications Script window

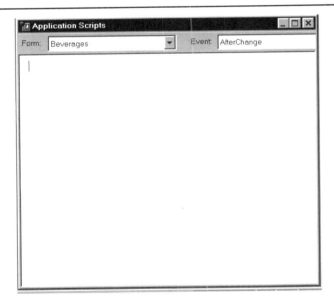

- Extensions opens the Available Extensions dialog box. See Figure 25.17.

PART

V

Advanced Techniques

FIGURE 25.17

The Available Extensions dialog box

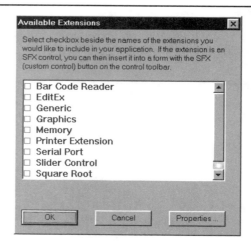

- Control Palette turns the Control Palette on/off.
- General Toolbar turns the General Toolbar on/off.
- Project Contents turns the Contents window on/off.
- Misc Toolbar turns the Misc Toolbar on/off.
- Status Bar turns the Status Bar on/off. The Status Bar is at the bottom of the screen just above the system tray.
- Preferences opens the Preferences dialog box. See Figure 25.18.

FIGURE 25.18

The Preferences dialog box

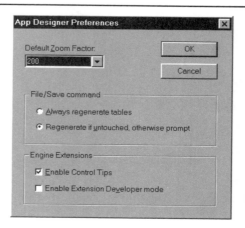

The Handheld Menu

The Handheld menu, shown in Figure 25.19, provides the commands and file management tools to move applications and files to the Palm device.

FIGURE 25.19

The Handheld menu

The Handheld menu includes the following commands:

- Download App & Tables downloads an application and its associated tables to your Palm device via the HotSync.
- Include Extensions In Download turns the extension transfer option on/off. This feature defaults to on when you create an extension, so you generally don't need to activate this option.
- Upload Tables uploads tables from the Palm device to your desktop computer. Use this feature to capture remote data (from the Palm) and move it to the central database on the desktop computer.
- Get User Info displays the username and ID of the Palm device currently in the attached cradle (see Figure 25.20). This info identifies the Palm device to the desktop database and ensures that the data transfers to the correct database. The ID information is the same information used by the Palm OS conduit during a HotSync.

PART

V

Advanced Techniques

FIGURE 25.20

*Palm III User
Information screen*

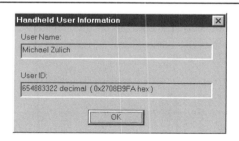

The Window Menu

The Window menu includes standard Window commands and manipulation features as shown in Figure 25.21.

FIGURE 25.21

The Window menu

The Window menu includes the following commands:

- Cascade cascades (lines up the open windows one behind the other) all open windows in the workspace pane.
- Tile tiles all open windows in the work space pane. Tiling places all open windows side-by-side, allowing you to view them all simultaneously.
- Arrange Icons neatly arranges icons in the work space pane.
- Open Windows lists all windows currently open and available for modification.

The Help Menu

The Help menu, shown in Figure 25.22, lists help topics and the About Box.

FIGURE 25.22

The Help menu

The Help menu includes the following Help items:

- Help Topics opens a Windows standard Help menu with Contents, Index, and Find tabs.
- About App Designer opens the information box for the App Designer. This box displays the version and serial number.

The Toolbar

What you would normally consider to be "the" toolbar is actually three different toolbars in Satellite Forms App Designer. As we saw in the View menu above, you have the option to view any combination (or none) of the toolbars. By default, the toolbars are all active.

The three toolbars (the General Toolbar, the Misc Toolbar, and the Control Palette) provide shortcuts to menu options, saving you some time and mouse clicks. As with every application, toolbars provide a degree of usefulness, however, when they contain 29 icons, as with Satellite Forms, they may become a little overwhelming. It all depends on your point of view, but fortunately App Designer uses tool-tips so you won't need to memorize each icon's function. Additionally, you can turn off any one or all of the toolbars through the View menu.

The General Toolbar

The General toolbar includes those buttons common to all GUI-based applications and familiar to each of us. From left to right, these seven tools are:

- New creates a new Satellite Forms application.
- Open opens an existing Satellite Forms application.
- Save saves the current application.
- Cut cuts the highlighted text or element and puts it onto the clipboard.
- Copy copies the highlighted text or element and puts it onto the clipboard.
- Paste pastes the contents of the clipboard to the location identified by the cursor.
- Help opens the help files with Content, Index and Find tabs.

 TIP To show or hide any of the toolbars, click View in the Menu Bar, then click the toolbar you want to turn on or off. A checkmark to the left of the toolbar name means that the toolbar is visible.

Misc Toolbar

The Misc toolbar provides custom control shortcuts to manage extensions. Extensions are controls, like the slider control, that add capabilities beyond those included with this application development tool. See the section on extensions later in this chapter. From left to right, these seven tools are:

- Manage Extensions opens the Available Extensions dialog box.
- Show Scripts opens the Applications Scripts dialog box.
- Compile Changed compiles edited/modified scripts.
- Compile Current compiles the current script.
- Compile All compiles each script in your application.
- Download App & Tables downloads applications and tables from your desktop computer to your Palm device.
- Upload Tables uploads applications and tables from the Palm device to the desktop computer.

Control Palette Toolbar

The Control Palette toolbar contains all of the available forms, design, and building tools, and automatically becomes available whenever you open the forms window. Just like the other toolbars, you can hide the Control Palette toolbar through the View menu option.

The Control Palette toolbar is the largest of the three available toolbars. From left to right, these 15 tools are:

- Title control displays a title bar across the top of the form.
- Text control displays static text, such as a field description or help field.
- Edit control inserts an editable text field.
- Paragraph control inserts a multi-line editable text field.
- Check box control creates a check box. Remember that check boxes are not mutually exclusive: there is no limit to the number of check boxes a user can select.
- Radio Button control creates a radio button. Radio buttons are mutually exclusive, so a user can select only one within a group.
- Button control creates a button and allows you to define its behavior.
- List Box control displays the contents of a linked table in tabular form.
- Drop List control allows you to create a drop-down list.
- Lookup control displays the contents of a lookup table.
- Ink control allows you to collect a signature or freehand drawing.
- Bitmap control displays bitmap images on your forms.

- Graffiti Shift Indicator control displays a state indicator for the Graffiti shift lock.
- Auto Stamp control records the current time and date into your database.
- SFX Custom control inserts the special Satellite Forms control.

Creating the Application in Satellite Forms

You may recall from Chapter 24 that our sample application is a simple but useful tip calculator. In the previous chapter you used cbasPad Tiny BASIC to create this application. You will now use Satellite Forms to do the same.

Some tools are more adept than others at handling the jobs you toss at it. Though Satellite Forms is certainly capable of mastering this application, we won't tap its strength. Satellite Forms really shines when used as the front-end and manager of a database. If you need to collect information on your Palm device, then Satellite Forms is your tool. Perhaps, if we added an additional wrinkle to the sample such as saving all of the restaurant bills to a database, you could fully use Satellite Forms' capabilities. We'll keep this sample simple and comparable to the cbasPad Tiny BASIC sample so that you can compare the application tools side-by-side. You'll also see that for every problem there is a correct tool—and a reasonable substitute.

We will design our tip calculator to determine a tip based upon the total restaurant bill, the total drink portion of the bill, and the quality of the service. We will also use the old rule of thumb that says the tip for any restaurant bill should be based upon the total food bill, and it should include the cost of drinks consumed. So, your tip calculator will give you the opportunity to remove or include the drink portion of the total bill into the tip calculation.

Since restaurant service varies with the quality of the establishment, among many other factors, the calculator must take that into consideration and provide a means to reflect the service quality in the tip. The calculator will have the ability to figure a tip of whatever percentage you feel is appropriate.

So we now have the basis for our tip calculation: we will take the total restaurant bill, offer the choice to address the drink bill, then calculate the tip based upon a percentage of the adjusted total. If we turn that statement into a logical expression, it would look like this:

```
Total Bill less Drink Bill times Tip Percent equals the Tip.
```

Now, let's turn that logical expression into a mathematical one:

```
(B-D)*S=T
```

where B is the Total Bill, D is the Drink Bill, S is the Tip Percent (or Service), and T is the calculated Tip. Alternatively, we can turn that one expression into two, to simplify the logic. We'll also turn the expression around putting it into standard computer assignment form:

```
NB=B-D
T=NB*S
```

where NB is the Net Bill (the Total Bill less the Drink Bill) and T is the calculated tip, which is the product of the Net Bill times the Tip Percent. We can use either the first expression or the second two expressions to calculate the tip.

No matter which application development tool you choose to use, proper planning is the cornerstone. But because Satellite Forms is a database development tool, proper planning is even more critical. Once you create a database, making changes to its basic structure can be very time consuming and difficult. You really want to get it right the first time—not that you won't have changes, but hopefully these changes will be minor tweaks and not major rewrites. We don't think that you could find an application that couldn't benefit from a few changes or improvements. Creating an application is a little like hitting a moving target—just when you think you've got it in your sites something changes. The problem that your application attempts to address will change as you the world around you changes, so the application will likely need constant modification.

Consequently, you really need to understand the problem that you are trying to address through the application. This understanding will help you design the best (we hope) application.

Coding the Application in Satellite Forms

As a database development tool, you can use Satellite Forms to build your application's front end and then, if necessary, the back end. The front end is comprised of the data collection and storage routines that reside on the Palm device. The back end is the database itself, the structure that stores the input information for future use. We will concentrate on the storage routines of the front end and develop a mechanism that will calculate the tip value of a restaurant bill.

To create your front end using Satellite Forms:

1. Create the tables that will hold your captured data. This step is optional for the tip calculator since you will not capture any data.

2. Create the data entry and viewing forms. This will determine how the data looks on the Palm LCD panel.

3. Add controls to your forms. Through controls, you determine how Satellite Forms handles your data.

4. Add scripts to the forms. Scripts give you the ability to write small Visual Basic-like code snippets so that you can fully manipulate the data.

5. Add SFX plug-ins and controls to further refine your application.

6. Configure the application's properties.

7. Download the completed application to the Palm device.

8. Upload collected data to the desktop computer (a feature we will not employ for this example since we are not recording data).

We'll follow this structured order to create the tip calculator, but skip Step 1 since we're not planning to capture data. Start at Step 2 and create the data entry form. This form will serve double duty as a data entry mechanism and as a means of reporting the calculated tip. The tip calculator will use controls (Step 3) in the form of program button. These buttons will have associated scripts from Step 4 that will calculate the tip. We'll skip Steps 5 and 6 and move to Step 7 to download the completed application to the Palm device. And since we are not capturing data, we'll not use Step 8.

OK, it is really that simple, so let's get started.

The App Designer

To create your front end, you'll use the built-in Satellite Forms tool called the App Designer. The App Designer gives you all of the features you'll need to lay out your forms (and tables if you used them), code your scripts, and pull the whole thing together.

Open Satellite Forms by clicking the App Designer icon from the Satellite Forms SE version 3.1 menu. This action opens the App designer desktop shown in Figure 25.23.

PART

V

Advanced Techniques

FIGURE 25.23

The App Designer (blank)

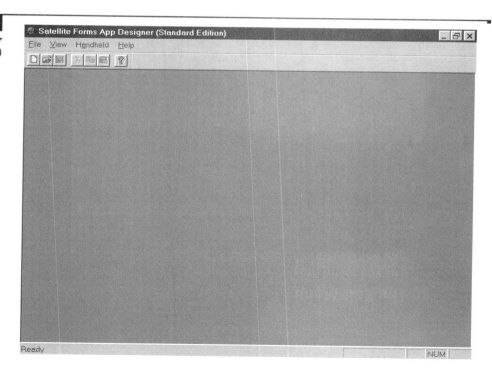

From the Menu Bar, click File/New or the New button in the toolbar to create a new application. This opens the Contents window on the left side of the screen. The workspace window remains on the right side of the screen, though slightly reduced in size. See Figure 25.24.

FIGURE 25.24

The new application window

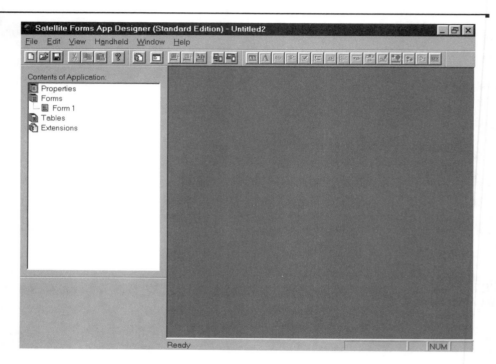

The Contents window uses a Microsoft Explorer–like hierarchical layout to graphically display the application's format. Four header icons (Properties, Forms, Tables, and Extensions) segregate the application into its component pieces.

Properties icon   Double-click to display the application's name and options.

Forms icon   Listed beneath this icon are all the forms used in your application.

Tables icon   This lists each table used in the application.

Extensions icon   Lists any extensions used in the application.

You can double-click or right-click each of these icons to display further information, properties boxes, or an edit menu.

Double-click the Properties icon to open the Application Properties dialog box. See Figure 25.25. Type your application's name (such as the Tip Calculator) in the Name of Application field. This name will become the application's identifier and will display wherever the application is listed. The Initial Form field holds the name of the first form that you create for the application. Since you're only planning to use one form, this field is not a big issue and you can accept the default information.

FIGURE 25.25

Application Properties dialog box

The Creator ID is a critical field that you must not overlook. As we explained earlier, an application's Creator ID must be unique to that developer. Fortunately, Puma Technologies provides several default values. You can accept any of these, create your own (like your initials and date of birth), or use your Palm Computing registered Creator ID, if you have one. Accept the default options at the bottom of the screen, and click OK to enter this information for your application.

Next, you should create your data entry/data display form. To create a new form, select Insert Form from the Edit menu, or right-click the Forms header in the Contents Window and select Insert Form.

PART

V

Advanced Techniques

FIGURE 25.26

New Form window

The Forms window, shown in Figure 25.26, provides some basic information that will make your forms designing experience a little easier. The name of the form displays in a banner at the top of the screen. Beneath the banner are four tools/information displays that simplify forms' design. From left to right they are:

- The Snap-to-Grid button provides a grid of blue dots across the form field and automatically aligns objects to the nearest set of dots. The Snap-to-Grid capability works to ensure that objects placed on the form line up both horizontally and vertically, just like drawing a line on graph paper.

- The Form Magnification control changes the size of the form from 100 percent (life size of 2.5 inches by 2.5 inches) to 500 percent. The default is 200 percent. To change the magnification, use the drop-down list and select a new option.

- The Origin control indicator provides the X/Y coordinates of the selected control. The grid coordinates range from 0 to 159 in both the X and Y planes, with 0/0 at the upper left-hand corner and 159/159 in the lower right-hand corner.

- The Control Size indicator displays the size of the current control through coordinate points.

We will create our tip calculator form using the Control Palette icons, and insert a title at the top of the form. Use the Text controls to display the static text; insert Edit controls to accept user input such as the total bill and tip percent; and lastly, insert

Button controls at the bottom of the form that will calculate the tip amount and clear the form. When complete, the tip calculator should look like Figure 25.27.

FIGURE 25.27

Completed Form

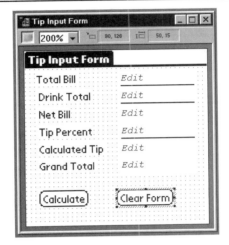

PART

V

Advanced Techniques

The Data Input Form

We'll start development of our form by inserting the title at the top of the form. In the Control Palette toolbar, click the Title control. This tool will place a title bar at the top of the form, in a folder-like tab format. The default title is the word Title. Double-click the title to obtain the Properties of Title Control dialog box shown in Figure 25.28.

FIGURE 25.28

The Properties of Title Control dialog box

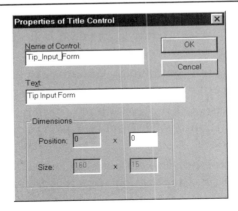

You can accept the Name of Control default, Title 1, since this is an internal identifier and will not display on the form. Alternately, you can give it a name such as Tip_input_form. To do this, go to the Text field and type in the name for the form: **Tip_Input_Form.**

 NOTE Control names cannot contain spaces, so use the underscore character.

 TIP In each properties box there is a Name of... field that contains a default value. You can accept these defaults, or change them to match the name of the form or variable. Whichever you choose, however, you must be consistent to avoid losing track of your position.

Accept the Dimension Information position and size defaults. The Position field determines where on the form the title will appear. Position 0/0 is in the upper left-hand corner. The Size field determines the dimensions of the title tab on the form. The size field will automatically adjust to accommodate the length of the text entered in the Text field.

When you are satisfied with all of the information, click OK to save. The App Designer will return you to the Form Window and display the new title across the top.

The Static Field   The next step is to add the static text fields. These fields include the Total Bill, Drink Bill, Net Bill, Tip Percent, Calculated Tip, and Grand Total fields. For the first, second, and fourth fields you should allow data entry/editing; the third, fifth, and sixth are calculated fields with no user interaction, so they will be read-only.

To enter static fields or labels, follow these steps:

1. Click the Text control icon from the Palette Control toolbar. The App Designer drops a text control block on the form. The text control block looks like a gray, hash-mark text box surrounding the word Text.

2. Drag this control to the desired location; just beneath the form title is a good place to start.

3. Double-click the text control to open the Properties of Text Control dialog box. See Figure 25.29. From this dialog box you can adjust or edit the label as required.

4. Accept the Name of Control and in the Text field type the label name Total Bill. You can change the font using the Attributes/Font drop-down box, or change the label's position and size. We suggest that you just accept the defaults and click OK.

Repeat these steps to create labels for the Drink Bill, Net Bill, Tip Percent, Calculated Tip, and Grand Total. Your input form should now look like Figure 25.30.

FIGURE 25.29

The Properties of Text
Control dialog box

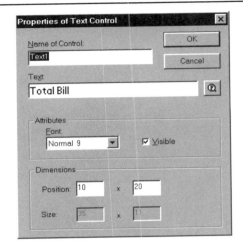

FIGURE 25.30

Input form with labels

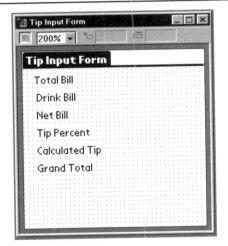

The Dynamic Fields   Now that the labels are in place, you can create the corresponding data fields. You could use drop-down lists or a lookup table field for the data fields, but the simplest method is to use an edit control. An edit control will allow you to enter data to that field via the Palm's built-in keyboard or Graffiti. Or you can use it to display data, either from a table in your database or as the result of a calculation.

To create the edit controls:

1. Click the Edit control icon in the Control Palette toolbar. The App Designer creates a field bounded by a gray hash-mark border surrounding the word Edit.

2. Drag this field to the desired location on the form and double-click to access the Properties of Edit Control dialog box. See Figure 25.31.

FIGURE 25.31

Properties of Edit Control

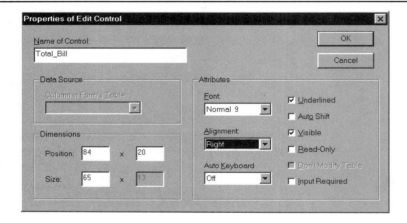

3. In the Name of Control field, change the default value to match the associated variable name, such as Total Bill.

4. The Data Source/Column in Form's Table field associates this edit control field to a column in the associated database table. Since you aren't using a database table, ensure that no columns are selected by accepting the NONE keyword.

   The Dimension field works just like this field's counterpart in previous forms.

   The Attribute section holds the Font, Alignment, and Auto Keyboard fields, plus check boxes for field characteristics.

5. Select the desired attributes.

The Font field works like the Font field in other control dialog boxes. The Alignment field gives you the choice of aligning data in the field to the left or right. The Auto Keyboard field provides five data entry mode choices through a drop-down list.

If you enable Auto Keyboard, the App Designer automatically opens the appropriate keyboard whenever you access the field. For example, if you select the Numeric setting, the App Designer will display the Palm's numeric keypad. This feature is particularly handy, making the application a little easier to use and ensuring that the proper information is added.

The column of check boxes under the Attributes section are field characteristics and provide added controls for the Edit Control field. You can describe an Edit Control field in further detail, or ascribe a certain behavior to the field. Here's what is available to you:

- The Underlined attribute underlines the field on the screen signifying that this is a data entry field.

- The Auto Shift attribute automatically shifts the keyboard or Graffiti into upper case for the first character you enter on text fields.

- The Visible attribute toggles the field from hidden to visible on the Palm's LCD panel.

- The Read Only attribute prevents user data entry into the field. This attribute is useful when displaying data from a table or, as in this example, the results of a calculation.

- The Don't Modify Table attribute controls whether or not the contents of the field will be saved to a linked table. This attribute is not applicable to this example since we are not using tables.

- The Input Required attribute determines whether or not the user must enter something in this field. By selecting Yes (clicking the check box), you prevent the user from proceeding beyond this point unless they enter something into the field.

The Tip Calculator Example   For the tip calculator example you need to create an edit control for each label created earlier. For the Total Bill, Drink Bill, and Tip Percent you should use right alignment, the Auto Keyboard set to Numeric, and the Underline attribute. For the Net Bill, Calculated Tip, and Grand Total, use right alignment and Read Only attributes.

To create an edit control for the Total Bill label, perform the following steps:

1. Click the Edit control icon in the Control Palette toolbar.

2. Drag the Edit control to the right of the Total Bill label. See Figure 25.32.

FIGURE 25.32

Edit control on form

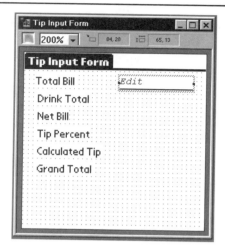

3. Double-click the Edit control to obtain the Properties of Edit Control dialog box.

4. Change the default control name to Total Bill. We will use this name later in our calculation.

5. Use the Dimension area to fine-tune the control's location, if required. See Figure 25.33.

FIGURE 25.33

New Edit control dialog box

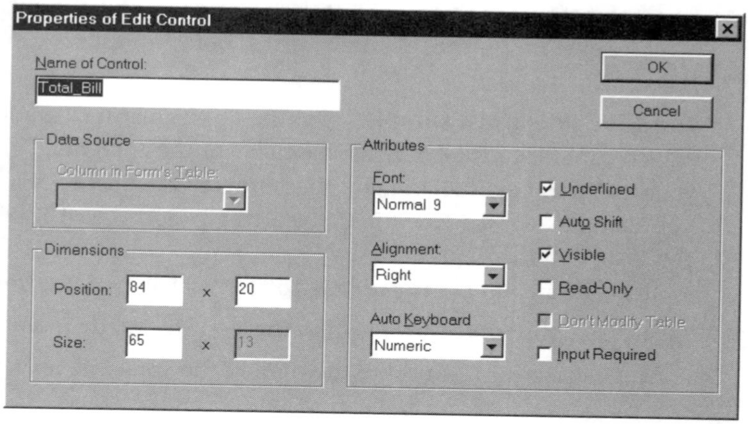

6. Accept the Font Attributes default.

7. In the Alignment field, select Right to right align the data added to the field.

8. In the Auto Keyboard field, select Numeric from the drop-down list. This will automatically display the numeric keypad whenever you enter the field.

9. From the check box, select Underlined as a visual queue for data entry, and Visible to completely display the field on the Palm's LCD panel.

10. Click OK to save the attributes.

Repeat the above steps for Drink Bill and Tip Percent, renaming the control for each to match the label. The completed form should look like Figure 25.34.

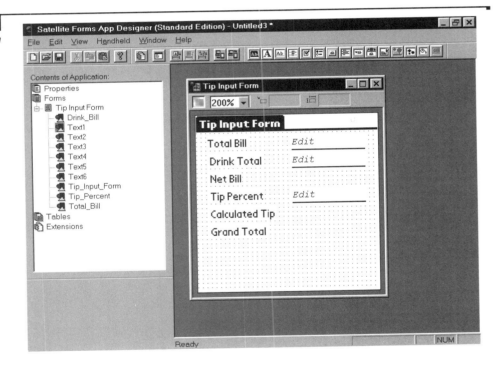

FIGURE 25.34

The completed form

For the Net Bill, Calculated Tip, and Grand Total fields, you need to follow a process similar to the above with a few minor changes. Try this:

1. Click the Edit control icon in the Control Palette toolbar.

2. Drag the Edit control to the right of the Net Bill label.

3. Double-click the Edit control to obtain the Properties of Edit Control dialog box.

4. Change the default control name to Net Bill. See Figure 25.35. We will use this name later in our calculation.

FIGURE 25.35

New Edit control dialog box

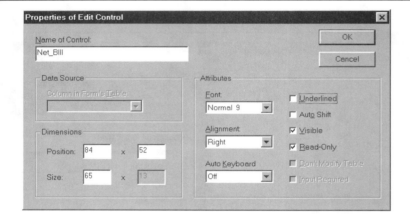

5. Use the Dimension area to fine-tune the control's location, if required.

6. Accept the Font Attributes default.

7. In the Alignment field, select Right to right align the data in the field.

8. In the Auto Keyboard field, select Off from the drop-down list. Since this is a calculated field, you don't need a keyboard for data entry assistance.

9. From the check boxes, deselect Underlined, select Visible to completely display the field on the Palm's LCD panel and Read Only to prevent data entry in the calculated field.

10. Click OK to save the attributes.

Repeat the above steps for the Calculated Tip and Grand Total, renaming the control for each to match the label. The completed form should look like Figure 25.36.

PART

V

Advanced Techniques

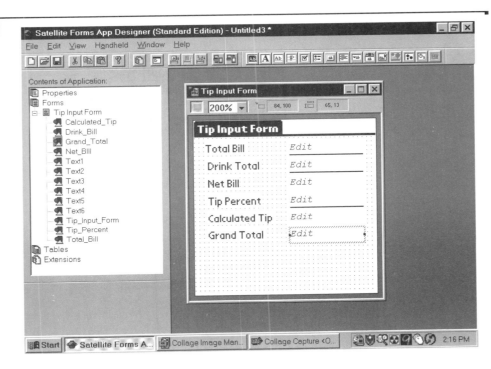

FIGURE 25.36

The completed form

Now that you have created labels and fields for all of the data, you need to include some means of performing an action—something to start the ball rolling, basically get the application to calculate the figures that we require. Remember, Satellite Forms is event-driven, so nothing will happen to your data without some event triggering an action or set of actions. You have several alternatives, some of which we'll investigate in the next section on scripting. Alternatively, we could use an old stand-by—a button.

You can create a button control or a series of controls that will determine the next set of actions. Specifically, you can create two buttons: one that performs the calculation and one that clears the form of all information. Fortunately, this is a fairly simple task in Satellite Forms because it supports a Button control that not only draws the button but supports characteristic attributes.

The actions that the button takes when pressed, however, are entirely up to you. Through a script, you can have a button do just about anything. In the next section, we'll look closely at scripts and create several for this application.

In the meantime, you need to invoke the Button control and create two buttons: one to calculate and one to clear the form. Here is the simple though lengthy process:

1. Click the Button control icon in the Control Palette toolbar.

The App Designer creates a button bounded by a gray hash-mark border.

2. Drag the button to the lower portion of the screen, as shown in Figure 25.37.

FIGURE 25.37

*Button control
on form*

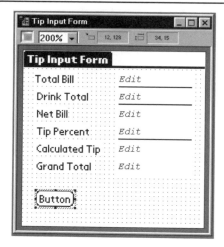

3. Double-click the Button control to open the Properties of Button Control dialog box.

4. Change the name of the control and text fields to read Calculate (see Figure 25.38).

FIGURE 25.38

*Setting properties for
the Calculate button*

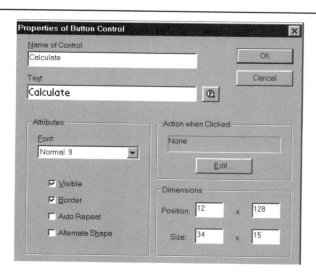

5. Click the Edit button beneath the Action when Clicked field to open the Control Action and Filters dialog box. See Figure 25.39.

FIGURE 25.39

*Control Action
dialog box*

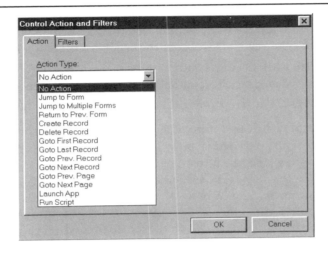

FIGURE 25.40

*Application Scripts
dialog box*

6. From the Action Type drop-down list, select Runscript. You can see it at the bottom of Figure 25.39.

7. Click the Edit Script button to open the Application Scripts dialog box.

8. From the Application Scripts dialog box, select the form name Tip Input Form from the Form drop-down list. See Figure 25.40.

9. From the Event drop-down list, select OnClick Calculate.

The large white workspace is where you will write the script for the Calculate button. We'll work out the details for this script in the next section.

10. Click the Close button in the upper right-hand corner of the Application Scripts dialog box. This automatically saves the button attributes.

11. Create one more button—Clear Form—using the above procedure.

Scripts   The basic form that you created provides a means to input and view data. The script, or program, provides the ability to process that data. Satellite Forms' scripting language is based on Microsoft Visual Basic, so if you are familiar with Visual Basic, this next section should be quite simple. We're going to assume that you have a basic understanding of BASIC, whether Microsoft Visual Basic or standard old Dartmouth BASIC—the same version used in cbasPad Tiny BASIC. So, we will not delve into the intricacies of how Visual Basic works, though we may investigate the details of Satellite Forms scripts a little more closely.

The script that you'll write will perform the basic mathematical calculations to generate the tip and the grand total. This script will be pretty simple and will look similar to the Tiny BASIC solution from the last chapter.

Your script must solve the mathematical question posed by this question "What is X% of my restaurant bill?" To arrive at the solution, we need to recognize the problem: we know the value of the total bill, we know the value of the any drinks, and we know (hopefully) the percent of the bill we want to leave as a tip. This takes us back to original equation:

```
Calculated Tip = Tip Percent (Total Bill-Drink Bill)
```

The first step in creating the script is declaring the variables using the DIM command. The line should something like this:

```
Dim Total_Bill, Drink_Bill, Net_Bill, Tip_Percent, Calculated_Tip,
Grand_Total
```

Next, code the equation. The App Designer accepts input from a form control when you identify the fieldname with the .data suffix. So throughout the script, any variable that will be used to capture or display information must have the .data suffix. For instance, our input field Net_Bill would be accessed as Net_Bill.data. So each of the variables we create here correspond to edit control names.

To calculate the net bill, we must subtract the drink total from the total bill, which looks something like this:

```
Net_Bill.data = Total_Bill.data-Drink_Bill.data
```

This format tells The App Designer to look on the form for the two variables, `Total_Bill` and `Drink_Total`.

The calculated tip is derived by the following line:

```
Calculated_Tip.data = Net_Bill.data * Tip_Percent.data
```

You arrive at the grand total through:

```
Grand_Total.data = Total_Bill.data + Calculated_Tip.data
```

So, the complete script should look like this:

```
Dim Total_Bill, Drink_Bill, Net_Bill, Tip_Percent, Calculated_Tip,
Grand_Total
Net_Bill.data = Total_Bill.data-Drink_Bill.data
Calculated_Tip.data = Net_Bill.data * Tip_Percent.data/100
Grand_Total.data = Total_Bill.data + Calculated_Tip.data
```

Once you've coded the script, you need to attach/insert the script to the Calculate button through the Properties of Button Control dialog box.

1. Double-click the Calculate button. This opens the Properties of Button Control dialog box.

2. In the Action When Clicked area, click the Edit... button.

3. In the Control Action & Filter dialog box, click the Edit Script... button to open the Application Scripts dialog box.

4. In the workspace beneath the drop-down list, copy the above script. Script will execute whenever you tap the calculate button.

   Now that you've created your script, it's time to compile it.

5. Click the Compile Changed icon in the Control Palette toolbar. This compiles the script and makes it ready for the Palm device. Of course, you'll need to correct any errors such as edit control names or simple typos.

6. Click the close button in the upper right-hand corner to save and close the edit. The completed script should look like Figure 25.41.

Repeat the above process for the Clear Form button substituting the following script. The complete Clear Form button script should look like Figure 25.42.

```
Dim Total_Bill, Drink_Bill, Net_Bill, Tip_Percent, Calculated_Tip,
Grand_Total
Total_Bill.data = " "
Drink_Bill.data = " "
Net_Bill.data = " "
Tip_Percent.data = " "
Calculated_Tip.data = " "
Grand_Total.data = " "
```

PART

V

Advanced Techniques

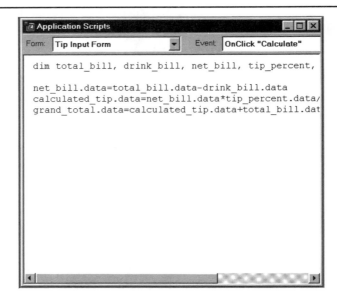

By setting each variable equal to a space, we are clearing the form of all data.

Using the New Form on Your Palm Device

Now that the scripts are compiled and the forms saved, you can download the application to your Palm device. This process is probably one of the easiest to perform. From the App Designer Standard Edition Menu Bar, select Handheld and then select Download App & Tables... option. Place your Palm in its cradle and HotSync. Once you've loaded the form on the Palm, you are ready to go.

To access and use the new application, perform the following:

1. Click the Sat. Forms SE icon from the App Launcher on your Palm device.

2. Select Tip_Calc from the list and tap it to open the form.

3. Tap your stylus on the horizontal line to the right of the Total Bill label. The form automatically displays the numeric keypad (just as you programmed it). Input all numbers without the dollar or percent sign.

4. Fill in an amount for the Total Bill, say $120.

5. In the Drink Bill area, input $20. That will leave a Net Bill of $100. (That's displayed after we calculate our bill.)

6. Input a tip percent, say 17 percent, as .17. That means that the calculated tip should be $17.

7. Tap the Calculate button. You should have a Net Bill of $100 and a Calculated Tip of $17. See Figure 25.43.

PART

V

Advanced Techniques

FIGURE 25.43

Completed calculation

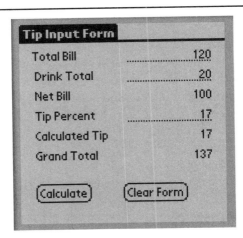

8. Tap the Clear Form button to clear the values and prepare for another calculation.

Looking back at the original formula, you can see that the tip calculator works exactly as it was designed to. That is, the application accepts three known values—the total restaurant bill, the total beverage bill, and the service fee or tip percentage—and returns the precise tip value.

Advanced Topics

You've just created a handy and useful application for your Palm device. Unfortunately, this application uses only a small fraction of Satellite Forms' power. As we said earlier, Satellite Forms is a database development tool, which we've used it to perform a simple set of calculations and nothing more. But what if we modify the original sample to include a database for the restaurant bills? What if we also wanted to track the restaurant name, whether or not the cost of the meal is a business or personal expense, and perhaps the date? This data would then feed a database that you could use to track your expenses.

You can rather easily modify the existing application to track this additional data. You can use the existing form, though you'll need to add a few more fields. You'll also need to create a table to hold the captured data. Once this data is in the table, you can import it to your favorite database manager for further processing. Satellite Forms stores data in dBase 5 format, so you should be able to import the table to virtually any other database tool.

Creating the Table

The data table is the vehicle by which you can store information captured through the Satellite Forms form and your Palm device. You may recall from our earlier discussion that the table resembles a spreadsheet, which consists of columns of categories like name and address, and rows of individual records (categories of data that pertain to a single entity like a person). Each row represents a new occurrence (in the restaurant example, this could be a meal eaten away from home), and each column represents the categories common to every occurrence (the restaurant name, the date, the dollar value spent, etc.).

You can use the same techniques and procedures that you used to create a form to create a table. Start by inserting the table into the application, then select Edit/Insert Table from the App Designer menu, and give the table a name like Meal Data (see Figure 25.44).

FIGURE 25.44

Creating a new table

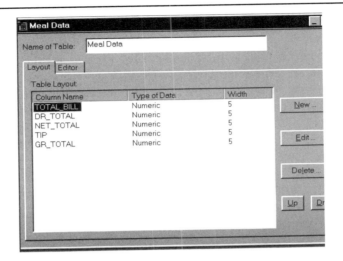

Click the New button to create a new field and change the name of Column field into a descriptor of the data you want to store, such as Total_Bill. From the Data Type field drop-down list, select numeric since we are dealing with number data, and make the Width field five digits long with two decimals to accommodate hundreds of dollars and tens of cents. Repeat this exercise for each variable on the form. To capture the additional data, you'll need to create columns for the restaurant name, the business/pleasure indicator, and the date and date stamp. See Figure 25.45.

FIGURE 25.45

Completed table

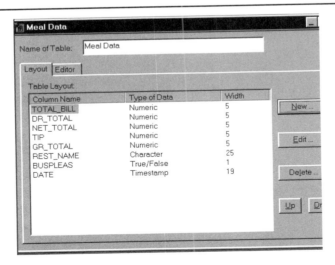

Modifying the Data Entry Form

The existing form will meet most of your needs, but could use a little modification. You need to make the form bigger to accommodate the additional information and link the form to the new table; then add a few new fields like a radio button for business expense and a text field for the restaurant name.

You can start the process by accessing the form's properties, increasing the Number of Pages variable to 2, and selecting the table name from the Linked Table field. This automatically attaches the form to the table and increases the form to double length. See Figure 25.46.

FIGURE 25.46

Modified form

Add a new text field for the restaurant name, a set of radio buttons for the business/pleasure indicator, and a date stamp. For each new field, go to the Properties of Edit Control dialog box and select the appropriate Data Source column from the table that the new field is attached to. The radio button works similarly through the Properties of Radio Button Control, depositing a value into the table. See Figure 25.47.

FIGURE 25.47

Properties of Radio
Button Control

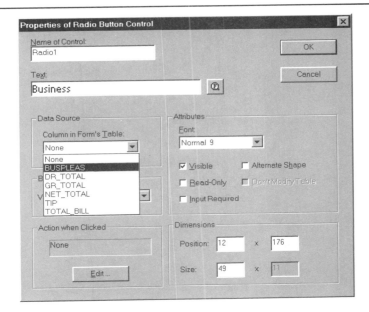

Remember to save the latest edits and then download the new application to your Palm device. That's about all that is required, though you can do even more with Satellite Forms than we have outlined here. Use this quick tour to whet your application development appetite and jump into the world of forms tools with both feet.

PART

V

Advanced Techniques

CHAPTER <u>26</u>

Creating a Sample Application in CodeWarrior

We started the exercise of creating a Palm application using a very friendly, albeit poorly documented piece of freeware called cbasPad Tiny BASIC. Tiny BASIC, you may recall, was a derivative of good old Dartmouth BASIC that we all learned somewhere during the course of our education. BASIC is usually a pretty simple tool to use: you can learn it quickly and develop applications to meet your needs in relatively short order. Of course, what you gain in simplicity you lose in capability. And, though you could use cbasPad Tiny BASIC to create a database, we wouldn't recommend it. You'd end up with more work than you would believe, not to mention the limitations imposed on you by Tiny BASIC.

The second tool that we used was Puma Technologies' Satellite Forms, a very different tool from Tiny BASIC. Satellite Forms is a forms-based application development tool, or rapid application development tool (RAD). You create the screens (forms) and tie them together to perform the task at hand. This baby costs quite a bit more than Tiny BASIC but adds considerably more functionality. You can readily use Satellite Forms to create a database and move information from the desktop computer to the Palm device and vice versa. Is it as easy to use as Tiny BASIC? No, but it offers many more features and capabilities. Again, what you lose in simplicity you gain in capability.

The last tool that we will use to develop the tip calculator application is Metrowerks' CodeWarrior, a true heavyweight in the application development world. Where cbasPad Tiny BASIC is simple with limited capability, and Satellite Forms is more complex with the commensurate capabilities, CodeWarrior is a full-function C/C++ compiler. Whatever you can do with any other version of C/C++, you can do with CodeWarrior. It is the de facto standard Palm development tool, sanctioned by Palm Computing for development use across the entire family of Palm devices/OSs.

CodeWarrior Release 5

CodeWarrior is a proprietary multi-language front-end development tool. With CodeWarrior, you can develop applications for virtually any platform. Metrowerks packages all of the necessary components to support the platform of your choice—in this case, the Palm OS. It provides all of the libraries, resources, compilers, and assemblers that you might need to generate the application of your dreams. Everything, including all of the documentation, comes on one CD-ROM. Metrowerks includes a Quick Start guide to get you up and running quickly, but relies on the electronic form of the documentation for all of the details.

Metrowerks markets various forms of CodeWarrior, but the Palm OS version comes in two flavors: Windows and MacOS. Each retails for around $300 (you might even be able to avail yourself of an educational discount and save some money), complete with all of the software tools that you'll need. In addition to the resources and libraries, Metrowerks includes a full-blown IDE, a screen developer called the Constructor, a debugger, an assembler, a compiler, as well as a copy of POSE to test your creation.

But you must also remember that for that $300 you get quite a bit more complexity. As a matter of fact, Metrowerks states quite clearly in their documentation that "to develop software in this environment, you should be an experienced C or C++ programmer, familiar with the desktop environment (MacOS or Windows) and its development tools." Though the C language may be the backbone of desktop programming, this book will not concentrate on teaching it. We'll assume that you don't want an in-depth lesson in C programming; if you do, there are some fantastic books on the subject. For more detail on C/C++ programming, we'd recommend any one of many C/C++ programming courses offered by your local university or community college.

CodeWarrior Details

As we mentioned earlier, CodeWarrior comes complete with all of the tools and features that you need to complete your own application. This includes an IDE, the screen creator called Constructor, a Palm simulator, a C/C++ code debugger, all of the necessary resources, and a compiler.

Programs in C/C++, or any other high-level language like Pascal or Java, must be compiled before you can run them anywhere other than on another system equipped with a C (or Pascal or Java) environment. C programs, like the other high-level languages, tap into a series of external functions and tools called libraries and resources. These libraries and resources must be present for the program to function. Simply put, the compile process incorporates the necessary portions of the ancillary libraries and resources into your application, making it completely transportable. Once compiled, you can move the program anywhere you like without the necessity for the ancillary libraries and resources.

The IDE

CodeWarrior's integrated development environment (IDE) is your home base for application development. From the IDE, you can access the editor, compiler, and linker. Think of it as a pre-compiler, a place where CodeWarrior connects your code to the built-in functions, which are the project manager and the debugger. Through the IDE (see Figure 26.1), you can access nearly all of CodeWarrior's features.

PART

V

Advanced Techniques

FIGURE 26.1

CodeWarrior IDE

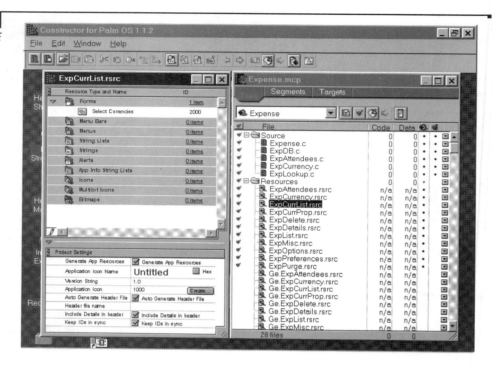

CodeWarrior's features include:

The Editor This feature provides a fairly complex degree of control over the source code, which is the raw text that provides instruction to the various CodeWarrior components. You can search, edit, and replace text throughout your application, as well as open the editor in several panes so you can view various parts of the application simultaneously.

The Compiler This feature turns your source code into what is sometimes called machine code, or an executable program.

The Linker This feature allows you to connect your source code to outside resources and functions and use them as if they were part of your source code. First you compile your source code to the outside resource, then you link. Code-Warrior's compiler then turns the source code into the executable program.

NOTE The compiler and linker are plug-ins, meaning that they are interchangeable modules that you can remove and replace to meet your programming needs. Metrowerks makes plug-ins for Windows and MacOS, as well as for C/C++, Java and Pascal programming languages.

The Project Manager This feature allows you to maintain and control all of the files that make up your application. Additionally, the project manager works with you to ensure that the proper plug-ins are available and operating when you put your project together. This is extremely helpful at compile time, allowing you to concentrate on the program itself and not on the required housekeeping chores.

The Debugger This tool lets you execute the program and step through your source code one line at a time, following the program's flow. You can set breakpoints (locations within the program where you may want processing to end) and watch points (locations where you can inspect the value of each variable and function), or you can just examine the code while it executes.

The Constructor

As if writing C/C++ code weren't difficult enough, developing a user interface screen that works with your code and looks good can quickly throw your development project off schedule. Fortunately, Metrowerks has thought of that and includes a really great little tool called Constructor (see Figure 26.2). Constructor is a drag-and-drop-like graphical utility that you can use to build your user interface. Constructor provides built-in GUI components like buttons, drop-down lists, data entry fields, etc., and works pretty much like Puma Technologies' Satellite Forms. Find the element you want to use, drag it to the desired location, and define its properties. That's all it takes. You can also build an icon for your application, which will display on the Palm's Application Launcher screen.

PART

V

Advanced Techniques

FIGURE 26.2

The Constructor

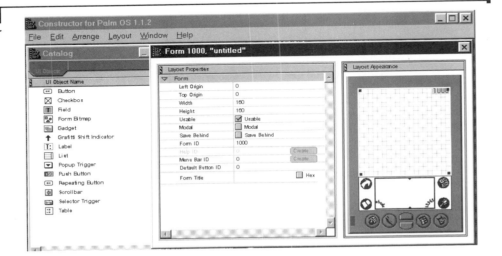

Possibly the most interesting of Constructor's features is its ability to automatically generate the C/C++ code behind the interface screen that you create. We and Palm Computing don't recommend that you tamper with the automatically generated code unless you are a truly proficient C/C++ programmer. So, now you have one less painful task to complete. There are a few more interesting features that we will examine more closely later on in this chapter.

The Simulator/Emulator

In case you don't have a version of POSE (the Palm OS Emulator) from Palm Computing, Metrowerks includes one for you. It's not the most recent version of the emulator, but it certainly will do in a pinch.

For the MacOS world, there is the Palm OS Simulator, which emulates the Palm OS on the Mac desktop computer. The OS Simulator is actually a Mac library that is automatically added to the project when you link your application to all of its associated libraries and resources.

The Palm OS Emulator for the Windows-based system is the same old version of POSE that we describe in detail in Chapter 27. It will emulate the Palm OS on your desktop computer allowing for easier testing and debugging.

In either case (MacOS or Windows), we recommend that you get the latest version of POSE from Palm Computing and use that for all of your testing and debugging. POSE offers the highest level of compatibility to the Palm device, and using the latest version ensures that your application won't run afoul of a real Palm device.

Installing CodeWarrior

Loading CodeWarrior is no different from loading any other program... Well, it may be even easier. We've all tried to install a new application only to find that the instructions bear no resemblance to reality. Luckily, CodeWarrior is not only simple to install, the installation documentation actually makes sense. So, here goes.

To install CodeWarrior on your Windows based PC, follow these steps:

1. Insert the CodeWarrior CD-ROM into your CD-ROM drive. If autoplay is enabled on your desktop computer, the CodeWarrior install program will start on its own. If autoplay in not enabled on your desktop computer, then look for and execute the `setup.exe` program in the root directory of the CD-ROM.

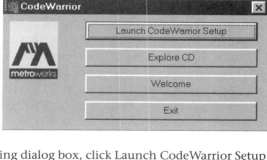

2. In the resulting dialog box, click Launch CodeWarrior Setup to begin the install. This results in a Welcome dialog box, which you can see in Figure 26.3. Click Next to continue with the installation.

PART

V

Advanced Techniques

FIGURE 26.3

Welcome dialog box

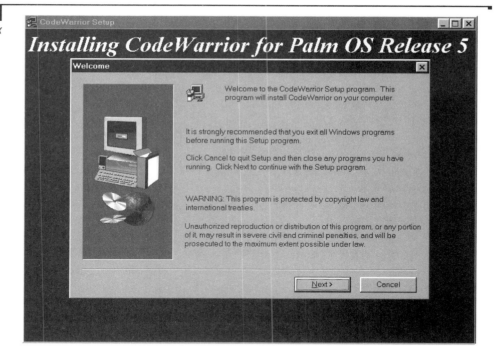

3. The install program displays the Metrowerks license agreement. Whether you read the agreement or not, you must click Next to proceed.

4. Next, you'll receive the Choose Destination Location dialog box, as shown in Figure 26.4. You can accept the default file location (recommended for simplicity) or select a new file location by clicking the browse button and navigating to the desired location. When you have selected the desired location, click Next in the Choose Destination Location dialog box.

FIGURE 26.4

Choose Destination Location dialog box

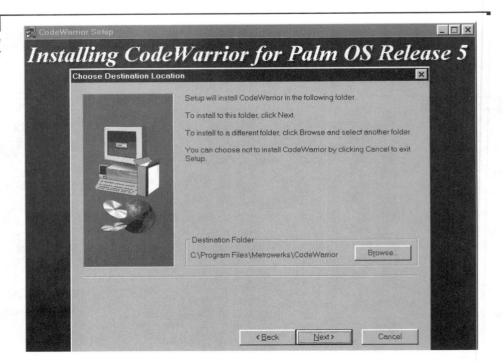

5. In the Select Components dialog box (see Figure 26.5), select the CodeWarrior Heaven radio button for a compete installation, including all documentation. This will use about 110MB of hard disk space. If you don't want the online documentation or can't afford that much hard disk space, then click the Minimal CodeWarrior radio button. This installation will use about 50MB. Of course, if you feel adventurous or you are an experienced C/C++ programmer, you can select the last radio button for a Custom installation and select those files that you want. We recommend either the first or second choice. Click Next to proceed with the installation.

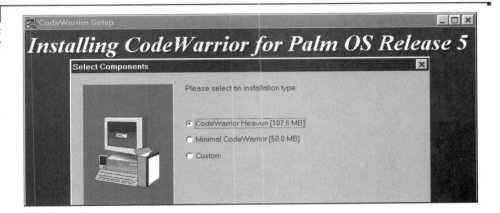

6. Select the menu location for the CodeWarrior folder and the CodeWarrior shortcut. Click Next to proceed with the install.

7. The setup.exe program now installs the CodeWarrior components that you've selected. The installation should take about 30–45 seconds depending on your desktop computer's speed.

8. When setup.exe completes the installation, you'll receive the Information dialog box (see Figure 26.6) telling you that the installation is complete and providing some clarification on using the Constructor. Click OK to continue with the installation.

The installation is complete. If you chose the complete installation, you should have six objects in the Metrowerks CodeWarrior folder: CodeWarrior IDE, Constructor for Palm OS, CodeWarrior Reference, CW ReadMe, CW Release Notes, and Uninstall CodeWarrior. See Figure 26.7.

PART

V

Advanced Techniques

FIGURE 26.6

*Information
dialog box*

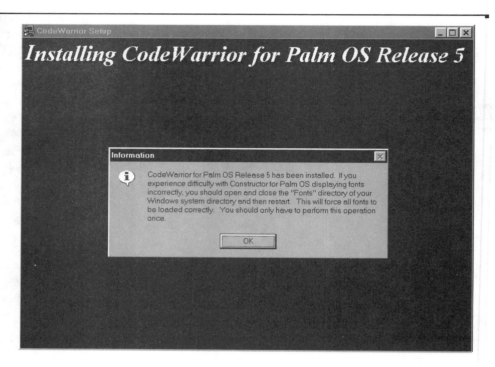

FIGURE 26.7

*Contents of
CodeWarrior folder*

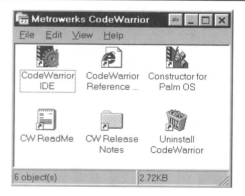

The Constructor

The Constructor is CodeWarrior's user interface (or GUI) design tool, that gives you standard, on-screen icons and elements. Through a simple drag-and-drop capability, you can quickly design a real, working screen. Each of the on-screen elements, from buttons to drop-down lists to data entry fields, is accompanied by a properties dialog box that allows you to define all the specifics, such as the size, location, variable identifier, and function of the on-screen element. We'll look at this process more closely in the following sections.

The Constructor also includes a bitmap editor that lets you create and edit images for icons. Big deal, right? Well, the bitmap editor gives you the power to make an icon for your application; the icon will sit on the Palm's Application Launcher. Of course, you can choose to use any other drawing tool that you prefer. The advantage to the Constructor's bitmap editor is its simplicity and availability. We'll look more closely at this feature, too.

The Constructor does one other thing that is truly helpful and quite interesting: it automatically generates the C/C++ code that defines the screen that you build. This is the true time and effort saver. To physically perform this "trick," Constructor employs Palm OS resources. An OS resource is the sequence of C/C++ code that describes the attributes of the on-screen element such as a button or drop-down list. In essence, the OS resource works like a C/C++ function; you don't need to know what code is behind the function (or resource in this case), you just need to be able to call it as necessary. Functions, as you may recall, perform a complex action such as a square root. In the case of resources, they describe the individual elements used to create the GUI. So there are resources for the physical on-screen elements such as buttons, icons, and errors. Basically, any action achievable through a GUI has some associated resource.

Resources

As mentioned above, Constructor manages Palm OS resources, making your job of creating a GUI a little bit easier. Constructor does all of the back-end work of generating the required code and assuring that the resources needed for the screen are available. You can use any of the eight Palm OS resources while designing your GUI or form, and Constructor will manage all of them.

- Use the application resource to create an application version (referred to as a tver) resource and an icon name (referred to as a tAIN) resource. The Palm OS uses the application version information as display information for your application.

- The form and control resource identifies the GUI (the form) and its elements, such as buttons (the control). A form resource is of type tFRM.

- Use the menu resource for menus and menu bars. This resource is included in any GUI design that makes use of menus. A menu bar resource is of type MBAR, while a menu itself is of type MENU.

- The character string resource (of type tSTR) holds non-editable text, such as labels or help text.

- Use the character string list resource (of type tSTL) to hold groups of associated character strings.

- Use the category name list resource (of type tAIS) to hold a group of default category names.

- The alert resources (of type Talt) displays messages and information that requires immediate attention. Generally, an alert consists of a dialog box with an icon, descriptive text and one or more buttons.

- The icon and bitmap resource (of type ICON and PICT respectively) manage icons and general bitmaps.

Constructor's Menu Bar and Options

Like every other application or application development tool, the Constructor employs a menu bar with multiple options and tools. These nine options and tools help to make the Constructor a little easier to use.

File   The File menu option contains all of the commands required to manage Constructor project files. The choices are:

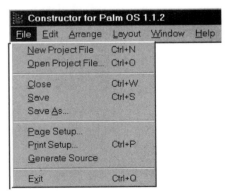

- New Project File (CTRL+N): Creates a new project file.

- Open Project File (CTRL+O): Opens existing project files through a standard Open File dialog box.

- Close (CTRL+W): Closes the active window. If you attempt to close a project before saving it, Constructor will give you the option to save before proceeding.

- Save (CTRL+S): Saves the active project file and generates the source C/C++ code for you.

- Save As: Saves the active project file but provides a standard Save dialog box, allowing you to change the file name or location.

- Page Setup: Provides the standard page setup dialog box, allowing you to change paper sizes, etc.

- Print Setup (CTRL+P): This is the standard print and printer setup dialog box for printing the active Constructor window.

- Generate Source: Saves the working file and generates the source code without saving the entire project.

- Exit (CTRL+Q): Exits the current project but notifies you of any open and unsaved files prior to closing the application.

Edit Constructor's Edit menu offers the standard file edit options as well as options to edit resources, panes, and menus. Some items in this menu are not always available but depend upon the active element. The Edit menu choices include:

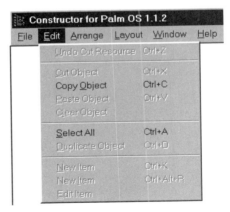

- Undo (CTRL+Z): Performs an undo for the last action undertaken, but only the last action. This option is only one level deep.

PART

V

Advanced Techniques

- Redo (CTRL+Z): Will redo the action removed by the undo option. The redo is also only one level deep.

- Cut (Object or Resource) (CTRL+X): Removes the highlighted text or element and moves it to the clipboard for pasting into this or another application.

- Copy (Object or Resource) (CTRL+C): Copies the highlighted text or element and moves it to the clipboard for pasting into this or another application.

- Paste (Object or Resource) (CTRL+V): Pastes the contents of the clipboard to the location identified by the cursor.

- Clear (Object or Resource): Deselects highlighted text or elements.

- Select All (CTRL+A): Selects all items in the active window.

- Duplicate (Object or Resource) (CTRL+D): Makes a duplicate of the highlighted text or element. Duplicate is similar to Copy except it does not use the clipboard and does not work outside Constructor.

- New Item (CTRL+K): Creates a new resource, menu, menu item, etc.

- New Separator Item: Inserts a menu separator when you edit menus.

- Remove Menu: Removes a menu item from the menu bar but does not remove the menu resource from the project.

- Edit Item: Opens a resource editor or the property inspection window if the editor is already open.

Window   All options that display or activate Constructor windows are available here. Not all options are available at all times, however.

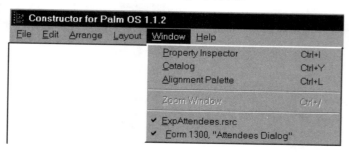

- Property Inspector (CTRL+I): Displays the attributes of resources, menu and menu items, or window panes.

- Catalog (CTRL+Y): Activates the Catalog window.
- Alignment Palette (CTRL+L): Activates the alignment palette.
- Zoom Window (CTRL+Z): Increases the magnification of the active window. This option has the same effect as the window's zoom box.

Arrange   The Arrange option provides the necessary tools to align and distribute items on your form. This menu is available only while you are working on forms with multiple items.

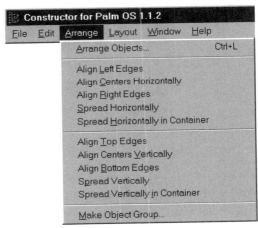

- Arrange Objects (CTRL+L): Opens the Arrange Objects dialog box.
- Align Left Edges: Aligns all selected items to the left-most in the group.
- Align Centers Horizontally: Aligns the selected panes between the left-most and the right-most items.
- Align Right Edges: Aligns all selected items to the right-most in the group.
- Spread Horizontally: Arranges the selected items evenly from left to right.
- Spread Horizontally in Container: Arranges the selected items from left to right within the edges of the boundary box that holds them.
- Align Top Edges: Aligns all selected items to the top-most item in the group.
- Align Centers Vertically: Aligns the selected panes between the top-most and the bottom-most items.
- Align Bottom Edges: Aligns all selected items to the bottom-most in the group.
- Spread Vertically: Arranges the selected items evenly from top to bottom.

- Spread Vertically in Container: Arranges the selected items from top to bottom within the edges of the boundary box that holds them.
- Make Object Group: Assigns one ID field to a group of objects. This option is used to assemble a group of push buttons and allow only one to be activated at a time.

Layout   You can access the Layout menu only after you have activated the form layout window. These options control item visibility and the layout grid.

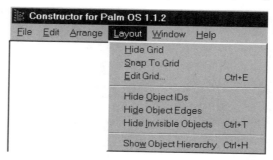

- Show Grid: Turns on the layout grid. The layout grid is a rectangular, graph paper–like matrix of dots used to align elements.
- Hide Grid: Turns off the layout grid.
- Snap To Grid: When activated, snap causes items placed on the layout grid to align to the nearest horizontal and vertical grid line.
- Don't Snap to Grid: Turns off the snap feature.
- Edit Grid (CTRL+E): Allows you to modify the grid size.
- Show Object IDs: Displays resource IDs in the upper right-hand corner of the item.
- Hide Object IDs: Does not display the resource IDs.
- Show Object Edges: Displays the otherwise invisible edges of panes, making it easier to arrange boxed items.
- Hide Object Edges: Hides the edge panes.
- Show Invisible Objects (CTRL+T): Displays items that have the Usable check box deselected.

- Hide Invisible Objects (CTRL+T): Hides items that have the Usable check box deselected.
- Show Object Hierarchy (CTRL+H): Opens the hierarchy window.

Options The Options menu is unavailable unless you activate the bitmap editor (more on that later), and when you do, several more menu options appear. All actions are performed on pixels, or picture elements, which are the smallest dots within any bitmap.

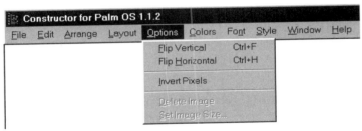

- Flip Vertical (CTRL+F): Rotates the selected pixels 180 degrees vertically.
- Flip Horizontal (CTRL+H): Rotates the selected pixels 180 degrees horizontally.
- Invert Pixels: Changes white pixels to black, and black pixels to white.
- Delete Image: Even though this option shows up in the toolbar, it doesn't work under any circumstance.
- Set Image Size: Sets the image size to fit the available space.

Colors The Colors menu is not available unless you activate a bitmap editor. Additionally, the selected resource must support a color palette, which is not generally the case with Palm devices.

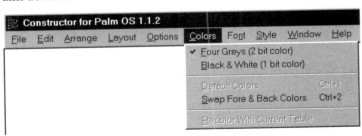

- Four Greys (2-bit Color): Multi-bit color available for the Palm OS 3.0 or later.
- Black & White (1-bit Color): Regular black and white icons.
- Default Colors (CTRL+1): Not usually an active selection.
- Swap Fore & Back Colors (CTRL+2): Changes the foreground color to the background color, and vice versa. This is active for Palm devices.

Font   The Font menu is active only when the bitmap editor is active. It lists all available fonts on the desktop computer.

Style   The Style menu is active only when the bitmap editor is active. It lists all typographical styles supported on the desktop computer.

 NOTE   Versions of the Palm OS prior to 3.0 can handle only 1-bit images (black and white). Palm OS Version 3.0 and higher will accept 2-bit (four-level grey scale) images.

Managing Projects

CodeWarrior refers to your application development effort as a project. Because Code-Warrior is comprised of several components (the IDE, Constructor, etc.), the project model works well and allows you to easily combine files created through the Code-Warrior components. By combining Constructor files and IDE files in the same project, you gain access to all of the resources used by either component. Constructor recognizes the resource types you used while creating your application in the IDE.

The Constructor Project window (see Figure 26.8) has two parts: the Resource Type and Name, and the Project Settings. The Resource Type and Name area uses a tree view display showing a branch for each possible resource type. Click the small triangle to the left of a resource, or double-click the resource, to open the list. To the right of the resource is the ID indicator, which lists the number of items used within that resource and, when the list is open, the resource ID numbers.

PART

V

Advanced Techniques

FIGURE 26.8

*The Constructor
Project window*

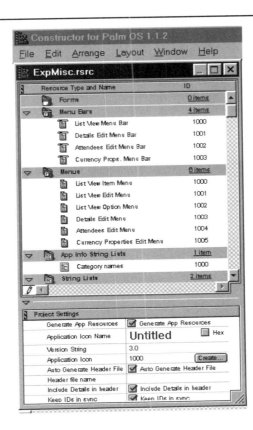

The Resource Type and Name/Project Settings window displays the resources and global project settings for the current constructor project. The Resource Type and Name section show the resources (as discussed above) associated with the current project. The Project Settings area lists the options that apply to the entire project, not just individual components. The Project Settings include:

- Generate App Resources: Includes both the version resource (tver) and the application icon name resource (tAIN) with the project resources.

- Application Icon Name: Holds the text that you want to place in the project's application icon name resource (tAIN) and becomes the name of the project. You are limited to 31 characters.

- Version String: Holds the text that will become the project's version resource (tver). This becomes the project's version number, like Release 5. The version string allows one decimal point to differentiate between major and minor revisions. The total field length is limited to 15 characters including the decimal point.

- Application Icon: Holds the application icon resource ID. In addition, every icon, form, menu bar, etc. is automatically given a resource ID by the Constructor.

- Auto Generate Header File: Tells Constructor to automatically generate the C/C++ header file that describes the resource used in the project. We recommend leaving this option checked so that Constructor does all of the hard work for you.

- Header File Name: Designates the name of the automatically generated header file. You can select your own file name or accept the default.

- Include Details in header: Adds descriptive comments to the header file when selected.

- Keep IDs in Sync: Maintains consistency among resource and form IDs. We recommend keeping this option active so that Constructor manages the ID numbers.

The Icon Editor

As part of the Constructor, Metrowerks includes a basic bitmap editor, useful for modifying and creating application icons and other bitmap images. Using Constructor's bitmap editor, you can create new icons for Palm OS 3.0 or modify icons developed in Palm OS 2.0 or older. Icons created for Palm OS 2.0 or older use 1-bit color for black and white, while icons created for Palm 3.0 use 2-bit or multi-bit color (four shades of gray).

Using the multi-bit Icon Editor, you can easily create two icons—a 1-bit and a multi-bit—and let the Palm OS select the appropriate icon. The Palm OS will automatically select the correct icon, even if both are present.

The easiest way to create a new icon is to modify an existing one. To modify an existing icon, follow these steps:

1. From the Constructor window, double-click the icon displayed in the Resource Type and Name window, shown in Figure 26.9. This opens the bitmap editor with the bitmap icon in the center of the screen and the editing tools to the right and left (see Figure 26.10). The editing tools are similar to other drawing packages, such as Windows Paint and Adobe Illustrator.

2. Make your icon edits and then close the window. The automatically saves the changes.

FIGURE 26.9

Resource Type and Name window

FIGURE 26.10

The Bitmap Editor

To convert older 1-bit icons to the newer 2-bit standard, follow this procedure:

1. From the Constructor window, double-click the icon displayed in the Resource Type and Name window. This opens the bitmap editor with the bitmap icon in the center of the screen and the editing tools to the right and left. The editing tools are similar to other drawing packages, such as Windows Paint and Adobe Illustrator.

2. From the Edit menu, click Select All, and then select Copy to copy the old icon.

3. Click the Multibit Icon heading in the project window, and from the Edit menu select New Icon Resources. This creates a new 2-bit icon.

4. Double-click the new icon to open it in the bitmap editor.

5. Click the B&W icon in the upper right-hand corner, then click the canvas. Choose Paste from the Edit menu.

6. Select the Color sample view and again paste the 1-bit image onto the canvas. The icon will now show in grayscale.

The CodeWarrior IDE

The CodeWarrior IDE is the starting and rallying point for all CodeWarrior development. That is, you can edit, compile, debug, etc. all of your program files from here. Think of the IDE as the portal to all of this functionality, providing you easy access to your files along with a series of useful tools. The Project window, a component of the IDE, gives you control over your projects. Remember that a project is just a collection of files (programs, icons, forms, etc.) and that the IDE is the best way to get to them.

There are several features within the IDE that you should become familiar with to draw the most out of your CodeWarrior development effort. The IDE menu and toolbar, shown in Figure 26.11, offers shortcuts and aids that make creating, editing, linking, and compiling programs much easier.

FIGURE 26.11

The IDE menu, toolbar, and Project window

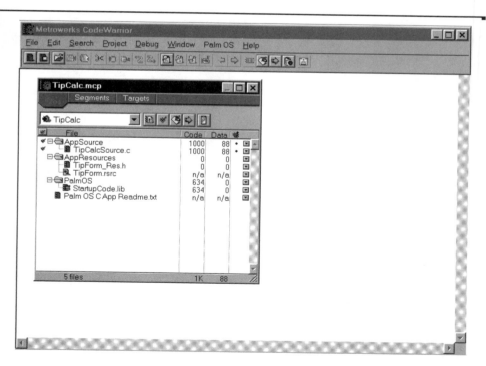

Though we discussed in detail each of the menus for cbasPad Tiny BASIC and Satellite Forms, we will only look at the highlights for CodeWarrior. CodeWarrior's IDE menu is quite extensive and would take a book to describe each menu item.

The File Menu

The File menu, shown in Figure 26.12, holds all of the commands for opening, creating, saving, closing and printing files and projects. In addition to the usual commands, the IDE supports the following:

FIGURE 26.12

The File menu

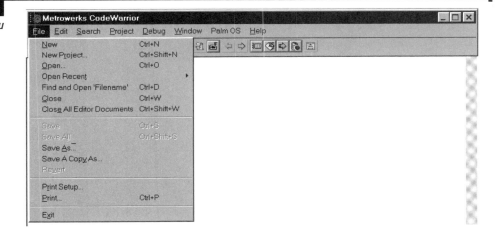

- Find and Open Filename (CTRL+D): Opens an existing file and searches for the current access path specified in the Target Settings window (more on that later).
- Revert: Returns the current Editor window to the last saved version.

The Edit Menu

The Edit menu supports the standard file editing features, such as cut, copy, paste, and undo/redo (see Figure 26.13). Unlike the Constructor, you can set multiple levels

PART

V

Advanced Techniques

of undo/redo through the Preferences panel (we will look at the Preferences panel later in this chapter). There are also several IDE specific commands.

FIGURE 26.13

The Edit menu

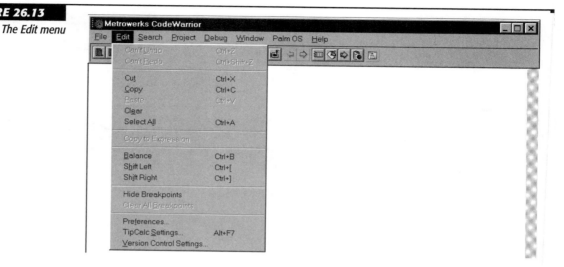

- Shift Left (CTRL+[): Shifts the line of C/C++ code one tab stop to the left.
- Shift Right (CTRL+]): Shifts the line of C/C++ code one tab stop to the right.
- Hide Breakpoints: Displays or hides the breakpoint window, but is available only when the debugger is active. Breakpoints are temporary start and stop points inserted into the code while debugging.
- Clear All Breakpoints: Clears any breakpoints, but is available only when the debugger is active.
- Preferences: Edits the global preferences for the IDE.
- Target Settings (ALT+F7): Displays the Target Settings window for the active build target.

The Search Menu

Within the Search menu, shown in Figure 26.14, are the commands that find, replace, and compare text, test strings, and files. There are also several file navigation commands.

FIGURE 26.14

The Search menu

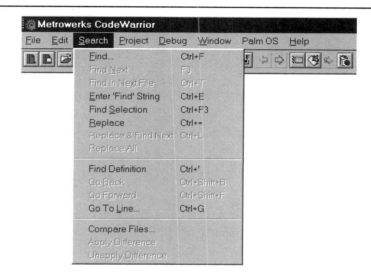

- Find Definition (CTRL+'): Searches all source code in the open project for a selected routine's definition, or code that describes its actions.
- Compare Files: Compares two files for similarities, reporting differences and then preparing them for merging into one file.
- Apply Difference: Accepts the reported differences, reported by the Compare Files command between two files.

The Project Menu

The Project menu provides tools to maintain project files, such as add and remove files and libraries, and compile and link files within a project. Figure 26.15 shows the Project menu tools.

FIGURE 26.15

The Project menu

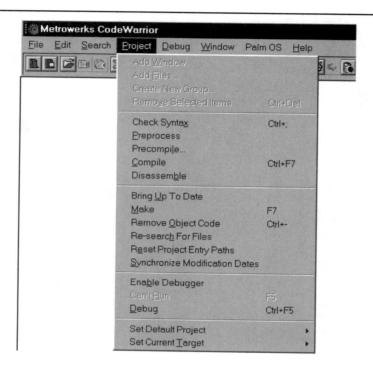

- Remove Selected Items (CTRL+DEL): Removes the selected items *permanently* from the project. Undo will not retrieve items removed through this command, so be very careful while using it.

- Check Syntax (CTRL+;): Checks the syntax of the source code in the active window and highlights syntactical errors.

- Bring Up To Date: Updates the open project by compiling all modified files.

- Re-search For Files: Refreshes cached locations for files.

- Reset Project Entry Paths: Resets project location data stored with each project entry.

- Run (F5): Compiles, links, and creates the stand-alone application, and then launches it.
- Debug (CTRL+F5): Compiles and links the project, and then launches the debugger.

The Debug Menu

Within the Debug menu (Figure 26.16) lists commands that let you manage program execution. You can set breakpoints and watchpoints to assist your debugging effort.

FIGURE 26.16

The Debug menu

PART

V

Advanced Techniques

- Kill (SHIFT+F5): Terminates execution of the current program.
- Reset: Resets the program, moving everything to the start point.
- Step Over (F10): Executes a single statement while ignoring all function calls.
- Step Into (F11): Executes a single statement and any function calls it may have.
- Step Out (SHIFT+F11): Executes the current function until it hits an exit.
- Stop: Suspends execution of the program.

The Window Menu

The Window menu, shown in Figure 26.17, provides controls over windows settings, tiling, and the debugger window properties.

FIGURE 26.17

The Window menu

- Toolbar: Toggles the toolbar submenu and provides control over the standard and floating toolbars.
- Browser Catalog Window: Displays the Browser Catalog window.
- Errors & Warnings Windows (CTRL+I): Displays the Errors & Warnings window.
- Project Inspector (ALT+ENTER): Displays the information about the current project.
- Breakpoints Window (ALT+F9): Displays the Breakpoints window that contains the currently set program breakpoints.

The Palm OS Menu

Through the Palm OS menu you can access and control the Palm Console and the Palm OS Emulator without leaving the CodeWarrior IDE.

- Open Debug Console: Sets up remote debugging through the Palm console. This is a test-only debugger.
- Launch Palm OS Emulator: Starts the Palm OS Emulator.

The Help Menu

The Help menu, shown in Figure 26.18, is a standard online help tool with topic, keyword, and feature search. Any information found in the online documentation can also be found in the online help.

FIGURE 26.18

The Help menu

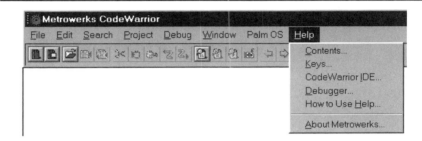

The IDE Project Window

The Project window displays information about the files, link order, and targets within the project. We all know what files are. The Project window discloses additional information about the files in a project, such as the file's type (source or resource) and its size (see Figure 26.19).

The segments, or groups of files listed beneath Source, Resources, etc., show the order in which the above files are linked. By default, files are linked in the order that they appear in the File menu, but you can adjust that order through the link order.

A target is a group of files used by the IDE to build an output file, such as an application or library. Additionally, files within any one target may be shared with other targets. Each target has its own set of options and can be configured to depend upon other targets on the project.

FIGURE 26.19

The Projects menu/ Files view

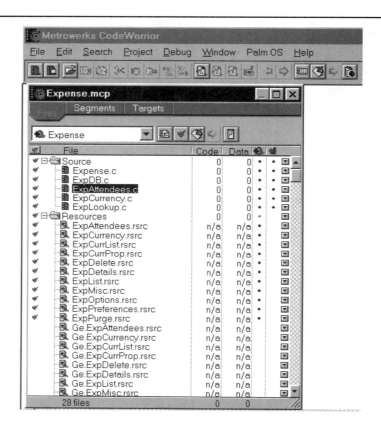

Files View

The Files view lists all of the files in the current project in a hierarchical fashion, grouped by category. You can open any file by double-clicking its name. This will open the editor and display the complete file.

To the right of each file are several columns that provide more information about the files in the project. Take a look at Figure 26.19 and follow along from the left-most column to the right-most column.

- The Touch column: Indicates whether the file needs to be compiled. A red checkmark indicates that the file must be complied.

- The File column: Lists each file's name, within each group, in the project.

- The Code column: Lists the size of the compiled, executable file in kilobytes. A listing of zero indicates that the file hasn't been compiled while an n/a indicates that the file has no executable code.

- The Data column: Lists the size of the non-executable data in kilobytes. A zero indicates that the file hasn't been compiled or does not contain a data section, while an n/a indicates that there is no data.

- The Target column: Indicates with a black arrow in a red bullseye icon that this file is included in the current build target, while a gray mark indicates that only some of the files are included in the target group.

- The Debug column: Signifies with its bug icon that it is the debug column. A black marker indicates that the IDE will generate debugging information for this file. A gray marker means that the IDE will generate debugging information for only a few of the files in the group.

- The Interface Pop-up column: Lists all associated files when you click this icon.

Segments View

CodeWarrior compiles files in the order that they appear in the Files view. This is the default mechanism, but through the Segments view (see Figure 26.20), you can re-order the files before compiling, allowing you to compile in virtually any order that you prefer. You must remember, however, that if the fourth file in order interfaces with the second file, then you must compile the second file before the fourth.

PART

V

Advanced Techniques

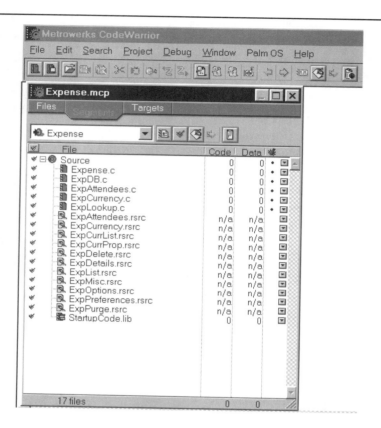

Targets View

The Targets view displays the list of targets in the project, as well as objects that the targets depend upon. Figure 26.21 displays the Project menu/Targets view.

PART
V

Advanced Techniques

FIGURE 26.21

*The Project menu/
Targets view*

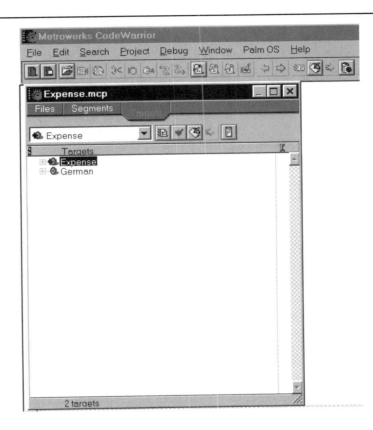

Setting IDE Preferences

You can easily customize the CodeWarrior IDE through the IDE Preferences window. These customizations affect global preference settings and, accordingly, the way that the IDE will work with every project. You can view the IDE Preferences window (see Figure 26.22) by clicking Preferences from the Edit option in the IDE menu.

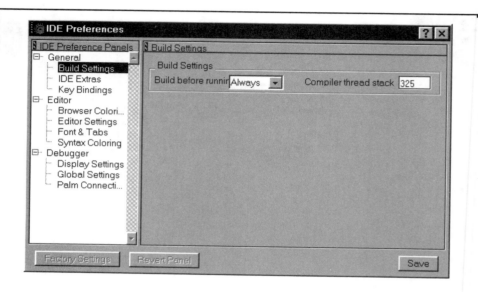

On the left side is the IDE Preference Panel, which lists three major headers: General, Editor, and Debugger. Listed hierarchically beneath each of these headers are the respective preference options. Click the plus sign to the left of a header to open it, and select the option that you wish to modify. When you select an option, this panel on the right will change and display the details pertaining to that option.

At the bottom of the Preferences panel are three dialog box buttons that act upon your modifications and determine their status. The three buttons are:

- Factory Settings: Returns all of your modifications back to their original, CodeWarrior defaults. This is a real savior for those times when you've made a host of changes but can't figure out what you've done.

- Revert Panel: Undoes the last series of changes and returns you to the previous setup.

- Save: Saves your changes.

General Preferences

The General Preferences adjust the entire IDE. There are three settings beneath the General heading:

- Build Settings: Control project builds, when to build, and the compiler thread size (the amount of memory space dedicated to the compiler).

- IDE Extras: Set the number of previously opened projects and files that will display with the File/Open command.
- Key Bindings: Let you customize the keyboard shortcuts for each group in the IDE menu bar.

Editor Preferences

The options listed within the Editor Preferences control editor features. They are:

- Browser Coloring: Uses different colors to differentiate among the various symbols. By default, this option is disabled.
- Editor Settings: Determines the editor's behavior including colors, default fonts, scrolling, drag-and-drop editing, and multiple undos.
- Font & Tabs: Sets the editor's default font and tab settings.
- Syntax Coloring: Allows you to set custom keyword, string, and comment colors, and make the source code a little easier to read.

Debugger Preferences

The options within the Debugger Preferences allow you to modify the Debugger options. They are:

- Display Settings: Let you choose variable and watchpoint colors and the method to display the debugger window.
- Global Settings: Determine how the debugger will perform and how it will address errors and unexpected occurrences.
- Palm Connection Settings: Allow you to determine the debug device, the device connection, and line speed.

Creating the Application in CodeWarrior

Developing an application in CodeWarrior is little different from any other development tool. You must determine what your application will do, lay out your application into its component parts, write the code that delivers the desired result, compile and link the application, and then debug the program (you'll almost always find yourself debugging your programs, even the simple ones).

You can use CodeWarrior's IDE to perform the above steps more effectively. The IDE takes some of the sting out of creating an application, though writing the application in C/C++ has a sting all its own. C/C++ programs are extremely complex and in some ways alien. Though it's said that C/C++ is similar to Pascal, which in turn is similar to many other structured languages, we won't see any similarity other than that they are both structured languages. A structured language, by the way, is any one of many newer programming languages that force a highly organized approach upon the programmer. This structure removes some ambiguity and confusion, or so is its intention. You'll see as we move through the C/C++ coding that there is still a bit of ambiguity and confusion.

We must also warn you that programming in C/C++ is not for the inexperienced programmer, the faint of heart, or anyone interested in a quick solution. These programs tend to be long and complex—a consequence of their design, as there is a considerable amount of overhead associated with each program. Additionally, Palm OS limitations further complicate and elongate the program. As you may recall from our earlier discussion of the Palm OS, older Palm devices, which use Palm OS version 1.0, do not easily handle floating point numbers (numbers with decimal places). This forces you to carefully think about your application development: do you expect your application to run on the Palm Professional and models 1000 and 5000? If so, you'll need to create your application with the floating point issue in mind. Don't misunderstand us—you can create programs that use floating point numbers, you just can't do it easily.

On the other hand, programming in C/C++ does offer the greatest control over the resulting application's function. Not only can you create a simple program like our tip calculator, but you can also create your own database or a virtually anything else that you can think of. One enterprising engineer that we know is anxious to develop his own CodeWarrior application to collect land survey data (good luck, Gordon!). The point is that C/C++ and CodeWarrior can open the world of high-end programming to you.

Let's review our application's goals once more. You are designing a tip calculator that will determine the tip of a restaurant bill based upon the total restaurant bill, the total drink portion of the bill, and the quality of the service. Your calculator will also accommodate your choice to include or exclude the drink portion of the bill in determining the tip value. The calculator will have the ability to figure a tip of whatever percentage you feel is appropriate.

So you now have the basis for your tip calculation: you will take the total restaurant bill, provide the opportunity to include or exclude the drink bill, then calculate the tip based upon a percentage of the adjusted total. Turning these words into a logical expression looks like this:

```
Total Bill less Drink Bill times Tip Percent equals the Tip
```

Turning that logical expression into a mathematical one yields:

```
(B-D)*S=T
```

Here, B is the Total Bill, D is the Drink Bill, S is the Tip Percent (or Service) and T is the calculated Tip. To simplify the logic, you can turn that one calculation into two, and then turn the expression around putting it into standard computer assignment form, which looks like this:

```
NB=B-D
T=NB*S
```

Here, NB is the Net Bill (the Total Bill less the Drink Bill) and T is the calculated tip, which is the product of the Net Bill times the Tip Percent. Either the first expression or the second two expressions (or any hybrid that you prefer) will calculate the tip.

Given the complexity of C/C++ programming and Metrowerks admonition that only experienced programmers should attempt development in CodeWarrior, we won't teach you how to use it, but merely explain what we have done. If you think that you'd like to use CodeWarrior to develop your application, let us recommend that you learn C/C++ programming first (check out Sybex's *Visual C++ 6 In Record Time*, by Steven Holzner). As we stated earlier, there are many good books on the subject and many local colleges and universities offer instructional classes. Start there, then turn your attentions to CodeWarrior.

Coding the Application in CodeWarrior

Probably the easiest place to start any CodeWarrior application is through the included Starter project and project stationery (see Figure 26.23). Metrowerks adds this folder and its associated files to every copy of CodeWarrior. The Starter project stationery is a template that includes sample source code and resource files, libraries, and a preset compiler and linker. Basically, the Starter project stationery provides all the necessary defaults and assures that your code will work—well, it assures that all of the necessary parts are included.

FIGURE 26.23

The Starter project location

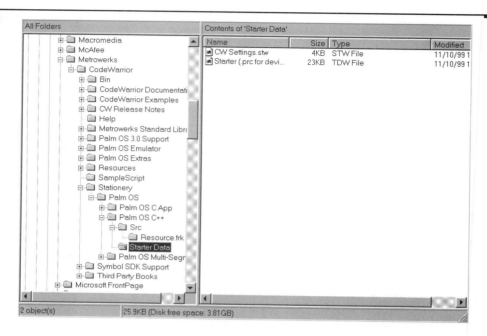

You will also need to create a user interface that will reside on the Palm device. Use CodeWarrior's Constructor to create your data entry form. Constructor is a visual, drag-and-drop tool similar in concept to Satellite Forms. It doesn't really matter which you create first—the Constructor form or the underlying C/C++ code—as long as you use all your variables properly. We'll start by creating a new project folder using the Starter sample.

Here's how to create a new CodeWarrior application using the Starter project:

1. Start the CodeWarrior IDE and select New Project from the File menu (see Figure 26.24). This will give you the New Project dialog box. Click the plus sign to the left of the Palm OS selection (it's probably the only option available unless you have acquired multiple device versions of CodeWarrior).

2. Next, select the Palm OS C App option and be sure that the Create Folder check box in the lower-left corner is checked. This last option ensures that you will have a separate folder for your project files. Click OK.

FIGURE 26.24

The New Project window

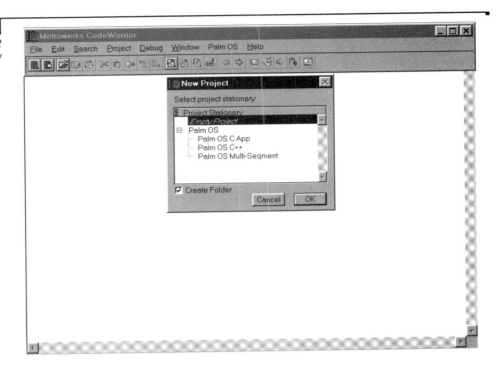

PART

V

Advanced Techniques

3. In the resulting Name New Project As dialog box, give your project a unique name with a MCP extension. For the Tip Calculator, use TipCalc.MCP, and click Save. CodeWarrior creates the new project file and folder with the name TipCalc.

The TipCalc file contains a standard source file comprised of many modules, some of which we will use and some that we will not. CodeWarrior includes them all since it's easier to delete the unwanted code than it is to put it there in the first place. For the Tip Calculator you will modify this standard source code.

Creating the Form Using Constructor

Now that you created a project folder with its template source file, you should create the data entry form. CodeWarrior's Constructor is your option for making this form (as if one selection constitutes an option). Actually, Constructor is really a pretty good interface design tool, and it interfaces perfectly to the rest of CodeWarrior.

So, to create your form, open Constructor and follow these steps:

1. From the File menu, select New Project File. This opens the Constructor's form layout window. See Figure 26.25.

FIGURE 26.25

The Form Layout window

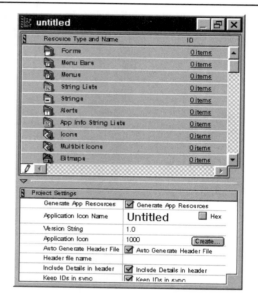

2. In the Resource Type and Name area, highlight Forms and then select New Form Resource from Constructor's Edit menu. This deposits a new form (as shown in Figure 26.26) named Untitled beneath the Forms header in the Resource Type and Name area. Change the form's name from untitled to CalcForm.

3. In the Project Settings area (beneath the Resource Type and Name area), click in the Header file name field and enter a form name. For the Tip Calculator, use TipForm_res to visually identify the form as a resource. Any name will do, with or without the _res.

4. Double-click the new form's name (Untitled) to open the Layout Properties and Layout Appearance windows as shown in Figure 26.27. The left side of this window lists the form's properties, such as title and ID, and the right side displays a graphic image of a Palm device. The left side is where you will create the form.

FIGURE 26.26

The Form Layout window with untitled form

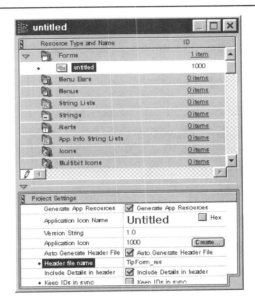

PART

V

Advanced Techniques

FIGURE 26.27

Constructor with Layout windows

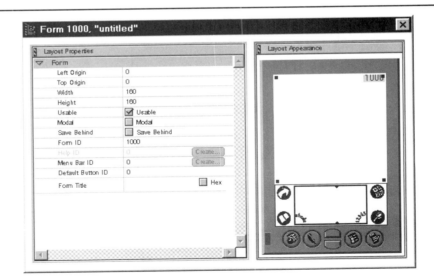

5. In the Layout Properties window, click the last field (Form Title) and type **Tip Calculator**.

6. Next, select Window/Catalog from Constructor's menu to bring up the list of drag-and-drop UI Objects. See Figure 26.28. This list includes buttons, labels, data entry fields, drop-down lists, and much more.

FIGURE 26.28

Constructor with Layout and Objects windows

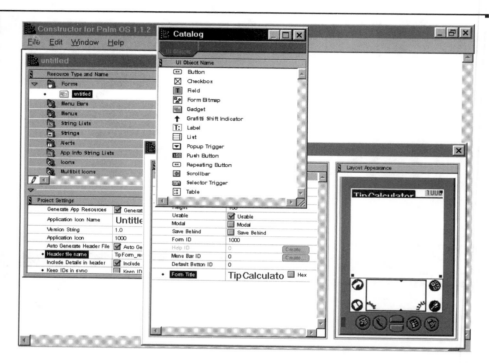

7. In a similar fashion to Satellite Forms, the CodeWarrior Tip Calculator form should have field labels on the left side and data entry fields on the right, with an action button at the bottom.

8. Drag a Label object from the UI Objects list (CTL+Y to display the object catalog) to the Layout Appearance window and drop it beneath the Tip Calculator title. Adjust its position accordingly. Use Label objects wherever you want to prevent data entry. The Layout Properties window now displays properties for the Label object.

9. Click in the Object Identifier field at the top of the Layout Properties window, and fill in the label's name: TotalBillLabel. A label's name is how the program internally addresses the label. Using the drop-down list, change the font to Bold (all labels are bold). Then click in the Text field and type in the information that will display on the Palm's LCD panel. For the example, use Total Bill since that is how you will address the label. See Figure 26.29.

FIGURE 26.29

Entering Label data into the Object Identifier field

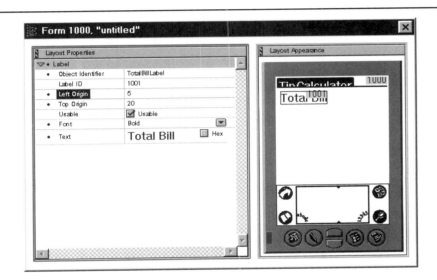

10. Drag a Field object from the UI Objects list to the Layout Appearance window and drop it to the right of the Total Bill label. Adjust its position accordingly. Use Field objects wherever you want to allow data entry. The Layout Properties window now displays properties for the Field object.

11. Click in the Object Identifier field at the top of the Layout Properties window, and fill in the field's name: TotalBillAmount. Leave the font as Standard, but change the Max Characters field to 6 and check the Numeric option at the bottom of the list. See Figure 26.30.

12. Repeat steps 8–11 and use the information in Tables 26.1 and 26.2 below to complete the form.

13. Now drag a Button object to the form and drop it at the bottom. Position the button accordingly.

PART

V

Advanced Techniques

FIGURE 26.30

Entering Field data into the Object Identifier field

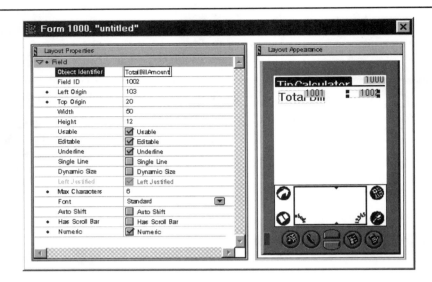

14. Click in the Object Identifier field at the top of the Layout Properties window, and fill in the button's name: Calculate. Using the drop-down list, change the font to Bold. Then click in the Text field and type in the information that will display on the Palm's LCD panel. For the example, use Calculate. See Figure 26.31.

15. Repeat Step 14 for the Clear button.

FIGURE 26.31

Button properties

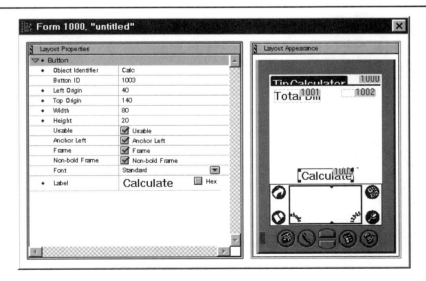

TABLE 26.1: SCREEN INFORMATION—LEFT SIDE		
Object Name	**Object Identifier**	**Text**
TotalBillAmount	TotalBillLabel	Total Bill
DrinkBillAmount	DrinkBillLabel	Drink Bill
TipPercentAmount	TipPercentLabel	Tip Percent
NetBillAmount	NetBillLabel	Net Bill
CalcTipAmount	CalcTipLabel	Calculated Tip
GrandTotalAmount	GrandTotalLabel	Grand Total

TABLE 26.2: SCREEN INFORMATION—RIGHT SIDE		
Object Name	**Object Identifier**	**Text**
Field	TotalBillAmount	N/A
Field	DrinkBillAmount	N/A
Field	TipPercentAmount	N/A
Label	NetBillAmount	None (leave blank)
Label	CalcTipAmount	None (leave blank)
Label	GrandTotalAmount	None (leave blank)

Once you've entered all of the above information, click File/Save from the Constructor menu. Constructor creates the form header file and creates an .h file, or a holdover, from CodeWarrior's Mac roots. The completed form should look like Figure 26.32 on the next page.

FIGURE 26.32

Completed Form

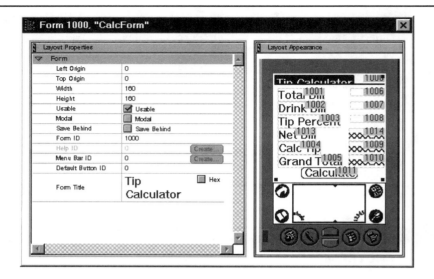

Writing the Code Using the IDE

Because you used CodeWarrior's Starter project as your template, you will also have Starter's source code and libraries attached to your project. You'll need to modify the source code, but you should use the libraries. This will make linking and compiling a lot easier, since you'll have all of the necessary components.

The Starter source code, `Starter.c`, contains considerably more "stuff" than you'll need, so your job is two-fold: modify the portions that you can use and delete those that you don't need. Some of the modules in `Starter.c` are standard bits that are used in all C/C++ programs. If you leave them out, your program will not work. Some of the modules in `Starter.c` must be modified to meet the specific needs of the application you are creating. And, of course, some must be removed to meet the needs of the Tip Calculator application.

Open the CodeWarrior IDE and, from the File menu, select Open. Navigate to the folder that you created earlier when creating the Tip Calculator form. Once you have found the folder, highlight `TipCalc.mcp` and click Open. This will open the TipCalc project, listing the newly created TipForm, `TipForm_res.h`, and the `Starter.c` source code. See Figure 26.33.

FIGURE 26.33

TipCalc Project Listing

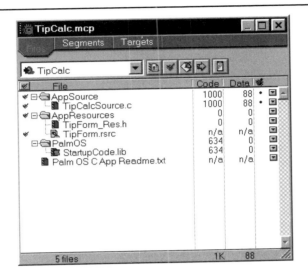

PART

V

Advanced Techniques

 NOTE To download the following code, go to www.sybex.com and navigate to the Mastering Palm Organizers page.

Double-click the Starter.c source code listing and either modify the code yourself (if you're a proficient C/C++ programmer), or delete the current contents of Starter.c and replace it with the code below. When you have completed the operation, save the file by clicking File/Save As in the IDE menu and name the file TipCalcSource.c.

```c
//Tip Calculator Program
#include <Pilot.h>
#include <FloatMgr.h>
#include <SysEvtMgr.h>
#include "TipForm_Res.h"

// The next section defines the variables and structures used
// in the program
    typedef struct
      {
      Handle Total;
      Handle Drink;
      Handle Tip;
      char NetBill[12];
      char CalcTip[32];
      char GrandTotal[32];
```

```
        } MealTipData;
 // Structure to hold our bill's information
        MealTipData mealTipData = {0,0,0,"","",""};


// This is the GetObjectPtr module that returns a pointer to the
// current form
      static VoidPtr GetObjectPtr(Word objectID)
      {
        FormPtr frmP;

        frmP = FrmGetActiveForm();
        return (FrmGetObjectPtr(frmP,
            FrmGetObjectIndex(frmP,objectID)));
      }


// This is the MainFormInit module that initializes the MainForm
      static void MainFormInit(FormPtr frmP)
      {
        VoidPtr item = NULL;

        item = GetObjectPtr(CalcFormTotalBllAmountField);
        if (item)
         FldSetTextHandle (item, mealTipData.Total);

        item = GetObjectPtr(CalcFormTotalDrinkAmountField);
        if (item)
         FldSetTextHandle (item, mealTipData.Drink);

        item = GetObjectPtr(CalcFormTipPercentAmountField);
        if (item)
         FldSetTextHandle (item, mealTipData.Tip);

        FrmCopyLabel (frmP, CalcFormNetBillAmountLabel,
             mealTipData.NetBill);
        FrmCopyLabel (frmP, CalcFormCalcTipAmountLabel,
             mealTipData.CalcTip);
        FrmCopyLabel (frmP, CalcFormGrandTotalAmountLabel,
             mealTipData.GrandTotal);


      }
```

```
// This module calculates the actual tip amount
    static short Calculate()
    {
      ULong mantissa;
      Int exponent;
      Int sign;
      Int offset;
      FloatType total;
      FloatType drink;
      FloatType tip;
      FloatType net;
      FloatType calc;
      FloatType grand;

// This command gets the total bill amount from the Palm device
      total = FplAToF(MemHandleLock(mealTipData.Total));
      MemHandleUnlock(mealTipData.Total);

// This command gets the drink amount from the Palm device
      drink = FplAToF(MemHandleLock(mealTipData.Drink));
      MemHandleUnlock(mealTipData.Drink);

// This command gets the tip from the Palm device
      tip = FplAToF(MemHandleLock(mealTipData.Tip));
      MemHandleUnlock(mealTipData.Tip);

// The following calculations determine the net bill amount, the
// calculated tip amount and the grand total
      net = FplSub(total, drink);
      calc = FplMul(net, tip);
      grand = FplAdd(tip, total);

// Magic floating point routines. This section takes the floating
// point results and converts them back to standard notation.

MemHandleLock(mealTipData.NetBill);
      FplFToA(net, mealTipData.NetBill);
      MemHandleUnlock(mealTipData.NetBill);
```

```
            FplBase10Info(net, &mantissa, &exponent, &sign);
            StrIToA(mealTipData.NetBill, mantissa);
            offset = StrLen(mealTipData.NetBill) + exponent;
            mealTipData.NetBill[offset + 3] = 0;
            mealTipData.NetBill[offset + 2] =
                        mealTipData.NetBill[offset + 1];
            mealTipData.NetBill[offset + 1] =
                        mealTipData.NetBill[offset + 0];
            mealTipData.NetBill[offset + 0] = '.';

            FplFToA(calc, mealTipData.CalcTip);

            FplBase10Info(calc, &mantissa, &exponent, &sign);
            StrIToA(mealTipData.CalcTip, mantissa);
            offset = StrLen(mealTipData.CalcTip) + exponent;
            mealTipData.CalcTip[offset + 3] = 0;
            mealTipData.CalcTip[offset + 2] =
                        mealTipData.CalcTip[offset + 1];
            mealTipData.CalcTip[offset + 1] =
                        mealTipData.CalcTip[offset + 0];
            mealTipData.CalcTip[offset + 0] = '.';

            FplFToA(grand, mealTipData.GrandTotal);

            FplBase10Info(grand, &mantissa, &exponent, &sign);
            StrIToA(mealTipData.GrandTotal, mantissa);
            offset = StrLen(mealTipData.GrandTotal) + exponent;
            mealTipData.GrandTotal[offset + 3] = 0;
            mealTipData.GrandTotal[offset + 2] =
                        mealTipData.GrandTotal[offset + 1];
            mealTipData.GrandTotal[offset + 1] =
                        mealTipData.GrandTotal[offset + 0];
            mealTipData.GrandTotal[offset + 0] = '.';

        return 0;
        }


// This is the event handler module that controls the bulk of
// the program
```

```
static Boolean MainFormHandleEvent(EventPtr eventP)
{
  Boolean handled = false;
  FormPtr frmP;


  switch (eventP->eType)
   {

   case frmOpenEvent:
      frmP = FrmGetActiveForm();
      MainFormInit(frmP);
      FrmDrawForm (frmP);
      handled = true;
      break;

   case ctlSelectEvent:
      if (eventP->data.ctlSelect.controlID ==
               CalcFormCalcButton)

      {
          Calculate();

       frmP = FrmGetActiveForm();
       FrmCopyLabel(frmP, CalcFormNetBillAmountLabel,
             mealTipData.NetBill);
       FrmCopyLabel(frmP, CalcFormCalcTipAmountLabel,
             mealTipData.CalcTip);
      FrmCopyLabel(frmP, CalcFormGrandTotalAmountLabel,
             mealTipData.GrandTotal);

       FrmEraseForm(frmP);
       FrmDrawForm(frmP);
       handled = true;
       }
    break;
   }
    return handled;
}
```

PART

V

Advanced Techniques

```
// This module loads the form
    static Boolean AppHandleEvent( EventPtr eventP)
    {
      Word formId;
      FormPtr frmP;

      if (eventP->eType == frmLoadEvent)
       {
       // Load the form resource.
       formId = eventP->data.frmLoad.formID;
       frmP = FrmInitForm(formId);
       FrmSetActiveForm(frmP);
       FrmSetEventHandler(frmP, MainFormHandleEvent);

       return true;
       }

      return false;
    }

// This module controls the event loop for the application
    static void AppEventLoop (void)

    {
      Word error;
      EventType event;

      do {
       EvtGetEvent(&event, evtWaitForever);


       if (! SysHandleEvent(&event))
          if (! MenuHandleEvent(0, &event, &error))
             if (! AppHandleEvent(&event))
                FrmDispatchEvent(&event);

      } while (event.eType != appStopEvent);
    }
```

```
// This module clears all variables after running the application
    static void AppStop(void)
    {

       MemHandleFree(mealTipData.Total);
       MemHandleFree(mealTipData.Drink);
       MemHandleFree(mealTipData.Tip);

      mealTipData.Total = NULL;
      mealTipData.Drink = NULL;
      mealTipData.Tip = NULL;

      FplFree();

    }

// This module initializes variables at start-up
    static Err AppStart(void)
    {

      MemSet(&mealTipData, sizeof(mealTipData), 0);

      mealTipData.Total = MemHandleNew(16);
      if (mealTipData.Total == NULL)
      {
       return 1;
      }

      mealTipData.Drink = MemHandleNew(16);
      if (mealTipData.Drink == NULL)
      {
       return 1;
      }

      mealTipData.Tip = MemHandleNew(16);
      if (mealTipData.Tip == NULL)
      {
       return 1;
      }
```

PART

V

Advanced Techniques

```
            FplInit();

            return 0;
        }

        DWord PilotMain( Word cmd, Ptr cmdPBP, Word launchFlags)
        {
            if (cmd == sysAppLaunchCmdNormalLaunch)
            {
            if (AppStart() !=0)
                return 0;
            FrmGotoForm(CalcFormForm);
            AppEventLoop();
            AppStop();
                }

            return 0;

        }
```

Once you've saved the file, click Enable Debugging from the Project menu. This turns on the CodeWarrior debugger. Next, click Make from the Project menu to link and compile your source code. The debugger will highlight linker, compiler, and syntax errors, making it a little easier to write error-free code.

 NOTE Once you have compiled and linked your application, you can load the resulting PRC file just like any other.

The TipCalcSource.c program uses standard C/C++ modules as outlined in the Starter.c template. It's also written the hard way, using Palm OS 1.0 function calls, so this application will run on any version of the Palm device. The Palm OS 1.0 is unable to handle floating point numbers directly, so a simple formula such as

NB=B-D

must be written as

NB = FlpSub(B,D)

which in and of itself is no big deal. However, the absence of real floating point manipulation takes on a life of its own when it comes to doing something with the value of NB. The resulting number is a floating point number, but Palm OS 1.0 and

CodeWarrior report it in scientific notation. You may remember that term from somewhere back in Chemistry 101. Let us refresh your memory: scientific notation reports all numbers in powers of 10, so 147 would look like 1.4700E02. How's that for pretty and easy to read? The digits to the left (1.4700) are called the mantissa. The E signifies that scientific notation is in effect, and the 02 is the exponent or the power of 10 by which you must multiply the mantissa. Got it? So here goes: the mantissa (1.4700) is multiplied 10 raised to the 2nd power (which is 10 squared or 100), resulting 147.

The fun begins when you try to convert a number in scientific notation back to good old standard floating point. To do this you must use a string manipulation routine that counts the number of digits in the result number, then slides the decimal to the right the number of digits represented by the exponent. It's not simple, but it does work.

You can simplify your life and your programming effort if you write your program for Palm OS 2.0 or higher. These devices support floating point manipulation and report resulting numbers in standard floating point notation. So, 147 is reported as 147.0000, and 2.35 is 2.3500. Not perfect, but much better, and certainly much easier to work with.

PART

V

Advanced Techniques

CHAPTER 27

Debugging with POSE

Debugging any program is usually hard work. Fortunately we have POSE, a Palm Computing tool to help us along with this arduous task. Keep reading and you'll find out more about what POSE is, how it works, and why it's a must if you're developing applications for the Palm operating system. And of course, we'll also show you how to use it to test and debug your applications.

What Is POSE?

POSE, the Palm OS Emulator, is an open source software tool that emulates the Palm OS on your Mac or Windows desktop computer. Unlike the other development tools that we have looked at, you cannot use POSE to create a program. However, POSE is the tool that you'll need to test the program you do create. Since POSE emulates the Palm firmware, it allows you to load, safely test, and debug your Palm application on your desktop computer. Using POSE allows you to put the data on your Palm device without putting it at risk for a forced reset.

Though it is managed by Palm Computing, POSE is still an open source software tool. That means that anyone can make changes, improvements, or modifications to the program, but Palm Computing requests that you inform them of the changes. Basically, Palm Computing sits as a judge and works to moderate modifications to POSE. The open source concept is used on other software products, most notably Linux, and adds to the product's overall strength by incorporating many different points of view and experiences.

Originally called Pilotsim, POSE was the brainchild of Greg Hewgill (we've seen this name several times before) in early 1996. He developed a software simulator for the Motorola 68000 chip based upon some original work accomplished for the Amiga. Both the Palm device and the Amiga use the MC68000 chip, and Pilotsim was originally written for the Windows environment only. Along the development road, the name Pilotsim became Copilot, and began to more closely emulate the functioning of the Motorola chip, though its emulation was not complete. Over the course of the next year or so, Copilot went through several beta releases—each one an improvement over the previous version.

By 1998, Palm Computing began to show great interest in the product. Prior to Copilot, Palm Computing only had CodeWarrior's Simulator for the Mac and was eager to obtain and develop a powerful tool for all Palm developers. After working out an agreement with Greg Hewgill, Palm took over development of Copilot and renamed the product the Palm OS Emulator or POSE for short. POSE is available as a free download in both Mac and Windows flavors from Palm Computing at www.palm.com/devzone/pose. A Linux version is expected in the near future as well.

POSE emulates the basic firmware of the Palm device. You must complete the emulation with a ROM file, available for each variety of Palm device. (We'll explain how to obtain and use a ROM file later in this chapter.) This ROM file adds the specific functions/features of that particular Palm device, making POSE a near perfect test environment. There are a few shortcomings that we'll get into later, but for now it's good to know that you don't need to own every Palm model to test your application. All you need to do is load the appropriate ROM file into POSE and you're ready to begin.

Technical Overview

To properly emulate a Palm device, POSE must emulate the Palm's CPU, memory, I/O ports, hardware registers, and LCD screen. Palm devices use one of two CPU varieties in the Motorola MC68000 family: the MC68328 (Dragonball) or the MC68EZ328 (DragonballEZ). Each of these uses the same instruction set as the original Mac—all based on the MC68000 chip. Fortunately, the ROM file includes the necessary information for proper emulation. So, the ROM for the Palm III is radically different from the ROM for a Palm VII.

Once you load a ROM file into POSE, the emulator boots using the definition in that ROM file, and begins the execution of machine language instructions or opcodes. These opcodes are read and acted upon here just as they are on the Palm device. The ROM image file acts as the Palm's ROM memory, and RAM is allocated on the desktop computer to emulate the Palm device. The specific amount of emulated RAM (this value is adjustable within POSE) is allocated as a block of memory on the desktop computer and is used as a RAM buffer. All memory puts and calls are made within this buffer.

Additionally, POSE offers the ability to automatically debug your creation through a feature called Gremlins. Gremlins is a pseudo-random event sequencer that mimics user input from multiple sources. Because of its pseudo-random nature, every action taken within Gremlins is 100% reproducible. This makes debugging an application a little bit easier, since you can reproduce the exact set of actions that caused a failure. We'll look more closely at Gremlins later in this chapter.

Installing POSE

After you have downloaded POSE from the Palm Web site (`www.palm.com/devzone/pose/pose.html`) and unzipped the file, you should have four files and a DOCS subfolder. The four files are the two POSE emulators and two utility programs.

- `Emulator.exe` is the main POSE executable.

- `Emulator_Profile.exe` is POSE with the profile options.

- `HostControl.h` is a C++ header file needed to run POSE.

- `ROM Transfer.prc` is used to extract and transfer ROM files from the handheld Palm to your desktop computer.

The DOCS subfolder holds all of the POSE manuals and documentation, including user guides and install notes. Oddly, some of these documents are PDFs (Adobe Acrobat files, which require an Acrobat reader that's downloadable for free from www.adobe.com), some are HTML files (readable by any Web browser), and others are plain old TXT files that can be read by any word processor, (even the Windows Notepad).

To start POSE, double-click the `Emulator.exe` file. This brings up the Palm OS Emulator dialog box with its four choices, as shown in Figure 27.1.

FIGURE 27.1

*Palm OS Emulator
Dialog box*

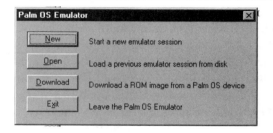

New

Click the New button to load a new or different ROM file. This feature lets you alternate among Palm device ROMs so you can emulate and test several different devices. POSE, by default, will open using the last selected ROM type. Within the New dialog, you can set the following parameters:

- The Device field allows you to select the Palm device that you want to emulate. Your choices run from the Pilot 1000 to the Palm VII.

- The Language field lets you choose the language type used to identify the silkscreen buttons on the POSE screen.

- The RAM Size field lets you choose the amount of memory to be allocated for your tests. Generally 1MB, or 1024KB, is a good starting point since most Palm devices have that amount of memory available. However, you can go as low as 128KB or as high as 8192KB, or 8MB. This latter amount is quite advantageous given the new, non–Palm Computing, 8MB upgrade memory chips available for most Palm devices.

- The ROM file field lets you browse and select a previously downloaded ROM file for use during your POSE testing. See the section on loading ROMs for more information on ROM files and how to use them.

Select the required options and press OK to start your POSE testing session.

Open

The Open button lets you use a previously saved POSE emulation session. You can load a new ROM file and test your application, and then save the environment for future testing. With this feature you not only save the configuration but also the current state of the emulated Palm device.

Download

The Download button lets you transfer a ROM file from an existing Palm device. Through this transfer you can copy the ROM file from your Palm device and use that data to test your application. Contrary to the name of the button, this will not download the ROM file from Palm Computing. See the section on loading ROMs for more details.

PART

V

Advanced Techniques

Exit

Every application must have a means for terminating its operation. Click the Exit button to end operation and leave POSE.

Loading ROMs

A ROM file is required for POSE to function. As a matter of fact, you can't even open the Emulator.exe application without a ROM file. Well, you can, but you can't get beyond the Palm OS Emulator dialog box.

The ROM file describes/defines the precise workings of the Palm device you are trying to emulate. Each Palm model has its own distinct ROM file that models the workings of that device right down to the CPU and registers. Since POSE is an emulator for all Palm devices, the ROM file is crucial. Think of the ROM file as the operating system for POSE.

There are two methods for obtaining a ROM file: You can petition Palm Computing or you can extract a copy of the ROM file from your Palm device. Each has its benefits and flaws.

Petitioning Palm Computing

You can petition Palm Computing for copies of a ROM file directly off the Web. All Palm asks in return is that you register with them and sign a license agreement. This last bit is a legal requirement that protects Palm from theft of intellectual property.

To register with Palm, access the Provider Pavilion at `www.palm.com/devzone/ pavilion.html`. Registration is free, but you have to provide some information. Just click Sign Up Now! and follow the menus. Palm Computing will provide you with temporary access on the spot, but complete access will take a few days. Palm will e-mail all of the relevant information to you, including your permanent login ID and password. You'll need the permanent ID to access the more interesting things, like ROM files.

Once you have your permanent ID, log into the Provider Pavilion and click the Development Resources Seeding Program under the Apply For Special Programs area. Now, here is where the process gets clunky: you must verify the information on the screen (this information is taken from your original sign-up form), modify anything that requires updating, and click the Submit My Application button. Next, you need to download a license form, print out the form, sign it, and mail—yes, mail—two copies with original signatures to Palm Computing. It takes Palm about two weeks to process the paperwork, at which time they will e-mail you a Web link with access to the entire Palm family's ROM files.

The advantage to this slow system is that once you are on Palm's list you will have access to ROM files for each Palm device, past, present, and—as new products roll out—future. With these files, you can effortlessly test your application across the entire product line—well, it lets you put effort into writing and testing your application rather than wasting it on getting hold of every variety of Palm device to use as a test bed. These ROM files also include a debugging feature that makes them ideal for application testing (more about debug versus non-debug ROMs later).

Extracting a Copy of a ROM File

The quick and easy way to obtain a ROM file is to extract a copy from your Palm device. POSE and Palm Computing provide the necessary software tools to make this a simple task. Here's what you need to do:

1. HotSync the `ROM Transfer.prc` file (it came along with POSE) to your Palm device. You do this by clicking the Install icon within the Palm Desktop software.

From the Install Tool dialog box, shown in Figure 27.2, click the Add button and locate the ROM Transfer.prc file, then click Open. Click Next.

FIGURE 27.2

Install Tool dialog box

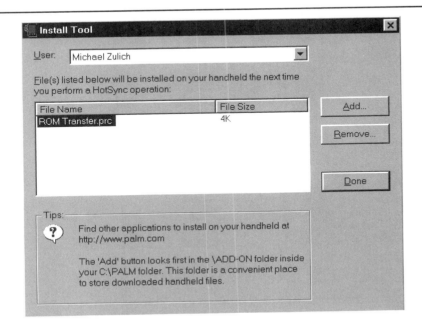

2. Put the Palm device in its cradle and perform a HotSync. The ROM Transfer.prc is now loaded on your Palm device.
3. From POSE, right-click and select Transfer ROM... from the POSE Features menu. This returns the Download ROM dialog box, shown in Figure 27.3. Click Next to proceed.
4. Select the COM port attached to your Palm cradle and accept the default transfer speed of 115,200bps, as shown in Figure 27.4. This is the fastest possible download speed and should work in all cases. Click Next.
5. From the Palm device, run the ROM Transfer application and in the Download ROM dialog box, click Next.

PART

V

Advanced Techniques

FIGURE 27.3

*Download ROM
dialog box*

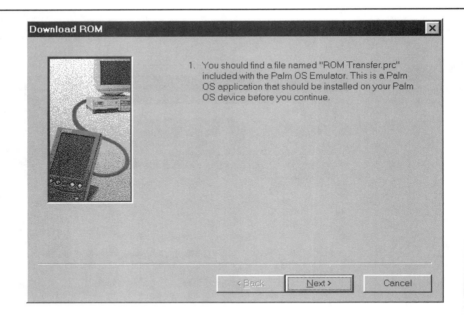

FIGURE 27.4

Pick the port speed.

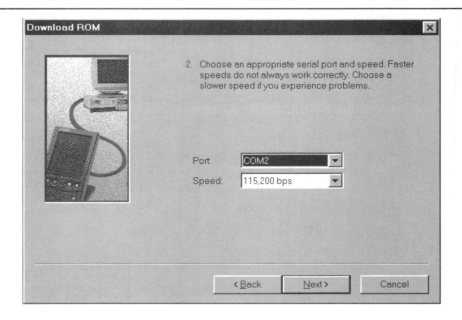

6. Be sure that the transfer speeds match on both the handheld Palm and the desktop software. Select 115,200bps to match our original selection. Click Next.

7. Click Next in the Download ROM dialog box to begin the download process.

8. Click Finish when the download is complete.

You've just downloaded, or more accurately, extracted, a ROM file from your Palm device. This process is identical for all Palm devices so you can extract a copy of any Palm device's ROM file for use in a POSE session.

 TIP If you encounter any difficulty in downloading (extracting) a ROM file, try lowering the transfer speed from the default 115,200bps to 57,600bps on both the Palm device and the desktop.

 WARNING Be sure that you have matched the transfer speeds on both the handheld Palm device in the cradle and the Download software. A mismatch of speeds will cause a transfer error.

Debug and Non-Debug ROM files

One of the key differences, and perhaps the only material difference, between a ROM file obtained directly from Palm Computing and one extracted from your Palm device is the presence of error checking codes. The ROM file obtained from Palm Computing is called a debug ROM and contains these codes. Used in conjunction with CodeWarrior or the Palm Debugger, these error codes will pinpoint the exact location within your code that is causing an error condition. Palm Computing recommends that you test every application using a debug ROM for obvious reasons.

 WARNING Because of the additional code required to create a debug ROM, and the complexity that it creates, you may sometimes encounter a false error. Palm Computing states that debug ROMs not only detect errors in the current OS version, but flag errors that may arise in future versions of the Palm OS. Whether or not that is an accurate statement, be advised that debug ROMs can be a little buggy themselves.

A non-debug ROM, or release version ROM, is obtained through the extraction process described above. These ROM files do not have the error checking codes but they fully and completely emulate the shipping version of the Palm OS—after all, you did extract that copy from a real-live Palm device (which presumably works just fine). Basically, it's best to use both ROMs when testing—the debug version first to uncover major flaws, followed by the release version to ensure compatibility.

Loading ROM files into POSE

Now that you have a ROM file (either through Palm Computing or extraction) you need to load that file into POSE. Click the Emulator.exe file to start POSE. POSE will respond with the Palm OS Emulator dialog box. Click the New button to bring up the New Configuration dialog box (see Figure 27.5) and start a new emulation session. To configure your emulation session:

1. Select the appropriate Device type. Be mindful not to select a Device type different from the ROM file type (if your device is a Palm III, then the ROM file must be for a Palm III as well).

2. Select the Display language for the soft buttons.

3. Select the appropriate memory level.

4. Select the ROM file. You can use the Browse button to locate the specific file.

FIGURE 27.5

New Configuration dialog box

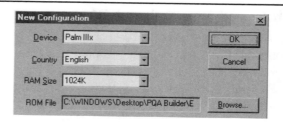

After you have completed the previous selections, click OK to start the POSE emulation session. POSE will combine the features defined in the ROM file with the attributes selected through the Palm Emulation dialog box to create a software copy of the Palm device.

WARNING Do not load the ROM file of one type of Palm device and select a different Palm device through the Palm Emulator dialog box. Doing so will deliver unreproducible results and an unstable POSE session.

POSE Features

When completely installed, POSE looks just like a physical Palm device made two-dimensional on your desktop computer screen. Palm Computing chose to use the design of a Palm III for the POSE interface, and it works just like the real thing. Place your mouse cursor over any of the buttons and click, and the POSE LCD panel will reflect the change. Press the on/off button to cycle POSE; you can even use Graffiti if you can write with a mouse. (See Figure 27.6.)

FIGURE 27.6

The Palm OS
Emulator

What you can see and use here are the standard Palm buttons and features. Since POSE is an emulation tool principally designed as an aid for testing and debugging, there is an additional set of features available. Right-click the POSE screen (or alternatively, press F10) for Windows, or select menu commands from the menu bar for a

Mac. This activates the POSE Features menu which is a drop-down list with 18 choices. (The Features menu is shown in Figure 27.7.) Here's a brief description:

FIGURE 27.7

POSE Features menu

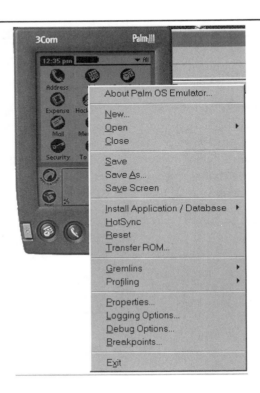

About Palm OS Emulator   Lists the credits for all of the important people involved as well as Web links to the Palm home page and other related locations.

New   Opens the New Configuration dialog box, shown in Figure 27.5, which allows you to specify the configuration options for your POSE testing session.

Open   Lets you open a previous POSE testing session saved with the Save command below.

Close   Closes the current emulator session without exiting POSE. You also have the option to save the details of the current session.

Save   Saves the current session for future testing and evaluation.

Save As...   Saves the current session for future testing and evaluation, but also allows you to create a new file name.

Save Screen   Saves the contents of the LCD panel as a BMP file on a Windows system or a PICT file on a Mac.

Install Application/Database   Lets you specify, load, and use a PRC, PDB or a .QA file for testing. This is the easy way to install your application into POSE.

HotSync   Simulates a HotSync between the Palm Desktop and POSE. To do this you'll need to connect two serial ports on your desktop computer via a null modem or a LapLink cable. This connection emulates the Palm cradle connection.

Reset   Emulates a Palm device reset and will clear memory while setting POSE to a "factory original" condition.

Transfer ROM...   Begins the ROM extraction process. We looked at this feature in detail a few sections back. After transferring your first ROM file, you can use the Emulator Dialog box or this POSE option to obtain ROMs from other Palm devices.

Gremlins   Gremlins is the pseudo-random automatic test feature of POSE which emulates a sequence of random taps, strokes, and button clicks. Click this feature and you'll receive the Gremlins Options menu: New, Step, Resume, and Stop. The Options menu lets you start a new Gremlins session (see Figure 27.8). The Gremlins Number is the seed for the random number generator, while the Number of Events is the number of iterations that Gremlins will process before stopping. The default value of –1 forces Gremlins to run until manually stopped through the Gremlin/Stop command in the Features menu. If you check the Continue Past Warnings check box, Gremlins will not stop if it encounters a program error warning condition. The box on the right lists all of the applications loaded into POSE upon which you could apply Gremlins. Select and highlight your application here. For logging options, see the section on logging options below. The Step option lets you step Gremlins through its paces, one action at a time. The Resume option lets you restart continuous emulation. And the Stop option terminates the Gremlins session.

FIGURE 27.8

New Gremlins menu

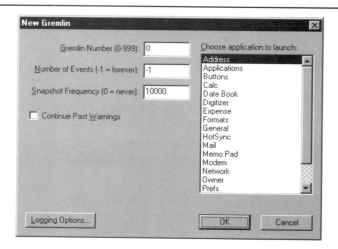

Profiling   The Profile feature is active only when using the profile version of POSE. Profiling an application is the process of measuring its performance or speed. Profile sessions identify bottlenecks and traffic jams in your code. If you are running the profile version of POSE (`emulator_profile.exe`), clicking this feature calls up the Profile submenu with Start, Stop, and Dump options. The Start option begins a profile session, the Stop option terminates the profile session, and the Dump option dumps the result of the last session to file.

Properties   Provides the basic options of a standard properties menu (see Figure 27.9). Here you can select the COM port used for HotSyncing, the color scheme and size of the POSE display, the disposition of the POSE session upon exiting the emulation, and the HotSync username.

Logging Options   Through the Logging Options dialog box (shown in Figures 27.10 and 27.11) you can choose to log events under Normal operation and/or Gremlin operation. The set of logging options is the same for both. By checking any of these options, POSE will log process information relating to the checked event. For example, by checking Serial Activity, POSE will log all activity that causes a call or an interrupt to a serial port.

FIGURE 27.9

*POSE Properties
dialog box*

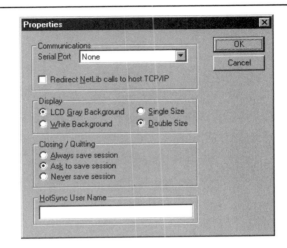

FIGURE 27.10

*Logging
Options/Normal*

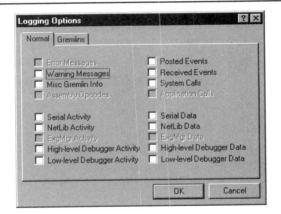

FIGURE 27.11

Logging Options/Gremlins

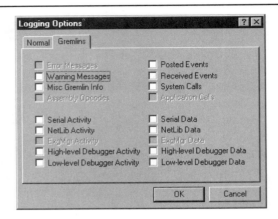

Debug Options   While testing in POSE, errors and warnings will cause a dialog box with details of the transgression to appear on the screen. You can suppress these warnings and control whether or not POSE will even monitor the condition. A checkmark enables the option while a blank box disables the option. The Debug options dialog box is shown in Figure 27.12.

FIGURE 27.12

Debug Options

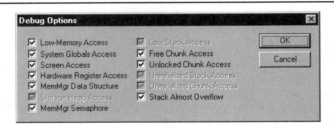

Breakpoints   Sets the breakpoint options for the code within your application. A breakpoint is a location within the program code where you would like processing to halt. You can use breakpoint when testing program segments—the breakpoint would prevent the application from running past the segment that you want to test. See Figure 27.13.

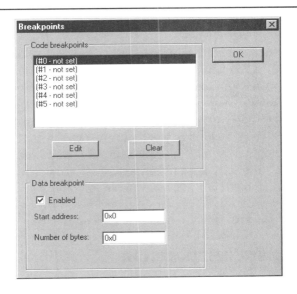

FIGURE 27.13

Breakpoints options

Exit   Terminates the POSE session.

You can access/activate any of POSE's hardware buttons through the mouse cursor. Additionally, POSE employs keyboard shortcuts:

Keyboard Key	Palm Action
ESC	On/Off
F1	The Date Book application
F2	The Address application
F3	The To Do List application
F4	The Memo Pad application
Page Up	Up key
Page Down	Down key

PART

V

Advanced Techniques

Testing and Debugging

Every new application, no matter how simple, should be tested for accuracy and compatibility. You don't know how the application will perform until you try to use it, and POSE is an excellent foil. It is the simplest method for testing across the entire Palm family—you don't need to own one of each Palm device type to determine if your creation will have problems on any given hardware. Of course, as we've said before, you shouldn't rely entirely on POSE; at some point in the development cycle, you should test your application on Palm hardware. But that level of testing can be cursory and performed merely as a physical confirmation of your findings in POSE.

The strength of POSE really lies in its ability to handle program bugs: It tracks whatever may lock up your Palm device and force a reset. No mystery, no guessing, no unknowns, and also no loss of data on the Palm device.

Loading Your Application

You can load your applications directly into POSE using the POSE Feature menu. Fortunately, you don't need to HotSync your application to POSE— a difficult task given that you must connect two serial ports through a null modem (see the HotSync section later in this chapter for details). POSE supports a Load Application option that allows you to load and install an application directly to POSE.

In a Windows-based environment, right-click the POSE window to obtain the Features menu (on a Mac, click the File Menu) and select the Install Application/Database option. Select the appropriate file, either a PRC or a PBD, from the appropriate drive and folder, and click OK to load the file into POSE. Be mindful that the newly loaded application will replace any previously loaded application with the same name. POSE, however, prevents you from overwriting a running application.

 TIP If you attempt to load a new application while the POSE Application Launcher is open, the Application Launcher will not immediately display the new application. POSE will load the PRC or PBD file, but you must exit the Application Launcher and return before you can see the new application listed.

HotSyncing to POSE

There are times when you must load software to POSE via a HotSync—to test the Hot-Sync or conduit capability, for instance. In order to perform a HotSync with POSE you need to connect two serial (COM) ports together on your desktop computer using a null modem or LapLink cable. This connection emulates the Palm cradle connection to your desktop, but assumes of course that you have two unused but active serial ports. One of your desktop computer's serial ports is most likely used for your mouse and, depending upon your desktop computer's configuration, you may not have two additional serial ports available.

In that case, you can disable the mouse and use the serial port previously used by the mouse along with the second serial port to connect the null modem or LapLink cable. This approach forces you to use the keyboard shortcuts and hotkey sequences that may or may not work for you. We find this approach quite cumbersome, but it is a viable alternative. See the previous section for keyboard shortcuts.

 TIP HotSyncing is a resource, primarily CPU, intensive operation. HotSyncing to POSE may result in a slow file transfers because there is only one CPU—the desktop computer's—involved in the process. Palm Computing recommends that after you establish the HotSync session, you click the POSE window, which will bring it to the foreground and give it processing priority. This should improve the HotSync performance.

PART

V

Advanced Techniques

Using Gremlins

If you use Gremlins, POSE's automatic test feature, testing your Palm application is actually quite easy. Gremlins mimics screen taps and button depressions in a pseudo-random order and records the results of these actions. All you need to do is activate the options you are interested in (by default all Gremlin options are inactive).

By selecting the Debug Options from the POSE Feature menu, you can activate any one or combination of 13 Gremlin debug options.

 NOTE You don't have to use Gremlins to use the Debug Options. You can set the Debug Options and manually test your application, and still benefit from the Debug Options. Gremlins is a useful feature that can speed up the production/test schedule of your application, and it's 100% reproducible. You may choose to run manual tests in addition to those run by Gremlins. Either way, we recommend that you set the Debug Options and let POSE track the internal program flow.

- Low-Memory Access flags reads and writes to memory address in the range 0 by 0000 to 0 by 00FF.
- System Globals Access flags, reads, and writes to memory in the range 0 by 0100 to the end of the trap dispatch table.

- Screen Access flags, reads, and writes to the LCD screen buffer.

- Hardware Register Access flags, reads, and writes to memory in the range 0 by FFFF000 to 0 by FFFFFFF.

- MemMgr Data Structure flags, reads, and writes to the heap headers, master pointer tables, memory chunk headers, and memory chunk trailers. These areas are restricted, and only the Memory Manager is allowed access.

- Storage Heap Access flags access by the application to the storage heap.

- MemMgr Semaphore records the duration of time that the application has possession of the Memory Manager. In general, the application should not hold this semaphore for more than 10 milliseconds.

- Low Stack Access flags access to the range of memory below the stack pointer.

- Free Chunk Access flags free-chunk access. Only the Memory Manager should access the contents of a chunk.

- Unlocked Chunk Access flags unlocked relocatable chunk access. Only the Memory Manager should access the contents of an unlocked chunk.

- Uninitialized Stack Access flags access from uninitialized portions of the stack. This checks access of uninitialized local variables.

- Uninitialized Chunk Access flags access from uninitialized portions of memory chunks. This checks access of initialized global variable access.

- Stack Almost Overflow flags any occurrence of the stack pointer dipping below the space allocated for it by the kernel. Basically, this option warns you when the application stack is near full.

Once you have selected the required Gremlins features, start Gremlins by right-clicking the POSE screen and selecting Gremlins/New. From the list of applications on the right-hand side of the New Gremlin dialog box, select the application to test and click OK. Gremlins will repeatedly perform a series of user interface actions: stylus movements, taps, button depressions, etc. Each Gremlins number represents a different series of user interface actions, so it is probably wise to try as many as possible. In addition, a Gremlin will repeat the same sequence of user interface actions so you can readily recreate a crash or condition that Gremlins found.

You should apply Gremlins to your application for at least a few hours, if not longer. Palm Computing suggests you do so for several days as a guarantee of smooth performance. At a minimum, you should run Gremlins for the time it takes to mimic the life span of the application. If your application can create data records, then you should test until you have created enough data to fill the Palm device's memory. If that is impractical, then look at hitting one million events (additions, deletions, etc.).

Either alternative seems like a lengthy process, but remember that Gremlins is an automated process; so you can turn on the logging feature and start a Gremlins test session, letting the tests run over night or for several days.

Though Gremlins runs through a series of pseudo-random user interface activities, it does not perform any actions that a user could not perform. It does not perform any special program calls or combinations—just the same sorts of things that the average application user could do. Basically, if Gremlins crashes your application you can rest assured that some user could, too.

Error Handling

Unless you're perfect or you can create perfect programs, you will encounter some problem or error while testing your application. Fortunately, POSE and Gremlins will let you know that you have a problem—and they'll do it unequivocally. POSE will flash an error dialog box to the screen and halt processing. The dialog box identifies the nature of the problem and affords several options for addressing it.

This dialog box provides an English-like error message that hopefully explains the nature of the error in clear and concise language. Unfortunately, POSE does not identify the location in your code that tripped the error. For that you'll need to link POSE and the debug option to a development debugger. The box also contains Continue, Reset, and More Info buttons. The Continue button attempts to ignore the error and continue processing. If the error is truly severe, this option will not be enabled. The Reset button emulates a Palm device soft reset. And the More Info button delivers a second dialog box with additional error information.

The More Info button provides state information such as memory location where the error occurred; variable, register, or function name; and program counter information. In addition to this information, POSE gives you three more buttons: Continue, Reset, and Debug. The Continue and Reset buttons function as described above. The Debug button will link you to an external debugger, if one is open. Otherwise, nothing happens when you click this button; it's kind of like those buttons at big city crosswalks that are supposed to alter the traffic lights, halt traffic, and allow you to cross the street (I've never seen one that worked!).

The nature of the errors that POSE reports fall into one of three categories: exceptions, memory access, or application error messages. If the CPU pushes the program counter and processor state onto the stack and then branches to a low-memory vector, you will receive an exception. If executing code accesses a memory location that it shouldn't, you'll get a memory access condition. Memory access conditions occur when your application, or any application, attempts to move beyond the Palm's RAM (only the Memory Manager can do that). Remember, applications run only in RAM, and the system files like the Palm OS run in ROM. If some command, action, function, etc. invokes the `ErrDisplayFileLineMsg` or `SysFatalAlert` system functions, you'll get an application error message.

Profiling

As described earlier, profiling is the action of determining an application's performance and the presence of bottlenecks and obstructions. Just because an application functions and delivers the expected results doesn't mean that the application is functioning smoothly or at its peak performance. For that we need to investigate the code more closely to uncover those areas where processing lags. A profiling tool, such as POSE with the Profile feature (`Emulator_Profile.exe`) is just the tool for this endeavor.

POSE is a passive profiler, which means it only observes the running code and does not interact with it. You do not need make any changes to the application's code or insert any special functions or subroutines. In contrast, an active profiler effectively becomes part of the application by intertwining itself into the application's code. To properly use an active profiler, you must modify your program code, however slightly, to accept the profiler. POSE, like all passive profilers, performs its magic through program counter sampling. The program counter is a register inside the MC68328 CPU chip that tracks the current execution location. You can see a small sample of the Profiler's output in Figure 27.14. The full sample report would take about 10 pages!

Since a passive profiler works by sampling the application's execution, more samples mean more accurate data. Hence, Palm Computing suggests you run a POSE testing routine such as Gremlins for an extended period of time. As a statistical technique, sampling relies on the number of samples taken, the sampling rate, and the environment that the profile is working in. Though more samples will lead to more accurate findings, there is no rule for determining how much is enough. The sample rate, and/or frequency of your samples, will add to the number of samples taken. Here we must be careful not to overdo the sampling, as too many samples add to the application's processing time and may lead to a false reading. We must also factor in the effect of any other applications that may be running on the test system. These other applications may remove CPU processing cycles from the application under test while not notifying the profiler of the reduction. So, to the profiler, your application looks to be processor-hungry. To avoid this, you should close down any unnecessary applications.

FIGURE 27.14

Sample Profile output

```
index parent       depth function name     count only cycles only msec
      only %        plus kids cycles plus kids msec    plus kids %
      average msec        max msec   interrupt msec    interrupt
count/debug
81    -1    0       functions   0     0    0.000 0.0  5457762
      329.000       0.0   -1.#IO  0.000 0.000 44
174   81    1       EvtGetEvent 11    28120 1.000 0.0  3884040
      234.000       0.0   0.154 0.158 1.010 1054
182   174   2       EvtGetSysEvent  11  22026 1.000 0.0  3844904
      231.000       0.0   0.121 0.124 1.010 1054
197   182   3       cjevwait    11    15406 0.000 0.0  3793296
      228.000       0.0   0.084 0.086 0.000 1000
202   197   4       cj_kpwait   11    10892 0.000 0.0  3756010
      226.000       0.0   0.060 0.061 0.000 1000
206   202   5       unknown $10C6A76E   11    7470  0.000 0.0
      3731684       225.000   0.0   0.041 0.042 0.000 1000
207   206   6       unknown $10C6A7B0   11    321692    19.000
      0.0   3724214     224.000   0.0   1.764 1.907 0.000 1000
208   207   7       unknown $10C6A83E   11    796956    48.000
      0.0   3402522     205.000   0.0   4.370 4.732 18.996
      122016
209   208   8       SysDoze     1016  111716    6.000 0.0  2345878
      141.000       0.0   0.007 0.007 18.996    2016
210   209   9       HwrDoze     1016  2051318   123.000   0.0
      2234162       134.000   0.0   0.122 0.127 0.000 1000
212   210   10      PrvShutDownCPU  1016  138140    8.000 0.0
      138140        8.000 0.0   0.008 0.008 97.998    2015
211   210   10      HwrDisableInts  1016  44704 2.000 0.0  44704 2.000
      0.0   0.003 0.003 0.000 0
213   208   8       unknown $10C6A85C   10    3672  0.000 0.0
      259688        15.000    0.0   0.022 0.023 0.000 110000
214   213   9       unknown $10C6A9E2   10    23896 1.000 0.0
      256016        15.000    0.0   0.144 0.480 0.000 102000
245   214   10      unknown $10C6A83E   2     31788 1.000 0.0
      136016        8.000 0.0   0.959 1.053 0.748 22040
247   245   11      SysDoze     40    4400  0.000 0.0  92560 5.000 0.0
      0.007 0.007 0.748 40
249   247   12      HwrDoze     40    80960 4.000 0.0   88160 5.000 0.0
      0.122 0.127 0.000 0
```

The Profile option in POSE offers the convenience of running on your code without the need for any modifications. But the quality of the data relies on the number and frequency of the samples taken and whether or not any other applications are active on the test system. Nevertheless, the advantages clearly outweigh the disadvantages, making the Profile feature in POSE a very handy tool.

APPENDIX <u>A</u>

Web Resources

The Palm organizer isn't just a tool: it's a culture. Just search the Web for the words "Palm organizer" if you don't believe us. There are tons of good sources of information, downloadable software, news, and tips. There are also some fairly useless sites out there, as well. Here are URLs and descriptions of almost two dozen of our favorite online resources for Palm goodies.

General Resources

These sites offer a little bit of everything—news, usage tips, downloads, and links to other sites. They serve as good jumping-off points for any Web exploration you may do.

www.palm.com

3Com's Palm Computing site is the best place to start if you want to get some general information on your particular Palm organizer and to know how it stacks up against the other models. Check back often for news of upcoming releases, to download operating system upgrades and patches, and to see what new accessories are available. The site also offers a really solid list of links for downloads, more information, and buying third-party stuff.

www.palm.net

Whether you own a Palm VII or are considering one, Palm.Net is the place to go for information on wireless network service options, such as what plans are available, whether or not there's coverage in your area, and more.

For those already signed up for service, the Palm.Net site provides a view of your account, some mailbox configuration options, a place to check on the status of the Palm.Net network, technical support, and new query applications to download.

www.webring.org

We know that the devices are no longer called PalmPilots, but the PalmPilot Web Ring hasn't changed its name to meet the times. Don't let the name deter you: there's lots of good stuff to be found here, especially along the lines of tips and tricks and freeware from small developers.

For the uninitiated, a Web ring is a chain of sites all based upon a single subject—in this case, all matters Palm. Just head to the URL listed above, and search on Palm. You'll come up with the general PalmPilot Web Ring, as well as rings devoted to games (the Palm Fun Ring) and e-texts (the Palm Etext Ring). Traverse the rings for a while, and you'll come across a number of the other sites we mention here, as well.

Shareware

We call this category shareware, but it also encompasses freeware. The difference between the two is small, but significant. Freeware is free software that you can download and use right away, without giving it another thought. Shareware applications can also be downloaded and used right away, but the expectation is that if you decide you like it and will keep using it past a trial period, you'll send some money to the developer. The fee is usually nominal, and helps these part-time developers keep coding good applications for you to use. So, if you like it, send the money—it's a worthwhile cause.

www.palmgear.com

If it's Palm-related, you can find it at PalmGear. The site offers tons of software to download, as well as news, deals on hardware and accessories, tips and tricks, a support FAQ…just check for yourself. We especially like the top 50 downloads and top downloads of the month areas, which are perfect when you know you want something new, but aren't sure what. Comprehensive and well-designed. What more could you ask for?

www.palmcentral.com

Palm Central offers yet another well-organized, expansive collection of software downloads. You'll find stuff here beyond the usual games and hacks. Check out this site if you're interested in development tools, enterprise solutions, and even law-related material. Of course, you'll also find all the requisite news, FAQs, tips and tricks.

www.pilotzone.com

If you're at all familiar with the world-renowned Tucows shareware site, you'll feel right at home at its Pilot Zone branch office. The offerings are comprehensive and arranged by category, so it's relatively easy to find what you're looking for. The best part of this site, though, is that just about every piece of downloadable software gets a 1 to 5 plane rating (plane/pilot—cute, huh?), so you don't waste your time on junk. The offerings in the development, docs, and PQA categories are particularly strong.

And, if you're hankering for a game you can play with another Palm user via IR, this is the place to start your search.

www.pickled.com

Pickled PalmPilot offers this fast, easy-to-use site full of downloads and other information. You can find the latest system updates here, as well as all the usual hacks, games, productivity applications, and uncategorizable goodies. It doesn't offer as vast a selection as some of the other sites do, but you can find some stuff here that won't necessarily turn up at the big sites.

www.palmpilotsoftware.com

PalmPilot Software is more than just a site full of downloads, though heaven knows there are plenty of those here. This well-designed offering from the ZDNet folks serves up really thorough reviews, witty articles, tips, tricks, and how-to-buy information. Everything is well organized by category, rated from 1–5 stars, and includes thorough download descriptions. If you can't find it here, you're really not trying.

www.download.com

CNet Download.com is yet another slick, well-designed site that's chock full of downloads, but not much more. Everything is well described and easy to find, but software titles are either given a Pick or no rating. There are some interesting titles here, but the offerings aren't as broad or deep as at some of the other sites.

Finding Information

Are you looking for ways to use your Palm organizer more efficiently? These sites can point you in the right direction. Besides just standard application tricks, some of these sites also include operating system details, reviews of new devices, accessories and applications, and some fun surprises.

www.the-gadgeteer.com

The Gadgeteer is a member of the Palm Web Ring and is heavy on the reviews and news. The site's owner, Julie Strietelmeier, writes pretty much everything. It's slicker looking than most non-commercial sites, but not so polished as to be pretentious. The best part of this site is its comprehensive list of Palm-related resources. It covers everything from IRC channels to User Groups, mailing lists, publications, and more. Feel free to skip Julie's Gear Diary; it rarely has anything to do with gear or anything but what's going on in Julie's head.

www.palmstation.com

Don't let the unappealing look of this site put you off. There's a very active community of Palm afficionados who regularly visit Palm Station to share tips, tricks, gossip, and conspiracy theories. There are also user-contributed reviews and news, as well as some software and the prerequisite links area. There's nothing slick about this site, but there's nothing commercialized about it either—and for our money, that's a big draw.

www.ugeek.com

U Geek bills itself as an "Online Technology Resource," and that's a pretty accurate assessment. The site as a whole is devoted to technical issues beyond the Palm platform. Check out the PDAGeek page for more Palm-oriented information. There you'll find some interesting product reviews and news, as well as a place to share your horror stories. You'll also find our favorite feature—the Easter eggs—which are funny little tricks hidden within your Palm organizer that can be revealed by following a particular series of actions. Don't miss the Dancing Palm Tree.

www.pda-archives.com/pilot.html

PalmPilot Archives provides an amazingly complete and well-organized archive of Palm related sites and software. It ranks related sites in order of popularity, and highlights a different site each week. The site doesn't offer software for direct download, but does offer a well-organized list of software categories and titles, and links to the sites where they can be found.

www.palmlife.com

PalmLife serves up a mix of opinionated product reviews, chat, discussion forums, Easter eggs, and other tidbits of Palm news. You'll also find some information on the Florida Palm Users Group. The site isn't particularly deep in its offerings, but it is well presented and interesting.

www.developer.com/roadcoders

RoadCoders is *the* site to visit if you're interested in programming for the Palm organizer. Some of the pioneers of the field have put together this site full of discussion forums, tutorials, and documentation for the Palm Computing Platform.

Online Magazines

Much as we hate to admit it, this book is not timeless. There are bound to be lots of Palm platform developments that happened after we went to press. For those of you who crave the latest information and just can't get enough Palm news, these online magazines should give you the fix you need.

www.palmzone.com

Don't be confused when you see that PalmZone's home page says HandGear.com—the site is in the middle of a transition to covering other handhelds besides the Palm (though we can't imagine why). You've come to the right place for reviews of new software and gadgets, and news about new software releases and other Palm developments. The articles here are well written, they have a small but well-chosen selection of downloads, and they promise to add some e-commerce as well. It's a site worth following, to see what it becomes.

www.palmpower.com

PalmPower is slick, well written, and thorough. This site delivers reviews, tips, techniques, and news in a timely, well-organized fashion. This is as good as e-zines get.

www.pmn.co.uk

The Piloteer Magazine site serves up news headlines for all manner of handheld devices, including (but not exclusively) the Palm organizer. The Web site is an adjunct to the Piloteer print publication, so you can try the content on for size here before you subscribe.

We rarely check out this site because we've subscribed to their daily e-mail newsletter. If you're really interested in the Palm platform, we'd advise you to do the same. You'll get all the news of the day delivered right to your mailbox for free. It doesn't get any easier than that.

Web Resources

www.tapmagazine.com

Like the Piloteer, Tap Magazine Online is an adjunct to a relatively new print publication. The site has a clever Palm organizer style interface that's very attractive, if not a tad too cute for our taste. But, the reviews, tips, and techniques are first-rate. Of course, you only get a taste of the content offered by the print pub—they really do want you to subscribe, after all.

Newsgroups

People helping people is what mailing lists and newsgroups are all about. These are but a few of the thousands of newsgroups and user groups lurking out there on the Internet. They're all based on the same premise: to provide an open forum where people with similar interests can share opinions, pose questions, and get answers from others in the same boat.

You'll need a news reader to access these lists (Microsoft Outlook Express works just fine). Or, you can go to www.dejanews.com and search for Palm to read what's out there.

Comp.sys.palmtops, Comp.sys.handhelds, Comp.sys.palmtops.pilot

These are all standard newsgroups, where you can post a message and hope for a polite, well-reasoned response. They're generally quite helpful, but they do have rules of engagement. Feel free to lurk for a while before you post if you're the timid sort who's afraid of getting flamed.

You may need to wade through some non-Palm discussions, but there's a lot to be learned here.

User Groups

Like newsgroups, there are hundreds of User Groups out there, devoted just to the Palm organizer. These groups hold meetings and events to discuss programming, and using and advancing the platform.

www.ne-palm.org

This is the New England Palm Users Group Web site. It delivers a smattering of news and reviews, but is most useful for its information on the group itself, including meeting times, special events, and more. Follow the link to their message board (www .insidetheweb.com/mbs.cgi/mb332061) for some really helpful threaded discussions.

APPENDIX B

When Bad Things Happen to Good Palms: Troubleshooting Tips

You change its batteries on a regular basis; you clean its screen; you tuck it away at night in a safe pocket in your briefcase. Yet, one day you press that little teal button and nothing happens. Your Palms just won't start. Or maybe it does start, but it freezes up and refuses to accept your frantic taps. Chances are, it's not your fault. Sometimes, even the Palms that are most cared for can go bad. More than likely, the damage can be undone.

What if you somehow did cause the Palm to behave this way? You were trying to look up a number in your Palm address application, dial your cell phone, and eat a giant soft pretzel all at the same time. What's wrong with this picture? That's right, boys and girls. That's one more activity than your hands can accommodate. Something is bound to hit the pavement, and too often that something will be your Palm.

Chances are, your Palm can even be saved after such a grievous breach of etiquette as a drop. Palm organizers may be small and cute, but these aren't fragile lapdog-like organizers. Palms are sturdy little beasts that will rarely fail of their own accord. Failure requires some user assistance.

Handling a Palm inappropriately, installing some funky third-party application, kicking, dropping, or immersing it in water—these are the sorts of things that could cause a Palm to go bad.

 NOTE Most third-party applications are perfectly safe. You should follow standard safe computing practices, though, to ensure that a rogue application doesn't wreak havoc on your Palm. Download applications only from reputable Web sites and always back up your data before installing anything new on your Palm. For more on third-party applications, see Part IV.

But not to worry. Most of the things that can go wrong with your Palm can be fixed by you—no matter how non-technical you may be.

What to Do When...

Hopefully, you're not encountering any problem so serious that it warrants a total replacement. But how can you tell? Try some of these solutions to specific problems first, before you panic.

Graffiti Doesn't Recognize Your Strokes

Your problem may be that you're simply not entering characters correctly. Check the Graffiti guide to make sure you're starting characters at the right place. Also, be sure to hold the stylus as close to a 90-degree angle to the screen as possible, and don't lift it from the screen until you've completed a stroke.

If those tips don't help, try recalibrating your screen. You do this through the Digitizer Preferences. See Chapter 4 for help on using this application.

The Screen Is Blank

Usually, this can be corrected by following one of these simple remedies. First, check your contrast knob. The little thing has a habit of spinning all the way to the brightest setting or all the way to the darkest setting all by itself. Either direction will cause a blank screen.

If this doesn't work, try replacing the batteries. We've been guilty of thinking the screen was at fault when really it was just a case of dead batteries.

The Palm IIIx Screen Is Streaky

This is a problem known as "crosstalk" that seems to be confined only to Palm IIIx organizers. It has something to do with interference in the display caused by a screen refresh rate that's ever-so-slightly out of range. You'll know you're suffering from the problem if you see vertical lines that are most prominent when there's a grid on the screen, like the Date Book's Month View.

Try adjusting the contrast wheel to eliminate the lines. If this doesn't work, you'll need to download the 3.1.1 system patch from the Palm Web site or try StreakHack, which we discuss in Chapter 21.

Beaming Doesn't Work

Chances are that this one can be solved by moving closer to the organizer that you're trying to beam to. The sending and receiving units need to be no further than about 3 feet from each other. Also, both parties should check that Beam Receive On is turned on. See Chapter 4 for help on setting this option. One last tip: To receive a beamed item, you must have twice the memory of the size of the item you're receiving. For example, if you're receiving an application that's 14K, you'll need 28K of free RAM. See the next section for tips on troubleshooting memory issues.

Can't Install an Application

Your organizer probably just doesn't have enough memory to accommodate the application. You can check the free memory on your organizer from the Application Launcher. Tap the Menu Button, then App ➤ Info. You'll see the amount of free memory, the size of all the applications installed on your organizer, the version number of your organizer's operating system and all its applications, the organizer's Flash ID, as well as how many records you have stored for each of the applications.

If you've verified that memory is the problem, delete an application or some records to make room for the new installation. If that doesn't work, check to see that you have the Install Applications option enabled in your HotSync options. Finally, follow the troubleshooting steps in the next section to fix any HotSync problems.

HotSync Doesn't Work

If you can't complete a local HotSync, first check to make sure that the cable from the cradle is firmly seated in the PC. Make sure your cradle is plugged into the COM port you've chosen. On the Macintosh, if your HotSync cradle is connected to the printer port, you need to make sure that AppleTalk is off. (From the Apple Menu, pick Chooser, then select AppleTalk Inactive.) On a Windows PC, make sure that an internal modem or PC Card modem isn't assigned to the COM port your cradle is connected to. Next, check to make sure your HotSync settings are correct (see Chapter 9 for help with this). Finally, make sure your Palm is seated properly in the cradle. Try removing it, and then replacing it in the cradle.

If you still can't complete a HotSync, quit any program you may have running besides HotSync, and turn off any startup programs or system extensions that may be grabbing the serial port your HotSync needs to use. E-mail programs, Internet software, and fax software are the most likely culprits here. You can also try picking a lower HotSync speed from the Setup menu (this works very well when you're having problems HotSyncing to a laptop computer).

If none of these steps work, try shutting down the HotSync software and restarting it. On a Macintosh, you can also try trashing the HotSync Preferences file (which you can find in the Preferences folder, nested within the System folder), then HotSync again. As a last resort, try uninstalling the HotSync software and reinstalling it.

Getting in through the Backdoor

This one is only for the adventurous who may be having problems HotSyncing lots of data to a slow or older machine. If you're getting Time Out errors waiting for the PC to respond, try using the Developer's Backdoor. Though it's intended for application developers, mere mortals can take advantage of the sneaky way in to make the Palm organizer wait forever for the PC to respond to a HotSync attempt. To activate this Backdoor, tap the Applications soft button, then tap the HotSync application. While holding down both of the Scroll buttons, tap in the top-right corner of the screen. You'll see a dialog box that says Developer's Backdoor: DLServer Wait Forever is ON. Tap OK and now try your HotSync. This mode stays active for one HotSync only, but if you complete that first one, the rest should work just fine in normal wait mode.

The System Freezes

If your Palm freezes up, the first thing to do is scream. Then take a deep breath and reset the Palm. There are three different types of Palm reset: the soft reset, the hard reset, and the in-between reset.

In the following sections, we'll explain what each reset does, which one to choose when, and how to execute each maneuver.

The Soft Reset

Fixing an ailing Palm is a lot like fixing an ailing human. You try the least painful, least invasive treatment first, and hope that will take care of the problem.

In the case of a petulant Palm, the first line of defense should be a soft reset. A soft reset simply tells your Palm organizers to stop whenever foolish task it's pursuing and start paying attention to you—right now. A soft reset is the preferred treatment because it doesn't erase any of your records. But you weren't worried about that happening because you HotSync regularly, right?

To perform a soft reset:

1. Unscrew the top of your stylus. Inside the cap, you'll see a short stick-like protrusion. This is the handy-dandy Palm reset tool.

2. Flip over your Palm organizer so its back is facing you.

3. Locate the Reset button on the back of the organizer. (It's actually just a little hole about midway down the back panel.) You can see the Reset button in Figure B.1.

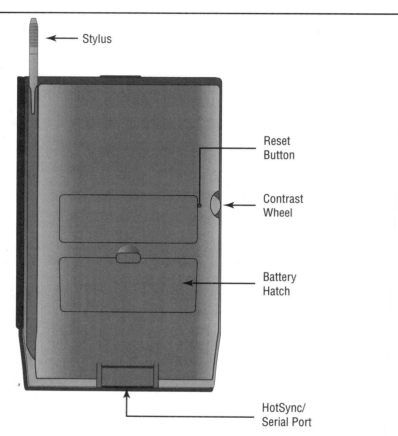

Stylus

Reset Button

Contrast Wheel

Battery Hatch

HotSync/ Serial Port

4. Insert the Reset tool into the Reset button (or hole, as we tend to think of it), and give a gentle push.

This will restart your organizer. You'll see the Welcome screen, followed by the General Preferences screen (where you set the date and time when you first powered up your Palm organizer). Don't panic. All your data is still there. This is just standard Palm operating procedure.

Don't believe us? Just press the To Do button to see that not a thing has budged.

When Bad Things
Happen to Good
Palms

 NOTE Think of the soft reset as the equivalent of restarting your Windows or Mac PC through the operating system software. For example, on a Windows PC, you'd choose Shutdown ➢ Restart. All that happens is that the operating system closes and reopens, flushing all the bad stuff from its memory in the process. Same thing happens when you perform a soft reset on your Palm organizer.

The Semi-Soft Reset

In most cases, a soft reset will wake up your Palm from its stupor and make it behave again. But, if you've installed a bunch of system enhancements (otherwise known as Hacks), a soft reset may not be powerful enough to get your Palm on the right track. It's time to stop pussyfooting around and call in the artillery—the semi-soft reset.

 NOTE We're eternally optimistic when it comes to our Palm organizer (not so much with life itself, but that's another story), so we choose to think of this option as the semi-soft reset. Those who perpetually believe that every glitch is a system-wide, unrecoverable meltdown may call this the semi-hard reset. We'll just explain it and let you give it whatever name you choose. Moe is rather catchy, don't you think?

The semi-soft reset lets you restart your Palm organizer without launching all the system modifications you installed. This way, you can figure out which Hack is causing the problem (hint: it's usually a conflict between the last one you installed and one already on there) and delete it before it causes any more trouble. You can read more about Hacks in Chapter 21.

To perform a semi-soft reset:

1. Unscrew the top of your stylus to access the Palm reset tool.
2. Hold down the Up Scroll hard button (it's the top half of the Scroll button). Don't let go!
3. While holding down the Up Scroll button, flip over your Palm organizer and insert the reset tool into the Reset hole.
4. Give a gentle push, same as you did for a soft reset.

This will restart your organizer with a fresh system file—no patches, hacks, or other nonsense loaded. You'll see the Welcome screen, followed by the General Preferences screen (where you set the date and time when you first powered up your Palm organizer). As with the soft reset, the semi-soft reset leaves all your data intact; it just shuts off anything that may be keeping your Palm organizer from running properly.

 NOTE The semi-soft reset on the Palm works a lot like starting your Windows PC in Safe Mode (only the basic drivers load) or holding down the Shift key while starting your Mac (to keep extensions from loading).

If all is hunky-dory with your Palm after a semi-soft reset, it's time to eliminate the Hack that caused the problem. To do this:

1. Tap on the Applications soft button to bring up the Application Launcher.

2. Tap on the HackMaster icon to bring up the HackMaster Extensions screen. You can see it in Figure B.2.

FIGURE B.2

No more bad Hacks.

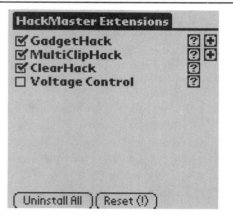

3. Tap in the check boxes for any Hacks you have installed to turn them off. Start with the Hack you installed just before your Palm organizer started behaving erratically.

4. Turn off your Palm organizer, and then power it up again to see if this did the trick. If not, repeat the semi-soft reset procedure and steps 1–3 to remove the Hack.

If the problem lies not in a Hack but in some other application or system patch that you've installed, you'll need to uninstall that application. To do so, follow the standard uninstall procedure detailed in Chapter 9.

When your system returns to a healthy equilibrium, perform a HotSync to back up all your data, and then perform a soft reset to restart your Palm organizer with all its add-ons running. You should be good to go at this point.

The Hard Reset

If you've tried the soft reset and that didn't work, then you tried the semi-soft reset and even that didn't get your Palm up and running, it's time to call in an air strike. In the Palm world, this is known as the hard reset.

The hard reset should be your weapon of last resort—heroic measures in medical terms, total annihilation in military terms, oh **** in common terms. In case that didn't make it clear enough for you, we'll spell it out—the hard reset is a drastic measure, to be undertaken only when you've exhausted all other possibilities and are really and truly desperate.

We may be acting a bit melodramatic here, but for good reason. A hard reset will get your Palm up and running (if anything can), but at the cost of your data. When you choose to perform a hard reset, you're wiping out everything on your Palm organizer and starting fresh.

This can be a very good thing—if you HotSync regularly. (Do it! Do it now! Before anything bad happens and your entire list of phone numbers is lost forever!) Starting fresh has some real appeal for those of us who install far too many untested applications on our Palms and just blindly expect them to run as if they were factory-fresh. Sooner or later all this wanton downloading has a way of catching up with you.

The hard reset erases all your data, any applications you've installed, as well as any Hacks, system upgrades, customizations, etc. It restores your Palm organizer to its fresh-from-the-box, everything-is-new-and-works state. If you have your data stored on your desktop PC, it's easy to restore it to your Palm once it's been revived by a hard reset.

 TIP The hard reset is also useful if you're passing your Palm organizer on to somebody else and want to make sure they don't get your Phone List or any of your other precious data. It's also a good idea to perform a hard reset before you start using a previously owned Palm. There's just no telling where the poor little device has been, or what's been done to it.

To perform a hard reset:

1. Unscrew the top of your stylus to access the Palm reset tool.

2. Press and hold down the Power button on the front of the organizer. (It's the teal colored button.) Don't let go!

3. While holding down the Power button, insert the reset tool in the Reset hole on the back of the organizer.

4. Give a gentle push, just as you would for a soft or semi-soft reset.

5. Take the tool out of the Reset hole, and then release the power button.

6. You'll see a message that says "Erase all data? Yes = 'up' button, No = any other button." If you're certain that this is what you want to do, press the Up Scroll button to finish the hard reset and launch the Setup application.

7. If you're really not sure about this whole hard reset thing, press any other button (not the Up Scroll button) to perform a soft reset.

And voila! If you went through with the hard reset, you now have a factory-fresh, as-good-as-new Palm organizer. Of course, your data will be gone, any formats and preferences you've set will be reset to the defaults, and any choices you've made when configuring your wireless preferences will be history. But, on the positive side, your Palm will still show the current date and time, and any applications that came pre-loaded on your organizer (including PQAs) will still be there. Best of all, whatever you did to make your Palm stop behaving will be forgotten.

 NOTE A Palm hard reset works similarly to reformatting your desktop PC's hard drive. Except, when you reformat a PC, you need to reinstall the operating system. The Palm organizer stores its operating system and all the standard applications in its ROM (read-only memory), which can't be altered by the user (that would be you!). So, no matter how many times you hard reset your Palm organizer, you'll never need to reinstall its operating system and core applications.

You can recover your data by performing a Custom HotSync, and choosing to have the desktop overwrite the handheld. This is a very important step: Don't under any circumstances choose Handheld Overwrites The Desktop because the blank applications on your newly restored Palm will wipe out all the data you carefully backed up to your desktop PC. Follow the instructions in Chapter 9 to restore your data via HotSync.

Replacing Your Palm Organizer

If you've performed a hard reset, and still your Palm organizer is acting freaky, you definitely have a problem. It may be time to accept the fact that even the best-loved

Palms can sometimes just break. They're not immortal, after all; they're just bits of electronic stuff crammed in a plastic case.

Besides behaving erratically, you'll need to have your Palm organizer replaced if

- The screen is badly scratched
- The screen is cracked
- The organizer drains batteries at an unusual pace
- Your Palm V won't hold a charge.
- Your Palm VII's wireless transmitter can't be recharged.

 WARNING There is nothing inside your Palm organizer that you can replace yourself—not even the transmitter. So don't even open it. If you do open up the organizer, your warranty becomes void and repairs will cost you.

In all these cases, the Palm Computing service and support folks will work with you to get a new organizer in your hands as quickly as possible.

If you're certain that your Palm is damaged beyond repair, don't just bundle it up and send if off to Palm Computing. First, call the Repair Information line at 888-956-PALM (888-956-7256). They'll talk you down from the ledge, and tell you what the procedure is for returning your device for repair.

We haven't (yet) busted up a Palm organizer, but we hear that the fine Repair folks will send you a prepaid, cushioned box to stuff your poor wounded organizer into, and then return your fixed up Palm (or possibly a replacement) within a few days.

If disaster should strike within the first year you own your organizer, and you haven't done anything to void your warranty (like open the device yourself), the repair is free. If your Palm organizer is outside the warranty period, the service will cost you somewhere around $100—still far less than buying a new organizer.

Replacing Your Antenna

Palm VII users have one more part to worry about than other Palm organizer users. That's the antenna. Now, if you put back your toys when you're finished playing with them, and don't use the antenna as a handle, you probably won't run into any trouble. But, in case you do, here's what you need to know to replace the Palm VII antenna.

First, call the Palm Computing folks for information about ordering a new antenna. You can reach them at 888-956-PALM (888-956-7256).

 WARNING Do not under any circumstances remove the antenna from your Palm VII until you are ready to insert a new one. You can damage the device by using the wireless communication features without the antenna.

When you have your new antenna in hand:

1. HotSync your organizer with your desktop PC, just in case.

2. Turn off your organizer.

3. Remove the AAA batteries.

   When you remove the old batteries, the organizer's built-in backup power maintains memory data for about one minute. If it takes you more than a minute to replace the antenna, you can perform a HotSync to restore any lost data.

4. Raise the antenna to a 180-degree angle. To be sure the antenna is raised to 180 degrees, place the organizer face down on a table and position the antenna straight out above the organizer, flat against the surface.

5. Grasp the antenna close to the pivot point with your thumb and index finger. (You can see the pivot point in Figure B.3.)

FIGURE B.3

Removing the antenna

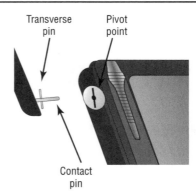

Transverse pin

Pivot point

Contact pin

6. Using your thumb, firmly push the antenna out of the pivot point.

NOTE Be careful not to move the pivot point, or you'll have a hard time inserting the new antenna.

Now that the busted antenna is gone, it's time to pop in a new one. To insert your new antenna:

1. Hold the new antenna at a 180-degree angle (straight up) from the pivot point.

2. Insert the contact pin into the center hole of the pivot point.

3. Align the transverse pin with its opening in the pivot point. (You can see all these bits in Figure B.3.) Push the antenna all the way into the pivot point. You will feel the antenna snap into place.

4. Lower the antenna to its at-rest position, alongside the organizer.

5. Replace the batteries you removed earlier.

6. If your data is gone, perform a HotSync to restore it.

You're ready to start connecting to the Internet wirelessly again. Just promise you'll be more gentle with the antenna this time, won't you?

General Maintenance

There's a lot you can do to keep your Palm organizer from ever needing to make a trip to the organizer hospital. For starters, you can just practice good Palm computing habits, like:

- Always use the stylus that comes with your organizer, or a replacement stylus, to write in the Graffiti writing area and tap on the screen.

- Always replace both batteries at the same time, and use only new batteries.

- Keep your organizer in a case, or keep the lid down on Palm III organizers, when not in use.

- Lower the antenna on a Palm VII when not performing a wireless transaction.

These are just some basic tips for keeping your Palm organizer in good working order. For the most part, if you observe these practices, your Palm's screen should stay clear, the electronics should stay grime free and in good working condition, and your antenna should stay attached to your organizer.

Cleaning Your Organizer

If you're a cleaning nut, come on over to our house and make yourself at home. Seriously, even a self-contained little device like a Palm organizer can use a bit of freshening up every now and then.

You don't need any special tools, accessories, or supplies to clean up your Palm's screen and case. If you have a paper towel and a little mild window cleaner, you're all set.

There are just two things to keep in mind when cleaning your Palm organizer:

- Do not under any circumstances immerse the organizer in water or spray cleaner directly on the device. If liquids seep in through the plastic case, your Palm will short out. Fry. Cook. Die, die, die.

- Do not use anything abrasive on your Palm organizer. Put down the steel wool, scouring powder, and sandpaper. If you wouldn't use it on a piece of fine crystal, don't use it on your Palm.

If you need to clean those mustard smudges off your Palm screen (or even just get some dust off):

1. Make sure your organizer is turned off.

2. Spray some gentle window cleaner on a piece of paper towel or a lint-free rag. Get it thoroughly damp, but not dripping wet.

3. Gently wipe the towel or rag across the surface of the screen, the back of the case, or the buttons (if you mucked those up, too).

4. Dry everything you just ran the damp towel over with a dry piece of towel or rag. Make sure no wet spots remain.

Now go ahead and use your nice, clean Palm organizer.

NOTE If you're the type who prefers a special tool for every job, you'll want to check out the Brain Wash screen-cleaning system from Concept Kitchen (www.conceptkitchen.com). The system consists of moist and dry towelettes for doing what we just explained. If your screen has some very minor scratches, you'll also want to get Concept Kitchen's Karma Cloth, which is used to gently buff your Palm organizer's screen.

Backing Up Your Data

The best form of Palm maintenance is HotSyncing. Keep your data current on your desktop PC, so you're never more than a HotSync away from a fully functional Palm.

We realize you're probably sick of hearing this, but frequent HotSyncing is the best way to ensure the safety and continued operation of your Palm organizer. And should something bad happen to the organizer itself, all will not be lost if you can just pull data back from the desktop.

So, when's the last time you HotSynced?

INDEX

Note to the Reader: Throughout this index **boldfaced** page numbers indicate primary discussions of a topic. *Italicized* page numbers indicate illustrations.

Continue Past Warnings option, 607
contrast wheel, 6-7, *7*, **15**, 629
Control Action and Filters dialog box, 528, *529*
Control Palette, 508
Control Palette toolbar, **512–513**, 522
Control Size indicator, 518
controls
    in Constructor, 550
    in Satellite Forms, **491–492**
converting
    Documents To Go files, 350
    images, **356–358**, *356–357*
    time to seconds, 440, 446
    Word and HTML documents, 384
Copy tool
    in Palm Desktop, 222
    in Satellite Forms, 511
copying
    memo text, 253
    PQA information, 317, *317*
copyright marks, 44
cos function, 475
countries
    default, 68–69
    for modems, 266
    setting up, **21**
coverage maps, 290, *291*
CPU resources for Hacks, 406
Crazy 8s game, 369
Create Appointment icon, 225
Create Contact icon, 225, 242
Create Event Banner icon, 225
Create Folder option, 576
Create menu
    Attach to command, 236
    Contact command, 242
    Task command, 250
Create Note icon, 255
Create Task icon, 225, 250
creator IDs, 421, **448**, 517

Credit Card option, 166
credit cards
    for Activate, 176
    in Expense, 166
crosstalk, 629
currency
    in Expense, **167–169**, *168–169*
    symbol for, 168–170
Currency option, 166
Currency Properties dialog box, 169
Current Sort option, 252
curve tool, 360
custom Address Book fields, **113–114**, *113*
Custom command, 425
Custom Currencies dialog box, 169
Custom dialog box
    for HotSync, 216–217, *216*, 426
    for Mail, 277, *278*
Custom installation, 199
Customer Support information, 182–183, *182*
customizing
    HotSync, **215–217**, *216–217*
    To Do List categories, **133–136**, *134–135*
Cut tool
    in Palm Desktop, 222
    in Satellite Forms, 511

D

Daily tab, 230, 233
Data Book tab, 223
Data column, 569
data input
    in programming, **435**
    in Satellite Forms, **519–520**, *519*
    dynamic fields in, **521–523**, *522*
    forms in, **533–534**, *533*
    modifying forms for, **536–537**, *536–537*
    scripts for, **530–532**, *532*

M

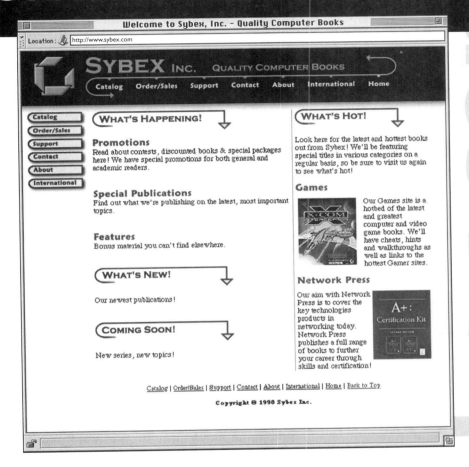

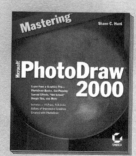